AF560684

DELHI

DELHI

Urban Space and Human Destinies

edited by

VÉRONIQUE DUPONT, EMMA TARLO, DENIS VIDAL

2026

First published 2000
Reprinted 2021, 2023, 2026

ISBN 978-81-7304-366-6

Published by
Ajay Kumar Jain *for*
Manohar Publishers & Distributors
4753/23 Ansari Road, Daryaganj
New Delhi 110 002

Published with the support of the
Institute de Recherche pour le Développement (Paris)

Printed at
Replika Press Pvt. Ltd.

Contents

Illustrations

FIGURES

MAPS

PLATES

Tables

Acknowledgements

This book is the outcome of a collective research project on the city of Delhi and its contemporary evolution. This Indo-French project was initiated in 1993, as a collaboration between the *Centre de Sciences Humaines* (CSH, New Delhi) and the French Institute of Research for Development (IRD—formerly ORSTOM, Paris), in association with the Centre for the Study of Developing Societies (CSDS, Delhi). It received financial support from *Action Concertée Sciences de l'Homme et de la Société* ORSTOM/CNRS (Centre National de la Recherche Scientifique) in 1994. A research team under the *Centre d'Etudes de l'Inde et de l'Asie du Sud* (CEIAS, Paris) was also formed on this subject.

The project was fuelled by an awareness of a need for new research on the social and cultural dynamics at play in the capital city of India. The CSDS took a keen interest in promoting research on Delhi and this led to the organization of the 'Delhi seminar'. This seminar was held on a regular basis from November 1994 to May 1996 at the Centre. It brought together members of the Delhi team with a number of other interested scholars and social activists who presented ongoing contemporary research for discussion. These regular sessions were succeeded by an international conference: 'DELHI GAMES. Use and control of urban space: power games and actors' strategies', held at the CSDS on 3 and 4 April 1998. Many of the contributions to this book have their origin in the proceedings of the conference.

The conference was jointly organized by the CSH and the CSDS and has received financial support from other institutions: IRD, the *Maison des Sciences de l'Homme* (MSH, Paris), the Economic and Social Research Council (London), the Institute of Development Studies (IUED, Geneva). We would like to express our gratitude to V.B. Singh, Director of the CSDS, who not only promoted the Indo-French project from its inception, but also took an active part in the research programme and in the organization of the conference. Our sincere thanks are also due to Chandrika Parmar for having been such an efficient and dynamic member of the organizing committee. We are also grateful to all the participants, contributors, chairpersons and panelists at the seminar, and all those who took part in debates. Those whose comments helped in the revision of the papers deserve a special mention: Bina Agarwal, R.C. Aggarwal, Pierre Audinet, Ashish Banerjee, Amita Baviskar, Tarun Bose, Roma Chatterjee, Malay Chatterjee, Dipankar Gupta, Saraswati Haider, Arup Mitra, Ashis Nandy, K.T. Ravindran, Dhirubhai L. Sheth, Tejbir Singh, P.S.A. Sundaram, Mohammed Talib, Patricia Uberoi, Shiv Vishvanathan, Marie-Hélène Zérah. We regret that we could not include all of the original contributions here.

The preparation of this volume would not have been possible without the help of Uma Krishnan. Finally, we would like to thank the former as well as the present directors of the *Centre de Sciences Humaines*, namely Bruno Dorin and Frédéric Grare, for their active interest in the publication, and for the financial support of the CSH.

Abbreviations

ABVP	Akhil Bharatiya Vidyarthi Parishad
AIIMS	All India Institute of Medical Sciences
ASI	Archaeological Survey of India
BHU	Benares Hindu University
BJP	Bharatiya Janata Party
BJS	Bharatiya Jan Sangh
BSP	Bahujan Samaj Party
CPWD	Central Public Works Department
CSD	Conservation Society of Delhi
CSIR	Council of Scientific and Industrial Research
DAV	Dayanand Anglo-Vedic
DDA	Delhi Development Authority
DIZ	Delhi Imperial Zone
DLF	Delhi Land Finance
DSIDC	Delhi State Industrial Development Corporation
DSMDC	Delhi State Mineral Development Corporation
DUAC	Delhi Urban Arts Commission
DUSU	Delhi Univeristy Students Union
HUDCO	Housing and Urban Development Corporation
INC	Indian National Congress
INTACH	Indian National Trust for Artistic and Cultural Heritage
ITC	Instructors' Training Camp
JB	Jamuna Bazaar
JD	Janata Dal
JJ	*Jhuggi-jhonpri*
JP	Janata Party
LF	Left Front
LLB	Bachelor of Law
MA	Master of Arts
MCD	Municipal Corporation of Delhi
MCD	Metropolitan Council of Delhi
MLA	Member of the Legislative Assembly
NCT	National Capital Territory
NDMC	New Delhi Municipal Committee
NF	National Front
NMML	Nehru Museum & Memorial Library
NWFP	North West Frontier Province
OBC	Other Backward Classes
OTC	Officers' Training Camp
PPS	Probability Proportionate to Size
RSS	Rashtriya Swayamsevak Sangh
SDM	Subdivisional Magistrate
UA	Urban Agglomeration
WHO	World Health Organization

1

The Alchemy of an Unloved City

DENIS VIDAL, EMMA TARLO,
VÉRONIQUE DUPONT

Wander around the fringes of the Jama Masjid in the 'old city' or among the ancient ruins of Tughlaqabad, and you may succeed in recovering something of Delhi's romantic appeal. However, the reality of India's vast capital is at once more diverse, more anarchic and at times more intriguing than the semi-mythical Delhi of tourist-book imagination. In this volume, which brings together research from several different domains, it is on these other aspects of the city that we wish to concentrate.

There is, of course, no single way of grasping the complexity of a city like Delhi. While questionnaires, statistics, maps and photographs can no longer fool us into believing their purported objectivity, neither can intimate quotations and case studies pretend to offer unmediated access to the truth. All are mere modes of representation with different strengths and weaknesses and, rather than privilege any single one of them, we have chosen to combine a variety of methodologies in our attempts to shed fresh light on different aspects of the city. This deliberate heterogeneity of approach is reflected in the backgrounds of contributors which span not only conventional social sciences such as history, anthropology, geography, demography and political science but also the visually expressive domains of architecture and photography. Many of the contributors are citizens of Delhi who have a long and intimate relationship with the issues they address.

It would be wrong, however, to surmise that in bringing together a diversity of approaches, our aim is to present an exhaustive portrait of the city and its inhabitants. As Delhi's own history amply demonstrates, there is often only a fine line to be drawn between the desire to create a totalizing image of the city and the confusion of that image with reality—hence the various attempts made by those in power to make the capital correspond to their desired image and to suppress those aspects which do not conform. Our aim, in this book, is quite different. We would rather convince our readers that it is impossible to examine any single aspect of the city without it straightaway unearthing other elements which defy all attempts to reduce Delhi's complex reality.

THE CITY THAT NOBODY LOVES

No one can doubt the fascination that Mumbai (previously Bombay) arouses throughout India, even among those who oppose much of what the city seems to represent. Similarly Calcutta has a legendary reputation not least amongst its own inhabitants who are often ready to defend it with zealous affection. No such loyalty and affection is found amongst the inhabitants of Delhi who are usually either indifferent or actively dislike the city in which they live. With the exception of a few chasers of djinns,[1] of the writer, Khushwant Singh,[2] some descendants of long-established Delhi families and a smattering of others (including some of the collaborators in this book)—hardly anyone is ready to declare a passion for Delhi; not even Ashis Nandy, whose taste and opinion usually flows against the general tide![3]

Admittedly Mumbai has its film industry to keep its exciting contemporary image alive and throbbing. Similarly, Calcutta's reputation is the product of continuous creative effort on the part of its cultural elites who, for more than a century, have expressed appreciation of their city, aided by the enthusiasm of the general populace. Things are very different in Delhi. Despite the new status it acquired as India's capital in 1911-12 and the sweeping changes which have transformed the city since independence, Delhi has somehow got stuck with an image based on stereotypes built as early as the fourteenth century and elaborated during the colonial era.

Take, for example, the image of Delhi as a city characterized by fragmentation. Most works on the capital cannot resist reiterating the claim that Delhi cannot really be considered a city in the true sense owing to the heterogeneity of its urban fabric. And so a consensus has been perpetuated since medieval times in which Delhi is defined as a 'city of cities'—an urban patchwork made up of various components, each of which is thought to bear the imprint of a distinct social, cultural and architectural identity.[4]

This insistence on the fundamental heterogeneity of the urban space is echoed by the insistence by most historians that it is also discontinuity that characterizes the history of the city. In what today certainly remains one of the best collective volumes on the city, the pioneering historian of Delhi, Percival Spear, depicts the city's development as a perpetual 'stop-go' movement, narrowly obedient to the political history of the moment.[5] Somewhat audaciously for an historian, Spear concludes his study by prophesying, 'it is then, with no positive case for continuance, that we may find that the glory of Delhi will depart almost as suddenly as it was thrust upon her in 1912'.[6] These words seem to echo Clémenceau's earlier pronouncement. Visiting New Delhi shortly after its creation, he declared, 'it will make handsome ruins'.

It is tempting to ask what lies behind this endless emphasis on Delhi's absence of spatial and historical continuity in recent times. Is it perhaps just an extension of the recurrent claim made in much colonial literature that South Asia did not have any genuine cultural, social or historical continuity until the arrival of the British? With its mythical reputation as the ultimate urban emblem of the power and decline of the various dynasties which ruled north India, Delhi does indeed seem the very incarnation of such a history. And it is this representation that the literature on the capital continues to convey. However, one of the most important advances made in recent sociological and historiographical writing about India is the questioning of this perspective. Such new research highlights the continuities that have been just as decisive as the fractures in the history of the subcontinent. Delhi is no exception to this rule, and we are today witnessing the beginnings of a historical revision of the city's past.[7] Yet most works on the capital continue to perpetuate outdated categories of analysis and perception.

The impoverished image of Delhi, that reduces it to the status of a hall of mirrors, each reflecting the power of the moment, may be colonial in origin, but it is not without contemporary relevance. For it is this idea that continues to inspire many of Delhi's bureaucrats and politicians even today. One only has to read A.G. Krishna Menon's contribution to this volume to realize the extent to which administrative powers continue to play an essential role in the urbanism of the city. No such equivalent is found in other Indian metropolis. And though it is true that since Independence, there have not been any urban or architectural creations as imposing as Tughlaqabad, Shahjahanabad and Lutyens' New Delhi, this is not for lack of political will. Politicians, administrators, architects and town planners have on the contrary dreamed of building 'a ninth Delhi'[8] or of 'reconstructing Shahjahanabad'.[9] And it would be wrong to think that these projects failed to come to fruition because they were considered too authoritarian for the demands of a new democratic India. A reading of Emma Tarlo's description of how Delhi's poor have been treated in various urban development projects since Independence, dispels any illusions on that score.

Thus political power remains undeniably central to the functioning of Delhi today. And this actually strengthens the need to break loose from the systems of representations which successive powers have tended to impose on the city and its inhabitants. Satish Sharma's contribution to this volume offers a striking visual demonstration. Meditating on his experience as a professional photographer in Delhi, he suggests that the visual imagery of India's capital is restricted and constrained partly by political and administrative controls. At the same time we should not underestimate the equally constricting demands of the marketplace with its tendency to perpetuate a colonially inspired 'exotic' or 'picturesque' imagery of the city and its populace. Satish Sharma explains how he has tried to elude these demands in his own work both by presenting the elite in a different light and by drawing attention to alternative popular photographic images of the city and its people. Such images challenge elite aesthetics and pre-occupations although they are not entirely uninfluenced by them.

Most of the contributions to this volume display a similar concern with challenging conventional images of the city and its populace. In the process, they contribute towards the building of alternative images of Delhi which are at once richer and less predictable for they refer to other social dynamics, other life experiences and other perspectives.

A DIFFERENT IDEA OF DELHI

Poor historical movies can be recognized by the fact that the actors live in decors which are exclusively contemporary to their times. Yet what characterizes every great city is not simply the way different architectural styles and forms of urbanism predominate in turn but also the way they coexist, both physically and ideologically. Delhi is a fantastic illustration of this principle, despite the oft-repeated temptation of its rulers to start from scratch by completely replacing much of the urban fabric. Both the city's architecture and its layout represent an interlacing of extremely varied styles, the coexistence of which is based on fragile foundations.

Hence it is only in the works of poets, novelists, historians, and above all, tourist guides, that Shahjahanabad is permanently destined to incarnate the rise and fall of the Mughal Empire, while New Delhi endlessly epitomizes the grandiose architectural folly of the declining British Empire. Such a perception ignores the fact that the uses and meanings of buildings change over time. For example, for over a century the Red Fort has served as a garrison, first for the British army, and later the Indian army. Furthermore it is from the entrance to the fort that the Prime Minister makes his annual Republic Day speech, thereby transforming the building into a symbol of Independent India. Similarly Rashtrapati Bhawan—once the British viceregal palace— is today the Indian presidential residence, much against the wishes of Gandhi, who had wanted it to be converted into a vast hospital complex.

In other words, with the exception of most religious buildings, the urban history of Delhi is as much about what has happened to monuments and neighbourhoods as about what they may have signified when they were first conceived. This point is brought out by Emma Tarlo and Narayani Gupta in their discussions of two very different aspects of the city's development. Emma Tarlo's ethnographic study of a resettlement colony for displaced squatters in East Delhi, reveals how the development of such urban spaces can not be understood unless we examine the relationship between policies, plans, life histories and critical events. She unpicks the numerous factors and circumstances that have transformed one particular colony both in terms of architectural composition and in terms of social demography. Here there is no straightforward transfer of plans into realities despite the level of authoritarianism behind resettlement projects.

At the other end of the spectrum, Narayani Gupta explores the controversies surrounding the preservation and/or destruction of Delhi's better known architectural heritage. She shows how the preservation of the colonial buildings and layout of Lutyens' New Delhi is largely the result of the extent to which political and administrative elites continue to invest in the area which is today one of the best preserved parts of the city. By contrast, Shahjahanabad (Old Delhi), has been less fortunate. Both its classification as a 'notified slum' and the intensification of commercial activities in the area, have been practically fatal to its architectural heritage. But it would be wrong to assume that the destinies of particular buildings are necessarily dictated by their religious identity or origins. For example, the tombs of the sultans of Lodi have been well protected owing largely to their incorporation into a well maintained public garden, enjoyed by people of all religious persuasions.

It is not only with the marching of time that we find a discrepancy between what a particular building is supposed to represent and what it actually seems to convey. Such a discrepancy may exist from the very moment of a building's conception. It is, after all, only in the dreams of rulers, the sketch pads of architects and the advertisements of real estate agents that architectural projects are ever in total harmony with the intentions of their promoters and the ideologies and lifestyles of their inhabitants.

Menon's discussion of Delhi's architecture since Independence brings out this point quite clearly. He shows how Nehru's ambition for India's capital did not differ much from that of many of his predecessors to the extent that he wanted the new architecture of the city to reflect his own idea of the era and government he personified. However, as Menon demonstrates, there is not much specificity to Delhi's modern architecture which, more often than not, expresses the dominant influence of the state bureaucracy and the scanty imagination of most of the Indian architects freshly trained abroad.

Menon's conclusions are based on the findings of a collective research project aimed at identifying the specificity of Delhi's architecture since Independence. By studying the features of a wide variety of buildings rather than simply selecting the usual few exceptional examples, Menon was able to identify various trends. Until the 1980s Delhi's architecture was characterized by a bland international modernism with occasional half-hearted revivalist attempts. Moreover, Menon interprets the bizarre success of the Austrian architect, Karl Heinz, in Delhi as a reaction to the boring nature of official architecture at the time. Karl Heinz enjoyed the patronage of elites in the private sector with his parodies of Swiss chalets and Tuscan and Andalusian villas. It is only in the projects of the 1980s onwards that Menon identifies a more systematic determination to innovate among Delhi's architects. This is true both for public and private sector projects.

All this suggests that the architecture and urban history of Delhi cannot be reduced to stereotypical descriptions any more than it can be reduced to meaningless debates about degrees of Hindu, Islamic, or Western influences. Neither is it necessarily possible to predict which circumstances and events most effect different aspects of the city's development. The future of Lutyens' Delhi today is, for example, threatened more by the progressive loosening of planning restrictions than it ever was by the transfer of power in 1947. Similarly, Shahjahanabad's architectural heritage has this century suffered more from the neglect of planners and the haphazard commercialization that comes with unrestrained economic development than from the dramatic transfers of population and ownership that accompanied Partition.

The increasing growth of economic activities in Old Delhi is a theme explored by Véronique Dupont in her study of the houseless population and by Denis Vidal in his study of the grain market of Khari Baoli. These studies both show how increased commercial activity has led to a redefinition of the urban fabric and the transformation of specific neighbourhoods. For example, one indirect consequence of the spreading commercialization of the old city has been a lowering of the population density in Shahjahanabad. This had in fact long been considered a desirable, if unattainable, aim by policy makers who had argued for the need to reduce the population density in order to make the area more habitable. As it is, the reverse logic has come into operation. The spread of commercial activities has made the area so uninhabitable that many of the more prosperous Old Delhi residents have chosen to leave in search of accommodation elsewhere. At the bottom end of the economic spectrum, others have of course been forced out under the slum clearance scheme which has been in operation since 1958 and which played a particularly important role in restructuring the profile of different areas of Delhi during the Emergency years of 1975-7. In these two years alone as many as 7,00,000 people were displaced to resettlement colonies, most of which were located on the outskirts of the city.

Such large-scale acts of displacement remind us of the precariousness of the lifestyles, homes and environments of many of Delhi's inhabitants. According to the statistics analysed by Véronique Dupont, practically half the population of Delhi lives in illegal settlements: either in unauthorized colonies, the existence of which is not officially recognized, or in squatter settlements which are perpetually threatened with demolition. The human and sociological consequences of such a situation cannot be underestimated as Saraswati Haider's research demonstrates.

The situation of illegality in which so many in-migrants find themselves leads not only to a permanent sense of insecurity but also to an inability to ameliorate the situation. Most squatters feel it is not worth investing their meagre incomes in their immediate environment when their homes might be destroyed by the authorities at any moment. On the other hand, that moment might stretch out for several years, if not decades owing to the political games of local leaders and politicians who patronize squatter settlements. In the meantime, the inhabitants of such areas carry on living in what are often deplorable conditions.

Though it is commonplace to consider that urban life does at least have the advantage of providing an element of individual emancipation for those who migrate from rural areas, Saraswati Haider's bleak portrait of the lives of squatter women refutes this. Not only do most of the women she interviewed appear to deplore the conditions in which they live (a fact which is hardly surprising), but they also feel that their lives and horizons have become even more limited and confined than they were in their villages of origin. Such women seem to benefit neither from a weakening of the restrictions imposed by the extended family nor from any increased intimacy that one might expect to develop within the nuclear family.

Another point which comes to light from this study is that for the first generation of in-migrants, their villages and regions of origin remain the most significant point of reference even when they have been living in Delhi for several years. This is perhaps the only really common feature of existence shared by the women of the squatter settlement studied by Saraswati Haider and the largely male 'houseless' population of the old city studied by Véronique Dupont. The latter also tend to retain their regions of origin as a key focal point socially, culturally and affectively. Yet the most interesting thing to emerge from research among those who sleep on the pavements and in the night shelters of the old city is that their situation is perhaps not as drastically socially or economically deprived as it at first appears. Véronique Dupont's findings suggest that houseless people do not constitute the poorest fraction of the population, either in Delhi where they are employed, or in their regions of origin where they usually have a permanent residence. By comparison to the squatter women studied by Saraswati Haider, the houseless population seem almost advantaged. Whereas the squatter women had usually come to Delhi against their own volition and virtually all regretted being there, the houseless men interviewed by Véronique Dupont were in Delhi as a result of choices they had made and usually had some motivation for being there. Most had been stimulated largely by economic reasons and, despite all the disadvantages accruing to their lifestyle in the city and the drastic financial constraints they endure, the majority of them had made a deliberate decision to live in a houseless condition in Delhi in order to be able to maximize their savings and avoid spending money on something as short-term as accommodation. In this sense, houselessness is part of a long-term economic strategy.

The decision that many in-migrants make to come to Delhi alone and take refuge on pavements and in night shelters can be better understood when one realizes the numerous pressures associated with even the most basic accommodation. Not only is there the difficulty of finding a place to live within easy distance from the workplace, but also the problem of the illegal status of most of the more affordable options. Those who choose to stay in an existing squatter settlement inevitably find themselves targets of varying degrees of economic and political blackmail. Many of Delhi's politicians gather their support by promising to regularize the situation of squatter families and to improve their standard of living in exchange for electoral support. At the same time, they often threaten them with dire consequences if they show signs of withholding support. If the politicians' many promises were fulfilled, then the deal would at least have some material worth. But, as squatters themselves realize, no politician would be so foolish as to redress the situation for this would mean relinquishing his or her hold over potential electors.

It is within this context that we can better understand how and why so many of the inhabitants of the resettlement colony studied by Emma Tarlo, did not resist the truly Faustian pact imposed on them during the state of Emergency. This was the time when many agreed to be sterilized or to pay others to get sterilized as a means of securing small plots of land on a so-called legal basis.

Tricks and machinations concerning land and property are by no means restricted to the urban poor and their patrons. In fact, they are nowhere more apparent than in the antics of those wealthy Delhites who, in recent years, have started posing as 'farmers' on the outskirts of the city. Anita Soni takes us on a revealing tour of the Mehrauli countryside in so-called rural Delhi where new farms seem to be proliferating at an unexpected rate. But before we can delude ourselves into believing that this is a new ecologically sound form of urban development, we are shown what lies behind the walls of these so called farms. Here we find, not simple rural farmhouses but palatial villas, not fields of crops but swimming pools and luxury gardens. The proliferation of these false farms not only violates existing property laws but is also ecologically disastrous. And so an area which should have been reserved as a 'green lung' for the capital becomes yet another drag on the capital's scarce resources.

Unlike the migrant workers who came to the area some years earlier to work in the stone quarries, the wealthy owners of unauthorized farmhouses are well placed for staying put. Most have sufficient political and financial clout to be able to minimize the risk of eviction.

POLITICS, COMMERCE AND THE REIGN OF INTERMEDIARIES

It should by now be clear that the history and sociology of Delhi is about the relationship between people and place played out in different parts of the city at different moments in time. Yet, as we have seen, the dynamics of this relationship are often highly complex and have been subject to a variety of misconceptions and oversimplifications. This is as true for the political sphere as for the architectural and spatial.

Christophe Jaffrelot's research challenges the common assumption that the long-standing success of Hindu nationalist parties in Delhi politics can be adequately explained by the traumas faced by the Hindu refugees who came to the capital following Partition. Whilst it is true that the huge influx of refugees altered both the religious make-up and the voting patterns of the people of Delhi, it is insufficient to interpret the rise of Hindu nationalism purely as a consequence of the Partition experience. What Christophe Jaffrelot's research reveals is that Hindu nationalism was already gaining popularity both in the Punjab and in Delhi in the decades leading up to Partition. Its main support came from the Hindu business communities in both areas. One effect of Partition was to increase the concentration of these business communities in the capital and it is this, rather than the Partition experience per se, which has inflated the fortunes of Hindu nationalist parties in Delhi.

Interestingly a similar interpretation is suggested by V.B. Singh's study of the 1996 elections in Delhi. His analysis confirms that despite the sweeping upheavals in the political life of the country in recent years, the social base of the two main parties, the Congress and the BJP (Bharatiya Janata Party) has remained relatively stable. The success, and also the limitations, of the

BJP seems to be directly linked to the fact that wealthy upper caste people, and in particular, business communities, are over-represented in the capital.

Although V.B. Singh and Christophe Jaffrelot's research is restricted mainly to the rise of the Hindu nationalist movement in Delhi, it nonetheless has wider analytical implications. Both reveal that political events are not necessarily the most significant factor in influencing voting patterns. Rather, it would appear that political life in Delhi is also governed to a large extent by the ideology of the business communities and by the way historical and political events favour or diminish their grip on the city. To ascertain the precise nature of this grip, one has to go beyond the purely political to examine the social and economic dynamics at play in Delhi.

As Saraswati Haider demonstrates, we cannot fully grasp how electoral policy functions in Delhi without also considering the crucial role played by the intermediaries (*pradhans* and others) who link the capital's poor to its politicians.[10] Similarly, whatever field of economic activity we have examined, whether the wholesale markets investigated by Denis Vidal, the stone quarries analysed by Anita Soni or the informal job market examined by Véronique Dupont, we find that intermediaries or brokers play an essential role.

Neither should it be imagined that direct state intervention necessarily diminishes the presence and puissance of intermediaries. As Anita Soni shows, the main consequence of the nationalization of the stone quarries on the periphery of Delhi, in 1976, was to add a new layer of intermediaries to the ones that already existed. However, the most extreme example of how intermediaries subvert state imperatives is found in Emma Tarlo's discussion of birth control politics in Delhi during the Emergency. Here we see the worst excesses of governmental authoritarianism diverted into a shocking new form of 'business transaction' as intermediaries created a new market in which land was traded for sterilization.

Given that the consequence of direct state intervention is to increase, rather than reduce, the presence of intermediaries, we might expect them to become obsolete with the current trend towards the globalization of the market economy. But Denis Vidal's study of the main grain market in Old Delhi suggests this will not happen. He shows that intermediaries, though they are in many ways parasitic, cannot simply be dismissed as impediments to the functioning of markets. While it is true that they generally gain a substantial profit from transactions, it is also true that they play a decisive role in defining supply and demand and in setting up business relations. This means that they play an important role in discovering new potential markets and facilitating the generalization of the market economy. Far from suggesting the diminution of Delhi's economic importance, the omnipresence of intermediaries is evidence of the extreme degree of commercialization prevalent in every aspect of life in the city.

It is time at last to challenge the long-standing opposition drawn between Mumbai as a city dominated purely by business concerns and Delhi as a city dominated almost entirely by politics and administration. This well-worn cliché has served to reassure those who wish to believe that economic life has remained largely independent of bureaucracy, just as it has served to reassure others that it is the state which ultimately controls the destiny of the nation. However, the contributions in this volume confirm that it is illusory to think of 'economics' and 'politics' as autonomous domains in Delhi, as elsewhere, and that it is artificial to draw a separation between the state and administration on the one hand from the market on the other. It should therefore come as no surprise when we learn from Philippe Cadène's maps that with the spread of liberalization, Delhi is coming to occupy an increasingly large role in the economy of India, to the detriment, not only of Calcutta, but also, Mumbai.

TRAJECTORY OF THIS VOLUME

The essays in this book take us from the specific to the general, although the relation between the two is always apparent. This means that although we begin in Part I with the experiences of people who inhabit comparatively marginal spaces—a squatter settlement, a resettlement colony and the rural fringes of South Delhi— we learn how their lives are intimately bound up with wider historical, political and economic developments. Life-histories therefore become a means to understanding the history and identity of various localities within the city.

That particular locations are defined partly by the people and goods that move through them is a theme taken up in Part II which shifts the focus to the area commonly known as Old Delhi. It begins with visual and verbal vignettes from the lives of a few of the thousands of men who earn a livelihood in the transport industry. Whether driving buses, bullock carts, trucks or rickshaws, these transport workers are essential to the social and economic dynamics of the city. So too are the houseless people who sleep on the pavements of Old Delhi by night and perform a wide variety of manual tasks during the day. Tracing their movements enables us to understand the logic behind the apparently perpetual stream of people attracted to Delhi's crowded commercial core while an examination of the role of intermediaries in the wholesale grain market of Khari Baoli helps unpack the dynamics of business relations which link a few narrow streets in Old Delhi to national and global markets.

Part III leads us out of specific localities towards a wider consideration of the buildings which help to define the identity and reputation of the capital as a whole. What becomes clear, whether we are discussing modern architecture, conservation history or photographic representations, is the complexity of the relationship between architecture and power in India's capital city. In Parts IV and V we take another step back to document and analyse political, demographic and economic developments. Here we are less concerned with the histories of individual people or buildings than with general trends which help characterize voting patterns and migratory flows to and from the capital. Finally, through a series of cartographic representations, we are able to take distance from Delhi by placing it within the larger Indian urban structure.

Though we end with maps and statistics which enable generalisations about the city, it is hoped that readers will not forget the human stories which lie behind—and too often escape—such neat formulations. Delhi represents very different things to different people and, in many ways, this book is the proof of it. Not only are the experiences of the women and men whose lives are portrayed widely divergent, but so too are those of the contributors whose attitudes to the development of the city vary from deep frustration and concern to occasional bursts of optimism. As editors, we have not tried to wipe out this diversity for we feel that it is this which rendered the collaboration lively. We hope that readers will share our feeling that such diversity of perspectives enriches the volume and prevents it from creating yet another totalizing image of India's capital city.

NOTES

1. W. Dalrymple, *City of Djinns: A Year in Delhi*, New Delhi: Harper Collins, 1993.
2. Khushwant Singh, *Delhi, a Novel*, Delhi: Penguin, 1989.
3. See: A. Baviskar, 'Towards a sociology of Delhi, Report on a seminar', *Economic and Political Weekly*, 5 Dec. 1998, p. 3102.
4. See for example: Ibn Battuta (1325) in *Historic Delhi: An Anthology*, H.K. Kaul (ed.), Delhi: OUP, 1985; G.R. Hearn, *Seven cities of Delhi: a description and history*, Calcutta: Thacker and Spink, 1909; A Shafi, 'A tale of two cities: Old and New Delhi', *Islamic Review*, 34(4), 1933, pp. 244-5; A. Banerji, 'Fifteen cities of Delhi', *Link*, 6(1) 15, August 1963, pp. 51-2; M.R. Anand, 'The many Delhis', *Marg*, 20 4°, 1967, pp. 4-8; M.P. Thakore, 'Sixteen cities of Delhi?' *Indian Geographer*, 8(1-2), 1963, pp. 84-119; C. Sarkar, 'Several cities in one', *Hemisphere*, 1(3), March 1971, pp. 2-10; P. Vestal, 'Seven cities of Delhi', *News Circle*, 18(4), 1972, pp. 22-8; B. Ghosh, 'Successive Delhis: from the sensuous architecture of the past to the insignificance and inappropriateness of the present', *Design*, 24(3), 1980, pp. 25-36; P. Singh, 'The nine Delhis: Historical Perspective', in *Delhi: the deepening urban crisis*, Patwant Singh, and Ram Dhamija (eds.), New Delhi, 1989, pp. 13-18; A.K. Jain, *The cities of Delhi*, New Delhi: Management Publishing Co., 1994.
5. P. Spear, 'Delhi the "step-go" capital' in *Delhi through the ages; Essays in Urban History, Culture and Society*, R.E. Frykenberg (ed.), Delhi: OUP, 1986, pp. 463-80.
6. Idem, p. 478.
7. C. Bayly, 'Delhi and other cities of North India during the "twilight"', in R.E. Frykenberg, op. cit., pp. 221-36.
8. G. Cullen, *The Ninth Delhi*, Delhi: Town and Country Planning Organisation, 1960.
9. Jagmohan, *Rebuilding Shahjahanabad: The Walled City of Delhi*, Delhi: Vikas, 1975.
10. See also the researches of Tarun Bose on political practices in Delhi and, in particular 'Power games in/and (un)authorised colonies', *Mainstream*, 1996.

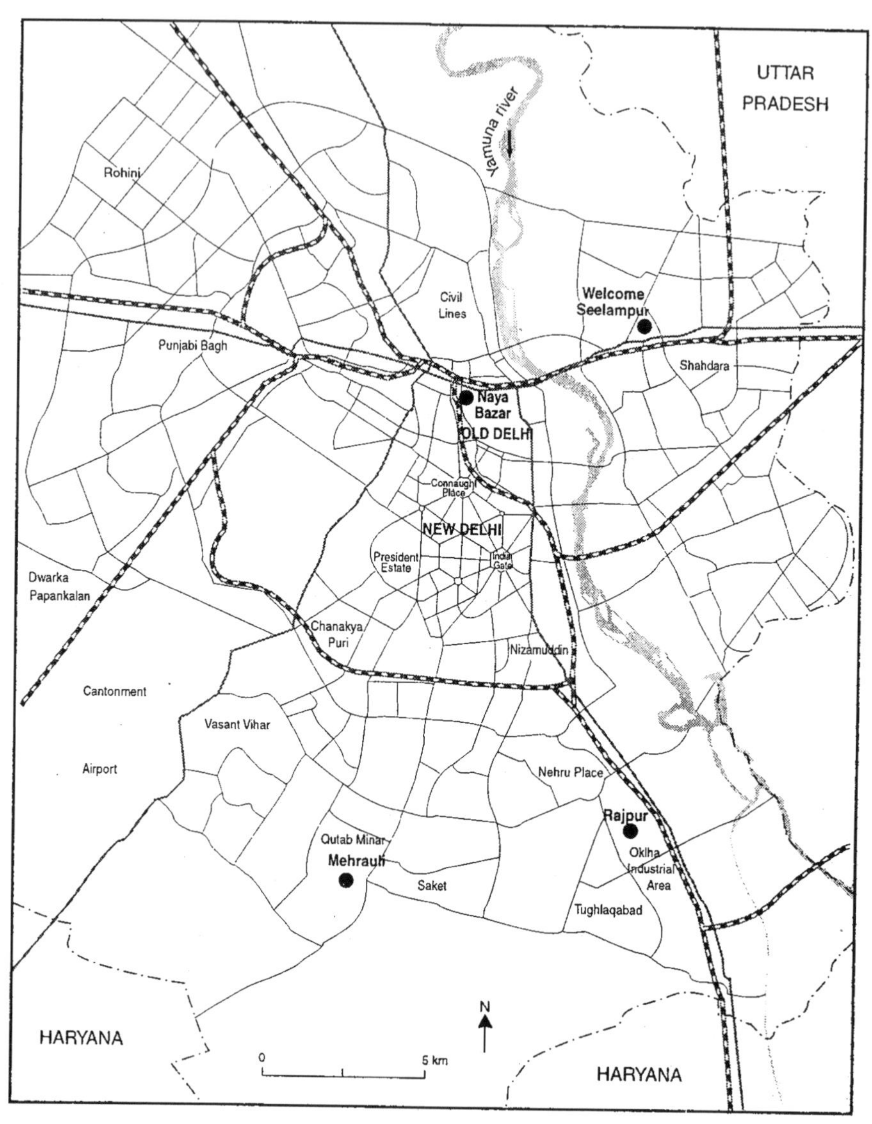

MAP 1.1 DELHI LOCALITIES STUDIED AND OTHER LANDMARKS.

PART I

LIFE HISTORIES—CITY HISTORY

2

Migrant Women and Urban Experience in a Squatter Settlement

SARASWATI HAIDER

Much of India's increasing urban population comprises migrants from rural areas where 39 per cent of people were still living below the poverty line in 1994[1] and where unemployment and under-employment rates are high even now. Women form part of this vast migration stream heading for the major cities, not to find work (though they may later take up employment) but more often to join their husbands who are in search of labour. The migrant men followed by their wives and some, or, all children, are invariably forced to find shelter in squatter settlements because of lack of affordable housing in the cities. Such rural dwellers catapulted into an urban milieu are often faced with radically different surroundings to which they have to adapt.

This essay attempts to document the experiences of rural migrant women as they confront their new urban environment—physical, social, economic, cultural and ecological. In particular, it focuses on personal narrations of their experiences of living in a squatter settlement in the capital city of Delhi. Narrations of this type offer deep insights into people's thinking and lives. They are able to capture the subtle nuances of thinking and behaviour which are missed in statistical figures. For instance, a statistical survey to investigate rural migrant women's physical and emotional reactions to their urban surroundings would not be able to capture the various patriarchal attitudes that underlie women's thinking and behaviour and have become an integral part of their mental make-up. Such attitudes are only revealed when women are left to talk at length through unstructured narrations. Similarly, the intensity of the stress women feel in their changed ecological surroundings and their struggle for survival in a situation where life seems to get confined to a ceaseless effort to gain access to basic minimum amenities would be lost in a statistical survey. Such information and insights can only be gained from keen observation and continuous dialogue with the protagonists of the research over a considerable period of time.

Such an approach is particularly necessary when conducting research amongst women in a squatter settlement because of the 'culture of silence' and unobtrusiveness to which they are expected to conform. For girls and young women, and to a large extent even older women, talking too much or flaunting themselves is considered improper behaviour—bold, brash and brazen. Girls are trained and socialized to do the work ordained for them, without asking questions or making protests.

Most rural migrant women living in Rajpur,[2] the squatter settlement in Delhi where I conducted my research, are a quiet lot and many of them are submerged in the 'culture of silence'.[3] To get them to speak about their personal feelings, thoughts and opinions was a difficult task. I wanted to avoid what is called an 'interview', with the researcher merely asking questions and the 'interviewee' providing answers often mechanically and soullessly. I was keen for a more involved engagement: to initiate a dialogue with my protagonists. But here my efforts were often thwarted, partly owing to the impenetrability and impassivity of rural migrant women, and partly due to the context of our encounter. I was a stranger to these women, coming from a different class, and these factors undoubtedly increased the communication gap, making it doubly problematic for the women to participate in a dialogue with me. Furthermore, I was often mistaken initially for someone from the government towards whose personnel the squatter settlement dwellers have much antipathy.

On the whole, using the mixed technique of dialogue and minimal questioning I was able to gain meaningful insights into women's personal, social and cultural lives in Rajpur: their sense of claustrophobia at being trapped in a heavily congested squatter settlement; their monotonous daily work in the effort to access basic minimum needs, especially water; their unending endeavour to make two ends meet somehow; their nagging fear that their hutment might be demolished at any time making them live in constant anxiety and insecurity; their curtailed freedom of movement; their muting; their reflections on their lives in an urban city—often only echoes of information given by their spouse; their almost non-existent relationships with their husbands; their alienation from the larger urban social and cultural milieu, all of which emerge fairly tellingly from the narratives of the women of Rajpur.

However, it must be stressed that if I have been able to elicit expressive, articulate narratives from my protagonists it is, I think, only because of the long time I have spent interacting with them—more than four years—over which time easy rapport eventually became established. Over this long period of association many women have been able to shed at least some of their inhibitions and overcome their initial suspicion of me. Today they view me not so much as a stranger, than as an elderly woman, who likes chatting with them and means them no harm.

THE SETTING

Squatter settlements are locally known as *jhuggi-jhonpri* (hutment) clusters or colonies (JJ clusters/colonies). Most inhabitants of these squatter settlements are rural migrants from all over India, especially the northern and eastern states. Squatter settlements in Delhi are proliferating at a rapid rate, from 929 JJ clusters in 1990[4] with a population of about 1.5 million[5] to 1080 in 1994 with a population of about 2.7 million and 1100 in 1997 with a population estimated at more than 3 million[6]—in other words almost one-third of the population of Delhi. With rural poverty aggravated following the introduction of economic reforms in India in 1991 and the accompanying curtailment in public expenditures in rural employment generation programmes, it is estimated that the number of JJ clusters must have gone up further by now.[7]

JJ clusters are spread all over Delhi. It is not unusual to find squatters' huts next to modern high-rise buildings or five-star hotels or in the nooks and crevices of the posh colonies of Delhi. As most of the JJ clusters are to be found on illegally occupied land they are unauthorized but the authorities are indecisive about what should be done with them. Because squatters live within a continuing sense of impermanence owing to the threat of demolition, their *jhuggis* are often makeshift dwellings of bricks and mud with thatched or tin roofs covered with polythene, or corrugated iron sheets. The *jhuggis* are very closely packed and if viewed from above the cluster looks like a beehive interspersed with very narrow alleys in a maze. Some more daring *jhuggi* dwellers have taken the risk of constructing permanent dwellings despite the insecurity. However, these homes are still very small and congested, housing more people than health norms permit.

JJ clusters always look dingy, drab and dreary—like grey patchwork quilts seen from above with a permanent smoke-filled haze hovering over them. This appearance lends them a peculiar air of mystery and they are looked on by middle-class city dwellers as ominous and dangerous places full of hidden vices. Most JJ clusters have a vacant piece of land next to them which serves as an open-air latrine. Sometimes they are located near stagnant ponds or along river beds. JJ clusters are often pervaded by a mixed odour of mildew, cooking food and stale clothes and tend to look damp, dark and derelict.

Working in Rajpur, visiting other JJ clusters and reading about squatter settlements in other developing countries, I get the impression that urban poverty in India is perhaps more dehumanized and dehumanizing than in other similar countries. It is unimaginable even to many Indians unless they see for themselves the squalid conditions in which the JJ dwellers live.

Rajpur is a large, unauthorized, illegally occupied settlement in Delhi, with a density of about 1.6 persons per sq. m. Situated on a hillock on land allotted to a government agency, it is surrounded by residential buildings functioning as small-scale manufacturing units. According to an unpublished survey by the Slum and JJ Wing of the Delhi Development Authority (DDA) in 1990 the cluster had a total of 2708 *jhuggis* with a population estimated at approximately 12,000. However in a more recent conversation with one of the active *pradhans*[8] of Rajpur I was told that the number of *jhuggis* is about 3,500 and the population approximately 16,000.

Rajpur has a large population of Scheduled Castes which constitute about 75 per cent of the settlement. The majority of inhabitants are from the state of Uttar Pradesh (62 per cent) with much smaller numbers from Bihar,

Rajasthan and Haryana. There are about 150-200 Muslim households, 1 Sikh household and the rest are Hindu.

Men outnumber women in Rajpur where 58 per cent of the population is male. Illiteracy is high at 52 per cent and of the so-called literates, 36 per cent had studied only up to the primary level. About 83 per cent of the population have a monthly income of Rs. 1000 or below. In other words the majority of families live below the official poverty line.

The Rajpur population is young, most inhabitants being between the ages of 18 and 45. According to 1990 statistics, 13 per cent of males were unskilled workers, 13 per cent had their own businesses and were self-employed owning small shops or buying and selling junk, 30 per cent were in service jobs and as many as 37 per cent were unemployed. Only 7 per cent were skilled workers. The employment data for women was not collected, but most Rajpur women are housewives. Most of the inhabitants (94 per cent) had come to Rajpur during the period 1977-85 and the majority are first generation migrants.

MIGRATION TO THE METROPOLIS: NOT A WOMAN'S DECISION

As far as Rajpur migrants are concerned, the decision to migrate to Delhi had, with few exceptions, been taken by the men of the household in consultation, and, after discussion, with the senior male members of the larger family unit.

Shanno, a Berwa (a Scheduled Caste employed in Delhi mainly as construction workers), whose husband hails from a village in the Jaipur district of Rajasthan and who, like most Rajpur women, is illiterate, said:

> In the village people like us who have no land do agricultural labour. My man's[9] family had some land. But very little—about 2 *bighas* [a *bigha* is about one quarter of an acre]. There was not much money in agricultural labour. That is why we came to Dilli [Delhi]. One of my man's relations told him that there were good prospects and jobs in construction work in Dilli. He worked and lived in Dilli. He told my man to come to Dilli also. My man wanted to move to Dilli very much after that. There were in all eight brothers and sisters: six brothers including my man who was the third eldest in the family. The land they owned was too small to be distributed among all the brothers [the sisters were not considered]. My man's father was dead. His mother was alive. We all lived together. All the brothers agreed that my man should move to Dilli and send them some money from there when he had got good work. I had no say in the matter. Women are not supposed to *tang adao* [obstruct] in these things. But my man had no money to move to Dilli. My man had decided to take me with him as he thought we could both work as construction workers in Dilli. We worked very hard to save enough money and then finally came to Dilli.

Most men of Rajpur had been marginal farmers with small landholdings or agricultural labourers, before coming to Delhi. As already noted, the decision to move to Delhi was normally finalized by men. However, occasionally a woman instigates her husband to leave his home in the village and move to a city in order to lead a separate life of his own, get his full share of earnings and have full control over his finances. This is what happened in Chanda's case.

Chanda, a Bawar (a Scheduled Caste claiming descendence from Brahmins) comes from a village in the district of Ballia in Uttar Pradesh (her husband's village):[10]

> My man was the youngest among his four brothers and three sisters. We had no land. All who could, worked as field labourers. We got earnings just enough to wipe our tears with: 20 rupees for me and 30 rupees for my man per day of work. All our money was given to my man's father and we had very little to eat. We were like birds thrown some grain; we had no money to spend on anything but food. My two older children were very small then. So, when my sister's *nandoi* [husband's sister's husband] happened to visit our village and told me about how in Dilli everyone can get a job and live much better I got after my man to shift to Dilli. My man is very simple and silent. He can never speak up for himself so I had to break the news to the family. Finally, they talked it over. My man's father and brothers did not like the idea. They would lose two workers and earners. But I got after my man. Ultimately my man, myself and two children came to Dilli and to Rajpur. I borrowed money from my brother. We stayed with my sister's *nandoi* at first though it was wrong for us to do so because wife-givers do not stay at the house of any one belonging to the family of wife-takers. But what could I do? I also took some money on loan from my sister's *nandoi* and purchased land for a *jhuggi*.[11] It cost me Rs. 2000. We built a flimsy *jhuggi* which cost me another Rs. 1000. But my fate is bad. Two years back our *jhuggi* got burnt down in a fire.

Most Rajpur migrants took their decision to move out of their villages on information given about good prospects in the metropolis by some relative or someone from the village who had settled in Delhi. The male migrant initially stayed with his relative, or, the man from his village who had enticed him to come to Delhi and with whom the migrant may have a fictitious kinship relationship.[12]

Usually, the wife just followed the husband—it not even being considered necessary to ask her if she wanted to migrate. Wherever her husband took her, was where she was meant to be. Most female migrants had followed this trajectory. Their interface with the urban milieu occurred because of their husband's decision to migrate and not through their own free will—something women are not supposed to possess.

INTERFACE WITH THE URBAN ENVIRONMENT OF RAJPUR

Wirth in his well-known theory of urbanism identified three demographic elements which play an important role in the emergence of a distinct urban mode of life: the large size of population, density of population and its heterogeneity.[13] The women who migrated to Rajpur had their first experience of urban living amidst large numbers of people when they arrived in the slum. They were forced to live in close proximity to other human beings, cheek by jowl. The women were used to having open spaces around their villages; but such open spaces are nowhere to be found in a squatter settlement.

Maya, an illiterate housewife, a Jatav by caste (Jatavs are a sub-caste of the Chamar caste whose traditional occupation was preparing and curing leather) from the Mathura district in Uttar Pradesh, recounts her first introduction to Delhi. Her experience was similar to that of most Rajpur women as were the health problems she encountered.

I was so frightened at the Dilli station when I stepped out of the *rail ka dibba* [train box, i.e. compartment] by all the people milling around me. As it is I was feeling sick because of the train journey. I had never travelled by rail. My heart was clutched by the hand of fear. On seeing the crowd at Dilli station, it beat like a drum. I was sure I would get lost. I was petrified. My man was hurrying far ahead while I ran following him far behind. I had no children otherwise it would have been difficult to keep them with me while running to keep abreast of my man. When I came to Rajpur I was stunned. There were such small huts: hundreds of them all built so close together. Even now, after so many years, every time I change clothes or have a bath in the *jhuggi* I feel everyone can see me. I still do not know who lives beyond the six or seven *jhuggis* that encircle mine. I felt breathless all the time and giddy and still do. There are no trees and one can see what is happening in other people's *jhuggis*. My neighbour's man beats her every other day and she shouts at the top of her voice. I get paralysed when I hear her. My man beats me too but not so badly. Most of our time we spend outside our *jhuggis* sitting on the threshold. One cannot hide anything here. I often remember the trees and greenery in the village and the clean air. Here the air is always filled with a bad smell and is stale. There is a stink here all the time. People are always quarrelling here. This whole place is like a chicken pen.

INTERFACE WITH BASIC URBAN SERVICES

Delhi's population is growing at a very fast rate every year though the growth rate has declined in the decade 1981-91.[14] The basic urban services required to fulfil the needs of the burgeoning population are in very short supply, well below the minimum requirement. Not surprisingly, basic amenities are better provided in areas where the rich live[15] while the worst provision is found in JJ clusters. However, the squatters of Delhi form important and sizeable 'vote-banks' whose votes can make or mar the career of a Delhi politician. JJ clusters in Delhi are hotbeds of politics.[16] And in such a context, the politics is largely a politics of basic amenities. In this section, I shall deal with the experience of migrant women *vis-à-vis* some of the essential amenities of daily life.

The Impermanence of Jhuggis*—A Constant Source of Insecurity*

The most harrowing anxiety of migrant women in Rajpur relates to the impermanence of their dwellings—their *jhuggis*—since the authorities remain undecided about the 'slum problem'.[17] Every now and then the rumour goes around that the Rajpur JJ cluster is to be demolished.

Says Sherbati, a woman from the district of Azamgarh in Uttar Pradesh whose husband works as a sweeper in the Municipal Corporation of Delhi (MCD):

The worst aspect of living in Dilli for me is that we are not sure when the *masheen* [bulldozer] will come and erase our assiduously and painstakingly constructed *jhuggis* in which our earnings of thick blood and sweat have been invested; so much time and labour. We are never sure whether we will be here tomorrow or not. Every two months the news goes around that the JJ cluster is to be demolished and we live in fear for several days. My heart is always troubled because of the anxiety about the fate of our *jhuggis*. Our life here is full of insecurity. Our joy and peace have gone. I do not know why they do not decide once and for all whether the Rajpur cluster is to be demolished or not. The *pradhans* also do not know whether the cluster is to be demolished. This hanging in mid-air is killing. In our village we had a makeshift hut but at least we knew it would keep standing. Our hut in the village could have been demolished by high-up people there but we did not live in constant fear that it could be demolished any time. My man's family tills the one *bigha* of land that we have in the village. My man's only brother wanted to buy our share of it but we did not sell. Life in Dilli is so uncertain. One does not know where we will be one day from another. Our land in the village is like a guarantee of a living space for us in our village, if nowhere else.

Kalavati, a woman of about 55 years is a Chamar from the Ballia district in Uttar Pradesh. Her husband has a pan-bidi shop (tobacco and pan stall) in their *jhuggi* from where only Chamars make their purchases. She told me:

I have been living in this cluster for a very long time and never have we had the certainty that our *jhuggi* will not be demolished. If they have let us live here for so many years, then why can't they let us live here permanently instead of playing cat and mouse with us? Our condition is like that of the snake and the mongoose: the snake can neither swallow it nor spit it out. This anxiety is like a mouse nibbling at a bag of flour and has eaten away my peace. At least in the village we were sure of a dwelling place. The *neta log* [political figures] come at election time and promise that they will not let our *jhuggis* be demolished—so my man tells me. My man says they promise to give us official papers for our *jhuggis* but nothing of the sort has been done for so many years. The *neta log* keep coming and going. My man says these *neta log* are all thieves. People from here are taken in bus loads—even children—to rallies organized by *neta log* to stop our *jhuggis* from being demolished; but my man says that this is all a sham and show. We remain where we are.

Shortage of Water: The Bane of Migrant Women's Lives

Almost all women in Rajpur complained about the shortage of water and about how their whole day seemed to go collecting and storing water for drinking, cooking and other purposes. Women's lives seemed to revolve around this one basic problem for which they are the ones who have to bear the brunt.[18]

Phulwati is a cleaner in a manufacturing unit situated opposite the cluster. She is a Balmiki (sweeper caste) from a village in the district of Sawai Madhopur in Rajasthan.

One's whole day goes worrying whether one will have water for the day or not. My *jhuggi*, as you can see, is on the upper side of the hillock so that water has to be brought up can by can [usually plastic cans in which automotive lubricant is sold] for drinking and cooking. My children are all small except one but he goes to school. My man goes out to work at 9 in the morning and does not return till 7 in the evening. I too work for three hours in the morning. I have the chore of going down from my *jhuggi* and climbing back up with a full can of water. I have to do this four or five times to procure enough water for the day for cooking and drinking. My man has his bath at the handpump and he or I bathe the children there too. We can't do it daily but we do it every three or four days. But how can I bathe at the handpump? The handpump which is close to my *jhuggi* has been out of order for the past whole year. No one has come to repair it. The other handpump is quite a distance away. When I wish to bathe I have to fetch water from the handpump and bathe inside the *jhuggi*. I can't bathe everyday because it requires so much extra work. It is all a lot of hard work and trouble. We do not drink water from the handpump but from the tap; yet all of us are always falling ill. Everyone told me that water from the handpump was not good to drink or cook with. The water problem is bad in Rajpur but it is especially tough for people like me—and there are many in the same position—those who live at the top of the hillock. In other families older boys bring water up by cycle. But I can't do that. In our village we had a well of our own and we could fetch water from it whenever we wanted. It was close to all our huts because it was a well meant only for us and not the high caste people. Here one has to keep waiting with one's heart a flutter for the water to come out of the taps. There is no fixed time when the water comes and sometimes the water does not come at all. I had thought that in a big city like Dilli, at least, there would be enough water for us but getting water here seems to be more difficult than it was in my village. The whole day here seems to go in fetching water.

Chanda, the tea shop owner bemoans:

I run this tea shop. How can I wait endlessly in a long line to fill water? My eldest child, who is a boy, goes far away to study in Govindpuri. He is not around in the cluster in the mornings and my daughter is not old enough to fetch heavy cans of water. Besides, one should not let young girls do heavy work. They may hurt themselves badly. Then who will marry them? We will then have a bigger problem on our head. My man goes to fetch water in the morning and we keep it here at the shop. But my man takes a long time because he cannot quarrel with the women who are all like hyenas at the tap when the water comes. There are often bad quarrels at the tap. My son gets water in the evening for me. He can fight. I don't live very far from the tap so it is not as bad as it is for the others. Water, I think, is the main problem in Rajpur. After all one cannot live without water.

I remember that the problem of water supply became a hot issue in one election.[19] The *pradhan* of Rajpur, Badlu, who is very wily, bargained for water pipes for the cluster with all the candidates. The candidates were aware that Rajpur had elected Badlu as leader. I heard someone here say that the candidates thought that the votes in Rajpur were all in the hands of Badlu. It was said that Badlu assured the candidates of all parties that the people behind him would vote for the candidate who would provide water pipes. One of the candidates—he was called Netaji (and when I saw him here in front of my shop, I thought he looked like a hairy bear)—was said to have spent at least one million rupees on the election. It was he who ordered pipes for 15,000 rupees to be delivered to the cluster. Do you know, Auntyji,[20] those pipes came within two hours. I saw it with my own eyes. But do you know I heard people say here at my shop that Badlu had made a pile of money after bargaining. The pipes just lay around for almost a year and then they were installed but they have not made much difference to the scarcity of water. In the village we had wells from which we could fetch water at any time. At least one was free from the anxiety whether there would be water or not. And in our village there was a pond where we bathed and washed our clothes whenever we wanted. Here it is impossible to bathe and wash clothes everyday. I have no time. My daughter washes the clothes. It is the women who have to do all the hard work of fetching water. At least my man helps. He is very simple you see. Other women's men do not help.

Sanitation: Too Much Other Work So Civic Cleanliness Neglected

The road in front of Rajpur is a dirt track and is always slushy with the overflowing dirty water of the open drains from inside the cluster. These pour into the open drains on the sides of the road but since these are always blocked, the water flows on to the road. All squatter settlements are unhygienic. Rajpur is no different. There are open drains full of muck and children's faeces with small piles of garbage alongside, although the narrow alleys have, at least, been paved by the authorities. It is women who are supposed to take care of cleanliness in the *jhuggis* and around them because this is considered women's work. Men never do it. Men never do any housework as long as there is a woman to do it. If they did housework when their wives were around, they would be ridiculed as their wife's lackey which would be an insult to their masculinity. Reproduced below is a conversation I had with Ramia, a woman of the Yadav caste (milkherds by tradition) from a village in Samastipur in the state of Bihar. Ramia's husband works in a manufacturing unit that makes polythene bags. Ramia's thinking and her day are more or less typical of the migrant women in Rajpur in general.

Saraswati Haider (SH): Ramia, is it difficult to clean the *jhuggi* every day?

Ramia (R): No. It is not difficult. I clean my *jhuggi* everyday. I have three young children. The youngest is two years old. He dirties the *jhuggi* very much. He urinates and sometimes defecates inside the *jhuggi* also so I have to clean the *jhuggi* everyday otherwise my man would be very angry. It is not difficult. Not more than it was in the village where I had to clean the cow-shed, clean the house and apply cow dung to the floor and sides of the cooking area [cow dung is used as a cleansing agent]. I had to sweep our two rooms. I did all the work in the house of my man's family which included his father and mother, a young sister, an elder brother and his wife and two younger brothers. Since I was the youngest daughter-in-law I had to do the major part of the housework.

SH: But I see that you dump the garbage just outside your *jhuggi*. Is it too much trouble to walk to the refuse dump? [There are three dumps constructed by the MCD at the side of the dirt road at the base of the cluster which are supposed to be cleaned by MCD sweepers everyday but apparently are not because I have always seen them overflowing with garbage and spreading a horrible smell all around.]

R: Yes it is. I have so much to do everyday. I get up at about 4 in the morning, make rotis and vegetables. My eldest daughter, who is 11 or 12 years old, helps me make the food. She studied up to Class VI but after that my man stopped her going to school. It was the right thing to do because I needed her to help me in the house. Besides, she has learnt how to read and write. That is enough for a girl. After all what will she do with too much education? We have to marry her soon and then she will only be doing housework and looking after children. She doesn't need high education for that. She needs to be trained to do housework and look after children so I make her help me in the house.

SH: Do you feed the children in the morning? You must be giving them milk to drink?

R: From where do I have money to give my children milk? I buy a kilo of milk for Rs. 15. I give half of it to my youngest child during the day and the rest I use to make tea. My man has tea in the morning and in the evening when he comes back from work. My older children—my two daughters, also drink tea and have something to eat in the morning. My second daughter goes to the Municipal Corporation school here in Rajpur. She is in class IV. I have to get her ready. She leaves at about 7:30 in the morning. She walks to the school which is close by.

SH: You must be fetching water after that.

R: No. I then clean the *jhuggi* with my daughter helping me. I put away all the bed clothes, sweep the floor and clean the cooking area.

SH: And you dump the garbage outside the *jhuggi*.

R: Yes. I don't have time to walk down to the dump to throw the garbage and I can't send my daughter down alone. One has to guard a daughter very closely. So, I keep the garbage in front of the *jhuggi*. All of us in the alley here pay 10 rupees per month to a sweeper woman to clean the alley and the drains and throw the garbage in the dump. The government sweepers don't bother to clean the alleys. They only clean the dirt road in front of the cluster and they don't even do that everyday. About five women come and I always see them sitting, chatting and smoking bidis. They do no work. Leela, the sweeper, is lazy and doesn't come everyday to clean the drains and alley litter. We shout at her but it has no effect. And, when she cleans the drains she just dumps the muck by the side of the drain and does not go to throw it in the dump. She says she needs a barrow to take all the garbage to the dump. How can we buy an expensive barrow and give it to her?

SH: I see that your children defecate in the drain.

R: Not all. Just my youngest one. Where else can he defecate? He just sits wherever he likes and defecates. All children do that.

SH: Where do your other children defecate? Don't you use the government latrines? [The authorities have built pourflush latrines with the help of the organization, Sulabh International. There are in all 200 latrines: 80 for women and 120 for men. The men have to pay 50 paise every time they use the latrines. The women and children don't have to pay anything. The latrines have been built in two blocks on one side of the cluster.]

R: The other children defecate in the open on the main road. I have to accompany them because they are both girls. We don't use the government latrines because they are too far away on the other side of the cluster. If they were nearer perhaps we could use them. The women who live near the latrines use them and also the children. The girls are accompanied by their mothers. Some are not. But I am very careful about my girls. The men, however, use the government latrines. But my man prefers to defecate on vacant land on the other side of the cluster near the government latrines and so do many other men. One doesn't have to pay 50 paise then.

SH: Where do you defecate?

R: That is why I get up at 4 in the morning and, even earlier in summer, and go to defecate while it is still dark on the main road next to my *jhuggi*. For the last four months, some mobile latrines have been brought here by the government. I use them sometimes. But generally, they are never clean. The government sweepers who are supposed to clean them do not do it often enough. When the latrines are too dirty I have no option but to squat on the road.

SH: And suppose your stomach is upset?

R: My oh my, then it is a problem. I have to hunt for some private place. It is agony. If I don't find a private place then I use the government mobile latrines no matter how filthy they are. What else can I do?

SH: When do you find time to store water?

R: I go down to the tap—the taps are all at the bottom of the cluster—at about 10 o'clock. I don't have a watch; so I just go by intuition. I sit at the tap in line, waiting for the water to come. Most women sit in groups and chat. I chat sometimes about this and that but usually I do not talk to the women. My man does not like me to chat with them because most of them are low caste people and untouchables. We are not untouchables. We are of a high caste. Lord Krishna was from our caste.

SH: When do you finish storing water?

R: I stop when it is time for my man to come home to eat. His factory [the small manufacturing unit where her husband works] is close by. My daughter meanwhile prepares some dal [pulses] and washes all the utensils. My man eats the roti and vegetable of the morning and the dal. He wants fresh food to be cooked every time he eats. But how can I cook fresh food three times a day? I don't have the money. My second daughter comes back from school a little later than my man. He has usually left for the factory when she comes. Then she and my eldest daughter eat. I then give some dal with mashed roti to my little one and feed him breast milk. It is only then that I get time to eat. When we have all eaten I sometimes bathe my daughters and my little son in the *jhuggi*. I don't bathe my daughters at the handpump. After all they are girls. If there is water left over, then I bathe. My children and I don't bathe every day. My daughters and I don't bathe in the bathrooms made by the government. Most women don't. They like to bathe in the privacy of their *jhuggis*. [The MCD has built 48 bathrooms where water is available all 24 hours from a tubewell. Twenty-four bathrooms are for women and 24 for men.]

SH: Don't you have any spare time in the day?

R: Not often because most of the time I have to go to the handpump to wash clothes. Sometimes after all the chores are done then I sit on the threshold of my *jhuggi* and chit chat with other women who also sit on their thresholds till it is time to fill water again. Then down to the tap I go. By the time I finish this, it is time for my man to come home. Before he comes back I quickly clean up the *jhuggi* once again with the help of my daughter. My man comes, smokes a bidi—he smokes about 30 bidis everyday—then he goes to bathe at the handpump. He bathes everyday. After he has bathed he goes out to meet his relations here or have a chat with the other men at a tea shop and my daughter and I get down to cooking rice which we can eat in the evening with the dal cooked in the afternoon. My man drinks everyday. He comes back late only after he has had his alcohol. He is usually in a foul mood then. If something is wrong in the *jhuggi* he shouts and screams at me. He also beats me sometimes .

SH: Don't you feel bad when he beats you?

R: What is there to feel bad about? It happens so often that it has become part of my life. I don't say anything. What can I say? My man has his food when he comes home. He always complains that I am lazy and give him stale food to eat, but, how can I cook fresh food every time he eats? He gives me so little money and he spends so much on his bidis and alcohol. But if I say this, he will probably throw me out of the house. So I keep quiet.

SH: When do you sleep?

R: I sleep late at night after every one has gone to bed. After our meal my daughter and I wash the utensils. Before I eat, I feed my little one some rice and dal. I breast feed him again when I lie down to sleep with him at my side. He doesn't sleep until I breast feed him. It is only after my child goes to sleep that I sleep.

Most women's lives in Rajpur follow almost the same pattern as Ramia's. They are at work the whole day washing, cleaning, fetching water and cooking. It is even more difficult for those who combine this work with a job.

Urban Health Services: An Unsatisfactory Experience

One of the advantages of being in a big city is that it has better health facilities than rural areas. In Rajpur free health services are available at the government dispensary but the dispensary is about 2 km away from the JJ cluster of Rajpur and, like all government dispensaries, is under-staffed and medicines are almost always unavailable.

Champa is the wife of a Dhobi (traditionally, a caste of washermen) named Charan, who irons clothes on a big table in front of his *jhuggi*. Charan comes from a village in the Jaipur district of Rajasthan. Champa says:

We never go to the government dispensary. It is too far away and one has to wait for ages in a long line. That is what my man told me. Besides I cannot go to the dispensary on my own. I have never stepped out of Rajpur alone. My man does not even like me to go far away from our *jhuggi*. My man went to the dispensary once when he was ill. He went early in the morning and did not come back until late afternoon. There was only one doctor there. My man told me he was very young. If he was so young, how could he know medicine well? The medicine required was not available so my man had to buy it from a shop. It cost him 70 rupees and he did not even get well after that. He then went to Dr. Srivastava in the cluster who cured him. He took only 30 rupees and gave the medicines himself. Now, whenever the children are ill, my man takes them to Dr Srivastava. He lives near by and is good. Our time is saved and we get well too.

There are about 25 private doctors in Rajpur, however, only one of them is qualified in allopathic medicine. Dr Srivastava is one of about 24 doctors who practise Ayurvedic medicine but whose qualifications are sometimes dubious. Says Shanno:

Once I went to Kiran to show myself. There, they examine you free and give you medicine without charging anything but they put such a huge needle in my arm and removed so much blood that I almost fainted. I screamed and cried. They took so much blood that I felt weak and got back home with great difficulty. I felt weak for two whole days. I will never go back there. I now go to Dr Ramesh. He is good. He is here in Rajpur and gives a small injection and one recovers. He charges 20 rupees but at least he doesn't take blood in such a painful way as the doctors at Kiran do.

Chanda, the tea shop owner, said 'The medicines given by Kiran never work. They are given free so they cannot be good.' The migrant men and women have apparently come to believe that nothing good comes free. If you want something of good quality you have to pay for it. Kiran is a non-governmental organization working in Rajpur providing primarily education. The All India Institute of Medical Sciences (AIIMS) in Delhi has a permanent clinic on the Kiran premises. There is one doctor, one supervisor and one technician who does blood tests and refers patients when necessary to clinics. For more sophisticated tests and treatments, they refer the people of Rajpur to AIIMS. However, the migrant women in Rajpur do not seem to appreciate the good work being done by the clinic. Says Nasreen, a Muslim woman who comes from a village in the Ghaziabad district of Uttar Pradesh and is the wife of Ahmad Khan, a junk dealer:

Once when my child was ill he [her husband] took him to Kiran. They asked him to take the child to the hospital. We were very frightened. One only goes to hospital when one is very seriously ill and all medicines fail. It is said that if once you go to the hospital you seldom come back. The hospital was also very far away. If the child was going to stay in the hospital who would stay with him? My husband [Muslims can use the term 'my husband' though not their husbands' names] then decided to take the child to Dr Hari. Dr Hari examined the child and gave medicine but the child did not get well. Then my husband took him to a doctor in Govindpuri who charged 50 rupees and gave medicines worth 60 rupees and the child recovered. However, he is ill again. We do not know what to do. May be we should get the child an amulet. Someone must have cast the evil eye on him.[21]

The migrant women of Rajpur have a firm belief in the evil eye and often blame someone for having cast the evil eye when their children fall ill. They feel that the effects of the evil eye cannot be cured by allopathic medicine but by *tona totka* (a form of exorcism) which only specialists who know *jhad phoonk* (literally shaking off and blowing off) can cure. These specialists, known as *jhad phoonk wale*, are found mainly in the villages.

Sukhiya is a Kuril (a sub-caste of Chamars) whose husband is without work but does nothing about it. They come from a village in the Ghazipur district of Uttar Pradesh and have two children: a boy and a girl. Sukhiya works as a sorter of cloth cuttings.

Auntyji, the evil eye is very bad. I always put a black spot on my younger child's cheek because he is extraordinarily healthy and fair and so can very easily become the target of someone's evil eye. A black spot protects from the evil eye. Once my son fell very ill and foreign medicines could not cure him. There is no *jhad phoonk wala* here so I told my husband that we must go to our village where there is a very good *jhad phoonk wala* who performed some rites and my son started getting better after we did that. Sometimes another person's soul can come and possess you or someone can do magic on you and you become very ill and don't recover. Then, only *jhad phoonk* can cure one.

Many women recounted similar things. They spoke about *jhad phoonk* with more conviction than they did about doctors and allopathic medical treatments available in the city. Their urban experience of modern medicine which they mistrust and take with a considerable hesitancy has not shaken off their faith in the evil eye, possession by spirits, goddesses, and *jhad phoonk*.

INTENSIFICATION OF THE HOUSEWIFIZATION OF WOMEN IN RAJPUR

Almost all migrant women in Rajpur worked as agricultural labourers in their native villages, either on the family's land or for other richer farmers or both. However, in Rajpur, they are not allowed by their husbands to work outside their own *jhuggis* as long as the husbands are earning, even if the latter earn only just enough to provide the barest of minimum to feed the family.

Saviti is the wife of Rambir, a Gujjar (buffalo breeders and sellers of buffalo milk, now often big landlords) who comes from a village in the Samastipur district of Bihar. Rambir has two buffaloes and sells milk in Rajpur. Saviti says:

My man's family has 3 *bighas* of land in the village. During the sowing and harvesting season I used to help with work in the field. I also worked as an agricultural labourer when the food and earnings from the land were not enough. My man did not mind me working outside the house in the village but here, in Rajpur, he wants to keep me as a prisoner in the *jhuggi*. He does not want me to step out of the *jhuggi*. He only allows me out to fetch water from the tap which is not far. I don't even know what the other side of Rajpur is like. The earnings from milk sales are not enough and it would be helpful if I worked. One woman here works in a tailoring factory [garment sewing unit]. She told me she could get me a job in that factory. I know tailoring. My husband was very angry when he heard about it. He said: 'As long as I am alive you should not have to work. I am the man. It is my job to earn. Your work is to look after the housework and children. Isn't that good enough for you? Why should you want to go gallivanting off to a factory to work?'

Rani is the wife of Surju, a Chamar who works in a manufacturing unit which makes television parts. Rani is very good looking. She told me,

I get very bored sitting at home. Till now, I have only one child and he goes to school. I told my husband that I would like to work. He got into a rage. He said: 'You want to go to work in order to show yourself off. You want other men to see you?' That was not correct but he is always saying that I want to play around with men. He also said that women of good families don't work. It is only low caste women who work. He said I was illiterate and did not know what the world was like. I would be easily fooled and was sure to go astray since I was very fickle. So I just sit at home and chat with my women neighbours, like a bird trapped in a cage.

The men, however, do not mind their women assisting them as shopkeepers if the shop is situated within their own *jhuggis* or sorting out cloth cuttings at home as part of a recycling trade. These activities are seen by the men as an extension of women's housework because they are done inside the *jhuggi*. The domestication of women and the 'tyranny of the household' are poignantly felt by the women of Rajpur. Their lives seem to have become more cloistered since their arrival in Delhi. Life seems more dominated by housework than it was in the village.

The men however often practice double standards. If they drink or spend money on other expensive habits or do not work, they do not seem to mind their women working as cloth sorters in other people's *jhuggis* where other men are engaged in recycling work. But even in these cases, men do not allow their wives to leave Rajpur. All the shopping is done by men; all the decisions are taken by men. The women only decide what rations are needed and what should be cooked. Without economic independence and self-sufficiency the women are greatly handicapped and are compelled to become captives of men in their own homes— subordinated and exploited.

WOMEN'S PLACE IN THE SOCIAL STRUCTURE OF RAJPUR

Rajpur not a Community but a Conclave of Chettos

Heterogeneity was the third main characteristic of urban development identified by Wirth.[22] The inhabitants of Rajpur conform to this pattern, coming from different regions and castes. However, they are homogeneous in one respect: they are almost all poor with the stigma of poverty attached to them—a stigma they find hard to get rid of even if they are able to amass great wealth. As 'the poor' they are first and foremost segregated within the city of Delhi. Cities are almost always unequally and unfairly structured[23] and the poor are generally confined to squatter settlements and inner city slums. Perhaps the most significant divide in the city is the social stratification on the basis of wealth. However, wealth does not necessarily ensure integration into the 'culture of the rich'. The poor-become-rich may be able to find a home in an affluent area of the city but, in all probability, they will not be able to participate in the social and cultural life of the area. In fact they are more likely to be ignored, alienated and possibly even ostracized.

The Rajpur *jhuggi* dwellers, both men and women, are extremely conscious of their identity as 'the poor'—perhaps more than they were in their villages where caste identity seemed to matter more. The chasm between the poor and the rich seems to be wider in the city. Shanno echoes the sentiments of most Rajpur women when she argues: 'In this city it is the rich who rule the roost. This is a city of big people. We poor people are like dust to be trampled on.'

Srimati, the wife of Shyamu, a Kachchi (vegetable growing caste) from a village in the district of Varanasi in Uttar Pradesh said: 'No matter how rich we may become we will always remain poor. It is a stain which cannot be washed away by money.' Here one is reminded of Oscar Lewis' observation that one may get rid of poverty but it is more difficult to get rid of the 'culture of poverty'.[24] Lewis' concept of the 'culture of poverty' was much attacked, perhaps because the issue of poverty is so closely linked to the politics of poverty. However, the notion should not be so easily discarded. If the 'culture of poverty' is effectively difficult for the poor to shrug off, one must not forget that many non-poor have a vested interest in keeping the poor where they are. The wealthy also consider the poor the 'dangerous class'.[25]

The Rajpur residents may be homogeneous as 'the poor' but the squatter settlement is definitely not a melting pot but rather a house divided. It has not become a community with a 'we' feeling.[26] The Rajpur cluster is split into ghettos: regional ghettos and within these, caste ghettos and within these, kinship ghettos. There is, therefore, segregation within segregation. Of all these ghettos the caste ghetto seems to matter most to Rajpur inhabitants when it comes to the question of residence. Women seem to have adopted their caste prejudice from men although they seem less stringent in their attitudes.

Shanti is the wife of Gopal who belongs to a village in the Mathura district of Uttar Pradesh and is a Thakur (a high caste). Shanti's *jhuggi* is surrounded by a number of Jatav families (a sub-caste of the 'untouchable' Chamars) who are also from Mathura but she says:

> He [her husband] does not like living here among these low caste people. He has forbidden me ever to enter their *jhuggis* or accept water or food from them. I have only two children—both boys. They both go to school, so I have quite a lot of time at my disposal and often do not know what to do. Sometimes I cannot help but sit on my threshold and talk to the women living in the surrounding *jhuggis* but I am always afraid he might see me. If he does he will beat me. He wants to move to a *jhuggi* in another part of Rajpur where better caste people live. But ideally, he would like to live in an area where Thakurs or other upper castes from Mathura reside because there is a lot of difference between Thakurs from Mathura and Thakurs from other regions. He bought this *jhuggi* in a hurry because he could not find anywhere else to live. Now he regrets it.

Kin Orientation

There are some cases where three generations of the same family are living in Rajpur. They live not in joint family set-ups but in separate households, each with their own cooking stoves. The Rajpur migrants are very much oriented towards their immediate kin.

Shiela is the wife of Bhulwa, a Kahar (a caste whose occupation was to cook food and wash utensils—a non-untouchable caste) from a village in the Jaunpur district of Uttar Pradesh. Bhulwa runs a roadside eating joint. Says Shiela:

My man's younger brother and one of his two sisters who stays with her father have their *jhuggis* close to ours. Both the elder brothers who also live here have children. So do I: two daughters and two sons. My man visits his family everyday. However, we are never invited to have a meal with them. We also do not invite them for a meal. Somehow the custom of having meals in the house of one's own relatives does not exist here. It is only on festivals that we have meals at his father's place. But then for the important festivals, we go to the village where my father-in-law's elder brother lives. At festivals when we have a meal at his father's we all contribute food. My man does not visit anyone else's *jhuggi* in Rajpur; not even those of people of our own caste and region. He may sometimes visit some people who are from our village and who are like relatives to us. The question of my man visiting people of our caste from other regions or lower castes does not arise. My man does not do anything without taking advice from his father and elder brothers. The males of the family are very close to each other but not the women. I do not have a close relationship with any of his family members, not even the womenfolk. I do whatever is expected of me as my man's wife and that's all.

A migrant man who does not have his larger family in the Rajpur JJ cluster leads an isolated and lonely life without the support of kin and without friends who are usually people from the migrant's village. Other friends are mere acquaintances and not much is expected of them.

The Rajpur migrants seem to be trying to preserve their primary groups without becoming members of the secondary groups commonly found in cities like trade unions, associations for different activities and societies of various kinds.[27] When men do not become members of secondary groups, it is out of the question for their wives to do so. The migrants seem content in maintaining close relationships with their immediate kin or, at most, with their own caste mates from their native village or *biradari* (a group of separate lineages of the same caste spread over a number of villages).

Telling me about the *biradari*, Champa, who is a Chamar by caste from a village in the Ballia district of Uttar Pradesh, and who is married to Laakhan, a tailor in a leather garment sewing unit said, 'The *biradari* is very strong and has very long hands. One can't dare go against the *biradari*.' All Rajpur migrants, especially the women, for whom strictures are tighter than for men, greatly fear the wrath of the *biradari* which acts as the collective conscience of the community.

Husband-Wife Relationships

It is commonly believed that the affective ties between husband and wife tend to become stronger and closer in nuclear households like those found in Rajpur. But this does not appear to be the case in Rajpur. The couples live together but often seem to remain totally alienated from each other. Says Ramkali, who is the wife of Chandu, a Nai (barber caste) from the district of Azamgarh who wants to open a barber's shop but has not yet managed it,

> My man only comes home to eat and sleep in the *jhuggi*. Otherwise he is out all the time. He does not like sitting alone with me or playing with his children. When he does speak to me it is either to order me to do something or to tell me what I have done wrong. He does not discuss any of his problems with me. He says women cannot understand men's problems. I always feel frightened that I may do something he doesn't like. He beats the children if they make the smallest mistake or are just a little bit naughty and he never fondles them. Actually even in the village men hardly speak to their wives. Never, in fact, in front of other people for it would give the impression that a man is paying too much attention to his wife. The man and his wife have very little time alone. Conversation between them is minimal. The men and the women are also not supposed to show too much affection for their children. However, my man was not so angry all the time in the village. Here his temper seems to have become very bad. He is always ready to scream and shout and beat me up.

The migrant man, no doubt, faces many frustrations and humiliations as he tries to eke a living in an alien, hostile, impersonal urban milieu. These frustrations and humiliations fill him with bitterness and anger which he takes out on his wife who is there for him to subordinate and oppress, just as he himself is subordinated and oppressed by others. Wife beating is very widespread in Rajpur but what is surprising is the extent to which women seem to take it as natural behaviour and often even condone it.[28] It is not uncommon to hear women argue: 'My man beats me but he also loves me, so if he beats me what does it matter?' When I asked Shanno why she did not leave her husband when he beat her, she said,

> Leave my man because he beats me? All men beat their wives some time or other. If women were to leave their men because they beat them, then all women would leave their men. They beat us when we have not done something they have told us to do. Sometimes we do not do the things they ask because they are bad. But most often they beat us because they know more about the world than we do and we go off and do foolish things because we are ignorant. If a child does something you don't like, don't you beat him? But you would not throw him out of the house because he has not listened to you and the child would not leave the house just because he was beaten. So why should a woman leave her man if he beats her? He beats her because he is a man. That is how he shows that he is a man and that it is he who takes care of the family.

Most women in Rajpur are not aware that they are oppressed or perhaps are afraid of realizing the reality which would make their lives more miserable than they already are. This is not to say that women are unaffected by their oppression. However, the humiliation and bitterness do not result in revolt but in doing what their men ask them to do. I have seen many a woman in Rajpur beat her children mercilessly with a face distorted in hate as if she were venting her suppressed anger and seething fury on her subordinate helpless mites.

CULTURAL LIFE IN RAJPUR

Most women of Rajpur have never visited the monuments, museums, cinemas and other cultural attractions of the city. They remain closeted in Rajpur and their main leisure activity seems to be watching television. Many Rajpur inhabitants have second-hand black and white televisions. Those without them, watch television by sitting outside the *jhuggis* of others. Says Ganga, a Chamar whose husband is at present without work,

I love watching TV. I don't have one myself but I watch it at my neighbour's. They are lower level Chamars than us so I don't enter the *jhuggi*, because if my man found out that I had, he would beat me, so I sit outside and watch. I love watching films though the lives of the people in them seem to be so different from ours. Our boys and girls do not go running around together and doing all those shameful things that boys and girls do in films. It would give them a bad reputation if they did. I loved watching the *Ramayana* and the *Mahabharata* on TV. My man, however, does not like me watching TV. He thinks I shirk work to do it.

Another entertainment that the people of Rajpur enjoy are the three *Ramlilas*, performed in the squatter settlement. These are enactments of the *Ramcharitmanas* or the story of Lord Rama. The *Ramlilas* are performed during the festival of Dussehra, a festival which celebrates Lord Rama's fight and victory over the evil Ravana, the Lord of Lanka who had kidnapped Sita, Rama's wife. No woman acts in the *Ramlilas*. Men perform both male and female roles. Most women are, however, forbidden to watch the *Ramlilas* because these are usually performed after dinner late at night when women are expected to stay inside.

For the most important festivals of Holi and Deepawali almost all migrants return to their native villages. All important *rites de passage* are also performed in the village especially wedding ceremonies and *gauna* (when the bride leaves for her husband's house which may be a couple of years after the marriage or earlier depending on the age of the girl). Most migrants in Rajpur are of the firm belief that a girl should be safely ensconced in her husband's house before she starts menstruating. Sherbati says, 'It is better to have marriage and *gauna* performed in the village. There, all the relatives can assemble. We sing and dance and everyone enjoys themselves. Here not all relatives would be able to come and it would not be so much fun.' The migrants of Rajpur make it a point of attending the marriages and *gauna* of their relatives back in their villages and they usually also return to mourn deaths.

Just as the people of Rajpur do not seem to have a social or cultural life away from their villages so it is with their religious life. They remain deeply attached to the village shrines of their caste gods and, more often, goddesses. But no such shrines are present in Rajpur, though there are two temples of Hanuman and one temple of Rai Das. The people of Rajpur do not seem to go to any temples in Delhi except that of the goddess Durga at Kalkaji which is within walking distance of Rajpur. Whatever cultural practices the migrant women follow, they follow in their villages which they think of as homes, while the *jhuggis* in Rajpur are considered no more than places of residence.

CONCLUSION

It is often assumed that life in major cities is less restrictive than life in small rural communities. However, the narratives of the women of Rajpur seem to suggest otherwise. In the context of a Delhi squatter settlement, women's lives seem to become increasingly confined and dependence on their men and acceptance of their fate reinforced. Life is dominated by the grind of performing daily chores and the potential benefit of urban life remain outside their reach.

NOTES

I would like to thank Véronique Dupont, Emma Tarlo and Denis Vidal for giving me the opportunity to write this paper and for their editorial observations and suggestions. I would also like to thank Taqui Haider for the continued encouragement, moral and intellectual sustenance that he has always provided.

1. Human Development Report, UNDP, New York, Oxford: OUP, 1997, p. 51.
2. Because of the sensitive nature of data collected on local politics the name of the squatter settlement and all other names in the essay have been changed.
3. For an explanation and amplification of the concept of this 'culture of silence' see Paulo Freire, *Pedagogy of the Oppressed*, Harmondsworth: Pelican Books, 1973; Paulo Freire, *Cultural Action for Freedom*, Harmondsworth: Penguin Books, 1974; Susan Gal, 'Between Speech and Silence: The Problematic of Research of Language and Gender', in *Gender at Crossroads of Knowledge: Feminist Anthropology in the Post-modern Era*, Maria di Leonardo (ed.), Berkeley, Los Angeles: University of California Press, 1991, pp. 175-293.
4. N. Sridharan, 'Indian Slums: Problems, Policies and Issues', in *Housing the Urban Poor: Policy and Practice in Developing Countries*, Brian C. Aldrich and Ranvinder S. Sandhu (eds), New Delhi: Vistaar Publications, pp. 385-400.
5. Voluntary Health Association of India, *A Tale of Two Cities*, New Delhi: Voluntary Health Association of India, 1993, p. 16.
6. *The Times of India*, New Delhi, Thursday, 15 May 1997.
7. Abhijit Sen, 'Economic Reforms, Employment and Poverty: Trends and Options', *Economic and Political Weekly*, vol. XXXI, nos. 35, 36 and 37 Special, March 1996, pp. 2459-77.
8. The *pradhan* is the headman of a community. There are about 35 *pradhans* in Rajpur. The *pradhans* serve as vote-brokers for politicians at election time and make various gains for themselves in the process.
9. Among orthodox Hindus it is considered disrespectful to speak one's husband's name. The women of orthodox upper castes tend to refer to their husband as 'he' or 'him' whilst lower castes use phrases like 'my man' or 'Bhim's father' (Bhim being the name of the child of the couple).
10. Among the mostly patriarchal, patrilineal, patrilocal communities in India once the woman is married she is absorbed into her husband's family and her husband's village comes to be seen as her village rather than her natal village.
11. There is at present a brisk trade in *jhuggis* because of the paucity of land. *Jhuggis* in Rajpur today can be purchased for anywhere between 10,000 to 15,000 rupees.
12. In a rural person's village all residents of the village have, if not a blood relationship, fictitious kinship with each other, and are addressed by kinship terms. See Saraswati Haider, 'An Ethnographic Profile of Family Kinship among Eastern Uttar Pradesh Chamar Migrants

in a Delhi Squatter Settlement', *Guru Nanak Journal of Sociology*, vol. 18, no. 2, Amritsar, October 1997, pp. 1-32.

13. Louis Wirth, 'Urbanism as a Way of Life', in *On Cities and Social Life*, Louis Wirth Selected Papers, Chicago: University of Chicago Press, 1964, pp. 60-83.
14. See Véronique Dupont, 'Spatial and Demographic Growth of Delhi since 1947 and the Main Migration Flows', in this volume.
15. See Girish K. Misra and J. Sarma, *Distribution and Differential Location of Public Utilities in Urban Delhi*, New Delhi: Centre for Urban Studies, Indian Institute of Public Administration, 1979; Voluntary Health Association of India, op. cit.
16. See Emma Tarlo in this volume.
17. See Saraswati Haider, 'Delhi Slums in the Season of Fresh Promises', *Mainstream*, vol. XXXVI, no. 8, 14 February 1998, New Delhi, pp. 27-9.
18. There are in Rajpur four sources of water supply. There are pipes of the main delivery system located at the base of the hillock on which Rajpur is situated. There are no taps but 12 points of delivery which are incisions in the pipes to which plastic tubes have been attached which, when water does not come, lie on the ground submerged in filthy water pools. One such attempt at a tap serves about 290 families. The water comes irregularly and never for more than six hours a day. People in Rajpur are aware that hand-pump water can be contaminated. They also say that the water drawn from the hand-pumps tastes foul and is very salty. Thus they take water for drinking and cooking from the main supply taps. There is always a crowd, mostly comprising women and children, when the news goes around that water is coming from the taps. Often there are vicious quarrels. There are about 35 hand-pumps in the cluster, i.e. one hand-pump for approximately 100 families. The crowd is less at the hand-pumps but most of the hand-pumps are out of order. There are two tube-wells operated by an employee of the MCD. The dwellers of Rajpur have the same reservation about tube-well water as they have about the hand-pump water. The motor of the tube-wells is operated for three hours in the morning and three hours in the evening provided there is electricity which often is not there. Recently the MCD has started sending a tanker of water for Rajpur. There are, however, illegal taps in several *jhuggis*.
19. The Delhi Assembly elections of 6 November 1993.
20. In Delhi most old people are addressed as Auntyji or Uncleji now rather than by Hindi kinship terms which were used earlier. Ji is a suffix of respect.
21. For belief in the evil eye, see David F. Pocock, 'The Evil Eye', in *Religion in India*, T.N. Madan (ed.), Delhi: OUP, 1995, pp. 50-62.
22. Wirth, op. cit.
23. See Blair Badcock, *Unfairly Structured Cities*, Oxford: Basil Blackwell, 1984.
24. Oscar Lewis, *The Children of Sanchez*, New York: Random House, 1963; Oscar Lewis, 'The Culture of Poverty', *Scientific American*, 214(4), 1996, pp. 19-25.
25. See Lydia Morris, *Dangerous Classes: The Underclass and Social Citizenship*, London and New York: Routledge, 1994; Beverley Skeggs, *Formation of Class and Gender: Becoming Respectable*, London: Sage Publications, 1997.
26. About the notion of 'we' feeling, see Robert Bierstadt, *The Social Order*, Bombay, New Delhi: Tata McGraw Hill Publishing Co., 1970, p. 2891.
27. On the notions of primary and secondary groups, see Bierstadt, op. cit., pp. 272-301.
28. See Saraswati Haider, 'Women's Oppression and Their Reaction in a Jhuggi-Jhompri Cluster', paper presented at XX All-India Sociological Conference, Mangalore, 29-31 December 1993.

3

Welcome to History: A Resettlement Colony in the Making

EMMA TARLO

This essay is a response to a half-forgotten conversation held some time in March 1997 in a resettlement colony, locally known as the Welcome. My assistant and I had been working there on and off over a period of two years, talking with people about their pasts and building up a social and political history of the colony. Inevitably, many of the residents of Welcome initially felt ill-equipped to act as local historians but once we explained that we were more interested in personal histories than official ones, most were both willing and able to rise to the challenge and, in narrating their pasts, simultaneously told us much about the history of the city. But occasionally, we encountered situations in which the gulf separating the researcher and the researched seemed unbridgeable. And so it was on that March afternoon when we met a young university-educated man who asked us what we were doing in the colony. Try as we might to explain our project, this young man just would not understand. 'There is no point in coming here if you are interested in history', he told us. 'Welcome has no history. This place is nothing. If you want history then you must go to the Red Fort, or to Qutb Minar. . . .'

We spent no more than a few minutes with this young sceptic but I remember finding the encounter particularly frustrating. What distinguished him from most other people of the colony was his high level of education and it was precisely this, which seemed to act as a total barrier to mutual understanding. This man knew what history was all about. He had read the books. He wanted to correct our error and ignorance by re-directing us to the 'real history' of Delhi—the stuff of history books as he knew them. I was in no mood for trying to explain recent developments in historical writing about India. The very idea of 'subaltern studies' seemed somehow farcical in the circumstances. This man had found confidence through education and who was I to tell him that his opinion was dated, that the intellectual climate had changed and that nowadays history was as much about people as about monuments and dates?

This essay attempts to re-develop the argument I had tried so unsuccessfully to put forward on that March afternoon—that a resettlement colony like Welcome is a useful window through which to explore recent historical events and, more particularly, how urban spaces like resettlement colonies are structured and re-structured through such events. The essay is located between two genres of academic discourse: the literature on urban development with its emphasis on the city as a product of planned—though not entirely controllable—development and the literature on urban violence with its emphasis on how the urban landscape is scarred and reconfigured through violent and disruptive events.[1] In the first discourse critical events like wars, riots and moments of extreme political tension are either ignored or passed off as mere accidents of history—outside the domain and concerns of urban planners. In the second discourse, the opposite tendency is the norm. Here so much emphasis is given to the event—which is usually the motivating factor for the study—that it becomes difficult to relate event to structure. Veena Das' attempt to locate the Sikh massacre of 1984 within the local fabric of life in the resettlement colony of Sultanpuri[2] and to demonstrate more generally how social structure comes into being through events proves a notable exception, but even here our understanding is built primarily around events (their build-up and aftermath) and it becomes difficult to relate the drama of the short-term to everyday life in the long-term.[3] Similarly, references to the demographic changes that followed the Hindu-Muslim violence of 1992 give us little basis for understanding how to place these changes either within individual life histories or within the development of urban space over time.

In this essay I argue that if we are to understand the socio-dynamics of space among the urban poor we need to develop an approach which examines the relationship between structure and event, not just at a given moment, but over time for urban spaces like resettlement colonies are structured as much through a succession of historical events at a national level as through local politics and urban planning. There are two main aspects to this. On the one hand, it is often historic events which create the political environment in which urban plans become realities. On the other hand, historic events often disfigure urban plans and this occurs with such regularity that in the final analysis it is tempting to perceive them less as impediments to urban development than as the hidden agents of urban development itself. It is this dynamic that I want to explore through the life-histories and experiences of people resettled in the colony of Welcome. The first half of this chapter focuses on the birth of the colony, exploring the points of intersection where policy, location and event conjoined in its formation. The second half focuses on the restructuration of the colony by examining the role of three particular events, all of which have led to a redistribution of people in space—not just in Welcome—but also in Delhi if not India as a whole.

THE BIRTH OF A COLONY

Welcome: A Window in Time and Space

A brief glance at a map of Delhi would seem at first to confirm the sceptic's view that Welcome is a marginal space of little relevance to the development of the city. Indeed the colony is only identifiable to those who know it by its official name of Seelampur.[4] Seelampur, situated in the Shahdara district of East Delhi, slips off the edge of many Delhi maps which pay little attention to developments east of the river even though the area is today densely populated. To all intents and purposes Seelampur is just a name, indicating a place somewhere in the unfashionable fringes of the area known collectively as 'trans-Jamuna'—a phrase which itself reveals the 'West-is-Centre' logic of the city.

But if one were to take the same map and mark all the spots from which the residents of Welcome hail and where their homes were demolished prior to their resettlement (Map 3.1), the development of Welcome would no longer seem so peripheral to the development of the city as a whole. On the contrary, it would become apparent that Delhi would look quite different were it not for the succession of demolitions out of which the colony of Welcome was born and through which new roads, parks and public buildings sprouted throughout the city. For with each new influx of evicted slum dwellers to Welcome, there was a corresponding transformation in the use of space in the city centre. And since Welcome draws its population from over eighty different locations situated in all corners of the capital, from areas as diverse as Chanakyapuri in the south to the Jama Masjid in the heart of Old Delhi, the birth of the colony is inextricably bound with the morphology of the city as a whole.

A map indicating demolitions may look more like a bombardment plan than a development plan (the similarity is by no means incidental), but it reminds us of the very tangible links traced by members of the resettled population to the different locations in the city where they used to live and work. This link often tends to be forgotten, not least because the slum clearance policy is built on the logic of erasure, designed to wipe out the ugly and sordid face of the metropolis—the cramped and over-populated '*jhuggi jhonpri* clusters' and the 'inner city slums'. These were the aspects of Delhi that offended the eyes and noses of respectable middle class citizens who did not want to see them at the time and who certainly do not wish to preserve their memory. Describing such places, the authors of the Draft Master Plan for Delhi remarked: 'The ugly hutment colonies pox-mark practically every part of the city. The majority of the occupants live in huts or filthy shacks built of poor material. They are mostly located in forsaken and insanitary places, bordering railway lines, open drains, open spaces earmarked for dumping refuse, etc.'[5] In such statements metaphors of disease and refuse intertwine as if *jhuggi jhonpri* clusters—and by extension their inhabitants—were not only saturated with refuse and contagion but were in a sense their material embodiment. What both refuse and disease share in common is the necessity of elimination. 'Cancerous growths' must be removed just as garbage should be collected and dumped outside the boundaries of the city. When a factory worker from Welcome remarked, 'They said they wanted to remove poverty, but actually its not poverty they want to eliminate, its the poor,' he described how it felt to be on the other side of such equations in which people and their condition fuse into one.

Once we re-establish the links between those resettled and the spaces where they once lived and worked it becomes less surprising that the residents of a single resettlement colony like Welcome should have a wide range of memories and experiences not only of urban policies but also of the vagaries of history more generally. In fact, I would argue that far from being marginalized by national policies and events, the urban poor often find themselves deeply implicated within them for they lack the political, economic and educational resources with which to build a shield in moments of crises. Whether singled out as the target group of a policy or simply exposed to critical events like wars or so called 'communal riots', the residents of Welcome have, more often than not found themselves caught at the very centre of the action. But before turning to their accounts of events, I want first to introduce the colony from the perspective of urban policy.

Welcome: A Guided Tour of Resettlement Policy

At one level Welcome is undeniably a product of urban planning—a colony conceived on paper, carved up in chalk and parcelled out to evicted slum dwellers in small portions of land. Despite the high level of unauthorized construction, the colony's plan is discernible even today. Enter Welcome from the Grand Trunk Road which stretches eastwards out of Delhi towards the Uttar Pradesh border and you will walk past three lanes of double storey tenement blocks, each 40 sq. yd. in dimension and evenly spaced—Welcome's respectable facade. However, the main body of the colony is a lego-like conglomerate of over 4,000 small brick houses arranged in blocks along narrow *gulis* (lanes) equipped with open gutters, plinths and taps. The colony is divided into two phases, officially known as Phases 3 and 4. Phases 1 and 2 are situated in the separate but neighbouring colony of New Seelampur, which predates Welcome and from which Welcome must once have been an offshoot (Map 3.2).

If Welcome's plan is discernible at ground level, it is less clear in the skyline. When plots were allocated to the displaced in the 1960s and 1970s, the latter were expected to construct their own houses with the result that the colony has grown haphazardly over time. The narrowness of the plots has forced residents to develop their space vertically, with the result that those who can afford it have constructed buildings of several storeys, usually on shaky foundations. In Phase 4 where this has become the norm, many of the streets resemble parts of Old Delhi with their tall narrow structures, balconies and roof spaces crammed with families and workshops. Besides plots and tenements, Welcome has a smattering of public buildings, small parks, toilets, temples, mosques, an *idgah* (Muslim ceremonial ground), cemetery and several markets—all of which to some extent break up the monotony of this excessively inhabited space. Some of these were written into the original plans for the colony; others have developed over time through the initiative of local residents.

Welcome also has its unofficial section situated at the back of the colony where the ground plan gives way to a crazy maze of meandering *gulis* which follow no discernible logic. Here houses vary from four-storey brick and concrete constructions to tiny makeshift hovels—all jammed together in what is a claustrophobic and precarious space. This unauthorized area is locally known as the Janata Colony (people's colony). Both officials and residents refer to it as a '*jhuggi jhonpri* cluster' but the term belies the fact that many of the houses have been there for over 20 years and have the appearance of permanence.

At one level it is possible to read the structure and layout of the colony as a statement of the successes and failures of resettlement policy over time. The tenements at the entrance represent a period of relative optimism when the ideas of slum clearance and resettlement were still in their experimental phase. It was back in 1958 that the Advisory Committee appointed for Delhi had first devised an initiative known as the Jhuggi Jhonpri Removal Scheme (JJRS). The aim was to remove squatters from government land and to allocate them plots of 80 sq. yd. at subsidized rates in new areas earmarked for resettlement. The plots would contain the basic amenities of latrine, tap and plinth but it would be up to resettled families to construct their own homes. A census of squatters was carried out in 1960 and slum clearance began in the same year. New Seelampur which pre-dates Welcome contains some of these original 80 sq. yd. plots.

However, the scheme soon ran into difficulties. Not only were there many evicted slum dwellers who were unable or unwilling to pay monthly instalments, but there were also many others who sold their plots to developers and returned to the city centre where they constructed new *jhuggis* near their places of work. This in turn encouraged a new wave of squatters who had learned that there was money to be made by squatting on government land. As a result of these difficulties the scheme was modified in 1962. Squatters were classified as 'eligible' or 'ineligible' according to whether or not they had been in Delhi before July 1960. The former were to be resettled on new conditions; the latter dispersed in the hopes of discouraging other migrants from squatting in the city. It was at this time that the DDA decided to develop built-up tenements for those eligible squatters whom they felt would be able to pay suitable rents. The poorer eligible squatters were to be taken to 'provisional camping sites' where regular plots and tenements would be developed at a later date.

The 400 odd tenements built in Welcome are a product of this short-lived phase when it was still thought that some evicted slum dwellers were capable of paying to live in built accommodation. It was not long before the construction of tenements was abandoned altogether, as were the 80 sq. yd. plots. Instead plots of 25 sq. yd. were developed and allocated on a leasehold basis with very minimum subsidized rents. By 1964 even ineligible squatters were allocated temporary camping sites since it had proved impossible to distinguish the eligible from the ineligible who, needless to say, refused to disappear from the city in the manner the authorities had hoped. Phase 3 of Welcome, which was developed gradually between 1963 and 1969, is a product of these modifications in resettlement policy when 25 sq. yd. became the standard size for a residential plot and 12 sq. yd. for a commercial plot. Phase 4 is a product of the accelerated slum clearance and resettlement activities that took place in Delhi during the Emergency years of 1975-7 about which we shall discuss more later.

If the planned area of Welcome can be read as an embodiment of resettlement policy over time, the unofficial area at the back of the colony can be read as an embodiment of its failure—a reminder that the development of squatter colonies is a never ending process. In fact recent studies have revealed that far from solving the 'slum problem', resettlement colonies have proved fertile ground for attracting new migrants who tap into the already meagre facilities provided to the resettled population, leading to the development of what Sabir Ali has called 'slums within slums'.[6]

However, the evolution of Welcome is more than simply the evolution of urban policy. When one speaks to residents of the colony, it soon becomes apparent that each block of the colony has a very specific history which links it not only to a phase in urban planning but also to a specific location in the city and often to a particular moment or event. These foundation narratives do not deny the importance of policy, but they situate it within a tangled web of other factors. From the accounts of the resettled, it is possible to make an alternative reading of the distribution of space in Welcome—one in which policy, location, political agenda and event are intermingled in complex ways.

Welcome: Some Narratives of Foundation

We begin this alternative reading of the morphology of Welcome in Phase 3 of the colony by talking to residents in blocks which bear the initials JB. JB stands for Jamuna Bazaar, once a notorious slum located between the wall of the old city and the river Jamuna—now an area dominated by park land and major roads. Through the narratives of local residents we learn of the complex web of factors that culminated in the erasure of Jamuna Bazaar and the creation of the JB blocks in Welcome.

AN EX-RICKSHAW DRIVER: I was about eighteen when I first came to Jamuna Bazaar. Those were still the days of British rule and there were very few *jhuggis* there at the time. The slum grew at the time of Partition with the coming of Punjabi refugees, but many of them were powerful people who were able to get land and tenements. Only the poor ones stayed on in Jamuna Bazaar. Most of the people there were poor people like me from UP [Uttar Pradesh].... In those days there used to be two parties—the Congress and the Jana Sangh. To get votes and seats one or other used to come to the colony and tell us that they would prevent the place from being demolished.... Actually they had been trying to remove people from there for some time but the issue was always shunted to the background because of the vote factor. This process went on for many years....

In 1960 Jamuna Bazaar was surveyed in the census of squatters and targeted for demolition. However, it was not until 1967 that an effective demolition drive was launched in the area after several minor attempts.

A TEA STALL OWNER: Initially the government was offering plots of 80 sq. yd. in New Seelampur. But people refused to move. Our leaders told us we couldn't be taken off. There was one *pradhan* [local slum leader] who assured us that he would force the government to give us land at Jamuna Bazaar itself. But of course that never happened.... By the time the bulldozers came they had reduced the size of plots to 25 sq. yd. and were no longer offering help with materials and construction. Some were taken to Seemapuri and couldn't get plots in Welcome for some years; others came directly here.

A SWEEPER: We used to live near the cremation ground at Nigam Bodh Ghat [in Jamuna Bazaar]. One day they organized a big meeting and told us that because of the bad smell coming from the burning bodies and because of the frequent problems with flooding, they were going to move us to a new place. Of course nobody believed them because this kind of talk had been going on for years. But a few days later the police came and told us to remove our belongings because the whole area was going to be cleared. We collected some things—I took corrugated iron and asbestos from my roof and some bricks. These were loaded into trucks along with our household possessions and we were taken off here. Basically the place was like an empty field at that time with orchards all around but they had marked out plots with white chalk and they handed out possession slips and told us to stay put.

Such accounts reveal that the JB blocks in Welcome are linked to the erased slum of Jamuna Bazaar not only through the memories of the displaced but also through the bricks and materials they carried with them. Initially they literally built their homes in Welcome out of the rubble of the previous slum. But the narratives also reveal how the resettlement policy was tangled up in a web of political factors with the result that for many years the threat of demolition was balanced out by the promise of protection from local leaders and political parties. To find out what finally tipped the balance we turn to the account of Jagmohan, ex-director of the Delhi Development Authority (DDA) who regards the clearing of Jamuna Bazaar and, in particular, Nigam Bodh Ghat as one of his early triumphs. Interestingly in his account, it is not the slum dwellers who needed to be protected from the stench of the burning ghats, but the other way round. He recalls,

Once, in the late fifties, Dr Rajendra Prasad, former President of India went to Nigam Bodh Ghat in connection with the death of one of his relatives. Apart from the fact that he was deeply moved by what he saw, his national pride was hurt by the reaction of some diplomats who could hardly stand the stench, filth and flies all around. On return, with poetic pain and anguish, he wrote a letter to the Chief Commissioner.

He suggested that immediate steps should be taken to remove the slummy conditions, improve the environment and restore the sanctity of Nigam Bodh Ghat. Yet such was the stranglehold of the slum politics, nothing was done for years. The area remained a spectacle of national shame and human misery in its worse form.[7]

The factor that finally enabled its transformation from a place of 'national shame' to one of 'national pride' was the Government of India's decision to transfer slum clearance operations from the locally-run Municipal Corporation into the hands of the centrally-administered Delhi Development Authority. This, combined with the use of Section 144 of the Criminal Procedures Code which gave the police the right to fire on anything said to resemble a crowd, provided a suitable environment for the demolitions to be carried out quickly and effectively in June 1967. Jagmohan describes with enthusiasm the rapidity with which the whole area and its inhabitants were erased: 'In about 3 days the clearance and simultaneous resettlement was completed. Immediately after the shifting, bulldozers were pressed into service. The area was levelled, and the work of developing the river front and the laying of the garden taken in hand. Horticulturists, engineers, planners and administrators worked around the clock to translate a dream into a reality. A new missionary zeal had gripped the entire set-up.'[8] For the displaced people who found themselves dumped with their small piles of rubble outside the city in the peak of the summer, the dream was more of a nightmare. Indeed, many people recall not daring to sleep during those early days in Welcome when they feared attack from snakes and goondas (ruffians) at night.

Taken together the contrasting but complementary narratives of Jagmohan and the ex-residents of Jamuna Bazaar reveal that the transfer of people and bricks from this centrally located slum to the newly developing colony of Seelampur (Welcome) was contingent not only on slum clearance policy but also on the political circumstances which created a suitable environment for such policy to be put into practice. They also reiterate the point that the development of individual blocks in Welcome cannot be seen independently from the redevelopment of different sites within the city. All blocks in Welcome are built on a similar act of erasure—each one recalling something which no longer exists. While the JB blocks recall the redevelopment of Nigam Bodh Ghat, other blocks recall the development of Rajghat Samadhi or the clearing of national monuments like India Gate. Yet others trace their origin to the creation of space for new monuments of national significance such as the international trade pavilions at Pragati Maidan.

Sometimes it was a sudden unpredictable event which precipitated a particular act of slum clearance, resulting in the founding of another new block in Welcome. Near the JB blocks is a block which evokes the memory of a terrible fire at the *jhuggi* colony known as Dairy Kisan Chand. The fire, which took place in 1961; had destroyed much of the colony but it had also provided the justification for the Municipal Corporation to demolish the rest on the grounds that it was unsafe for human habitation. Many of the survivors were shifted to the colony of Srinivaspuri where they were given 80 sq. yd. plots and compensation money. Those who ended up in Welcome are the ones who had tried to defy the authorities by rebuilding their *jhuggis* back on the spot where the fire had taken place. They had succeeded in remaining there a few years more until a new wave of demolition drives resulted in their being washed up in Welcome's 'black waters'.[9]

Not far from this block is a small block of people who used to live in *jhuggis* at Jamuna Bridge. In their case it was war with Pakistan that finally precipitated their displacement to Welcome, although they did not obtain official plots for several years as one man—ironically a demolition worker for the Municipal Corporation of Delhi (MCD)—explained:

DEMOLITION WORKER: We were living in *jhuggis* at Jamuna Bridge at that time. There were lots of blackouts. The government was worried that the Pakistan forces would drop a bomb on the bridge. They instructed us to remain in darkness, but someone lit a fire, so the police told us we were a threat to security and would have to be moved. Then they came and demolished our *jhuggis* and dumped us here. It was September 1965.

AUTHOR: Were you given plots?

DEMOLITION WORKER: No. Because it was an emergency situation. We were just thrown in the park [area of Welcome] so we built ourselves *jhuggis*. There was nothing here in those days. It was just a wild place full of serpents and roaming goondas. Later they demolished our *jhuggis* here as well and tried to take us off and give us plots in Seemapuri. There had been some fighting between Hindus and Muslims and that was why they said we had to move. Most people went, but some 40 families stayed on. We just rebuilt ourselves new *jhuggis* here in Welcome.

AUTHOR: So how did you finally get this plot?

DEMOLITION WORKER: That was during *nasbandi ka vakt* (the sterilization time). They were going about demolishing *jhuggis*, but they said we could get plots in Welcome if we got sterilized. So we got sterilized to get these plots.

In this brief extract of a conversation, we see a complex interweaving of policy, location and event. On the one hand, this man is dependent on municipal policy for he earns his living as a demolition worker. On the other hand, he has thrice found himself at the receiving end of demolition drives which were linked as much to specific political conditions as to urban planning. It is quite possible that the *jhuggis* under Jamuna Bridge had, like the *jhuggis* at Jamuna Bazaar, long been intended for demolition but it was the 22-day war with Pakistan that provided the context in which that plan became a reality. It also provided a pretext (real or imagined) for blaming slum dwellers for their own eviction for in the memory of the demolition man and other members of his block, it was the *jhuggi* dwellers who brought the demolition on themselves by lighting a fire under conditions of blackout. Whatever the reality, the urgency of the situation seems to have resulted in their not being allocated official plots but rather being dumped temporarily in the open park land of the colony where they simply built themselves new *jhuggis*. The consequence of their unofficial status was that each time new political tensions surfaced, first in the form of localized violence between Hindus and Muslims, and later in the form of Sanjay Gandhi's sterilization drive, the DDA felt justified in dealing with the situation by razing the area to the ground and trying to move the inhabitants elsewhere. Finally, after his third experience of demolition, the man was faced yet again with the prospect of displacement. But this time there was an alternative path. The year was 1976. Indira Gandhi had declared a state of internal Emergency and her son, Sanjay, had launched his infamous sterilization drive. The DDA, anxious to fulfil sterilization targets, was offering plots to those who agreed to have the operation. A deal was struck and the demolition man, who needless to say was busy demolishing the *jhuggis* of others during the Emergency, was finally able to secure an official plot in Welcome.

For the people of Jamuna Bridge there had been no simple continuity between their experience of demolition and their experience of resettlement. In fact, most of the people displaced from Jamuna Bridge went on to experience further displacement and soon found themselves allocated plots in the resettlement colony of Seemapuri a few miles further towards the UP border. According to one old woman, 'those who were clever went to Seemapuri and sold their plots and then returned to Welcome. But those who weren't just stayed put'. Whatever the case, the 36 families who eventually obtained their plots in the block through sterilization were undoubtedly the stubborn few who had tried to escape the dictates of urban planners. Then there were the others, the four families who have built temporary homes adjacent to the block but who do not have official plots. These are the ones who submitted sterilization certificates in 1976 only to be told that all the plots had been taken. Determined not to be defeated one such woman explained, 'We have occupied this piece of land in the hope that if they demolish this, then they will provide us with an alternative place.' Her gesture is backed by the local *pradhan* who comments with assertiveness, 'if the government ever wants to start causing trouble over this, they will have to take my permission first'. As far as local residents are concerned, these four unofficial plots are part of their particular block for their inhabitants share the same collective history of struggle and determination in the face of external war, internal emergency and demolition squads.

It would of course be possible to trace a different foundation narrative for every residential block in Welcome, just as it would be possible to map the resettled population of each block to a specific location in the city. But constraints of space do not permit such detail. Suffice it to say that the reading of space offered by the residents of Phase 3 of Welcome is far more rich and complex than any reading possible from the perspective of urban planning. And if we enter Phase 4 of the colony, we find that the entire area has been created through a similar interface of policy and event for it was developed and populated during 1975-7 when the DDA's slum clearance operations thrived under the climate of coercion created by Emergency regulations. This was a time when the entire city was perforated with demolitions as about 15 per cent of the population was dispersed from the city centre in a mere

19 months. In the spaces left behind by these acts of erasure new parks, trees and public buildings sprouted all over the city whilst a ring of poverty accumulated and thickened around its edges. Of the 7,00,000 or so people displaced, some 1,800 families ended up in Welcome bringing with them memories of the sites of erasure out of which all resettlement colonies are inevitably built. Blocks in Phase 4 of the colony trace their foundation histories to a whole range of inner city locations, including controversial areas like Dujana House, Kala Mahal and the Jama Masjid in the old city. These were not so much *jhuggi jhonpri* clusters as dilapidated inner city areas which had long been classified as 'notified slums'—a term which gave the DDA the authority to destroy them even before the internal Emergency of the 1970s, although it was the Emergency conditions that enabled them to exercise that right.

Viewed in this light even the *jhuggi* area known as the Janata Colony at the back of Welcome can be understood less in terms of the failure of slum policy and more in terms of a blatantly political gesture made at a precise historical moment. For, as local residents reveal, despite the spontaneous-looking appearance of this slum, it was in fact cultivated and nurtured by politicians just one week before the defeat of the Emergency government in March 1977:

A LOCAL PRADHAN: There were some 17 families who had got sterilized but could not get plots at the hands of the DDA. H.K.L. Bhagat[10] assured them that he would provide the land. However, when we reached the spot on 15 March we found some other people already pitching *jhuggis* there. H.K.L. Bhagat thought only the 17 people should be put up there but another Congress leader supported the setting up of the colony for everybody. The colony was inaugurated on 16 March 1977 and once it was established we all took a vow not to move from this place.

LOCAL RESIDENT: The Janata Colony was created by the Congress. They made it in order to try to get votes at a time when they were losing power because of the Emergency.

That the slum was a product of Congress manipulations is confirmed not only by the accounts of other residents of the colony, but also by the fact that, in 1977, several attempts were made to demolish it under the directorship of the new Janata Government which replaced Indira Gandhi's Emergency Government. The first of these attempts was halted by protesting residents lying down in front of the bulldozers; the second was greeted by a hunger strike organized by prominent people of the slum. Despite the fact that the Janata Party had built its following partly through its violent condemnation of Emergency slum clearance measures, it nonetheless did not hesitate to employ similar measures to try to get rid of a slum patronized by its main rival, the Congress. It is likely that the population of the Janata colony swelled more rapidly than even its founders had anticipated for the demolitions of 1975-7 had created a floating population of desperate displaced people in search of space in the capital.

We have traced the foundation of different areas and blocks in Welcome by examining the web of spatial and temporal factors that facilitated the enactment of the slum clearance and resettlement initiatives which formed part of a long-term urban plan devised in the late 1950s. In this sense the narratives of the people of Welcome tell us how the colony has developed through the playing out of internal politics and external events in different locations all over the city. But this is not to imply that once shifted to Welcome, the resettled population—who might more appropriately be called the unsettled population—ceased to play a part in historic events. As the example of the Janata Colony reminds us, national events are also played out within marginal spaces like Welcome. In this sense Welcome provides a window not just onto Delhi but onto historic processes that have effected north India as a whole for within each decade of the colony's existence a critical event of national significance has led to a reshuffling of its population. This means that any reading of the colony purely in terms of urban planning takes us one step further from the reality of its development. What the following examples reveal is the extent to which the socio-dynamics of space amongst the urban poor in Delhi is subject to a constant process of reconfiguration as national events are played out at a local level.

HISTORIC RECONFIGURATIONS, OPERATIONAL PLOTS

That the Emergency of 1975-7 was a significant moment in the history of Welcome is evident from the fact that this was the time when Phase 4 of the colony was developed. The accounts of those displaced from Jamuna Bridge also reveal that some people living unofficially in the colony had been able to secure official plots through sterilization at that time. It would however be wrong to conclude that the allocation of land on a sterilization basis was restricted to one small corner of the colony. On the contrary, the sterilization drive, which became so notorious during the Emergency, had a profound effect on restructuring the colony as a whole. Official records of the slum department reveal that there is not a single block in Welcome that was not affected by it.[11]

To understand the impact of the sterilization drive on the socio-dynamics of space in Welcome, it is necessary first to situate it within the context of family planning policy more generally. Like the resettlement programme, family planning had always been unpopular in India and suffered from severe problems of implementation. Apart from a few mass sterilization camps in Kerala which were deemed 'successful' at the time, few decisive attempts had been made to curb the population growth, not least because the issue was destined to lose the government votes. However, by the 1970s India was under considerable pressure from the international community, which was predicting a global population disaster with India at its centre. This external pressure no doubt formed the background to the decision to prioritize family planning during the Emergency. Following earlier experiments in Kerala it was decided that sterilization was the most efficient method of birth control and that men should be targeted since vasectomy was both cheaper and easier to perform than tubectomy.[12] Strangely, it was not the Prime Minister, Indira Gandhi, who took responsibility for promoting this policy, but her inexperienced son, Sanjay who made family planning part of his four (and later five) point programme. Since it was well known that people would not want to volunteer themselves for the operation, a package of 'incentives' and 'disincentives' was drawn up with the aim of ensuring the participation of all government departments. The directors of each department were issued targets accordingly and told to levy sterilization cases from their employees.

In this sense the DDA was no more implicated in family planning activities than any other government department in Delhi. All departments—whether concerned with education, transport, health, electricity or housing—were expected to accumulate sterilization certificates and most did so by threatening to withdraw the salaries of those employees who had two or more children unless they got sterilized. In Welcome all the government employees with whom we spoke, with the exception of two railway coolies, had in 1976 been forced to submit their bodies for sterilization in order to retain their pay. But although this 'disincentive' proved an efficient means of coercing the poorest and least powerful government servants into sterilization, it seems to have been less successful at higher levels in the administration.[13] At the same time high level officials were anxious to prove their enthusiasm for family planning since careers and budgets depended on their success in meeting and, if possible, exceeding sterilization targets. This meant that once they had exhausted their own workforce as a resource, they began to cast their nets a little wider in an attempt to draw in sterilization cases from the general public. This they did by denying basic services to civilians until such time as the latter agreed to pay for the services by getting themselves sterilized. In 1976 a whole range of activities from school admissions to ration became dependent on production of a sterilization certificate. As one man in Welcome put it,

> The time was such that you had to produce that *nasbandi* card [sterilization certificate] wherever you went and if you wanted any work of yours to be done. If you went for hospital treatment they wouldn't treat you unless you had that *nasbandi* card. It was exactly like it is now with Seshan's identity card.[14] That *nasbandi* card was needed at every place and in all Government offices.

Discussion of the multiple routes through which a large number of the residents of Welcome were manoeuvred into getting themselves sterilized is beyond the scope of this essay.[15] My aim here is to concentrate uniquely on DDA-related sterilizations since these were the ones that led to a radical re-distribution of land within the colony. Records held by the slum department of the DDA reveal that just over 28 per cent of the plots in Welcome were officialized in 1976 through sterilization. These were distributed throughout the colony although the concentration of sterilizations differed from block to block.

Analysis of the records pertaining to Welcome combined with

conversations with both housing officials and local residents reveal that the process by which the DDA levied their cases was highly complex. Basically in September 1976 production of a sterilization certificate became the new pre-requisite for the allocation or regularization of resettlement plots in the area. Effectively applicants were given two choices: either they got sterilized themselves or else they paid someone else to get sterilized, thereby attaining the status of a 'motivator'. Those who presented themselves as motivators were as entitled to plots as those who presented themselves on a self-sterilization basis. It was only the motivated people who were not eligible for plots since they had received money instead from the motivator. As one man in Welcome succinctly put it, 'it was a forcible deal on the part of the government'. This deal did not present itself to those residents who already had official plots in Welcome and had all the documents of entitlement relating to the demolition of their previous slum. But for those already living in the colony without the relevant documents or those, whose homes were unofficial or had just been demolished, the deal was a matter of land or no land. Only by sacrificing their reproductive capacity, or by paying others to sacrifice theirs did they gain the right to live in the colony. Since this was a time when demolition squads were out in force all over Delhi, the possibility of squatting on land elsewhere in the capital was not a viable option.

Essentially there were three main routes through which the DDA accumulated sterilization cases from people already settled in Welcome. The first was by demolishing all unofficial constructions in the colony and refusing to offer alternative sites to the displaced until they produced evidence of self or motivated sterilization. Effectively, this was the situation faced by the people displaced from Jamuna Bridge during the Pakistan war and there were many others who had been squatting unofficially in Welcome or in nearby colonies who suddenly found themselves homeless as a result of demolitions in September 1976. Jagmohan, who was in charge of DDA operations during the Emergency, has always denied that plots were allocated to displaced slum dwellers on a sterilization basis, but the DDA's own records as well as the testimonies of people in Welcome prove otherwise. Whilst blocks populated as a result of demolitions in 1975 contain only a small proportion of sterilization cases (13 per cent), those populated as a result of demolitions in 1976 are basically built on sterilization cases (83 per cent). These blocks are located on the extreme edges of the colony and are collectively referred to by many residents as the Nasbandi plots. In spatial terms, the dispersal of *jhuggi* dwellers from all over Welcome to the edges of the colony echoes the dispersal of *jhuggi* dwellers from all over the capital to the edges of the city.

The second route through which the DDA officials levered sterilization cases was by scanning the colony for what they called 'irregularities'. At the time of their resettlement all those who were allocated official plots had been made to sign affidavits in which they agreed to abide by a long list of rules which included not selling or letting out their plots. The resettlement process was intended to remove the poor indefinitely from the city centre.

However some of the people resettled in the 1960s had, by the mid 1970s, sold up and left the colony whilst others had let out space to tenants. In September 1976, DDA officials were on the lookout for such irregularities. Suddenly both tenants and purchasers, some of whom had been living in Welcome for over a decade, found themselves confronted with the bleak choice of sterilization (self or motivated) or eviction. Most chose either to get sterilized or to pay someone else to take their place on the operating table. The result was that absentee landlords lost their properties to their tenants who now became the official occupants of their homes and plots.

The third technique employed by the DDA was to make sterilization a medium of negotiation. People wanting transfers from other colonies or seeking to obtain a second plot now had the opportunity to do so by getting sterilized or 'motivating' someone else. Sterilization had in effect become a form of currency and there were some individuals who used the sterilization drive as a means of purchasing land they could otherwise ill afford. Others, though opposed to family planning themselves, turned the threat to their advantage by motivating the maximum number of people. Such was the case with the 30 scrap iron merchants whose old market on the Grand Trunk Road (near Welcome) had been demolished by the DDA. By motivating three people each, they were able to get double-sized plots in Welcome. The people they 'motivated' were mainly poor villagers from Uttar Pradesh who had come to Delhi either to seek refuge from coercive sterilization in their villages or because they had heard that there was money to be made through sterilization in the capital. Constraints of space preclude a discussion of the process by which the motivation structure operated on the ground—something I have discussed elsewhere at some length.[16] Suffice it to say that the market for sterilization that developed as a consequence of the DDA's initiative took the family planning policy out of the hands of the state and into the hands of intermediaries and black marketeers who cared little for the victims of their trade.

It is difficult to generalize from the experiences of the people of Welcome since one of the most remarkable features of the family planning campaign during the Emergency was the extent to which individual officers and ministers were given carte blanche to invent the rules. Certainly it seems likely that the other six resettlement colonies belonging to East Zone B of the slum wing suffered similar treatment at the hands of the DDA and there is some evidence to suggest that the offer of plots for sterilization was common in different parts of Delhi. Furthermore, the testimonies of some Welcome residents who paid poor villagers to get sterilized in their place reveal that in the rural areas of UP the pressure was equally, if not more, intense. In social terms, this pressure always accumulated downwards until those at the bottom of the hierarchy had little choice but to get sterilized. In spatial terms, it radiated outwards from the capital, with the northern states levying far higher sterilization tolls than those in the south.[17]

The sterilization drive of September 1976 had two main effects on the socio-dynamics of space in Welcome. The first was to disperse *jhuggi* dwellers from inside the colony, settling them in peripheral blocks where they were mixed up with strangers from their own and other religious communities. The second was to fix the position of those who had entered the colony as illegal purchasers and tenants. Through sterilization they now became official occupants whilst the original owners lost their rights to land in the colony. Ironically, all plots issued or regularized through sterilization were granted on a provisional basis and are still categorized as 'provisional' to this day. In spite of this, the emergency re-shuffle had a stabilizing effect on the colony for it gave the inhabitants of Welcome a feeling of security they had not previously experienced. It was only after the dramatic events of 1976 that people gained the confidence to invest in building permanent pukka homes in the colony. The fact that over a quarter of all families in the colony had sealed their rights to land in flesh and blood gave them a feeling of legitimacy as if somehow confirming the permanence of their relationship to their plots. Little did they know that when the MCD took over administration of the slum wing from the DDA immediately after the Emergency, one of the first things they contemplated was the cancellation of all allocations of land that had been made on a sterilization basis.

The Missing Community

Over twenty years have passed since the Emergency and in this time the inhabitants of Welcome have done much to impose their own logic on the colony. This is particularly apparent in the carving up of space for religious activities. The colony now has several large temples and shrines as well as many mosques, an *idgah* and a graveyard. A passer-by could easily be forgiven for assuming that Hindus and Muslims are the only religious communities represented in Welcome. However, near the entrance to the colony is a large building which, in 1997, was still under construction. From it there stuck a flag revealing that this was in fact a gurdwara (Sikh Temple) in the making. What was curious about the emergence of this gurdwara in Welcome was the apparent absence of Sikhs in the colony.

It was several months before my assistant and I happened to chance upon an old Sikh man in one of Welcome's markets. We were keen to talk to him and he was more than willing to explain the mystery of the gurdwara without Sikhs. The new building was in fact a replacement of an older gurdwara, which had been destroyed:

> In 1984 our gurdwara was burnt to ashes. Not a single brick of it was left. Before that time there used to be some 60 or 65 Sikh families in Welcome but now there can't be more than 15. Most of them left never to come back. Tell me, how can someone loot a house when the head of the family is sitting right there inside it? But this is exactly what happened here in Welcome in 1984.

The old man was of course referring to the Sikh massacre, which followed the assassination of Indira Gandhi by two of her Sikh bodyguards in 1984. His account seemed to suggest that Sikhs no longer felt secure in Welcome and led me to ask why he himself had stayed on, to which he gave the following reply:

> By April I will no longer be here. I am moving to the Ashram area. There are many people from our own community on that side of town. It's not good to live in an area where you are isolated from your own community. These days there aren't any Sikhs left in the plots [of Welcome]. The only few that remain are in the tenements area. I have made a good life in Welcome and have made good money from this place but one should not be greedy. Now it is time to leave.

We spent several hours listening to this man's account of how he had survived the massacre of Partition when most of his family had been killed escaping from Pakistan. 'They had created a second Pakistan for us' was the phrase he used to describe the anti-Sikh violence of 1984, although this time his life had been saved by Muslims. Welcome, with its small Sikh community, had not suffered the terrible losses experienced in some parts of the capital, but for the few Sikh families who did live in the colony the feeling of betrayal invoked by the episode had been enough to provoke a slow but systematic exodus. It is as if by erasing the gurdwara, the vengeful mobs had in effect guaranteed the erasure of the community from the colony.

How then should we interpret the emergence of the new gurdwara now under construction? Eventually we were able to track down the *granthi* (Sikh religious leader) and a few remaining Sikhs who lived in the tenement blocks and they confirmed that the congregation had dwindled along with the population with the result that there were only 5 or 6 people left who came to worship at the new gurdwara. Nonetheless the building was at least ten times the size of the old one and was being built entirely from money raised by Sikh networks in the absence of government compensation. By the time the building is completed it is likely there will be even fewer Sikhs in Welcome until perhaps only the building will remain as a hollow shell reminiscent of a community that once was. The replacing of a small and relatively insignificant building with a larger more prominent one has been even more striking in the neighbouring colony of New Seelampur where a huge gurdwara dominates the horizon despite the fact that the Sikh population of the colony has diminished and was never very large in the first place. What we are witnessing in colonies like Welcome and New Seelampur is a symbolic stamping of the urban landscape by a wounded minority who dare not live there but who none the less wish to make their presence felt. These new gurdwaras may remain physically empty most of the time but they act as powerful reminders of a community's symbolic refusal to be effaced.

Separate Paths

The departure of Sikhs from Welcome represents only a minor shift in the socio-religious make-up of the colony for the Sikhs had always been a minority community. Far more dramatic has been the segregation of the two dominant religious communities of Hindus and Muslims. Walking around the colony today one could easily get the impression that Phase 4 of the colony was conceived by planners as a Muslim area and Phase 3 as a space for Hindus. Only the unofficial Janata Colony at the back of Welcome gives the impression of being truly mixed. However, appearances are deceptive. The allotment documents held in the slum department reveal that many blocks of the colony used to house a mixture of both Hindus and Muslims even if the former dominated in Phase 3 and the latter in Phase 4. Officials of the slum department confirmed that the resettlement policy was designed to cut across social and religious divisions by mixing people up. However history has defied policy in Welcome. It is likely that religious segregation is a process that has long been occurring in the colony but there is little doubt that the process has accelerated in recent years. In particular, it was the violence following the destruction of the Babri Masjid in Ayodhya by right wing Hindu extremists in 1992 that has precipitated a systematic re-drawing of socio-religious boundaries within the colony. Walking around Phase 4 it is not uncommon to hear residents remark that there used to be several Hindu families in their block but that they have moved away in recent years. Equally, in Phase 3 we heard of Muslim families who had left the colony during the violence, some of whom never returned and others who moved to Phase 4 of the colony. The effect of these demographic changes is that those families who remain in areas dominated by the other community feel increasingly vulnerable like the Muslim woman in one of the JB blocks who told us, 'I don't feel safe living here any more. I'm alone in the house all day long. We are the only Muslims in this street. I have told my husband we cannot stay on. We have started looking for somewhere else but the problem is that this is cheaper.'

Discussion of the processes by which the residents of Welcome were drawn into some of the worst violence experienced in the capital in December 1992 is beyond the scope of this essay. Suffice it to say that the demolition of the Babri Masjid in Ayodhya seems to have functioned as an excuse for the playing out of local resentments within the colony. Just as the local Chamars of Sultanpuri had used the 'Sikh riots' as a means of re-structuring local relations of power in 1984,[18] so in 1992 Hindus in Welcome seem to have seized the opportunity to try to suppress, if not eliminate, the expanding and relatively successful Muslim community from the colony. This is not to say that all Hindus participated. But it is very clear from the debris left behind after the conflict that almost all of the property destroyed as well as the people murdered, injured and arrested belonged to the Muslim community. Though to some extent scattered, arson attacks had followed a clearly discernible pattern. They had started at a mosque adjoining a Hindu-majority area of the colony and had mostly been directed either at entire residential blocks containing mainly Muslims or else at Muslim-owned houses which were targeted within Hindu-majority blocks. Since a large proportion of Muslims in Welcome earn their living working in small manufacturing units for denim jeans and various crafts, what was destroyed was not only their homes but also their means to a livelihood.

Much has been written about the '1992 riots' and it is not my intention to add to this burgeoning literature here. But I mention 1992 to give a sense of how Welcome has been restructured not just through the violence of the moment—the murder and arson attacks directed mainly against Muslims—but also through the memory of that moment and the fear that something equivalent might one day occur again. In this sense Welcome is very much a scarred space, or perhaps it would be more appropriate to argue that Welcome's very existence is built up through a process of perpetual scarring—whether in the form of slum fires, demolitions, sterilizations, riots, or massacres so that, in the final analysis, it becomes difficult to isolate the scars from the body of the colony itself.

At one level the restructuring of Welcome might seem marginal to the development of Delhi as a whole. But, as I have argued from the beginning, resettlement colonies cannot be divorced from the development of the capital for they are quite literally born through the demolition and re-development of some other place. Similarly, as historic events get played out in Welcome, leading to the reconfiguration of people in space within the colony, so Welcome continues to contribute to wider demographic movements taking place within the city as a whole. Those Sikhs who left Welcome after 1984 have contributed to the building of Sikh-dominated settlements in other parts of the city; similarly those Muslims and Hindus who have moved to areas dominated by their own communities have contributed to the re-inscribing of geo-religious boundaries, not only in Delhi, but also in many other north Indian cities which experienced the traumas of 1992. In this sense the window that Welcome provides offers a very rich and extended view of developments well beyond the colony.

CONCLUDING REFLECTIONS

I began by expressing my frustration with a young man from Welcome who had tried to convince me that the colony had no history. It is doubtful whether I shall ever meet him again, but if I did, I hope I would be able to convince him that Welcome provides us with an interesting opportunity to take a fresh look and develop a new vocabulary for understanding how aspects of the city have been shaped over the years. As the colony grows and becomes restructured over time, this new vocabulary takes us further and further away from the language of urban planning. Land is allocated not according to rights but through 'forcible deals'; minorities are suppressed through a combination of arson and intimidation; boundaries are re-drawn through acts of mass violence. Blackmail, obliteration and segregation may not have much to do with urban policy but, I would argue, they do bring us nearer to understanding how history is lived and experienced by members of the urban poor who constitute a very significant proportion of the population of Delhi.

NOTES

I would like to thank the Economic and Social Research Council of Great Britain for funding this research. I am also grateful to the London School of Economics and Political Science, Goldsmiths College, University of London and Jawaharlal Nehru University in New Delhi for their institutional support. For his work as research assistant, I would like to thank Rajender Singh Negi and for their willingness to enter into conversation, I would like to thank the people of Welcome.

1. For some examples of the former, see H.D. Birdi, *Slum Law and Urbanisation*, New Delhi: Vidhi, 1995; Giresh K. Misra and Rakesh Gupta, *Resettlement Policies in Delhi*, Delhi: Institute of Public Administration, 1981; Sabir Ali, *Environment and Resettlement Colonies of Delhi*, Delhi: Har Anand Publications, 1995; Jagmohan, *Rebuilding Shahjahanabad*, Delhi: Vikas, 1975. For examples of the latter, see V. Das (ed.), *Mirrors of Violence: Communities, Riots and Survivors in South Asia*, Delhi: OUP, 1990; P. Brass, *Theft of an Idol*, Princeton University Press, 1997; J. Spencer, 'Problems in the Analysis of Communal Violence', in *Contributions to Indian Sociology*, 1992 (n.s.) 26, 2.
2. Cf. V. Das, 'The Spatialisation of Violence: Case Study of a Communal Riot', in K. Basu and S. Subrahmanyan (eds.), *Unravelling the Nation: Sectarian Conflict and India's Secular Identity*, New Delhi: Penguin, 1996.
3. Cf. V. Das, *Critical Events*, Delhi: OUP, 1995.
4. There are today three neighbouring areas known as Seelampur (sometimes spelt Silampur) in the Shahdara district of East Delhi: Old Seelampur—the 'village' area once located outside Delhi but today well incorporated within the city and dominated by a large wholesale cloth market; New Seelampur—one of Delhi's oldest resettlement colonies and Seelampur Welcome—a second resettlement colony and the one that concerns us here. Locally it is simply known as 'Welcome'. All three Seelampurs have a distinctive identity and are perceived as separate places by the people who live and work there.
5. Cited in Birdi, op. cit., 1.52.
6. Cf. Sabir Ali, *Slums within Slums: A Study of Resettlement Colonies in Delhi*, Delhi: HarAnand/ Vikas, 1990.
7. Jagmohan, *Island of Truth*, Delhi: Vikas, 1978, pp. 31-2.
8. Ibid., p. 33.
9. The Hindi phrase *kala pani* meaning black waters is frequently invoked by Welcome residents to refer to the sense of banishment they felt at being dumped in a far-off colony. It is a euphemistic reference to the Andaman Islands where prisoners used to be deported and holds similar connotations as 'Siberia' for Europeans.
10. H.K.L. Bhagat was the Congress Minister of State for Works and Housing during the Emergency. Local *pradhans* have long cultivated political links with him and used to refer to him as 'the King without a crown'. He has undoubtedly played a major role in both official and unofficial developments in the colony although his reputation is today tarnished by his alleged participation in the Sikh massacre of 1984 and, more particularly, by his failure to intervene during the Hindu-Muslim violence of 1992 when large sections of Welcome and the Janata Colony were burnt down.
11. For a more detailed analysis of slum department records pertaining to Welcome during the emergency, see E. Tarlo forthcoming, 'Paper Truths: The Emergency and Slum Clearance through Forgotten Files', paper presented at the workshop, *The Anthropology of the Indian State*, held at LSE in 1998, to be published in the volume *The every day state and society in Modern India*, eds. V. Benei and C.J. Fuller, Delhi: Social Service Press.
12. For critical insights into the coercive nature of pre-emergency family planning initiatives, see M. Vicziany, 'Coercion in a Soft State: The Family-Planning Program of India', Part 1: 'The Myth of Voluntarism' and Part 2: 'The Sources of Coercion', *Pacific Affairs*, 1982, vol. 55, no. 3, 1982, pp. 373-401 and no. 4, pp. 557-93.
13. Informal conversations with medium and high-level officials suggest that many, though not all, were able to avoid getting sterilized either by knowing people of influence or by getting credit for 'motivating' others to undergo the operation.

14. T.N. Seshan was the Election Commissioner who introduced identity cards following the 1993 elections in which a number of Muslims found themselves excluded from the electoral role on the grounds that they were considered Bangladeshi nationals. The man quoted here is a Muslim embroiderer who, like many Muslims in Welcome, had suffered exclusion from the elections and for whom possession of an identity card was essential if he wished to escape deportation from Delhi where he had lived all his life.
15. For details of this, see E. Tarlo, forthcoming *Unsettling Memories: Narratives of the Emergency in Delhi*, London: Hurst, especially Chapters 2 and 6.
16. Cf. E. Tarlo, 'From Victim to Agent: Memories of the Emergency from a Resettlement Colony in Delhi', *Economic and Political Weekly*, vol. XXX, no. 46, 1995, pp. 2921-8.
17. That Delhi functioned as the physical centre of Emergency measures is confirmed by Gwatkin's observation that the sterilization achievements of different states varied in relation to their proximity to Delhi, with the highest rates found in neighbouring states and lowest ones in states physically distanced from the capital. Cf. Gwatkin, 'Political Will and Family Planning: Implications of India's Emergency Experience', in *Population and Development Review*, vol. 5, no. 1, 1979, pp. 29-59.
18. For a detailed study of how the Sikh massacre provided a background for the playing out of micro politics between Sikhs and Chamars in the resettlement colony of Sultanpuri, see V. Das, op. cit.

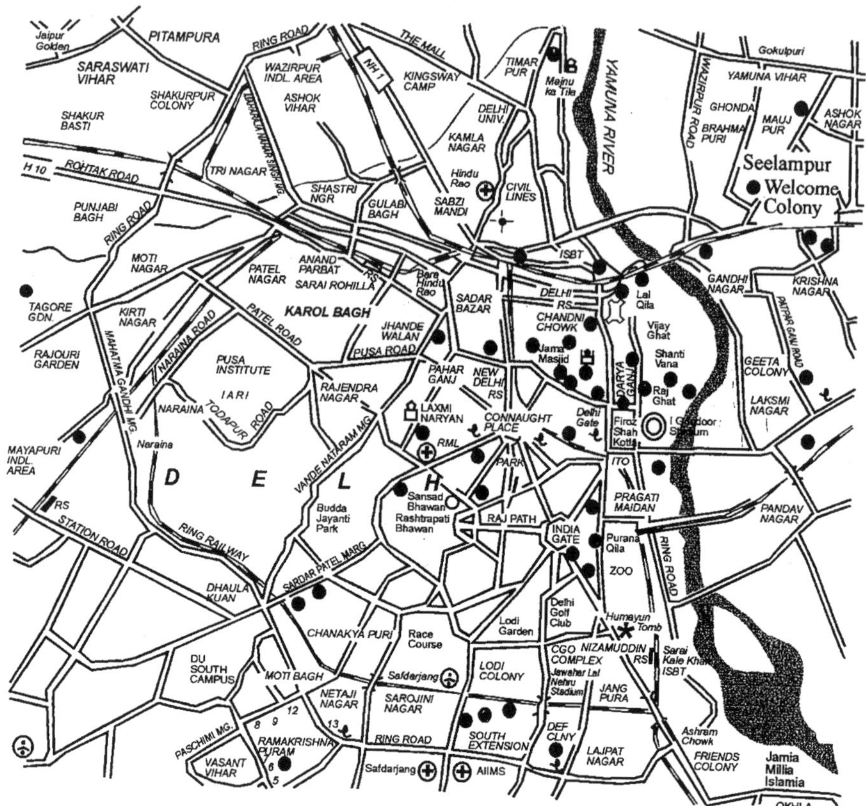

Note: Dots represent sites of demolitions.

MAP 3.1 MAP OF DELHI INDICATING THE DIFFERENT LOCATIONS FROM WHICH THE RESIDENTS OF WELCOME HAVE BEEN DISPLACED.

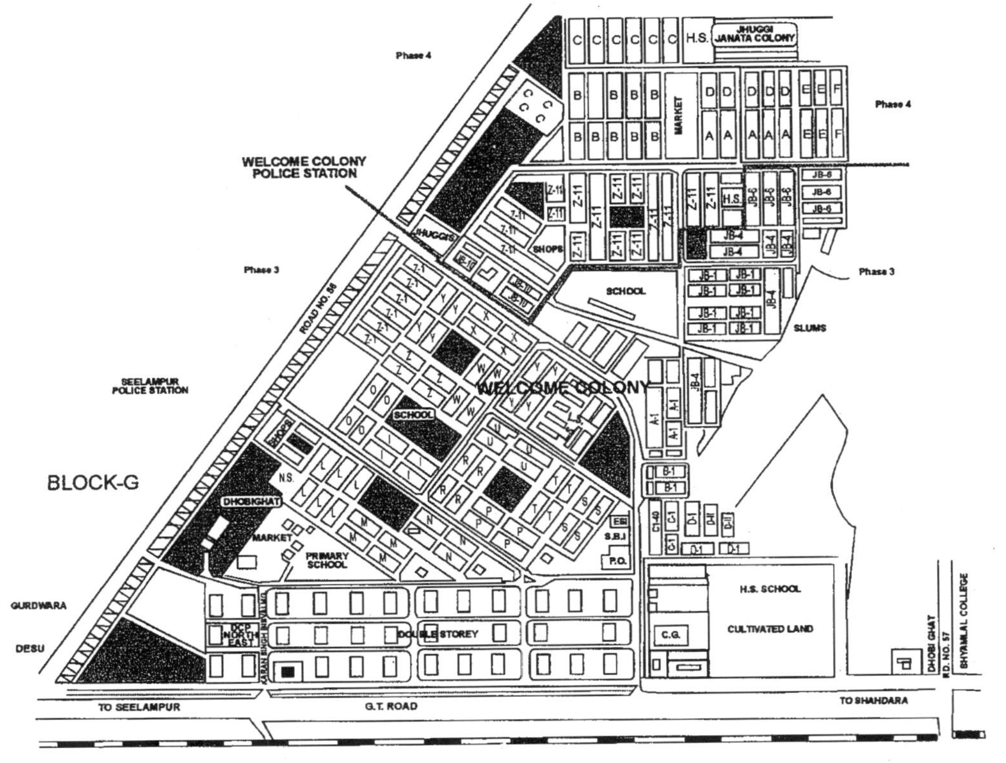

Note: Phase 3 developed 1963-1969, Phase 4 developed 1975-1977.

Source: Delhi Atlas: Colony and Area Maps (New Delhi: ISID and Delhi Police, 1993).

MAP 3.2 OFFICIAL PLAN OF WELCOME COLONY.

4

Urban Conquest of Outer Delhi: Beneficiaries, Intermediaries and Victims

The Case of the Mehrauli Countryside

ANITA SONI

This essay is not a product of pre-planned, methodologically defined research, carried out within a set time frame. Neither does it present quantified findings. Rather, it offers certain insights of the kind social activists are prone to obtain through prolonged exposure to grassroot realities and reflection on those realities. In this case, the ground realities of the area defined broadly as the 'Mehrauli countryside' have been observed and experienced in the course of a decade-long personal interaction with little known marginalized communities of rural migrants who settled in the southern parts of Outer Delhi, originally as quarry workers.

Ever since the 1960s, when they appeared on the scene as the much needed workforce for the emergent, village-based, quarrying industry of Delhi, these sturdy migrants from diverse occupational and ethnic backgrounds have remained present in Outer Delhi's rural milieu, adapting themselves with silent determination to profound changes in that milieu. Their continuing experience of material deprivation and insecurity, oppression and humiliation has been the only 'constant' during the consecutive phases of the progressive appropriation of the area by commercial urban interests.

I shall deal here specifically with one segment of Outer Delhi—the 'Mehrauli countryside'—which has been targeted for appropriation by a particular set of urban actors, the affluent buyers of luxury country estates which have been carved out of village farmlands and commons. In order to place this peculiar trend in a civilizational perspective, I consider it necessary to include in my frame of reference the whole area officially known as 'rural Delhi', largely falling in the Outer Delhi parliamentary constituency. I subsume major post-Independence developments in this area under the general theme of the 'urban conquest' of the hinterland. This has relevance to the whole of India and is the key principle of Delhi's metropolitan growth.

OUTER DELHI: CLASS-WISE DIFFERENTIATION OF UNREGULATED SPACE

Delhi, it is said, is unusual among the world's major cities in that it has managed to push out its growing numbers of poor to the physical fringes.[1] The traditionally rural areas of the Union Territory, corresponding to Outer Delhi and East Delhi parliamentary constituencies have, since the Emergency of 1975-7, been assigned the role of 'peripheries'—distant tracts of wilderness, fit to accommodate the masses of slum-dwellers, left to fend for themselves in poorly serviced 'resettlement colonies' (cf. Emma Tarlo in this volume). In the course of further development, those peripheries have been absorbing assorted segments of the urban middle classes—lower-middle, middle-middle and even upper-middle—in sprawling residential complexes planned by the Delhi Development Authority (DDA), as well as in mushrooming unauthorized colonies. New industrial areas have come up, accompanied by the proliferation of new slums and slum-like tenements.

Outer Delhi is, both in name and reality, synonymous with metropolitan periphery. With its nearly three million voters, it is the largest parliamentary constituency not only of the capital, but of the whole country. But it is also the least prestigious constituency, considered to be a dingy backyard littered with crime and corruption. Both the vast expanse of its north-western parts (notwithstanding the presence of affluent areas like Punjabi Bagh or Pitampura), and the overcrowded eastern part, from Okhla to Tighri, evoke these negative associations. There is, however, one area in Outer Delhi that, far from being regarded as 'periphery', attracts very favourable attention from the most enterprising and ambitious members of the upper class. It is an area markedly free from congestion and squalor, an area of yet unspoiled scenic beauty, tacitly 'reserved' for the privileged few with high incomes and high connections.

This 'special' segment of Outer Delhi has two components: urban and rural. The urban component includes the Tughlakabad Institutional Area, Saket, Qutb Enclave and Institutional Area, Jawaharlal Nehru University campus, Vasant Vihar and—as the southernmost frontier of metropolitan expansion—Vasant Kunj. Of these, Vasant Vihar and Saket are long-established affluent residential areas, similar in character to the 'posh' colonies of South Delhi. Vasant Kunj is a long stretch of multi-storeyed flats and apartments, built in the 1980s by the DDA, and housing mostly salaried employees and young professionals from high income groups.

A few urban estates with a 'touch of class' also belong here. Sainik Farms (south of Mehrauli-Badarpur road), Ruchi Vihar (behind Vasant Kunj), Andheria Bagh (at the location of the ancient mango orchards of the same name, near Mehrauli), are arrogant complexes of palatial mansions with gardens, enclosed behind tall boundary walls. They are, from the point of view of civic authorities, none other than unauthorized colonies, built illegally on agricultural land. But somehow, this derogatory definition is never applied to them. Rather, they are regarded as 'farmhouses'. Their denizens are celebrities of the city's cocktail circuit, and have the means to arrange their own electricity, water, drainage and sewage disposal services. They often indulge in massive power theft with the connivance of law-enforcement agencies.[2]

The area also has several urban villages—which were once agricultural settlements, but are now surrounded by the metropolitan domain, stripped of their entire land and left only with their old original living space (*abadi*), where traditional rustic architecture is rapidly being replaced with opulent modern kitsch likely to attract prosperous urban tenants and buyers.[3] Clusters of huts, officially referred to as '*jhuggi-jhonpri* colonies' (shanty towns), found in the vicinity of such villages, are not urban slums, but habitations of displaced rural people, including both landless sections of the original village population and former quarry workers, most of whom came to such places from the 1960s onwards.

The rural component of this area comprises the countryside south of Mehrauli, falling within the Mehrauli assembly constituency, and the western region south of the Mehrauli-Mahipalpur Road, falling in the Mahipalpur assembly constituency. For administrative purposes, villages of this part of rural Delhi are divided between the Mehrauli and Najafgarh Development Blocks, under the respective Block Development Officers. In theory at least, all of them are 'rural villages'. This tautological expression is official; it denotes the villages, whose land has not been acquired by the government, and is therefore presumed to be still in the possession of individual farmers. Rural villages are also shown in the land records as possessing their '*gram sabha* land' (land coming under the village assembly).

Some large villages like Dera (in the Mehrauli block) or Rajokri (in the Najafgarh block) have still retained some of their fertile agricultural land and traditional rustic ambience. But the dominant features of this once rural belt are the ubiquitous 'farmhouses', prized fiefdoms of the urban gentry. Their high and forbidding boundary walls, increasing in height with each passing year, criss-cross the whole countryside. The sight of open, green village fields has become a rarity.

Apart from their obvious use as luxury weekend resorts and lavish entertainment scenery for the new-rich, these farmhouses also function as venues for tax-free commercial enterprises. A farmhouse is considered agricultural property, and its owner is entitled to concessions intended for land-tilling farmers—exemption from income-tax and subsidized power for tube-wells. But all sorts of highly lucrative businesses thrive behind the conspicuously towering walls and opulent gates: floriculture, nurseries of decorative plants and trees, timber yielding eucalyptus plantations and even garment factories with export outlets. Another important business is the commercial renting out of farmhouse premises for marriage parties and banquets with catering services provided at exorbitant rates.

From an ecological point of view, these farmhouses are a disaster. All of them freely use electric power to extract groundwater through tube-wells, the number and pumpage volume of which have not been monitored by any state authority. The result is that the depletion of the groundwater table has been most catastrophic in precisely those areas where farmhouses have proliferated.[4] Commercial floriculture, in particular, involves the excessive use of groundwater—four times more than that required for food crops—and ruins the soil.[5]

The total number of farmhouses found presently in the Mehrauli and Najafgarh blocks of Outer Delhi exceeds 1800.[6] More are anticipated. Of late, there has been an unprecedented boom in the sale and re-sale of farmhouse plots not requiring land-use conversion legalities, thus opening vistas for further speculation. The metamorphosis of the Mehrauli countryside from an area of undisturbed rusticity into a busy playground of urban commercial interests has taken around forty years. The transition was not smooth at any stage. It has been a turbulent process, changing not only the physical landscape beyond recognition, but also upsetting the rural economy, social hierarchies and the ethos of villages.

Before proceeding to explain how this transformation has been achieved, what factors have played a part in it and in which ways different social groups and agencies are implicated, I want first to explain what is meant by the notion of 'urban conquest'.

NEW COLONIALISM OF THE URBAN RICH

The twin processes of industrialization and urbanization in developing societies can be viewed from opposing standpoints. The essentially optimistic assessment of the internal dynamics of fast-growing urban conglomerations focuses on the economic advantages and employment opportunities offered by big cities attracting large-scale migration from villages. Conversely, critics and adversaries of the 'development ideology', among whom are found some eminent social thinkers and environmentalists of the developing world, highlight the predatory and exploitative nature of urban domination over agrarian peripheries.

The concept advanced here is that of 'internal colonialism'. It is argued that:

> The exploitation of man and nature has not ended with the end of western colonialism. Urban-industrial enclaves in countries of the South are now ruthlessly colonising their own hinterlands, mostly settled by subsistence cultures. As in old style colonialism, displacement and dispossession continue to be justified and legitimised in the name of development and progress.[7]

This critical perspective seems to be relevant in the Indian context in general, and in the context of Delhi's urban growth in particular.

The agenda of development pursued by the rulers of independent India both in the era of Nehruvian socialism and in the recent 1990s era of 'liberalization', has preserved the colonial legacy of asymmetrical power relations between the dominant urban elite and the vast mass of the rural population. The laws that once served the purposes of the colonial administration now serve the interests of the independent government.

Foremost among these oppressive laws of colonial vintage is the Land Acquisition Act of 1894. It confers on the State the absolute right to acquire private or common village lands 'for public purpose'. No objection can be made regarding arbitrary definitions of 'public purpose'. Only individual property owners are entitled to compensation. The amount of compensation, again arbitrarily decided by the State, is always a small fraction of the market value of the land in question. Consequently, displaced farmers who lose their land in the interest of 'public purpose' cannot buy equivalent land elsewhere or establish themselves as respectable self-employed entrepreneurs. They end up as assetless job seekers in the urban-industrial sector.

Even more severely hit are the non-property owning sections of the rural population; landless labourers, tenant cultivators, cattle grazers, fisherfolk and artisans, all of whom are dependent on common natural resources, such as forests, pastures, wastelands and water belonging to the village community as a whole. Such people are not entitled to any compensation when the State appropriates commons under the Land Acquisition Act. Deprived of their source of livelihood, people are often forced to migrate to urban-industrial centres as unskilled wage labourers.

The acquisition of common lands by the State has invariably resulted in their commercial exploitation by unscrupulous profiteers. 'Whereas more than 80 per cent of resources were common in India at the beginning of this century, barely 20 per cent remain so now', according to the well known environmental lawyer, Chattrapati Singh. 'The benefits from common natural resources, whether in hills or in plains, have been almost wholly usurped by the industrial, mercantile, and urban-rich base.'[8]

Traits of 'internal colonialism' endorsed by the State representing the economic interests of the urban rich are discernible in the process of metropolization and 'megapolization' of Delhi during the 50 years since independence. They manifest themselves both at a national and local level.

As the supreme centre of political power, Delhi has assured itself preferential treatment in the allocation of national resources. The Central Plan outlay for Delhi is more than that for the entire State of Assam, for instance. As for the social and ecological costs of Delhi's escalating demands for resources, there is no statistical account of them—they are not quantifiable.

Delhi's huge and wasteful water consumption and large amounts of untreated industrial effluents and domestic sewage discharged into the Yamuna, has reduced the great river to a stinking drain, and inflicted terrible suffering on millions of people in villages and towns downstream from Delhi, poisoning even underground water in wells.[9] Additionally, Delhi's ever-growing demand for electric power is the main factor behind the displacement and dispossession of tens of thousands of villagers in Uttarakhand, around the Tehri Dam construction site, and in the Singrauli region of Madhya Pradesh, hosting the World Bank-aided Rihand Super Thermal Power Project, a source of heavy environmental pollution in the surrounding countryside. Of the electric power produced by the Northern Grid 65 per cent is consumed by

Delhi alone. It does not seem far-fetched to assume that the games of cynical politicians and their agents encouraging the colossal theft of electricity for domestic and industrial purposes in slums and unauthorized colonies (their crucial vote banks) are played out in the safe knowledge that any deficit that the Government of the National Capital Territory of Delhi may run into, will be paid from the national kitty and its burden passed onto the hinterland.

The direct colonization of Delhi's very own hinterland has been motivated primarily by the quest for additional urban space. In this, the government has followed the example set by the British rulers who built New Delhi as their imperial capital, taking away the land of several historic villages in the process. During the British period, about 40 villages were incorporated within the urban limits of Delhi. Since Independence, their number has risen to 185. The Land Acquisition Act of 1984 has served throughout as the legal instrument to enlarge urban space at the cost of agricultural landholdings and village commons.

The momentum of metropolitan expansion, especially since the 1960s, has not been created by the government's actions alone. The rural space in the areas near the newly created urban settlements became the target of feverish manipulations on the part of real estate speculators and land developers who lured the farmers into 'profitable' sales of land. As the building industry grew into a veritable empire of money and power, builders' mafias, in collusion with self-serving politicians and government officials, became active in cornering new chunks of rural land for the construction of palatial enclaves, housing VVIPs and their friends and relatives.

The swoop on rural land has practically eliminated the once powerful and assertive landed peasantry of Delhi Territory as a social class. Till the late 1980s, the village *panchayats* (councils), representing the locally dominant castes (Jats, Gujjars or Rajputs as the case may be) of the respective villages, held sway over the rural areas falling predominantly in Outer Delhi and decided the fate of political candidates. The old caste loyalties still exist and continue to figure in the electoral calculations of contesting parties, but their social context has changed.

At present, in the existing 195 rural villages of the National Capital Territory of Delhi (90 per cent of which fall in Outer Delhi), there are barely 40,000 families who still possess and cultivate agricultural land.[10] These are mostly small and marginal farmers, relying on their own family labour (except during the harvest season when they employ others), and although their performance as agriculturists is impressive (with yields of wheat per hectare 37 per cent higher than the national average; 1.74 thousand mega tonnes of annual production of food grains, and 6,00,000 mega tonnes of vegetables), it does not alter the fact that these 40,000 families—or around 2,00,000 people—dependent on land for their livelihood constitute no more than 15 per cent of the total rural population of Delhi, estimated in 1996 at 13,00,000.

The vast majority of Delhi's rural population (over 10,00,000) is employed either outside agriculture or is unemployed. Only a few ex-farmers who parted with their land, on their own accord or under duress, have succeeded in commerce (whether of the lawful or unlawful kind[11]). Others, after making a splash with their sudden fortunes, have ended up as small-time shopkeepers, auto-rickshaw drivers, factory workers and so on. Many unemployed youths from the rural villages have become petty criminals (Delhi Police records, especially in North-West Delhi, bear witness to this), or the hired bodyguards of politicians from amongst their caste-brethren.

On the whole, large-scale social disruption has been the inevitable consequence of the rapid and ruthless colonization drive in rural Delhi. Those who have suffered most on account of the acquisition and illegal sale of *gram sabha* lands are the landless sections of the rural population, belonging to the Scheduled Castes and Other Backward Classes. Non-implementation of the 73rd Amendment of the Constitution, passed in 1992 for the mandatory elections of village *panchayats* in rural areas (including Union Territories), following the supersession of the formerly (1984) elected *panchayats* by the Delhi Administration in 1990, has deprived these poor and oppressed sections of the opportunity to get their rightful share of representation in local governance at the village level.[12] The old *gram panchayats* were the preserve of landowning castes, who fiercely suppressed any stirrings of assertiveness on the part of the lower orders of village society. Predictably, the officialdom of Delhi has always sided with the 'haves' against the 'have-nots'.

Implementation of the 73rd Amendment would be the only way of stopping, and even reversing, the illegal sale of commons, by subjecting *pradhans* (elected village leaders) to scrutiny and public exposure by those vitally interested in preserving the commons as their livelihood base. However, the Delhi Government has preferred to declare the rural sector of the National Capital Territory as 'non-existent' for the purposes of participatory democracy under the new dispensation of the *panchayati raj* system (a decentralized democratic institution), and to incorporate rural villages and the constituents of municipal wards with up to 2,00,000 voters each (the 74th Amendment of the Constitution with reference to municipalities). All *gram sabha* lands, still shown in the records as belonging to the respective rural villages have therefore become the property of the Development Department of the Delhi Government. Ironically, the official in charge of *gram sabha* lands is still called the Director of *Panchayats.*

That the Delhi Government has designs on rural Delhi, or on whatever is left of it, becomes clear from a recently published, glossy prospectus entitled: 'Mini Master Plan for Development of Rural Delhi'.[13] Styled as the Sardar Patel Gramodaya Yojana (Sardar Patel Village Upliftment Plan), it visualizes the acquisition of 2,066 ha (hectares) of land in the existing 195 rural villages of Delhi. They are to be developed by the Development Department of the Delhi Government as a 'Special Area', provided with trunk infrastructure (water, sewerage, drainage, power) and roads. Barely 0.6 per cent of the developed area has been earmarked for 'Social Justice' use, that is for various community facilities classified as 'Multi-purpose

Community Centres', serving the host villages; 5 per cent has been allotted for the use of the Delhi Police ('Social Security') and various government departments; 7 per cent for parks, and the remaining 90 per cent is to be available as urban space for residential housing, industrial estates, commercial complexes, medical and educational institutions—all to be developed through the comprehensive involvement of private sector interests through the sale or lease of respective sites auctioned by the Development Department.

In other words, the Development Department of Delhi Government, formally in charge of rural development, has already stepped into the role of an urban development agency, a role previously monopolized by the Delhi Development Authority. Interestingly, there is a cryptic mention in the text of the brochure, that in some areas there has been 'resistance on the part of local people' against the construction of 'multi-purpose' community centres on village land, suggesting that the colonized know they will be excluded from sharing the benefits.

Delhi's urban spread has already claimed the entire National Capital Territory as its land resources reserve and now continues across the state boundaries of Uttar Pradesh and Haryana into the National Capital Region.[14] 'The new Indian landscape' emerging on the Haryana side has been graphically depicted by Baljit Malik:

> All you need to do is to drive past the airport to Gurgaon and Sohna. What unfolds is a panorama of aggressive urbanism—a six-lane highway with arterial roads cutting into farm lands being bought out by property developers and urban development agencies. True, *sarson* (mustard) fields of saffron and green are still there, the odd grove of guava and mango still clings to the disappearing soil. But these are desperate acts of survival before the grinding wheels of the bulldozers of development.
>
> You can see the bulldozers and trucks in their hundreds as they rip the Aravalli hills apart of their rock, soil and surviving vegetation. You can have your nostrils filled with smoke and dust as new industrial estates are carved out and trees and crops levelled to make way for air-conditioned country resorts and golf courses greened with vicious chemicals...
>
> . . . As the new hi-tech homes, offices and recreation grounds expand into the countryside, an even larger ancillary outcrop of *jhuggi-jhonpri* colonies comes into existence to service them. No planning, no infrastructure, no civic services.... Here, then, is where our dispossessed villagers find themselves.[15]

THE MEHRAULI COUNTRYSIDE: THE SEQUENCE OF CHANGE

The specific case of the Mehrauli countryside reflects all the general traits of urban 'colonial' invasion, analysed earlier, but also has its own peculiarities. It is on these peculiarities that I wish to focus, both with regard to the social categories of people defined as 'beneficiaries', 'intermediaries', and 'victims', and to the stages through which the conquest has progressed. For exemplification, I have chosen two separate areas of the broadly defined Mehrauli countryside. Both of them are known to me from direct observation over the past ten years. Reconstruction of their earlier history (prior to 1988) is based on the oral testimonies and reminiscences of local people, as well as from the few secondary sources available.[16]

One of these areas is the stretch south of Mehrauli, from Chattarpur up to the Asola-Bhatti Wildlife Sanctuary. It comprises the villages of Satbari, Chandan Hola, Fatehpur Beri, Asola and Bhatti, all falling in the Mehrauli assembly constituency. I shall refer to this area as the 'Asola-side'. The other area, situated to the west of Mehrauli, includes the villages of Masoodpur, Rangpuri, Mahipalpur and Rajokri, falling in the Mahipalpur assembly constituency. I shall call this area the 'Rangpuri-side'.

Mehrauli, the heritage town dating back to the Sultanate era, and summer retreat for the Mughal kings and nobles, has fallen on bad times but it has retained its importance for the villages around—both as the *tehsil* town, seat of the Subdivisional Magistrate (SDM) and as the major commercial centre where villagers make their special purchases of cloth, utensils and so forth on festive and ceremonial occasions. Before partition, the population of the Mehrauli region had a rich and sophisticated Muslim component. However, today, the old Muslim families who remain here have low social standing.

In the villages of the Asola-side, it is the Gujjars who rule the roost. They are feared by other local communities on account of their alleged propensity for bullying and aggressive display of caste solidarity in conflict situations. They were originally a nomadic tribe of cattle-grazers (as the 'forest Gujjars' in the Uttar Pradesh hills still are). The Gujjars of the north Indian plains were not settled as landed peasants by the British during the nineteenth century. They have never really become interested in agriculture, their main activity being animal husbandry, the milk and ghee (clarified butter) trade. Buffaloes and cows remain an indispensable part of every Gujjar household.

By contrast, the Jats, who dominate the rural scene of the Rangpuri-side (except for Rajokri, which is another Gujjar dominated settlement) have been hereditary farmers since time immemorial. Other caste groups are similarly distributed in both areas. There are some Brahmin farmers and Baniya shopkeepers, both higher in traditional status than Jats and Gujjars, but of lesser importance. The 'low order' in both areas include the Scheduled Castes, mainly Jatavs and Balmikis, who jointly constitute about one-fourth of the village population, and a smaller number of families belonging to the Other Backward Classes.

Till the late 1950s, the villages remained relatively free from urban influence. The rhythm of life was regulated principally by the agricultural cycle—ploughing, sowing and harvesting the wheat and millet crops. Tube-wells were unheard of and fields were irrigated with the help of the Persian wheel. Most essential items of everyday use were produced in and around the village—agricultural implements, earthen utensils, hand-woven cloth, string cots and mats. Religious festivals enlivened the busy routine with a splash of colour and gaiety. Village wells provided the venue for women to exchange gossip while drawing water in turn, and turbaned elders gathered in the evenings in the *chaupal* (community courtyard), passing the hookah around.

The urban invasion proceeded differently in each of the two areas. In the villages of the Asola-side it was triggered off by the Delhi Land Finance Co (DLF) conducting large-scale land purchase operations in entire rural Delhi from the 1950s onward. DLF agents swooped down on Gujjar farmers, taking quick advantage of the difficulties they faced in the rain-dependent cultivation of their fields. The DLF carved cheaply purchased agricultural land into plots of assorted sizes, provided road connections and electricity, and auctioned these developed estates to city-based, upper-class buyers. The installation of power-operated tube-wells enabled the new owners to use the rich subsoil water resources for the greening of their wall-enclosed fancy farms which were cultivated and guarded by hired migrant labourers from eastern Uttar Pradesh.

The Rangpuri-side had not been targeted for this purpose at that time. It did not have its first encounter with the Land Acquisition Act until the late 1950s, in the wake of the construction of the New Delhi airport at Palam, when the Airport Authority of India began to notify large tracts of land—including some in Mahipalpur village. Real estate agents soon leapt in, enticing farmers to sell their land before it became notified for acquisition by the government. Some land did change hands at this time, but for many years there was no visible sign of urban colonizers in these villages.

In the 1960s and 1970s both areas came under the influence of another factor which was to transform their old rural economy, linking it to the urban market. This 'long distance' colonization was conditioned by the rapid growth of the urban construction industry on a scale Delhi had never known before. The growing demand for building materials like granite, sandstone, red sand, silica sand and mica gave rise to the emergence of a village-based quarrying industry in the entire southern belt of Outer Delhi, from Badarpur in the east to Kapashera in the west.

In village after village, the *panchayats* began to throw open the hilly parts of *gram sabha* lands, till then a mixture of forest and pasture, for quarrying operations. Mining permits were issued to private parties by the Delhi Administration through the office of the Collector of Mines, while ownership rights over the respective mineral-yielding areas rested with the village *panchayats*, elected from among landowning castes. This allowed the *panchayat* members and their kinsmen to act as middlemen, procuring truckloads of minerals from the quarrying sites and supplying them to city buyers. Such middlemen have been given the generic name of 'mining contractors'. With the emergence of the lease system in the late 1960s, a whole quarrying area in a village came under the control of a single lease-cum-permit holder, typically the *panchayat pradhan* himself, who deposited a yearly lump sum with the *gram sabha* as lease money, and collected octroi from a large number of individual 'mining contractors', operating under his legal umbrella.

All over the Rangpuri-side, it was stone that was quarried—and the people who exerted themselves in these tough and dangerous quarrying operations were mostly Rajasthani migrants living with their families in small hamlets surrounded by the rocky wilderness of the quarries. Stone quarrying involved drilling holes in solid rock and blasting it with dynamite. The rocks, which were extracted with the help of crowbars and pick-axes, were further pounded by hand with hammers to produce stones of a marketable size. These were then procured by contractors who made oral agreements with the workers, offering them payment on a piece-work basis (to be paid per truckload).

The Asola-side had a different type of quarrying. Here, hidden beneath the earth's surface were rich deposits of *bajri* (red sand) in rock form. This red sand was extracted from crater-like 'pits' formed through the excavation of rock.

The red sand quarries, situated on the common lands of Asola and Bhatti villages, were worked by two categories of migrant labourers—the 'cutters' and the 'loaders'. The 'cutters' were mostly single males from western Uttar Pradesh and Bihar who had come to Outer Delhi, leaving their families behind in their native villages. They did the extraction work. This consisted of excavating a vertical face of rock with the help of pick-axes whilst being precariously suspended by a rope tied around the waist. The 'loaders' comprised two ethnic groups of traditional earth-craftsmen settled at the quarries and working as family units. Their task entailed repeated rounds of descending to the pit-bottom along a steep winding path, with mules or donkeys as carriers, loading the extracted mineral into sacks and transporting the load on the animals' backs up to the pit head.[17]

In both types of quarries the capital input by the contractors was limited to the purchase and operation of the vehicles. The procurement of minerals cost very little: around 5 per cent of its market value. The workers themselves bore all occupational expenses (in stone quarries, the main expenditure was on explosives for rock blasting; in red sand quarries, on fodder for animals; in both the purchase and maintenance of tools was the workers' responsibility). They also bore the occupational risks, without any onus of responsibility falling on the contractor for grievous injuries and deaths (from dynamite blasts in stone quarries and pit-wall collapses in the red sand quarries). Most important, the workers had no bargaining power; they had to accept the payment of a pittance for their labour, because their employers were the owners of the territory where quarrying sites lay. This exploitation of quarry labour has been the crucial factor leading to the rise of a powerful class of intermediaries linked in multiple ways to the needs of the urban market.

The formal takeover of Delhi's quarrying industry by the State in 1976 (through a policy decision of the Delhi Administration to hand over the control and management of all mines and quarries to the Delhi State Industrial Development Corporation—DSIDC) succeeded only in adding another set of middlemen from urban backgrounds, who used their official position to strike profitable deals with the village-based contractors.

The mines, as the quarries came to be officially called (Rangpuri Stone Mines, Rajokri Stone Mines, Bhatti Bajri Mines), were tacitly understood to operate within the informal sector. The idea of being subject to the government's control was, in the words of one senior official of the Delhi

State Mineral Development Corporation (DSMDC), which succeeded DSIDC in 1985, 'a legal fiction'. Since the rural areas of Delhi's fringe were treated as un-regulated legal and social space, there was no interference from either the Delhi Administration or the Union Government regarding the abysmal conditions of work, the lack of labour welfare measures, and the environmental havoc being wrought by the haphazard, profit-driven extraction of mineral wealth.[18]

To compound the lawlessness of the quarries, an ancillary stone-grinding industry, comprising hundreds of small units owned by city-based profiteers, was allowed to operate freely for decades, with massive use of electric power and without any check on air pollution from the primitive un-canopied 'stone crushers'. Large concentrations of those barbaric industrial units—exempt from the provisions of the Factory Act (since each of them employed no more than six to eight workers)—were situated close to the Harijan settlements of Rajokri, Lal Kuan and Mithapur villages, enveloping whole localities in a haze of stone dust, and causing incurable respiratory ailments among the population.

By the 1990s, the time had come for the quarrying activities in the Union Territory of Delhi to close down; a suitable ban was issued by the Delhi Administration in 1991 and made operational in 1992. The huge Bhatti Mines complex (Asola-side) was temporarily closed by the Directorate General of Mines Safety in mid-1990, following a fatal accident which claimed several lives). It was never re-opened.

Ostensibly, the belated awakening of the Delhi Administration to the need to preserve the green belt (where all quarries were situated) was the reason for prohibiting further pilferage of ecologically sensitive areas of the southern Ridge. However, subsequent developments in these areas reveal the presence of other incentives, more potent than environmental concerns. Since 1991 there has been a spurt in the proliferation of new farmhouses, boldly advancing into the (un) Protected Forest area on the Ridge and even into the outer zone of the Wild Life Sanctuary (created in 1986 out of the commons of Asola, Sahurpur, Maidan Garhi and Deoli villages, and extended in 1991 to cover the area of the Bhatti Mines). The colonization of the Mehrauli countryside has come full circle.

It would be wrong to assume that the termination of quarrying activities in the southern part of rural Outer Delhi has been the cause behind the spectacular increase in the number of farmhouses, and in the acreage of earlier existing estates (among them, two major religious establishments on the Asola-side: the Sant Yoga Ashram in Chandan Hola, and the Radhaswamy Satsang in Bhatti) at the cost of *gram sabha* land. In reality, the deals had been struck much in advance, during the years of the operation of the quarries, formally under the control of the government. Vacation by the DSMDC of its leasehold areas in Bhatti, Rangpuri and Rajokri was expected, and awaited, by the village-based intermediaries, ready to exercise their ownership rights over the land. Manipulation of land records in order to show that the DSMDC leasehold area, and parts of *gram sabha* land outside it, were in fact the private property of individual villagers, had been facilitated by a legal provision allowing the exchange of agricultural land in possession of a given farmer against four times as much area in the wasteland belonging to the *gram sabha*.

In the three decades in which the quarries operated, the intermediaries, for whom the mineral trade was not only the source of enormous, untaxed profits, but also the means to develop wide contacts and networks with the metropolitan power structure, showed increasing self-assurance. In their dual capacity as suppliers of raw materials for the capital's biggest and richest industry, and as facilitators of real estate transactions in their respective village territories, they have actively fulfilled the 'colonial' agenda of Delhi's metropolitan expansion. At the same time, they have not turned away from their rural identities. Lack of English education has never allowed them to mix with their urban trade partners as social equals—although, increasingly, they are sending their children to 'prestigious' English medium schools in the city. For their co-villagers, these middlemen have remained the *Chaudharis* (*Chaudhari* being the honorific title denoting originally the hereditary clan leader of a landowning peasant caste, and later, any member of such caste), and they duly prefix their names with that traditional title. Though now living in urban-style concrete mansions (with drab interiors and conservative women inside), and conversing on mobile phones while moving around in cars, they have nonetheless cultivated their image as 'sons of the soil'.

Having amassed wealth and influence, they prepared themselves for entering into the business of politics on their own strength. The 1993 elections to Delhi's first Legislative Assembly brought ample evidence that the new, non-agricultural, rural elite of Outer Delhi had arrived as a political force. Practically all the candidates of all contesting parties had been connected in the past, directly or by proxy, with the mineral trade and real estate business. Electoral campaigning was personality-oriented, and it was the richest candidate who could order the greatest number of giant cut-outs to be installed at the cross-roads, organize the biggest rallies and deploy mass communications technology in the most aggressive way, who was able to impress potential voters.

The switch to the Bharatiya Janata Party (BJP) in the previously Congress-dominated rural areas of Outer Delhi, which has coincided with the attainment of (limited) statehood by the National Capital Territory, reflects the rising aspirations of this new 'urbanized' elite, ready now for a bigger role and no longer willing to play second fiddle to the established power hierarchy of the Congress Party.

THE MARGINALIZED

Analysis of the changing socio-economic configuration of the Mehrauli countryside would be incomplete without giving a profile of the largest group whose cheap labour built the fortunes of the contractors and contributed substantial profits to the Delhi Administration's coffers. I have already indicated the physical conditions of their work in the stone and red sand quarries, and the mode of their employment as piece-rate workers in the informal sector. I have also mentioned the primitive un-mechanized 'production system' which allowed their exploitation as unskilled casual labourers to remain unchanged as long as the quarries were in operation, in spite of the official trappings of public sector management under DSIDC (1975-84) and later, DSDMC (1985-91). What remains to be told is the inside story of the quarry workers' lives: how they came and where they were from, what their past backgrounds were, what memories, traditions, attitudes and values they carried, what problems they had to cope with in their everyday existence at the quarrying sites and what prospects awaited them after the closure of the Delhi quarries. To answer these questions, let us again turn to the Rangpuri-side and Asola-side to present the specific cases of quarry labour settlements still in existence, though precariously so, at the old sites of the Rangpuri Stone Mines and the Bhatti Bajri Mines.

The first case is a *basti* (settlement) of around 400 households figuring in the 1993 electoral rolls of the Mahipalpur assembly constituency, as a separate polling area with 1,200 voters under the name Rangpuri Pahar Nala. It is situated on the *gram sabha* land of Rangpuri village, in the middle of a *pahar* (vast hill), divided in two parts by a *nala* (rain-channel). The inhabitants are all Rajasthanis mainly from the districts of Jhunjhunu, Sikar, Nagaur and Alwar, and the *basti* has, even now, a decidedly rural Rajasthani flavour—with women's *odhnis* and men's turbans in the bright red and yellow colours of the desert—and neat mud-walled courtyards. They belong to different castes and communities, most of whom have become alienated from their traditional professions. The Ballais (previously weavers, of ancient tribal origin) predominate, followed by the Raigars (leather craftsmen) and the Khatiks (wood-cutters). Tribal communities are represented by the Banjaras[5] (in medieval times prosperous transporters of goods) and the Meos (Rajputs later converted to Islam. The region of Mewat is named after them).

The *basti* was settled in the 1960s. The first workers came in teams led by their own headmen who arranged for individual mining permits from the Delhi Administration and negotiated their wage terms with the local Jat landlords. Later on, new migrants arrived mostly through kinship and village links. Often migration occurred in stages of movement from one location to another, as people searched for a place providing regular employment opportunities.

Many workers of Rangpuri Pahar Nala maintained an amphibious relationship with their native villages (circular migration), working for about six months in the quarries then leaving for their villages during the summer and monsoon seasons which were slack periods at the quarries and coincided with important agricultural and festive seasons in the villages. In several instances employment in the quarries allowed the workers to rise in social status in their native villages where they invested their savings in the construction of large houses—symbols of the new aspirations of their communities.

At the quarry sites their life was full of stress. Subjugation by local contractors became more oppressive as the latter grew in economic status (initially they did not possess vehicles other than bullock carts) and took advantage of the workers' financial hardships by advancing *peshgis* (loans) payable by deduction from already meagre earnings. Indebtedness to 'contractors' created conditions akin to bondage labour, lowering the self-respect of the workers' communities and inviting sundry attempts at the sexual exploitation of their wives and daughters. It was largely in order to counter this menace that help was sought from the prominent human rights activist, Swami Agnivesh, to form a labour union in the area.

The quarrying sites were not provided with even basic amenities like drinking water. Women—who also worked at the quarries, breaking granite stones with 12 kg hammers to produce *rodi* (gravel) had to trek to far away wells in the fields of Rangpuri village to fetch their supplies. Similarly, food provisions had to be brought from the village market. Only in the late 1980s did the workers succeed, with help from voluntary bodies, in securing ration cards (and along with them voting rights), and sanction for a few deep bore wells from the Slum Wing of the DDA (now under the Municipal Corporation of Delhi—MCD). An informal school and part-time health centre were provided on behalf of the Institute of Social Sciences, New Delhi.

The Rangpuri stone mines had been leased out by DSIDC to a private party, the *pradhan* of Rangpuri village, who at one point obtained a stay-order from the District Court against the increased octroi rates payable to DSIDC, and assumed independent ownership rights by default. The government officials continued, however, to attend their office in a small building at the Rangpuri Stone Mines Complex Check-Post, maintaining good relations with the *pradhan* and other local intermediaries. It paid them well in the end, when after the closure of the Rangpuri quarries, they acted as conduits to attract VIP buyers of *gram sabha* land.

At present the Rangpuri Pahar Nala *basti* is surrounded by a sea of farmhouses (the biggest of them raising its towering wall right at the edge of the *basti* which partakes of its illicit electricity connection). It is in these farmhouses that the former stone miners of Rangpuri find employment now as construction labourers and as menials doing odd jobs in flower nurseries. Some of them are transported in batches by agents of land developers to work for daily wages in Gurgaon and other places in Haryana where construction activity is currently at its peak.

The case of the labour villages in the Bhatti Mines area is more dramatic. In a bizarre turn of events, the three decades old, properly established human settlements with their unmistakable rural ambience have been officially construed as 'encroachment by slum dwellers' on the land of the 'Wildlife Sanctuary', notified in 1991 out of the mammoth complex of red sand quarries, which had suddenly been closed one year earlier on grounds of being unsafe. The worker-settlers—now defined as 'squatters'—are to be relocated as per the Supreme Court order of 9 April 1996, to a site earmarked by the authorities on the *gram sabha* land of Jaunapur village which, while being a part of the same ecological space, falls outside the 'notified Ridge' in the zone left open for urban colonization. (Out of the total 6,200 ha area of the southern Ridge, as much as 2,030 ha have been cornered by farm-houses, and 200 ha are owned by government agencies promoting non-forest land use projects.)

Peaceful but resolute protests voiced by the Bhatti Hill settlers in the form of several rallies and dharnas (forms of public protest) with support from social activists of the National Alliance of People's Movements and Joint Women's Programme, and with instant endorsement by leading environmentalists from Delhi, has temporarily delayed execution of the court order but the implementing agencies—the Slum Department of the MCD and the Forest Department of the Delhi Government—have not abandoned their efforts to get the 'encroachers' evicted. The moot point is that the Slum Department of the MCD has already received around Rs. 300 million sanctioned by the Expenditure Finance Committee, Ministry of Finance, Government of India, for the 'model' relocation project, and money has been paid in advance to various contractors for developing the site.

On Bhatti Hill, there are three labour villages close to the Haryana border, known as Sanjay Colony, Balbir Nagar and Indira Nagar with 7,000 registered voters. They were settled in the late 1960s and formally established as 'DSIDC Labour colonies' in 1975 by the then Lt Governor of Delhi, Jagmohan, at the instance of the late Sanjay Gandhi. In subsequent years, the worker-settlers secured, step by step, important civic amenities like fair price shops, schools (primary and secondary), a hospital, a regular bus service and electricity. The endemic shortage of water in the area—the quarry workers had to buy water from private operators to meet their daily requirements, increased by the presence of work animals in every household—was sought to be tackled by the laying of an elaborate piped water network, completed in 1992, but effectively sabotaged by the private water sellers.

The loaders, who constitute the bulk of the population in the three villages, and remained in residence when the unattached cutters moved out to other places after the closure of the mines, comprise mainly two groups—the Odh and the Kumhar. The Odh, a caste of hereditary earth diggers, were once nomadic tribals who spread in medieval times from Gujarat to Orissa. They have functioned as rural engineers for centuries, known and praised as skilful constructors of indigenous rain harvesting systems: ponds, lakes, check-dams and canals, which were the base for irrigation before the advent of tube-wells. Even today, the Odh find employment as a specialized category of construction workers engaged in digging operations (basements of high-rise buildings, underground passages in Delhi have always been dug by Odh labourers who work as family units, women alongside men, and keep donkeys to transport the load). The 17 Odh *gotras* (clans) found at the Bhatti Mines migrated from Sindh and Multan as refugees in 1947, and worked at several major construction projects in northern India before settling down in Bhatti where, for the first time in their tribal history, they founded a village of their own called Bhagirath Nagar (later renamed Sanjay Colony).

The other group found in large numbers in all three labour villages are the Kumhar, a well known artisan caste of clay potters, calling themselves Prajapat (after the divine clay moulder of Hindu mythology). Once an indispensable component of every village, now displaced from their hereditary occupation and native habitats by the relentless pressure of market forces, the Kumhars are proud of their ancient heritage and painfully conscious of their degraded status as anonymous 'unskilled' wage labourers. The Kumhars settled in the Bhatti Mines area hail from the Alwar and Bharatpur districts of Rajasthan and the Rewari and Mahendergarh districts of Haryana. The women know several crafts besides pottery decoration (operating the potter's wheel being the men's preserve), and the whole community possesses a keen aesthetic sense.

Both the Odh and the Kumhar families living at the Bhatti Mines regard themselves as respectably settled villagers. Drudgery in the quarries has been their means of earning a livelihood—an occupational choice related to their ethnic past as earth craftsmen. Over the years they have built for themselves neat rural-style dwellings, both mud cottages and brick structures (the latter being a status symbol), with wide courtyards, enclosures and sheds for animals (mules being more sturdy were of greater use in deep quarrying pits than donkeys, but also very expensive to keep) and planted trees around for cool shade. The trees are cherished as household members, and new saplings regularly watered in spite of prevailing arid conditions. The past seven years of desperate survival struggle since the loss of regular employment at the Bhatti Mines have been marked by the increasing misery, indebtedness and marginalization of these workers. Since June 1990, they have spread far and wide in search of employment, primarily in the red sand quarries of the adjoining Faridabad district of Haryana, but also in sundry construction sites and brick kilns all over the National Capital Territory—all the while holding on firmly to their homesteads at the Bhatti Mines. As years pass they find that employment opportunities in traditional quarrying have shrunk under the impact of mechanization. Most families have been forced to dispose of their mules and come down to the level of assetless casual labourers hiring themselves out for stone pounding, carrying head loads, doing paltry jobs at godowns and farmhouses in the surrounding area. Needless to say, no employment prospects have been visualized for them at the resettlement site in Jaunapur where they are unlikely to settle. They might at the most, sell the tiny plots proposed to be allotted to them against the payment of Rs. 10,000 and depart on further journeys in search of work and dignity.

In the meantime, the Bhatti Wildlife Sanctuary even more fictitious than the adjoining Asola Wildlife Sanctuary, notified back in 1986, and, unlike the latter, not demarcated by a boundary wall or even wire fence, has been serving as a thoroughfare for heavy, smoke-spouting vehicles carrying mineral loads from the Haryana quarries and illegal mining areas within the National Capital Territory. The troubled legacy of the Bhatti Mines will not be easily forgotten.

CONCLUSION

I have attempted to trace the underlying regular patterns of domination and coercion (administrative as well as socio-economic) in the apparently spontaneous process of the urbanization of Delhi's rural environs during the 50 years of India's Independence. These patterns reveal colonial-style asymmetrical power relations between the expansionist urban elite (co-opting the emergent rural commercial class) and the subjugated hinterland. The inherited colonial structure and outlook of the state administration, along with the continuation of unchanged colonial laws, reinforce this inequality whilst middlemen from rural elites enable it.

In the southern parts of Outer Delhi, direct colonization by the urban elite has been taking place. Important patterns of change include: monopolization by the upper class of the 'select' prime areas (as opposed to the large motley peripheries in the north-west and east Outer Delhi); transformation of the once rural belt of the 'Mehrauli countryside' into a quintessential 'farmhouse belt'; the large-scale involvement of the local rural elite as intermediaries in real estate speculation; and the success of this rural elite in appropriating the village commons in the Ridge area for commercial sale, initially of mineral resources, and finally, of the land itself.

These developments, unfailingly condoned by government agencies, concurred with well-defined actions of the Delhi Administration (since 1993, the Government of the National Capital Territory of Delhi) targeting the whole of rural Delhi: the incessant drive to create additional metropolitan space through the forcible acquisition of agricultural land; the earmarking of whole tracts in the green rural belt for the dense, ill-planned resettlement of urban slum dwellers; and the arbitrary supersession of village *panchayats* in order to take over the common lands of remaining 'rural villages'.

Both in its actions, and in its inaction, the Delhi Government has been serving the interests of the 'colonizers' in dispossessing, displacing and banishing the surviving remnants of the old agrarian society from the colonized territories. The injustice and humiliation heaped on the people of the Bhatti Mines is just one example of it.

NOTES

1. See Jayati Ghosh, 'The Expansionist City', *The Frontline*, Chennai: 20 May 1994, p. 110.
2. A recent press report quotes a senior official of the Delhi Electricity Board confessing to his helplessness in curtailing massive power theft by resident owners of Sainik Farms: 'Their modus operandi is simple—a thick wire encased in a PVC pipe runs beneath the boundary wall into the house. The other end of the wire is connected to the street light. . . . All of them steal power for so many air-conditioners, refrigerators, TV sets and absolutely latest gadget. . . . But they somehow get to know beforehand about the raids and switch on their generators when we strike.' Gaurav C. Sawant, 'The Bijli Burglars who Live in Farmhouses', *Indian Express Newsline*, New Delhi, 15 July 1997.
3. For a photographic evocation of Delhi's urban villages, see Charles Lewis and Karoki Lewis, *Delhi Historic Villages: A Photographic Evocation*, New Delhi: Ravi Dayal Publishers, 1994.

4. The deteriorating ground water situation in the capital, especially in the Mehrauli and Najafgarh blocks, was assessed by the Central Ground Water Board in 1995 and attributed to 'excessive pumpage in residential areas and farmhouses'. The Chief Secretary, Government of NCT, Delhi, P. V. Jayakrishnan, stated in the Supreme Court: 'The number of tube-wells installed in Delhi and the quantity of water being drawn by them is not being maintained or regulated by any single authority of the Govt of Delhi and MCD has no control over the installation of tube-wells.' Manisha Deveshvar, 'Groundwater Table Fast Depleting in Capital', *Indian Express*, 19 August 1995.
5. Devinder Sharma, 'A Choice Between Flower and Food', *Indian Express*, 12 March 1998.
6. The estimate according to Delhi Police sources, in connection with a spate of attacks on defenceless servants in farmhouses falling within the South-West Zone and the outcry of the owners demanding better police protection. (Unlike urban farmhouses usually inhabited by the owners, the countryside farmhouses have hired employees as the only occupants in the owners' absence.) Agency report in *Indian Express*, New Delhi, 25 February 1998.
7. Claude Alwares, *Science, Development and Violence: The Twilight of Modernity*, New Delhi: OUP, 1992, p. 21.
8. Chattrapati Singh, *The Framework of Environmental Laws in India*, New Delhi: INTACH, 1993, p. 6.
9. See Dwijen Kalia, 'The Murder of a River', in Anil Agarwal and Sunita Narain (eds), *Dying Wisdom: Rise, Fall and Potential of India's Traditional Water Harvesting Systems*, New Delhi: Centre of Science and Environment, 1997, p. 78: 'The city engineers instead of laying down sewers, simply discharge the polluted water into the 19 channels that originate in the Aravali hills. At one time these channels acted as streams for draining off rainwater, and in the process recharged many wells. . . . However, now these channels carry more industrial pollutants and domestic sewage than rainwater. As a result, on their way to the Yamuna, they pollute all the water bodies.'
10. This and the next figures regarding the agricultural component of rural Delhi are taken from the November 1997 publicity brochure of the Government of NCT, Delhi, Development Department. The population figures are from 'Delhi Data', *Indian Express Newsline*, 13 February 1997.
11. See Tarun Bose, 'Power Games in (Un)Authorised Colonies', *Mainstream*, 1996.
12. For further details on the implementation of the *Panchayati Raj* system, see M.A. Ommen, *Panchayati Raj Development Report 1995*, New Delhi: Institute of Social Sciences, 1996.
13. Government of NCT, Delhi, Development Department, *Sardar Patel Gramodaya Yojna—Mini Master Plan for Rural Delhi, Progress of Schemes at a Glance*, 1997.
14. Commenting on the theme of this paper, the discussant, Professor Mohammad Talib, pointed to a parallel from American history where the continuously advancing 'frontier' was seen as the dividing line between 'civilization' (represented by robust white pioneers) and 'savagery'. He further observed that 'Delhi's civilisational frontier treats the villages on its margin as an unregulated legal and social space', allowing for several violations. The unstated implication of the perceived analogy across the historical and geographical differences, is that the 'pioneers' pushing onwards into 'enemy country', assumed the right to grab the land, exploit the natural resources, and rob the 'natives' of their cultural heritage. The nineteenth century ethnocide of North American aborigines, and the contemporary destruction of peasant and tribal habitats and cultures in India have had at their root similar civilizational arrogance. In the latter case, the pioneers need not even be 'robust'; the conquest is fully programmed by global techno-capitalism.
15. Baljit Malik, 'Downside of the Mantra of Liberalization', *Indian Express*, 4 July 1995.
16. Primila Lewis' narrative (Primila Lewis, *Social Action and the Labouring Poor: An Experience*, New Delhi: Vistaar Publications, 1991) contains plenty of factual information on developments in the Mehrauli countryside since the early 1970s, especially in Mandi village where the 'Action India' voluntary group organized a cooperative of quarry workers and helped local Harijans to get possession of *gram sabha* land. The PUCL investigative report (PUCL Bulletin April 1983, special issue on: *The Sands of Death: A Case Study of Bhatti Mines,*

published by Inder Mohan for People's Union for Civil Liberties, New Delhi) and Justice V.S. Deshpande's Court of Enquiry Report (Govt. of India, *The Gazette*, 1983) depict the situation in Bhatti Bajri Mines in the early 1980s.

Professor Mohd. Talib's (Department of Sociology, Jamia Millia Islamia, University, New Delhi) doctoral dissertation titled: 'Some Social Aspects of Class Formation Among the Migrant Labour: A Case of a Labour Settlement in Delhi', submitted in 1988 but unfortunately never published, presents a sensitive penetrating analysis of the socio-economic and psychological reality of migrant workers in the stone quarries of Tughlakabad, *c.* 1984.

17. For further details on the conditions of quarry workers, see Indira Chakravorty and Jyoti Mudgal, *Conditions of Quarry Workers in Delhi*, New Delhi: Centre for Education and Communication, 1991.
18. The only high-level intervention occurred in 1983 when after a spate of fatal accidents in the Bhatti Mines, the Ministry of Labour, Government of India, appointed a Court of Inquiry under justice V.S. Deshpande. His famous report, entitled 'From Private to Public Interest', severely indicted the 'illegality and immorality' of the system of operating the mines, condoned by the DSIDC, and gave several precise recommendations for safeguarding public interest 'firstly in the welfare of the labour working in the mines, and secondly, the scientific exploitation of valuable national resources' [Report by the Court of Inquiry under S. 24 (4), Mines Act 1952 (Justice V.S. Deshpande, former Chief Justice, Delhi High Court): *From Private to Public Interest*, Govt. of India, *The Gazette*, New Delhi, 20 August, 1983]. But the recommendations of the Deshpande Report were never implemented, except for the reorganization of the mining department of DSIDC to form a 'new' managerial entity, the Delhi State Mineral Development Corporation (DSMDC), even more corrupt than the previous one.

PART II

PEOPLE AND GOODS ON THE MOVE

5

Images and Voices of Transport Workers in Old Delhi

SYLVIE FRAISSARD

In the heart of the commercial centre of Old Delhi, thousands of people earn their livelihood in the transport industry, carrying passengers and goods in an amazing variety of vehicles. We have identified at least 14 different methods of transport. Whether working on foot, by horse, cycle or car, each transporter performs a very specific function. Here I would like to introduce 14 transport workers who speak to us of the advantages and disadvantages of their particular jobs.

* Interviews and photographs: Sylvie Fraissard; interpreter and translator: Dhananjay Tingal.

Plate 5.1 KULBIR SINGH
48 years old.
Delhi Transport Corporation Bus Driver.
Native place: Vishnugarh, Delhi.

'If we speak sweetly to our passengers, then they will speak sweetly to us. I have no problem with my work.'

Plate 5.2 DHARMA
40 years old.
Goods Cycle Rickshaw Puller.
Native place: Mahendragarh (Haryana).
Migrated to Delhi ten years back.

Plate 5.3 SONA
37 years old.
Hand Cart Puller.
Native place: Sikar (Rajasthan).
Migrated to Delhi twenty years back.

'When you don't have a job, you are forced to take up any kind of work, just to fill your stomach.'

Plate 5.4 SRIRAM
58 years old.
Horse Cart Puller.
Native place: Delhi.

'There is no other work available and we have to earn. If I did not do this job, then from where would I get my bread? There is lots of misery in this work.'

Plate 5.5 RAJNATH TRIPATHI
22 years old.
Auto Rickshaw Driver.
Native place: Gorabhpur (Uttar Pradesh).
Migrated to Delhi twelve years back.

'I am not happy doing this. Hunger has forced me to it. I am educated and want to get a government job or work in a factory. But it's impossible without someone to push you up.'

Plate 5.6 RAJENDER PRASAD
40 years old.
Blue Line Bus Driver.
Native place: Meerut (Uttar Pradesh).
Migrated to Delhi twelve years back.

'There is a lot of competition in Blue Line buses; the owner wants his money every evening. If we have not earned much, then we get a scolding.'

Plate 5.7 JITENDER SINGH
25 years old.
Bullock Cart Driver.
Native place: Etah (Uttar Pradesh).
Migrated to Delhi twelve years back.

'I like this work. In this we are masters of our own will and no one can boss us about or trouble us.'

Plate 5.8a Khari Baoli Bazaar.

Plate 5.9a Ajmeri Gate.

Plate 5.8b Khari Baoli Bazaar.

Plate 5.9b Ajmeri Gate.

Plate 5.10 KULDEEP SINGH
48 years old.
Four Seater Driver (*Phut-Phut*).
Native place: Delhi.

'Now the only problem is increasing traffic because of which we have to drive very carefully.'

Plate 5.11 DEEPAK DE
23 years old.
Passenger Cycle Rickshaw Puller.
Native place: Murshidabad (West Bengal).
Migrated to Delhi two months back.
'I only came here to earn money and will not stay in Delhi for ever. I want enough money to be able to return to my village and open a sweet shop.'

Plate 5.12 GULAB KUMAR CHAUDHARY
20 years old.
Taxi Driver.
Native place: Darbhangah (Bihar).
Migrated to Delhi four years back.

'I don't have a ration card or an identity card. I don't even have a house. This taxi is my home and this is where I sleep.'

Plate 5.13 OMVIR SINGH
48 years old.
Tempo Driver.
Native place: Mathura (Uttar Pradesh).
Migrated to Delhi twenty-five years back.

'There is no future in this occupation, especially in Delhi. There is no union of drivers and coolies, so they are easily exploited. Jobs and earnings are given according to caste.'

Plate 5.14 VIRPAL
20 years old.
School Rickshaw Driver.
Native place: Barelly (Uttar Pradesh).
Migrated to Delhi three years back.

'This work is a big responsibility. The children have to be taken care of. The rickshaw has to be driven carefully and the kids have to be fetched and carried on time.'

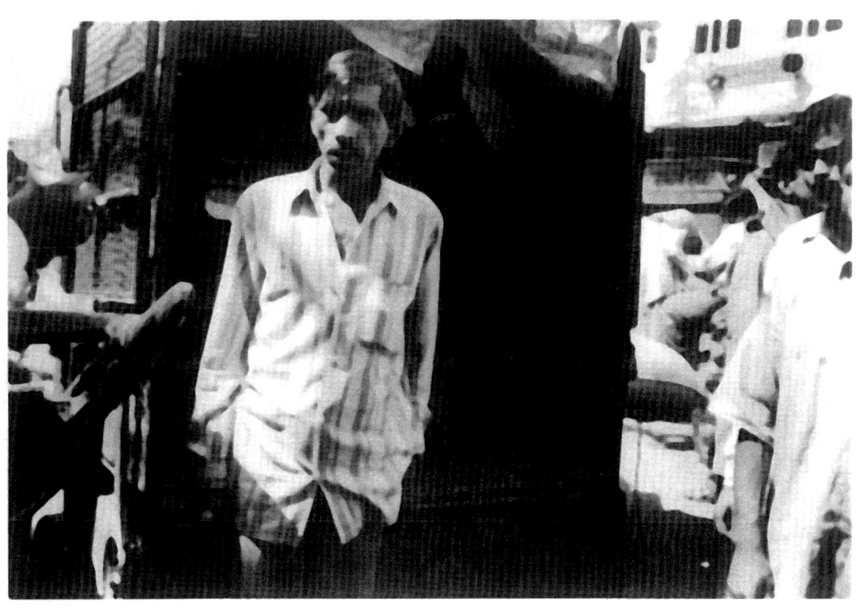

Plate 5.15 SRINIVAS
35 years old.
Three Wheeler Goods Carrier.
Native place: Meerut (Uttar Pradesh).
Migrated to Delhi seven years back.

'We get trouble from the police in many places. They take bribes. If we don't give them, they fine us for no reason.'

Plate 5.16 VIJAY KUMAR
30 years old.
Truck Driver.
Native place: Kangra (Himachal Pradesh).
Migrated to Delhi four years back.

'Since I am far away from home, anyway, it does not make any difference if I'm on my truck, or in Delhi or in Mumbai.'

6

Mobility Patterns and Economic Strategies of Houseless People in Old Delhi

VÉRONIQUE DUPONT

The sight of people sleeping at night on the pavements in large Indian cities like Delhi, Mumbai, Calcutta and Chennai conjures up an image of extreme poverty. More than any other category of the population, pavement dwellers appear to be living in conditions of acute deprivation from shelter and basic services; and it is no surprise to hear them being described as 'the unfortunate victims of diverse kinds of physical and social crisis among our rural and urban societies'.[1] At the macro-level the presence and increase of the shelterless population in big cities has been analysed as 'an inevitable outcome of the urbanization process',[2] a consequence of industrialization and economic development which induces the migration of the rural poor to major cities leading to a pressure on both land and housing.[3]

While it is not my purpose to deny this side of the reality, I would like to propose a more qualified appraisal of the practice of pavement dwelling and to show how the study of houseless people can also highlight other dimensions of the process of metropolization. In the same way that 'rural to urban' migrants should not be considered merely as pawns pushed and pulled by macro-economic forces but also as actors in a position to shape the urbanization process, so pavement dwellers in big cities should not be considered merely as the victims of dire poverty, but also as dynamic agents capable of implementing their own economic strategies and of finding appropriate responses to specific urban environments. Furthermore, the houseless migrants surveyed in Old Delhi exemplify how population mobility contributes to the restructuring of geographical space by transcending the rural/urban dichotomy. As observed in many developing cities, there is a process of functional integration between the metropolis and the settlements of its catchment area as the result of circular migration and the attendant flows of money, goods, information and ideas.[4] Admittedly, the shelterless migrants are not the only ones to practise this form of mobility between their native villages and the city of their in-migration: such a type of circular mobility is also observed among migrants settled in slums or among those belonging to the higher socio-economic strata.[5] Nevertheless, the residential practices of the houseless population, perhaps more than those of any other category of city dweller, highlight a vision of the city as a space reshaped by migrants: 'a space of movement that envisages the city not as a place of sedentariness, but as a cross-roads of mobility'.[6]

In line with this perspective, this essay aims to investigate the mobility patterns and economic strategies of shelterless people who sleep in the streets of Old Delhi at night through a detailed micro-level analysis of their situation. At the same time, the specific focus on the shelterless people of the Walled City of Delhi—the historical core of the capital—allows us to illustrate the relationship between the transformation of urban space, population movements and social recomposition, and to show how urban space is subject to competing interests. The findings of this essay are based on primary data from my own socio-economic surveys: these are outlined in the paragraphs that follow along with a brief review of other available data, which suggests the need for reflection on the concept of houselessness.

CONCEPT OF HOUSELESSNESS AND SOURCES OF DATA

Secondary Data Available

Although the pavement dwellers are generally perceived as 'the poorest of the urban poor'[7] the issue of houselessness is often overlooked[8] in the abundant literature dealing with the urban poor and the urbanization problems.[9] Primary survey data is relatively scarce[10] as compared to the numerous studies of the inhabitants of slums and squatter settlements. In particular, there is a striking absence of research which deals specifically with the pavement dwellers of the capital city of Delhi.[11] A direct consequence of this paucity is a lack of accurate information about this segment of the population. Even its number remains in doubt: 22,516 according to the 1981 Census and about 50,000 according to the 1991 Census.[12] These figures are obviously underestimates, due in part to the problems of identifying and enumerating this specific segment of the population during census operations, which devote little time to this category of people.[13] According to a more realistic estimate provided by the Slum and Jhuggi-Jhonpri Department of the Delhi Development Authority in 1985, the number of houseless people in Delhi is approximately 1 per cent of its total population. This would mean about 1,00,000 persons in the mid-1990s.

The heaviest and most conspicuous concentrations of pavement dwellers are found in the Old city and its extensions, where the Municipality has—logically—opened 10 of its 18 night shelters (6 in the Walled City proper). These represent three quarters of the total sleeping capacity of about 4,500 spaces provided for shelterless people in the entire urban agglomeration. As expounded in the next section, the morphological and economic characteristics of the historical core of the capital city contribute to its specific attraction to a floating population without shelter. The decision to focus this investigation on pavement dwellers in Old Delhi was influenced by these factors.

The Concept of Houselessness

Apart from the problem of widely diverging numerical estimates, another difficulty with the secondary data on the houseless population of Delhi—and indeed of other cities—is the absence of consensus regarding terminology. Various terms are used: 'homeless', 'houseless', 'roofless', 'shelterless' people or 'pavement dwellers', but these do not always cover the same group of population. Furthermore, the same term may de defined quite differently in different studies. For instance, in studies on pavement dwelling, while some focus specifically on 'truly shelterless persons',[14] others also include pavement dwellers with some kind of temporary shelter,[15] and in certain studies on Delhi, the inmates of municipal night shelters are also included.[16] The Census of India uses the notion of 'houseless population', defined as persons who are not living in 'census houses', the latter referring to 'a structure with roof'; hence the enumerators are instructed 'to take note of the possible places where the houseless population is likely to live such as on the roadside, pavements, in hume pipes, under staircases, or in the open, temples, mandaps, platforms and the like'.[17] It is worth pointing out that similar problems of reliable estimation and clear definition of the houseless population are also encountered in surveys conducted in American and European cities.[18] As rightly noted by Bienveniste, 'Homelessness is not a characteristic that defines a sub-group, but rather a situation common to heterogeneous populations at some time in their lives.'[19] This also points to two major characteristics of this segment of the urban population: its heterogeneity and mobility (as this essay will highlight), not to mention the invisibility of certain sections of it.

Specific Survey of Houseless People Conducted in Old Delhi

In this study of houseless people in Old Delhi, the population under focus consists of persons without any form of shelter of their own, in other words those who sleep at night on the pavements (entirely in the open or partly protected by verandas), in other open spaces or in night shelters run by the municipality and who do not have any personal fixed abode in the city. Persons who squat on the pavements by erecting temporary constructions or structures are hence outside the scope of this study; in any case, such situations are usually not found within the Walled City on which my surveys have been focused. While presenting the findings of this case study, I shall refer to the population surveyed by using the terms 'houseless' people, 'shelterless' people or 'pavement dwellers' interchangeably.[20] I deliberately avoid using the term 'homeless' since it implies not only a situation of deprivation in terms of shelter but also a loss of familial moorings. This term is commonly used in the North American context where it may correspond to social reality,[21] but, as we shall see, it is inappropriate in the context of Indian cities where houselessness does not necessarily mean homelessness. The concept of family stretches beyond the limits of a simple 'household' or 'home' in the Indian context where familial segments may be spatially scattered, but tightly linked through economic and emotional ties. Thus, I use here the terms 'shelterlessness' or 'houselessness' to refer to a concrete situation (the lack of physical shelter) in a specific place at a given time (in Delhi during the period of observation); but it must be borne in mind that the situation currently observed in Delhi does not necessarily represent a permanent state and it may be compatible with the existence of a house and/or a home somewhere else (especially in the native village).

The research on which this study is based was composed of two types of surveys: a statistical survey carried out in January-March 1996, covering a total sample of 248 individuals selected by area sampling from the main concentrations of pavement dwellers in the Walled City and the six night shelters run by the municipality in the same area; and in-depth interviews conducted simultaneously with a sub-sample of 36 individuals that were randomly selected.[22]

THE WALLED CITY OF OLD DELHI: THE TRANSFORMATION OF URBAN SPACE AND POPULATION MOVEMENT

The Walled City of Old Delhi, otherwise known as Shahjahanabad—the historic core built by the Mughals in the seventeenth century—exhibits features typical of traditional Indian cities, with a mixed land-use pattern combining a high concentration of residential units with an important aggregation of commercial and small-scale manufacturing establishments. However, what is remarkable in the case of Old Delhi are the extremely high residential densities (on average 616 persons per hectare in the Walled City in 1991, with a maximum of 1596 in one of the census divisions) combined with an equally impressive congestion of economic activities.

Population Deconcentration and the Intensification of Economic Activities

This situation is in fact the result of a two-pronged process which has affected the dynamics and urban morphology of the old city core. On the one hand, there has been a decline in the resident population, first noticeable in certain areas during the decade 1961-71,[23] and which has since continued to spread. Hence, although the present residential densities are still excessively high in the Walled City, they were significantly higher in 1961, with an average of about 740 persons per hectare. But at the same time, the Walled City has recorded a dramatic increase in the number of its commercial establishments (shops, workshops, warehouses and wholesale markets) as well as manufacturing workshops, including noxious industries and hazardous trades. For example, the number of registered commercial establishments increased by 700 per cent in two decades, from 22,000 units in 1961 to 1,55,000 units in 1981.[24] Moreover, as Mehra has rightly underlined,[25] the official statistics underestimate the extent of this growth in economic activities, since they do not include the informal sector of employment.

While the decongestion of the population from the urban core is in line with one of the objectives of the Delhi Master Plan—although the actual extent of the population decrease remains far below that initially proposed[26]—the proliferation of commercial and industrial activities is in direct contradiction with the objectives of urban planners. Thus, in the 1990 Master Plan, we read: 'in case of the Walled City, the objective is to clean the area from noxious and hazardous industries and trades to check further commercialization and industrialization of this area and to revitalize the same to its glory of the past'.[27] In fact, these recommendations of the Master Plan, perspective 2001 (published in 1990) provide ample evidence of the failure of the earlier 1962 Plan, and highlight instead the significant role of private actors, whose economic rationale goes against institutional intentions.

The Transformation of Urban Morphology and Social Recomposition

The overuse of the physical space and building infrastructure in the Walled City—both in terms of residential and economic use—has contributed to the degradation of its housing stock. However, the 'cycle of deterioration' was at the outset a perverse outcome of rent control policies which led to inadequate income generation, thereby discouraging landlords from incurring expenses in maintaining their buildings.[28] As time went on, practically all areas of the Walled City became classified as 'slums' under the Slum Areas (Improvement and Clearance) Act of 1956.

The transformation of the urban morphology of the Walled City and its decaying housing conditions must also be understood in relation to the social recomposition of the residing population. The better off sections of the population have tended to move out of the old city, in search of better housing conditions in less congested residential areas, leaving behind mainly people from low-income groups, in particular tenants who would not be able to afford alternative accommodation elsewhere in the urban agglomeration.[29] Besides, the proliferation of commercial and manufacturing activities, along with the related services which provide a large number of informal job opportunities, has attracted a floating population of male migrant workers whose residential integration remains extremely precarious.[30] Thus, at night many of them are found sleeping under the verandas in bazaars, on pavements and other open grounds, or in night shelters run by the municipality for houseless people. The fact that the two main railway stations and the main inter-state bus terminal are located within the Walled City or in its immediate vicinity has also played a role in contributing not only to the general economic buoyancy of the old city and increased employment opportunities in the area, but also to the movement patterns of shelterless migrants. Upon their arrival in the city, they are in immediate proximity to (or easily directed to) locations where opportunities for unskilled labour are high, and where sleeping space can be found in pavement dwelling areas or in night shelters.

The Economic Functions of the Old City and Occupational Opportunities for the Houseless

The different types of occupations performed by the houseless people surveyed show how the economic functions of Old Delhi are directly reflected in the major occupational groups of this population (Table 6.1). There is first of all the large category of handcart pullers and pushers transporting goods in and out of the wholesale markets of the old city (24 per cent of the respondents were engaged in this work as their principle occupation). Loading and unloading activities in the markets, and the carriage of luggage to and from the two main railway stations also provide considerable employment opportunities for the pavement dwellers. The transport of passengers by cycle rickshaw in this densely populated and very buoyant market area, with two adjoining railway stations and the inter-state bus terminal, is another activity attracting a significant number of houseless workers (20 per cent of respondents cited it as their main activity). Altogether, the sector of transport seems to absorb the majority of the houseless workers based in the Walled City (52 per cent of respondents cited it as their main activity). This would appear to be a major distinctive characteristic of the occupational structure of this shelterless population, as compared to the male population of urban Delhi as a whole, but also as compared to the

TABLE 6.1. OCCUPATIONAL PATTERN OF THE HOUSELESS POPULATION OF OLD DELHI, 1996

Occupation	*Main occupation*		*Other occupations*		*All occupations*	
	No.	%	No.	%	No.	%
Clerical workers	2	0.8	–	–	2	0.6
Sales workers (vendors, shop assistants)	10	4.1	1	1.2	11	3.4
Cooks, waiters and related workers	54	22.2	46	56.1	100	30.8
Other service workers (domestic servants, barbers, etc.)	2	0.8	2	2.4	4	1.2
Production workers including mechanics and repairmen	16	6.6	2	2.4	18	5.5
Construction workers including painters	22	9.1	7	8.5	29	8.9
Loaders, unloaders and porters	21	8.6	10	12.2	31	9.5
Handcart pushers or pullers	58	23.9	7	8.5	65	20.0
Cycle rickshaw drivers	48	19.8	6	7.3	54	16.6
Other drivers (motor vehicle)	1	0.4	1	1.2	2	0.6
Rag pickers	5	2.1	–	–	5	1.5
Beggars	3	1.2	–	–	3	0.9
Other workers	1	0.4	–	–	1	0.3
Total	243	100.0	82	100.0	325	100.0

Non-workers = 5.

The occupations taken into account include all types of work carried out in Delhi during the 12 months preceding the survey. Hence those occupations carried out outside Delhi during the reference period have been excluded.

Source: Own sample survey—1996.

TABLE 6.2. PERCENTAGE DISTRIBUTION OF THE HOUSELESS POPULATION OF OLD DELHI BY INDUSTRIAL CATEGORY

Industrial category	*Houseless population of Old Delhi 1996**	*Male population of Old Delhi 1991***	*Male population of the whole of urban Delhi 1991***
Agriculture, livestock, mining, quarrying	0.0	0.6	1.3
Manufacturing, processing, repairs	6.2	32.0	26.4
Construction	9.0	2.8	7.9
Trade, commerce, restaurants, hotels	28.4	38.3	26.4
Transport, communication	51.9	7.9	8.8
Community, social and personal services	4.5	18.3	29.2
Total	100.0	100.0	100.0

Source: * Own sample survey—1996.
Sample of 243 workers classified by their main occupation (non-workers = 5)
** *Census of India 1991, Delhi, Primary Census Abstract.*

male population residing in the Walled City: the sector of transport and communication employed only 8 to 9 per cent of the corresponding workers in 1991 (Table 6.2).

Another specificity of Old Delhi lies in the many labour markets (in the strict neo-classical sense of the term) which take place in different locations of the Walled City. Some of them are specialized in recruiting particular types of workers, such as waiters, cooks and related service workers for marriage parties and other functions which require catering services and the setting up of temporary tent structures to host large numbers of guests. The demand for these types of workers is subject to seasonal fluctuation, with peaks corresponding to the most auspicious periods for marriage ceremonies. Such employment opportunities draw many houseless workers, many of whom do such work as a supplementary seasonal or temporary activity. While the occupational category of waiters, cooks and related service workers accounts for 22 per cent of the main occupations reported by the respondents, it accounts for 56 per cent of the supplementary occupations reported (Table 6.1). On the other hand, marginal activities such as rag picking and begging which are often associated with the plight of the urban poor, absorb very few of the houseless surveyed in Old Delhi (2 and 1 per cent respectively in the sample). Rag picking is more specifically carried out by children and teenagers.

Services Developed for the Houseless

A range of services specifically oriented towards the needs of the houseless population have also developed in the Old City. The government itself, taking cognizance of the plight of the houseless, started constructing night shelters in the early 1960s, 6 out of the 18 functioning today being located within the Walled City. In the night shelters run by the municipality, for a nominal rate of Rs. 3 per night,[31] each inmate is provided with a blanket and a floor carpet, and has free access to the toilets and bathrooms usually available in the same building.

Some small private entrepreneurs, perceiving the shelterless situation of so many as a good business opportunity, rent out sleeping place and bedding facilities to pavement dwellers. Quilts are available on hire for an average rate of Rs. 5 per night, and cots with bedding for an average rate of Rs. 15 per night. Most of the entrepreneurs involved in this business also provide sleeping space to their customers: at night they encroach on some sections of the pavements, in particular those covered by verandas, as well as pedestrian over-bridges and precincts, or other open grounds, on which they spread plastic ground sheets or place their cots. In the sleeping areas which are entirely exposed, overhead plastic sheets are also arranged on rainy nights to protect the sleepers. The bedding facilities are particularly in demand in the winter, when the temperature at night can go down to as low as 3° C. However, the offer of a relatively protected sleeping place, and of cots for those who can afford it, is also taken up during other seasons. Since the renting out of quilts and cots in public spaces is carried out without authorization, it inevitably leads to police interference, which at worst results in the eviction of both quilt owners and pavement dwellers; and, in order to minimize this risk, bribes are paid to the police by the informal entrepreneurs. However, a substantial proportion of the pavement dwellers do not rent bedding facilities; rather they have their own blankets and sleep on pavements covered by verandas or in open spaces where access is free[32]—though not necessarily free from police harassment.

Another type of service developed for pavement dwellers is the provision of hot meals from roadside food stalls directly set up on the pavements, on a temporary basis usually for just a few hours every night at dinner time. Roadside tea stalls are also a common sight in and around the pavement dwelling areas and are sometimes operated by the same entrepreneurs who rent out quilts.

THE LIFE SPACE OF HOUSELESS PEOPLE: THE CITY PAVEMENT AND THE VILLAGE

In this section I shall attempt to reconstitute the life space of pavement dwellers and to identify its structuring poles through an examination of their conditions of integration in the city, the relations they maintain with their native places and their future plans. At a micro level, this will allow us to assess the significance of moorings in the native village or town for the majority of houseless people in Old Delhi, and to highlight the relevance of the basic unit of social organization, the family. This, in turn, will help us better understand the trajectory and present living practices of pavement dwellers. At a macro level, it will provide important indications of the degree of integration between urban and rural spaces, the city pavement and the village. As a prelude, a brief outline of the socio-demographic profile and migration history of houseless people will help us better portray the characteristics of this population.

Socio-Demographic Profile

The first salient feature of the houseless population in Old Delhi is that it is almost exclusively male, composed of single men or men living in a single state. Access to the night shelters run by the municipality is, in fact, restricted to males. Among the main pavement dwelling areas identified in various open spaces of the Walled City, very few women and families (less than ten) could be seen during the headcount, and their presence was moreover confined to one or two localities. Therefore, the sample surveyed comprised male individuals only. The predominance of single men (unmarried or not) among pavement dwellers is especially pronounced in the Walled City as compared to some other parts of Delhi such as Nizamuddin where pavement dwellers are also located but where familial units are more conspicuous. At the same time, it is also a distinctive characteristic of Delhi as a whole when compared to other Indian metropolitan cities. This is clearly shown by the sex ratio of the houseless population in the first four megalopolises as recorded in the 1981 Census.[33] Here we find 187 females to 1000 males in Delhi urban agglomeration, as against 453:1000 in Calcutta, 278:1000 in Bombay and 955:1000 in Madras. The average size of the shelterless households found elsewhere further confirms the specificity of the capital city: 1.9 in Delhi as a whole, as against 4.8 in Calcutta, 2.0 in Bombay and 4.1 in Madras.

The quasi absence of familial units on the pavements of the Walled City is reflected in the age composition of the shelterless population. Although the presence of street children living on their own is one of the most disquieting features of the city, in demographic terms they represent only a very minor group among all the pavement dwellers (less than 5 per cent of respondents were below 15). The majority of the pavement dwellers (54 per cent of respondents) are young people belonging to the age group 15-29 years.

More significant from the point of view of social integration is the marital status of this population. Of the respondents 78 per cent in the 15-29 age group and 43 per cent of those aged 30 and above had never married. To better appraise the specificity of the houseless population, these figures can be compared to the corresponding percentages found in the 1991 Census for the male population of the Delhi urban agglomeration as a whole. Here we find that while 62 per cent of those in the 15-29 age group were unmarried, only 3 per cent of those aged 30 and above remained unmarried. The remarkably high percentage of houseless persons who remained unmarried at a relatively advanced age indicates a certain degree of social marginality among the houseless, and is a manifestation of the individualization process, whether chosen or endured. The circumstances of people's migration to Delhi and their life stories more generally will provide some explanation of this situation.

The percentage of houseless people in Old Delhi belonging to Scheduled Castes and Tribes is a good indicator of whether or not members of this population hail from the most underprivileged sections of society. In the sample population, 13 per cent of respondents reported belonging to a scheduled caste or tribe. Given the sampling errors, this represents a proportion very close to that recorded in the total male population of the Walled City at the 1991 Census, namely 11 per cent. Interestingly, it is also almost similar to the proportion of Scheduled Castes and Tribes recorded in the 1971 Census among the houseless population in the territory of the Delhi Municipal Corporation, namely, 12 per cent for males. On the other hand, the proportion of Scheduled Castes and Tribes among the pavement dwellers of Old Delhi is significantly lower than their share in the male population of the entire Delhi urban agglomeration, that is 19 per cent at the 1991 Census. Though no comparison can be drawn with census data, it is noteworthy that the majority of the houseless surveyed in Old Delhi (56 per cent) belong to upper castes or communities, the remaining share corresponding to Other Backward Classes (31 per cent).

The proportion of illiterates is an alternative indicator of socio-economic backwardness. In this respect the houseless population in the Walled City appears clearly disadvantaged, containing 38 per cent of illiterates, whereas, according to the 1991 Census, the proportion of illiterates in the total male population of the Walled City was 24 per cent, and in the total male population of urban Delhi only 18 per cent.[34]

Migration History

Migration is a common experience shared by almost all houseless people in Old Delhi (96 per cent of the respondents are from outside Delhi) and the large majority of migrants (61 per cent of the sample) have come directly from their native place to the capital. Most of them (69 per cent) hail from rural areas with the largest single group coming from Uttar Pradesh (47 per cent), followed by Bihar. The large proportion of people from the neighbouring state of Uttar Pradesh conforms to the general pattern of migration to the capital city; what seems more remarkable is that the catchment area of the Old Delhi pavements extends farther to eastern and southern states such as West Bengal, Orissa, Andhra Pradesh and Tamil Nadu. These findings are consistent with the survey of pavement dwellers in Old Delhi conducted by the Delhi Development Authority in 1989, according to which 98 per cent of the respondents were migrants, most of them coming from Uttar Pradesh and Bihar. For comparative purposes, it can be recalled here that, at the 1991 Census, migrants accounted for 40 per cent of the total male urban population of Delhi, with 45 per cent of them coming from Uttar Pradesh.

Analysis of the reasons which motivated departure from the native place (or home) and migration to Delhi (or arrival on the pavements) reveals contrasting situations. One striking feature is the impact of familial tensions and quarrels: children beaten up by a drunken father or ill-treated by a stepmother, cases of disputes over family property after the death of the father, quarrels with a spouse, brother, parent or other relative, etc., are frequently quoted in the migration histories of respondents.[35] For those who migrated to Delhi under circumstances of familial crisis, the main concern was to escape an unbearable situation, and it is small wonder that their arrival in Delhi was often ill-prepared, and that their choice of destination was uncertain or even left to chance while catching the first departing train. In case where flight from home was followed by the severing of all familial links, it comes as no surprise that the young unmarried migrant will generally remain unmarried, since he is no longer in a position to benefit any more from the support of his family who under normal circumstances would arrange the marriage.

In greater conformity to the general pattern of migration expected for a large metropolis, the majority of respondents (66 per cent of the migrants) chose to come to Delhi for reasons related to better employment opportunities and economic prospects. This includes the many migrants from rural areas or small towns, whose incomes in the native place were not sufficient to sustain their families, as well as young people anxious to earn an income on their own outside familial agriculture. The decision to come to Delhi was sometimes made without specific information about the labour market there, and was based more on the general assumption that Delhi, being a big city, must provide opportunities. This attitude is exemplified in the sayings that in Delhi 'everybody can accommodate himself' or 'everybody can find a job if hardworking'. Some pavement dwellers, especially some children and young people, were initially attracted by the capital city as a place to visit but eventually stayed over, because they too found greater economic scope in Delhi.

Conditions of Integration in the City

In addition to the economic attraction exerted by the capital city, a migrant's choice to come to Delhi is often influenced by the presence of relatives, parents or co-villagers already working in the capital and conveying information about job opportunities. The importance of relatives and friends in transmitting information to prospective migrants has been highlighted in migration studies,[36] and the houseless migrants of Old Delhi, like other labour migrants, make use of familial and social networks whenever possible. Help related to finding a job or starting work as self-employed was most prominent in migrants' accounts, followed by help related to accommodation or a place to sleep.[37] In the majority of cases, it was the migrant who approached the network of relatives or co-villagers, showing that the houseless condition does not necessarily mean that pavement dwellers operate in a familial and social vacuum. However, the economic and housing conditions of the relatives already settled in Delhi may put limits to the type and duration of help extended to new migrants, especially as far as accommodation is concerned. In a few examples, after an initial stay with his parents or relatives in a slum hut or one-room tenement, the migrant was compelled to leave due to lack of space and to stay in a night shelter or a pavement dwelling area. The persons working in the occupation or sector of activity in which the migrant eventually becomes absorbed also play an appreciable role in introducing him to new work, including sometimes training, and showing him cheap (or free) and convenient places to sleep.

In fact, the work place and the community of workers in the same type of occupation come to provide the main network of socialization for the houseless people during their stay in Delhi. In the wholesale market of Khari Baoli especially, many handcart pullers can be seen staying together in groups at night, sleeping on their carts or under the verandas of the market, and cooking food collectively on pavements. Another important network of socialization among houseless people in an urban setting is based on village or regional affiliation. The survey revealed several interesting examples of migration channels rooted in familial or village tradition. This was the case with some of the pavement dwellers working as cycle rickshaw drivers, handcart pullers or construction labourers in Delhi. Working on a seasonal basis during the lean agricultural months, some were perpetuating a practice initiated by their fathers, or by other villagers. They followed a migration channel already well established, going to the same labour markets, the same rickshaw garages, and sleeping on the same pavements. Such groups of villagers can be found in the wholesale spice and grain market of Khari Baoli or under the verandas of Asaf Ali Road. In the latter place, for example, there was one group of some 25-30 persons who came from the same village in Uttar Pradesh, lived together on the pavement despite belonging to different castes, and sometimes even cooked together. Moreover, they returned together to their village for the main festivals, and each month one member of the group went back to the village taking the remittances from all the other villagers working in Delhi in order to redistribute them to their respective families. Thus, a community life had been reconstituted among the pavement dwellers, based on belonging to the same place of origin, and this link transcended caste differences, at least during the temporary stay in Delhi, where earning money was the predominant preoccupation.

Relations Maintained with the Place of Origin

As revealed by the in-depth interviews, most of the houseless people surveyed still have family members staying in their native place and the majority of them visit their native place and family more or less regularly (at least once in the last two years according to the survey) or intend to do so in the case of very recent migrants who have been in Delhi for less than one year.[38] A notable proportion of the houseless migrants also maintain contacts with their families through letters. Another revealing indication is the practice of remittances or support in kind provided to the family: about half of the respondents who still have family members in their native place provide financial support, often supplemented by gifts of clothes or household items at the time of visits. Reciprocal exchanges in favour of the migrant in Delhi are rare, which is only to be expected given the fact that it is precisely the unsatisfactory nature of economic conditions in the native place which pushed many migrants to leave in the first place.

However, contrary to what might be expected, the houseless migrants in Delhi do not necessarily hail from the poorest rural families, and apart from having familial houses in their native places, many of them come from families with agricultural land, though the size of properties is generally small. For those migrants who have not broken away from their families, familial assets in the place of origin represent a form of security, since they involve rights on land and a share of the family property. Conversely, the protection of their rights over familial properties provides an incentive for migrants to maintain relationships with their native places and send remittances to their families. As observed frequently in the process of rural-urban migration in developing countries, access to agricultural land can be used as a lever by the village community to control migrants from afar and to benefit from the economic returns of their work in the city.[39]

Attachment to the family is further revealed by future plans to return to the native place (in the near or distant future), a wish that was shared by the majority of houseless migrants interviewed. Those who wished to return to their native places, often made plans for future investments. In particular, many planned to open up a general store or some other type of shop in the village, to buy more agricultural land or to invest more generally in agriculture. To realize these projects, the individuals interviewed planned to raise funds from their own savings, supplemented, if necessary, by a familial contribution. Some of these investment projects may not be realized, yet some seem viable given the saving capacity of the workers concerned. This shows a definite degree of economic dynamism among certain houseless persons, and conveys an image not of abject poverty, but of economic calculation involving temporary sacrifice in terms of housing conditions in the city as a short-term measure geared towards improving economic conditions in the native place.

The above investigation makes it possible to draw up a typology of the houseless migrants living in Old Delhi as regards their degree of attachment to their family and native place. Concerning the significance of familial units for houseless individuals living alone in Old Delhi, two distinct—and opposite—patterns can be identified, with a whole range of intermediary possibilities. Corresponding to the highest degree of familial integration, one can find seasonal migrants coming to Delhi every year to work for a few months, usually during the lean season for agriculture, and directly supporting their families in the native place. Close to this group in terms of their integration are married migrants whose wives and children (if any) remained with the extended families in their native place and to whom remittances are periodically sent. There are also unmarried migrants contributing to the familial income. Both such groups visit their families regularly. These remitter-migrants exemplify familial solidarity which transcends residential unity: this is a common feature of the migration process, especially rural-urban migration, both in India and in other developing countries.[40] What needs to be underlined here is that the houseless condition of the migrant in the city does not prevent him from exercising this solidarity; in fact, as I shall show in the next section, it is this very condition which allows him to support his family financially.

At the lowest end of the scale of familial attachment are those individuals who ran away from home following an acute familial crisis often involving violence (quarrel, dispute, etc.), and who eventually severed all links with their families and home. Whilst most of the children interviewed belonged to this category, there were also some young adults who had felt compelled to take this radical step, and even some older men who experienced familial crisis at a relatively advanced age. Given the circumstances of their departure from home, these migrants or escapees cannot rely on familial networks for their integration within the city. Among this section of houseless people, which nevertheless remains a minority, a process of individualization and anomie, more forced than chosen, may be at work as a consequence of the breaking away from the basic social institution of the family. Such traumatic experiences at the origin of the shelterless situation of those men should not be confused with the few examples of pavement dwellers who made a deliberate decision to withdraw from family life and material attachments in order to live a life of renunciation—or close to it.

In sum, living alone and without shelter does not necessarily imply social marginality. The majority of the houseless surveyed in Old Delhi maintain relationships and various links with their families in their native places which remain their basic contexts of reference. As a matter of fact, the importance of the native village as a structuring pole of the migrants' life space might be more marked for houseless migrants (barring those who have severed all links with their families) than for those migrants whose residential integration is less precarious: thus, this local reference which also contains a mythical dimension probably helps the pavement dwellers to better accept their present living conditions in Delhi and to justify the hardship and degrading aspects of their situation. 'City dwellers by compulsion, yet villagers by heart' is a phrase which summarizes the dual identity of the majority of houseless migrants.

ECONOMIC AND RESIDENTIAL STRATEGIES

In this section, I shall further investigate the economic and residential strategies of the houseless people surveyed in Old Delhi, examining economic conditions, choice of sleeping places, and willingness to move and to pay for a dwelling. I shall attempt to appraise the elements of choice and constraint, by asking the following question: to what extent is the shelterless situation the consequence of exclusion from access to the urban housing system and to what extent does it also correspond to a residential strategy aimed at improving individual or familial economic conditions? And is shelterlessness merely a transitory stage preceding a person's better integration into the urban housing system or does it correspond to a permanent way of life or at least a prolonged one lasting the duration of a person's stay in Delhi?

Economic Conditions

One striking feature of the economic condition of this segment of population is the great variety of situations encountered. The different types of occupation performed by houseless people have been already described (see Tables 6.1 and 6.2), in relation to the economic characteristics of Old Delhi. The proportion of respondents who did not report any income generating activity in Delhi remained marginal (2 per cent of the sample).[41] These were essentially very recent in-migrants who had been in Delhi for less than one month and were still looking for jobs. From this point of view, the shelterless population of Old Delhi proves to be an integral part of the metropolitan labour force. This accords with the findings of previous studies on pavement dwellers and night shelter inmates in Delhi.[42]

In terms of money earned, the houseless workers appear to form a very heterogeneous section of the labour force: the average monthly earnings (for the twelve months preceding the 1996 survey) ranged from Rs. 300 (in the case of a child helper in a tea stall) to Rs. 4,500 (in the case of a pavement dweller involved in some illegal trade combined with other legal occupations),[43] with 60 per cent of respondents earning between Rs. 1,000 and Rs. 2,000 per month (for their main occupations only). Furthermore, intra-occupational income differentials are very large.

The incomes generated by the houseless workers place them in the low-income group, yet, with the exception of one case, all the respondents of the sample would be above the poverty line of Rs. 310 per capita per month, considered to be the expenditure required for a daily calorie intake of 2100 per person in urban areas at 1995-6 prices.[44] This would appear to apply even after taking into consideration the remittances sent to the family outside Delhi. In proportion to their income levels, the saving capacity of the majority of the houseless is also far from being marginal. Remittances to the family and future plans for investment following their return to their native place are other encouraging indicators of the economic potential of a good number of them. In this respect, the findings of this survey corroborate the conclusions of other studies on the urban poor, such as Kundu's assertion that 'the thesis regarding economic marginality of the people in urban informal sectors, slum dwellers, pavement dwellers and others is an exaggeration'.[45]

Yet, the insecurity of employment and the uncertainty of getting sufficient work constitute widespread concerns. Going daily or periodically to the labour market to get recruited by a contractor or to the wholesale markets and bazaars to find assignments, is the common fate of construction workers, service workers in the catering industry, loaders and unloaders, handcart pushers (who help the main pullers and are recruited by them), and other casual labourers. Among the houseless working as employees, only a very small minority have secured salaried jobs. As for self-employed workers such as handcart pullers and cycle rickshaw drivers, they have to hire their cart or rickshaw everyday without any guarantee of the number of trips—of goods or passengers—they will be able to obtain. The situation for street vendors, roadside mechanics, and others self-employed in the informal sector is similar in terms of general precariousness and corresponding irregularity of income.

As a response to this risk of unemployment and irregularity of work, houseless workers have developed the strategy of combining several occupations and being flexible about changing work. Thus, almost one-third of respondents reported having had more than one occupation in Delhi in the last year (most reported two). These occupations are often alternated according to the changing opportunities of the labour market, in particular according to seasonal patterns; sometimes different activities are also carried on simultaneously throughout the year (see also Table 6.1).

All of this means that, although most of the houseless surveyed in Old Delhi had not experienced unemployment during the preceding year (among those who had few reported significant unemployment periods), the insecurity of employment and the consequent lack of guaranteed regular income are some of the most significant features of the economic condition of these workers and a critical factor for understanding their shelterless condition.

Financial Constraints

Given the economic condition of the pavement dwellers, financial constraints undoubtedly constitute a major obstacle in obtaining housing. However, the significance of this factor has to be appraised in relation to other factors and to be considered in a long-term perspective. Financial constraints are likely to be most stringent at the initial stages of pavement dwelling when the migrant first arrives in Delhi and is yet to be absorbed into the labour market. Later, the key constraint is not so much the average level of income as the lack of guarantee of a regular income. This element of uncertainty restrains many shelterless casual workers from contemplating accommodation on rent even if they have the financial potential to pay for it, for they do not wish to entail regular and fixed expenses which cannot be adjusted in relation to actual earnings. On the other hand, expenses for hiring a quilt or a cot outside or for entrance to a night shelter are incurred on a daily basis and are therefore easily adjustable to daily earnings.

Further elements for understanding the residential strategies of pavement dwellers are revealed in their frequent practice of changing sleeping locations during the year. In particular, seasonal patterns can be observed, with various possible combinations. For example, in the summer, preference is given to sleeping on open grounds, non-covered pavements, road dividers, or in parks; during the rainy season, verandas, night shelters, cots or mattresses on hire in sleeping areas protected with ground and overhead plastic sheeting, are more in demand; and in winter preference is given to quilts on hire, night shelters and verandas. Some pavement dwellers have been repeating the same seasonal patterns with the same combination of locations for years. This flexibility in sleeping places also helps us understand how pavement dwellers who can afford to spend Rs. 3 per night for access to a night shelter, or Rs. 5 for hiring a quilt, or up to Rs. 15 for a cot and bedding, are not necessarily ready to spend the equivalent monthly amount to rent a room. Whereas taking a room on rent entails regular and fixed expenses throughout the year, resorting to a night shelter or bedding on hire involves daily expenses which can be reduced to zero during certain periods of the year when climatic conditions are favourable.

Even for those houseless persons with a sufficient and regular saving capacity to rent a room (alone or by sharing it with one or two other workers) priority may be given to remittances to the family or to long-term savings for future investment in the native place. In other words, preference may be given to the family's living conditions in the native place over the migrant's living conditions in Delhi, and to the future over the present. In such cases, it cannot be said that there are absolute financial constraints preventing the houseless migrant from renting a room, but rather relative ones resulting from his own choice and priorities.

Proximity to the Workplace

Another major factor for understanding the shelterless situation of many workers in Old Delhi and their choice of sleeping place is the location of their workplace. Closer proximity to the place of work or source of employment opportunities is one of the reasons respondents gave for staying initially on the pavement or in a night shelter, and more frequently to explain their choice of a specific place to sleep. The actual 'residential' location of the houseless is more revealing than their explicit answers. Most of the respondents interviewed in Old Delhi work in the Walled City itself, or in the adjoining areas, within walking distance from their place of sleep. If we consider the statistics pertaining to the people's main occupations, 80 per cent of the houseless workers surveyed walk to their place of work, the average time of commuting being only 16 minutes each way, with 57 per cent of them taking 10 minutes or less. The cost of transportation to work is consequently reduced to nil. Even amongst those respondents who claimed to give priority to the quality of their sleeping environment, in terms of choosing areas which contained acquaintances and good facilities, most still remained within walking distance from their place of work or from the labour market.

The relative importance given to staying close to the source of employment opportunities depended to some extent on types of occupation. For casual workers who have to go daily to a labour market to get recruited, such as workers in the catering services and construction labourers, this proximity factor appears primordial. In order to get more job offers, and to be in a better position to bargain with contractors, it is necessary to reach the labour market early in the morning, and hence not have to waste time commuting. For handcart pullers or pushers and loaders working in market areas, transportation activities do not start very early in the morning (usually around 10 a.m.) but they often continue late into the night, which makes it more convenient to sleep in the market itself, and more profitable for getting assignments. Since the nature of the work requires intense physical strength, the transportation workers are usually exhausted after a day's work; sleeping in the same location (or nearby) enables them to avoid the additional tiredness of commuting. Furthermore, in the market they are able to sleep on their handcarts or under the verandas of the buildings, and usually do not face harassment by the police since they are known to work there. The position of the cycle rickshaw drivers (whose work is also physically demanding) is mixed. Those who keep their rickshaws at night can sleep on them and have more flexibility in their choice of location, providing they can park their rickshaws safely. But for the drivers having to hire their rickshaws every morning from their owners' garages, staying within close proximity to the garage is important. Even for those houseless workers whose occupations and modes of recruitment do not require them to stay near sources of employment opportunities, proximity between sleeping place and workplace is highly sought after in order to reduce—or eliminate entirely—the cost of commuting.

The residential mobility of houseless people in Delhi further highlights the significance of the strategies aimed at staying closer to the workplace. In addition to seasonal patterns of mobility governed by climatic conditions, we find people changing their 'residential' location in relation to occupational mobility.[46] The houseless people adjust their choice of sleeping place according to employment opportunities, to the location of a particular labour market, or to the possibilities of sleeping at the workplace itself.

The vital importance of proximity to the workplace was highlighted in another urban context by a famous Supreme Court ruling concerning the eviction of pavement dwellers in Mumbai.[47] The judgement delivered acknowledged that the pavement dwellers needed to live near their place of work, 'the time otherwise taken in commuting and its cost being forbidding for their slender means. To lose the pavement or the slum is to lose the job'.[48] Thus, for this population, squatting on the pavement proved to be a prerequisite to earning a livelihood.[49]

It is worth referring here to a report from the 1950s by the Bharat Sevak Samaj concerning the then slums of Old Delhi about which it was written: 'On the whole it is amply substantiated that nearness to the workplace is one of the most important factors forcing them to live where they are living today, in the slums.'[50] This conclusion continues to have relevance for the pavement dwellers who today inhabit the same part of the city.

Perennial versus Transitory Shelterlessness in Delhi

An investigation of the length of time people remain shelterless and of their future plans and willingness to pay for a dwelling throws some light on another important issue: the perennial versus transitory nature of the shelterless situation in Delhi. A notable proportion of houseless people have been living in this condition for ten or more than ten years (17 per cent of the sample) though this does not exclude regular visits to their native place. For this category of pavement dwellers, and especially for those staying in the same night shelter or sleeping place for several years, or repeating exactly the same seasonal movements sometimes for the past ten or even fifteen years, their houseless condition seems to have become a permanent way of life, or at least permanent enough to last the duration of their working lives before they retire to their native place.

Although many people express a desire to move to better accommodation, this is unlikely to be realized in many cases owing to constraints similar to those already underlined in the case of houselessness. The minority of houseless people who had attempted to move to proper dwellings gave the following reasons for their return to pavements and night shelters: difficulties adjusting to other persons with whom they shared the same room (a common way of reducing housing expenses) or the realization that their work and income were suffering owing to the distance from their place of work. Hence, the desire and even actual attempts to move off the streets cannot be taken as indicators that the shelterless situation is merely a transitory phase leading eventually to better integration into the urban housing system.

The arguments of those houseless persons who stated that they had no intention of moving to better accommodation, are also worth considering. Interestingly, those reporting their unwillingness to pay for a dwelling were not necessarily those with the least earning and saving capacity. They gave two reasons for their position. Some claimed they did not intend to stay in Delhi for a long period, and therefore found it irrelevant to take a room on rent. Others made it clear that their priority was to maximize savings, especially in order to send remittances to their families. Consequently, they tried to minimize expenses for housing and transportation in Delhi, sometimes even reducing them to zero. Being alone in the city without their families, some houseless migrants did not perceive proper accommodation as a need. As a matter of fact, most of the houseless interviewed did not plan to settle in Delhi permanently, but hoped eventually to return to their native place or to migrate to another city. Hence, they perceived their stay in Delhi as limited in time, even if this transitory situation may eventually last the entire duration of their working lives.[51]

Coming back to questions raised at the beginning of this section regarding the interpretation of the shelterless situation, we can sum up the main arguments which have emerged from the surveys of houseless people in Old Delhi. Employment conditions and financial constraints undoubtedly prevent or limit the possibilities of access to a dwelling. Nevertheless, this factor has to be considered in combination with other explanatory factors, forming a system in which choice is often present. The residential practices of the majority of the houseless reveal an economic rationale oriented towards maximizing savings and remittances to their families in their native place, by minimizing their housing and transportation expenses. Such economic behaviour also conforms to the explanatory framework propounded by the 'New Economics of Migration', in which 'migration decisions are not made by isolated individual actors, but by larger units of related people—typically families or households—in which people act collectively not only to maximize expected income, but also to minimize risks . . . to their economic well-being by diversifying the allocation of household resources, such as family labor', in particular by sending family members to work in urban labour markets.[52] When the logic of staying shelterless in Delhi is an integral part of familial strategies rooted in the native place, priority being given to the economic condition of the family in the village at the expense of the migrants' living conditions in Delhi, then, the shelterless situation is likely to last for the duration of their stay in the capital.

The role of rational choice in the residential practices of houseless people has been highlighted in other studies—although the exercise of choice for this segment of the urban poor is obviously restricted by strong economic and social constraints.[53] The importance of proximity to the source of livelihood is also emphasized. This factor is crucial not only for understanding the residential practices and location choices of the houseless, but more generally of the urban poor.[54] The failure of many attempts to relocate slum dwellers and squatters in settlement colonies outside city centres is often due to inadequate consideration of the importance of easy physical access to earning opportunities.

CONCLUSION

In the use of urban space, Old Delhi is particularly subject to competing interests and strategies from different actors, both institutional (the planning authorities) and private (traders, entrepreneurs, pavement dwellers). Despite the attempts of town planners to regulate this process, the proliferation of commercial and industrial establishments in the old city core during the last decades accelerated the deterioration of old buildings, and has attracted a floating population of migrant workers whose residential integration is extremely precarious. This has further engendered the development of 'unauthorized' economic and residential practices: the nightly occupation of pavements and other public spaces by houseless migrants and by private entrepreneurs renting out bedding facilities. Yet, these small informal enterprises, though without license, help compensate for inadequate civic services, namely the insufficient capacity of the night shelters run by the municipality.

Statistical and anthropological surveys conducted on a sample of shelterless persons in the old city permitted us to examine their mobility patterns and their economic and residential strategies. Only a minority have broken away from their families. Although they live alone in Delhi, the majority of the houseless migrants maintain regular links with their families in their native place, which remains their primary place of reference. Through their circular mobility, the houseless labour migrants contribute towards integrating rural family enterprises such as agriculture with the urban labour market, village with city, in such a way that they form part of a single economic system.

The houseless population of Old Delhi also forms an integral part of the metropolitan labour force, which in terms of income seems to be able to stay above the poverty line. Yet, the lack of guaranteed and regular income constitutes a general concern. At the same time, their saving capacity, remittances and plans for future investment, all represent encouraging indicators of the economic potential of a notable portion of the houseless. Finally, the large variety of individual situations encountered indicates that the houseless are not a single category of 'urban poor', nor are they necessarily 'the poorest of the urban poor'.

Although financial constraints provide the background to the shelterless situation, the residential practices of pavement dwellers and night shelter inmates should not be interpreted purely in terms of exclusion from access to a dwelling. Rather, it is important to recognize the economic rationales of individual migrants who try to maximize remittances to their families by cutting or eliminating housing and transport expenses. It is within this context that they give priority to sleeping locations near the workplace or labour market. It therefore stands to reason that the condition of the pavement dwellers has to be viewed in relation to their needs and priorities. This is a prerequisite for planning appropriate urban housing policies.

To conclude this analysis, a comprehensive explanatory framework for the mobility and residential patterns of houseless migrants can be formulated at three different levels. At the macro level, rural-urban labour migration, including that of the houseless workers surveyed in Old Delhi reflects and is induced by the unequal economic development between rural areas and the capital city. Furthermore, the economic characteristics of Old Delhi contribute to the specific pull exerted on a floating population of unskilled labourers. At the family level (which proved relevant in the majority of cases), the economic and residential strategies of houseless migrants is led by the principle of risk aversion, through the diversification of the allocation of family labour. This would appear to be the guiding logic of migration in developing countries more generally. Finally, at the individual level, the economic and residential practices of the houseless are geared towards maximizing savings by minimizing housing and commuting costs, as well as ensuring better economic returns by staying near to the main locations for employment opportunities. This type of strategy is common amongst the urban poor—in the case of the pavement dwellers it is pushed to its logical extreme.

NOTES

The research for this paper is part of a study on patterns of population mobility in the metropolitan area of Delhi. This is a collaborative project between the French Institute of Research for Development (ex-ORSTOM) which financed the study, and the two Delhi-based institutions: the *Centre de Sciences Humaines* and the Institute of Economic Growth which provided institutional, logistical and intellectual support. I am most grateful to these institutions for their assistance and co-operation. This project has also received financial support from the CNRS (*Action Concertée en Sciences Sociales ORSTOM-CNRS*) as part of a collective research programme on the city of Delhi, and from the *PIR-Villes*, for comparative analysis of residential practices in Delhi and Bogota), as well as from the CSH as part of the research theme on 'Urban dynamics'.

Sincere thanks are also due to the team of field investigators and research assistants who helped collect, code and edit the data. Those who deserve particular mention are: Dhananjay Tingal with whom I conducted the in-depth interviews, Mohammed Baber Ali, Sandeep Chauhan, Bhuwan Kumar, Jay Prakash and Ravi Shekar.

This contribution draws on an earlier paper prepared with Dhananjay Tingal for the 14th European Conference of Modern South Asian Studies in Copenhagen (21-4 August 1996), and later revised: V. Dupont and D. Tingal, 'Residential and Economic Practices of Pavement Dwellers in Old Delhi', Delhi: Institute of Economic Growth, *Working Paper Series*, 1997, no. E/186/97.

1. R.K. Arora and A.K. Chhibber, 'Chilled nights on pavements in Delhi. A Socio-Economic Study of the Children Staying in Ran Baseras in Winter', New Delhi: Socio-economic division, Slum and Jhuggi-Jhonpri Department, Delhi Development Authority, mimeo, 1985, p. 1.
2. NIUA, *Dimension of Urban Poverty. A Situational Analysis*, New Delhi: National Institute of Urban Affairs, Research Study Series no. 25, 1986, p. 90.
3. D.B. Gupta, S. Kaul and R. Pandey, *Housing and India's Urban Poor*, New Delhi: Har Anand Publications, 1993, p. 29.
4. V. Dupont, F. Dureau, 'Rôle des mobilités circulaires dans les dynamiques urbaines. Illustrations à partir de l'Equateur et de l'Inde', Paris: *Revue Tiers Monde*, Tome XXXV, no. 140, Oct.-Dec. 1994, pp. 801-29.
5. For Delhi, see A. Basu, K. Basu and R. Ray, 'Migrants and the native bond. An analysis of micro-level data from Delhi', *Economic and Political Weekly*, vol. XXII, No. 19-20-21, Annual Number, May 1987, pp. AN-145-54; and B. Banerjee, *Rural to Urban Migration and the Urban Labour Market (A case study of Delhi)*, Delhi: Himalaya Publishing House, 1986, Chap. V.
6. A. Tarrius, 'Territoires circulatoires et espaces urbains', *Mobilités, Les Annales de la Recherche urbaine*, no. 59-60, June-September 1993, Paris: Plan Urbain, METT, pp. 51-60 (p. 51, *our translation*).
7. N.V. Jagannathan and A. Halder, 'Income-housing Linkages. A Case Study of Pavement Dwellers in Calcutta', *Economic and Political Weekly*, vol. XXIII, no. 23, 1988, 4 June 1998, pp. 1175-8.
8. For exceptions, see S. Manzoor Alam and F. Alikhan (eds.), *Poverty in Metropolitan Cities*, New Delhi: Concept Publishing Company, 1987; A.M. Singh, A. de Souza, *The Urban Poor, Slum and Pavement Dwellers in Major Cities of India*, Delhi: Manohar, 1980; A. de Souza, (ed.), *The Indian City: Poverty, Ecology and Urban Development*, Delhi: Manohar, 1983.
9. To mention some of the more recent studies: H. Nagpaul, *Modernisation and Urbanisation in India: Problems and Issues*, Jaipur and New Delhi: Rawat Publications, 1996; D.B. Gupta, S. Kaul and R. Pandey, *Housing and India's Urban Poor*, New Delhi: Har Anand Publications,

1993; A.K. Jain, *The Indian Megacity and Economic Reform*, New Delhi: Management Publishing Co., 1996; A. Kundu, *In the Name of the Urban Poor. Access to Basic Amenities*, New Delhi: Sage Publications, 1993; NIUA, *Dimension of Urban Poverty. A Situational Analysis*, New Delhi: National Institute of Urban Affairs, Research Study Series no. 25, 1986; NIUA, *Profile of the Urban Poor: An Investigation into their Demographic, Economic and Shelter Characteristics*, New Delhi: National Institute of Urban Affairs, Research Study Series no. 40, 1989; E.M. Pernia (ed.), *Urban Poverty in Asia. A Survey of Critical Issues*, Hong Kong: OUP, 1994; P. Suri, *Urban Poor. Their Housing Needs and Government Response*, Delhi: Har Anand Publications, 1994.

10. One can however mention:

- for Calcutta: P. Dhar, 'Pavement Dwellers in Calcutta. Strategies for rehabilitation and Urban Development', unpublished thesis, Delhi: School of Planning and Architecture, 1985; N.V. Jagannathan and A. Halder, 'A Case Study of Pavement Dwellers in Calcutta', *Economic and Political Weekly*, vol. XXIII, no. 23, 4 June 1988, pp. 1175-8; no. 49, 3 December 1988, pp. 2602-5 and vol. XXIV, no. 6, 11 February 1989, pp. 315-18; ISI, 'Calcutta 1976: A Socio-economic Survey of Pavement Dwellers', Calcutta: Indian Statistical Institute, 1977; S. Mukherjee, 'Under the Shadow of the Metropolis—They are Citizens too', Calcutta: Calcutta Metropolitan Development Authority & Calcutta Metropolitan Planning Organization, 1975.

- for Mumbai: P. Ramachandran, 'Pavement Dwellers in Bombay City', Bombay: Tata Institute of Social Sciences, Series no. 26, 1972; SPARC; '*We the Invisible*', *Report on Pavement Dwellers in Bombay*, Bombay: SPARC, 1985.

- for Delhi: R.K. Arora and A.K. Chhibber, 'Chilled Nights on Pavements in Delhi. A Socio-economic Study of the Children Staying in Ran Baseras in Winter', New Delhi: Socio-economic division, Slum and Jhuggi-Jhonpri Department, Delhi Development Authority, mimeo, 1985; Bharat Sevak Samaj, 'A Roof Over the Head', Delhi : Delhi School of Social Work, 1964; DDA, 'Survey of Pavement Dwellers in Old Delhi', unpublished study, New Delhi: Slum and Jhuggi-Jhonpri Department, Delhi Development Authority, 1989; J. Kuruvilla, 'Pavement Dwelling in Metropolitan Cities. Case Study Delhi', thesis, New Delhi: School of Planning and Architecture, Department of Housing, 1990-1.

This list is not exhaustive.

11. The main reference dates back to 1971: this is the special study on the houseless population carried out by the 1971 Census operations (S.R. Gangotra, *Houseless in Delhi*, Census of India 1971, Series 27, Delhi, Part X (a), Special Study, Delhi: Government of India, 1976). The other references are unpublished studies, poorly circulated: the pioneer report of the Bharat Sevak Samaj (op. cit.), a non-governmental organization dedicated to the cause of the poor; a special study conducted by the Slum Wing of the Delhi Development Authority (DDA) on the children staying in night shelters in winter (Arora and Chhibber, op. cit.); a sample survey of about 1069 pavement dwellers in Old Delhi, conducted in 1989 by the Slum Wing of the DDA (op. cit.), and whose report was unfortunately untraceable even in the concerned administration; a thesis completed at the School of Planning and Architecture based on a sample survey of 71 pavement dwellers and 30 inmates of government night shelters in different localities of Delhi (Kuruvilla, op. cit.).
12. A figure quoted in an unpublished report of the Slum and Jhuggi-Jhonpri Department of the DDA ('Programme of Night Shelters for the Homeless in Delhi', Slum and Jhuggi-Jhonpri Department, New Delhi: Delhi Development Authority, 1994), although the corresponding census table has not yet been published.
13. Census enumerators are instructed 'to take note of the possible places where houseless population is likely to live' in their enumeration block(s). This recognizance has to be done during the enumeration of all the households and persons living in 'census houses' (including all types of dwellings), and while this main census operation usually lasts 20 days (between 9 February and 28 February in 1991), the enumerators have only one night to survey the houseless population. Thus, for the 1991 Census, they were told 'On the night of February 28/March 1, 1991, but before sunrise of March 1, 1991, you will

have to quickly cover all such houseless households and enumerate them.' (Census of India 1991, *Instructions to Enumerators for Filling up the Household Schedule and Individual Slip*, New Delhi: Office of the Registrar General & Census Commissioner for India, Ministry of Home Affairs, 1991, p. 64.)

14. Jagannathan and Halder, 1988, op. cit., p. 1175.
15. Ramachandran, op. cit.; Kuruvilla, op. cit.; SPARC, op. cit.
16. Arora and Chhibber, op. cit.; Kuruvilla, op. cit.
17. Census of India, op. cit., p. 64.
18. See, J.M. Firdion, M. Marpsat, 'La statistique des sans-domicile aux Etats-Unis', Paris: *Courrier des Statistiques*, nos. 71-2, December 1994, pp. 43-51; and J.M. Firdion, M. Marpsat, and M. Bozon, 'Est-il légitime de mener des enquêtes statistiques auprès des sans-domicile? Une question éthique et scientifique', Paris: *Revue Française des Affaires Sociales*, 49ème année, 1995, nos. 2-3, pp. 29-51.

    As these authors show, in the United States, where numerous pioneering statistical studies of homelessness have been conducted, estimates of the homeless population varied from 3,00,000 to 30,00,000 in 1982-3.
19. C. Bienveniste, '*Toward a Better Understanding of the Homeless and Exclusion from Housing*', Paris, Actualités du Conseil National de l'Information Statistique, no. 17, May 1996, p. 1.
20. Hence, when referring to the survey and unless otherwise stated, the term 'pavement dwellers' will be used to designate the houseless population sleeping either in various open spaces or in night shelters. In fact, as shown later in this essay, there is a significant level of circulation amongst houseless people who move between various open spaces and night shelters.
21. J.D. Wright and B. Robin, 'Les sans-domicile aux Etats Unis', Paris: *Sociétés Contemporaines*, no. 30, 1998, pp. 35-66.
22. For a detailed presentation of the methodology used, see V. Dupont, 'City History—Life Histories: Changing Equations. Migration Surveys and Biographical Data Collection in Delhi', New Delhi: Centre de Sciences Humaines, *Contributions CSH 97/7*, 1997.
23. J. Brush, 'Recent changes in ecological patterns of metropolitan Bombay and Delhi', in V.K. Tewari, J.A. Weistein, V.L.S.P. Rao (eds.), *Indian Cities. Ecological Perspectives*, New Delhi: Concept, 1986, pp. 121-49.
24. DDA, *Zonal Plan Walled City. Draft*, New Delhi: Delhi Development Authority, 1993.
25. A.K. Mehra, *The Politics of Urban Redevelopment. A Study of Old Delhi*, New Delhi: Sage Publications, 1991, p. 50.
26. For example, at the time of the preparation of the Delhi Master Plan (1958-9), the planning division 'A', which includes the Walled City and its extension, contained a population of 6,07,000. The Master Plan predicted that its population would be reduced to 3,22,600 by 1981. However, 'the population of this division according to 1991 Census is 6,16,000 indicating that the dedensification proposals of Delhi Master Plan could not be realized' (Jain, op. cit., p. 85).
27. DDA, *Master Plan for Delhi. Perspective 2001*, Prepared by Delhi Development Authority, New Delhi: Delhi Development Authority, 1990, p. 46.
28. HSMI, *Renewal of Historical Housing Stock in Old Delhi*, New Delhi: Indian Human Settlement Programme, HSMI Studies 1, Human Settlement Management Institute, 1988, p. 4.
29. See TCPO, *Seminar on Redevelopment of Shahjahanabad: the Walled City of Delhi (New Delhi, 31st Jan.- 1st Feb. 1995), Report and Selected Paper. Resume of the Seminar*, New Delhi: Town and Country Planning Organization, Government of India, Ministry of Works and Housing, 1975, p. 16.
30. See Mehra, op. cit., p. 46.
31. This rate—as well as others mentioned in this essay—refers to the situation at the time of the survey, that is January-March 1996. In 1997 the entry rate for night shelters was increased to Rs. 4.
32. In the sample surveyed in winter, 40 per cent of the shelterless persons were sleeping in night shelters, 34 per cent in pavement dwelling areas with bedding facilities on rent, and 26 per cent in open spaces without renting any bedding facility.

33. The corresponding data for the 1991 Census were still not published when this essay was written.
34. In the 1991 Census, figures relating to literacy pertain to the population aged 7 and above.
35. Of the total sample of houseless migrants surveyed 24 per cent cited familial tensions of this type as their primary reasons for migrating to Delhi. Furthermore, about one-third of the 36 respondents selected for in-depth interviews mentioned similar tensions as significant to their migration trajectory.
36. Banerjee, op. cit., p. 79.
37. The question of the degree and type of help received by the migrant at the time of his first arrival in Delhi is however ambiguous since the perception of help or support is highly subjective and varies from one respondent to the other. For example, information about possible night shelters or pavement dwelling areas, or about specific labour markets and employment opportunities was considered a form of help by some respondents, while others in a similar situation narrated their arrival in Delhi as an ordeal in which they had to manage entirely on their own without outside support. Such discrepancies should be borne in mind when interpreting the fact that about two-thirds of the 33 decision-making migrants surveyed for in-depth interviews stated that they received some kind of help at the time of their arrival.
38. Of the 36 respondents to in-depth interviews, only 3 did not have any family members left in their native place. The statistical survey further confirms the significance of the familial house and visits to the family for houseless people.
39. C.Z. Guilmoto and F. Sandron, 'Approche institutionnelle de la migration dans les pays en développement', Paper presented to the XXIII General Population Conference, IUSSP, Beijing (China), 11-17 October 1997.
40. A.M. Shah, *The Household Dimension of the Family in India,* Delhi: Orient Longman, New Delhi, 1973; R. Skeldon, *Population Mobility in Developing Countries: A Reinterpretation,* London-New York: Belhaven Press, 1990.
41. In this study, beggars are counted as workers, contrary to the conventions applied in official statistics like those of the census reports and National Sample Surveys. However, it should be remembered that less than 1 per cent of the houseless people surveyed in Old Delhi reported beggary as a source of livelihood.
42. See Arora and Chhibber, op. cit., p. 5.
43. In fact the highest income reported was that of a transient pavement dweller—a ticket checker who had a permanent government job in the railways, with a monthly salary of Rs. 4820. He had been transferred to Delhi some three weeks earlier and whilst waiting to get government accommodation, he was sleeping on a hired cot on open ground located just opposite Old Delhi Railway Station, his place of work.
44. This figure is calculated on the basis of the last published official estimate, that is Rs. 209.50 per capita per month in urban areas at 1991-2 prices, converted to present value by applying the index numbers of consumer prices for industrial workers in Delhi for the corresponding period. For a discussion on the concept of poverty line in the context of the houseless population of Old Delhi, see Dupont and Tingal, op. cit., pp. 23-6.
45. Kundu, op. cit., p. 23, cited in M. Lee, 'The Mobilisation of Informal Sector Savings: the USAID Experience', paper presented at the International Workshop on Mobilisation of Informal Sector Savings, 8-12 December 1986, New Delhi: Society for Development Studies.
46. For example, among the houseless people surveyed who were previously staying in another place in Delhi (173 cases out of the total sample), 63 per cent reported 'better conditions of accommodation' (which included consideration of climatic factors) as the main reason for their last change of sleeping place, while 24 per cent gave 'employment related reasons'.
47. Namely a Public Interest Litigation case known as '*Olgas Tellis* v. *Bombay Municipal Corporation*' (*Supreme Court Cases,* 1985 (3), pp. 555-90); see also S. Ahuja, *People, Law and Justice. Casebook on Public Interest Litigation,* New Delhi: Orient Longman, 1997, Chap. 8.
48. *Supreme Court Cases,* 1985 (3), p. 575.
49. In this case, the recognition by the Court of the conditions of the pavement dwellers did not prevent the Court from placing 'the prevention of public nuisance on public streets

higher on its list of priorities than poverty' and declaring that these pavement dwellers were illegal (Ahuja, op. cit., p. 341).

50. Bharat Sevak Samaj, *Slums of Old Delhi,* Delhi: Atma Ram & Sons, 1958, p. 197.
51. Or may be even their entire remaining life, insofar as the future plan of returning to the native place may never get realized.
52. D. Massey, J. Arango, G. Hugo, A. Kouaouci, A. Pellegrino and J.E. Taylor, 'Theories of International Migration: a Review and Appraisal', *Population and Development Review,* 19, no. 3, September 1993, pp. 431-66.
53. For example, in the conclusion of his primary survey of pavement dwellers and night shelter inmates in Delhi, Kuruvilla states: 'The choice of the pavement is mainly for reduction of expenses on housing, proximity to employment opportunities, . . . availability of facilities, services, food and water and maximise savings to send back home. Thus it becomes a deliberate rational decision to live on the pavement' (Kuruvilla, op. cit., pp. 85-6). Jagannathan and Halder, in their study of the pavement dwellers in Calcutta, also infer: 'Pavement dwellers of the main stream vocations have chosen this lifestyle to protect their access to earning opportunities. In addition . . . a substantial proportion are temporary migrants, who remit savings home to the village.' Further: 'The majority of pavement dwellers live without shelter as a deliberate rational decision, by which the expenditure on housing is reduced to zero' (Jagannathan and Halder, 1988, op. cit., p. 1177).
54. See for example: Bharat Sevak Samaj, 1958, op. cit., p. 107; Gupta, Kaul and Pandey, op. cit., p. 86; Suri, op. cit., p. 273; Kundu, op. cit., p. 65.

7

Markets and Intermediaries: An Enquiry about the Principles of Market Economy in the Grain Market of Delhi

DENIS VIDAL

> If it is so, then the interaction of anthropology and economics may come for once to be more than an exchange of exotic facts for parochial concepts and develop into a reciprocally seditious endeavour useful to both.
>
> CLIFFORD GEERTZ

Situated at the western edge of the Walled City, Naya Bazaar offers an impressive sight. Here, concentrated in a very small section of the old city, is not only the heart of the grain market of Delhi, but one of the most important grain markets for the whole of north India. According to market people, only 20 per cent of the grain which is negotiated here would be consumed in Delhi itself. It is also the main centre for grain export outside India. Naya Bazaar must be one of the most congested areas of Delhi both during the day and at night. With the exception of Sundays and a few moments of relative quietude at dawn and dusk, there is no respite in this place which functions not only as a commercial centre but also as home to hundreds of coolies who work here during the day.[1] The traders themselves, who once used to live above their shops, have slowly moved away to quieter places of residence outside the walled city.

Along the main road and in a few adjacent streets, one finds during the day a constant flux of coolies, *dalals* (intermediaries), employees and traders, jostling together in the most indescribable chaos, made worse by the astonishing variety of vehicles. But, what really gives the place its identity and dominates the urban landscape is the mass of large jute bags full of grain, which seem to fill every possible vacant space in the area. However, the perpetual train of vehicles, advancing slowly in the desperate attempt to load or unload their sacks of grain in shops where bags never seem to cease accumulating is a rather deceptive sight: the bags which arrive at Naya Bazaar constitute only a fragment of the grain trade. This is just the semi-wholesale market oriented towards the relatively small clientele of individual shopkeepers in Delhi and its neighbourhood. The main part of the trade (the wholesale trade) is less visible; it is negotiated mostly in the hundreds of small offices which occupy each floor of the rather dilapidated buildings in the area. And apart from the omnipresence of telephones, account books and computers which are becoming increasingly common, the only apparent manifestation of the innumerable transactions which represent hundreds and thousands of tons of cereals per day is the sight of a few grams of grain in small plastic bags which circulate from hand to hand between traders and intermediaries throughout the entire market.

IN SEARCH OF THE PRINCIPLES OF MARKET ECONOMY IN INDIA

Historians of economic thought have remarked on the paradoxical circumstances which gave birth to the development of economic theory in England. On the one hand, it was a time when people seemed painfully conscious of the diminishing importance of local fairs and markets where buyers and sellers negotiated the price of agricultural goods directly between themselves. According to economic historians, this happened because of the extension of regional trade in the grain market which led to the increasing influence of big traders and trading intermediaries.[2] But in spite of this—or more plausibly because of it—this was also the time when the concept of the market as we know it today was developed. In this standard conception of the market, the active involvement of intermediaries in the functioning of every stage of the market process tends to be either ignored or underestimated. Furthermore, it is taken for granted that any interaction which does not favour the direct encounter between buyers and sellers can only constitute an impediment to the functioning of the market. An anthropological approach to markets can, however, offer a very different perspective. It obliges us to recognize that the activity of market intermediaries is at the very centre of market mechanisms. As the ethnography of the grain market at Naya Bazaar illustrates, it is not that intermediaries block the market process but rather that they create it.

More generally, there is a strange disjunction between the approaches used for analysing the market and those used for analysing other economic institutions. While it has been taken for granted that the best way of explaining market institutions is to uncover the logic and rationality which underlie them, it seems obvious to many that such an approach would not be very helpful if applied to other institutions. The main reason for this discrepancy is that the market economy tends to be regarded as the only form of economic organization whose principles of functioning are not determined by cultural values and social principles but rather by an independent logic of its own. This methodological bias has been aptly analysed by the sociologist, Mark Granovetter, in a well-known article concerning 'the problem of embeddedness'.[3] He highlights the contrast between two equally unsatisfactory tendencies in the study of economic institutions in the social sciences: on the one hand, the tendency of economists to adopt an 'undersocialized' conception of human action, especially when they study market institutions; on the other hand, the tendency of sociologists and social anthropologists to adopt an 'oversocialized' perspective whenever they study any form of economic activity which cannot immediately be identified as a market process.

There is little doubt that the study of economic institutions in India has greatly suffered from this double bias. There has been a tendency to consider market institutions as alien to the fundamental characteristics of Indian culture and society and as essentially an import from the West. As a result, the economic history and sociology of India has for a long time been particularly distorted: not only have the importance of market institutions and market processes been underestimated in Indian sociology and history, there has also been a contrary tendency to exaggerate the importance of other forms of economic logic (like the so-called *jajmani* system) in Indian society. It is only in recent years that economic historians and social anthropologists have begun trying to revise such a perspective.[4]

While it no longer makes sense to deny the importance of market institutions in the history or sociology of India by attributing them to influences of only relatively recent origins, this change of perspective has potential consequences which have not yet been fully realized. One might be to shift the nature of the debate, which has long been at the centre of economic sociology and political discourse in India. We need to get beyond the endless discussion of the degree to which Western principles of political economy and economic theories should or should not be applied to societies like India—a debate, which takes us from Max Weber to Polanyi and others. There are other questions which are surely much more central to our understanding of economic processes. In particular, we might consider how research done in the Indian context might enable us to challenge the use and legitimacy of economic theories, which may be inappropriate not only in the Indian context but also more generally in other social and cultural settings. In other words, the real challenge today is not simply to avoid the two traps of cultural relativism and pseudo-universalism; rather, it is to consider fully the epistemological consequences of those analyses which contradict the dominant models of economic and sociological thought whether in India or in other parts of the world, rather than simply reducing them to the status of local oddities. It is this direction that I have tried to follow in my own analysis, based on an empirical investigation of the functioning of the grain market in the bazaars of Old Delhi.

Bazaars and Markets

One of the most interesting attempts to contrast the market with another form of economic institution was made in the 1960s by Clifford Geertz in his well-known article about the economic logic of the bazaar in Morocco.[5]

The merit of Geertz' analysis was his avoidance of the trap of assuming that one should give a central role to social and cultural factors in explaining bazaar transactions on the one hand, but discarding them automatically while describing market principles on the other. The core of Geertz' demonstration may be briefly summarized as follows: what distinguishes the bazaar from the market is not local traditions as such but rather the way in which economic actors get access to relevant information in both cases: the sort of interaction which prevails in the bazaar

> is an expression of the fact that such a market rewards a *clinical* form of search (one which focuses on the diverging interest of concrete economic actors) more that it does a *survey* form (one which focuses on the general interplay of functionally defined economic categories). Search is primarily intensive because the sort of information one needs cannot be acquired by asking a handful of index questions of a large number of people, but only by asking a large number of diagnostic questions of a handful of people. It is this kind of questioning, exploring nuances rather than canvassing populations, that bazaar bargaining represents.

Geertz concludes his article by explaining that 'here as elsewhere in the bazaar, everything rests finally on a personal confrontation between intimate antagonists'. Geertz also rightly notices that clientelized transactions do not necessarily exclude a more extensive form of survey in the bazaar. Rather, such surveys constitute preambles to the real transactions to be made among a 'firmly clientelized buyer and seller exploring the dimensions of a particular, likely to be consummated transaction'.[6]

Neither a Market nor a Bazaar

At first sight it would appear that Geertz' analysis is relevant to most bazaars and markets of India. It certainly appears appropriate for analysing the general behaviour of buyers and sellers in the different markets of Old Delhi. However, there are certain reservations. The type of behaviour Geertz describes and on which he bases his analysis applies only to retail transactions. It is only in this case that one can draw an effective contrast between 'extensive' and 'intensive' forms of search for economic information; or that one can oppose anonymous styles of market interactions with more personalized ones between buyers and sellers.

However, an analyses of the sort of commercial transactions which take place between buyers and sellers at the wholesale level in Indian markets and bazaars, changes not only the style but also the whole process and inner logic of the transactions. Not only can one no longer contrast different sorts of economic transaction on the basis of the knowledge that buyers and sellers individually possess, but more fundamentally, one can no longer consider the confrontation between buyers and sellers as a central element of the market institution. Rather, as I shall demonstrate, it is the presence of intermediaries and the different functions they assume that defines the characteristics of the market. In exploring the reasons why market intermediaries play such a fundamental role, my aim is not simply to highlight the specificities of wholesale markets as such, but rather to go beyond this to reconsider our understanding of the market economy as a whole.

THE GRAIN MARKET IN DELHI

Naya Bazaar, in spite of its importance, constitutes only one of the elements of the grain market in the capital. Due to historical circumstances in the commercial development of the city, it is, for example, in the smaller market of Rui Mandi near-by that the wholesale market for cereal is concentrated. One will also find in adjacent areas separate grain markets of lesser importance, selling on a retail basis the produce which they have just purchased in Naya Bazaar. Similarly, all around the market, one finds areas where different sorts of trades and services, which cater to the specific needs of grain traders are concentrated. There are, for example, street corners which specialize in recycling jute bags or in making and renting the *thelas* (trolleys) which coolies use for transporting grain.

As long as trains were the main means of transporting grain, the centrality of the old city remained a relative asset for stocking grain in spite of the congestion. However, this is no longer the case. Almost all traders nowadays prefer to use trucks which, though slightly more expensive, are both faster and more reliable. It is only in the case of big traders negotiating entire shipments of grain, generally for export, that transportation by trains is still preferred. As a result, it has become both advantageous and cheaper to have godowns outside the old city. Godowns are now disseminated throughout the periphery and in the immediate vicinity of Delhi. A significant number of them are concentrated in the northern part of the capital known as Lawrence Road. There, besides the hundreds of godowns which give a strange deserted look to the area, are numerous small factories where some of the grain which transits through Delhi is also processed before being resold and sent again outside the city. While the majority of traders, commercial intermediaries and accountants are still located at Naya Bazaar, it is at Lawrence Road that one finds the most important contingent of coolies, peons and factory workers associated with the grain market.

The People

It is difficult to estimate the number of people whose activities are directly linked to the grain market in Delhi. Such an attempt poses methodological problems. However, it may be convenient in this essay to offer an approximate estimation of the numbers of people involved in the different activities which play a prominent role in the organization of the market as a whole.[7]

— the number of *palledars* (coolies) can be estimated at 10,000, with just under a third working in Naya Bazaar and the other two-thirds working mostly in Lawrence Road and other godowns disseminated throughout the city. Most of them are associated with particular traders but a few work on a freelance basis.

— the number of peons can be estimated at between 2,000 and 3,000.
— the number of accountants between 3,000 and 4,500.
— the number of traders between 3,000 and 5,000.
— the number of intermediaries is something which the market people themselves find most difficult to evaluate. While the official number seems to stand at around 5,000, not all of them are effectively active in the market at the same time. Only one or two thousand of them are based at Naya Bazaar and no more than half of them are constantly active. The others live outside Delhi and do not necessarily come regularly to the market.
— the number of people associated with the various modes of transport which cater almost exclusively to the needs of the grain trade may be estimated at between 5 and 10,000.
— the number of workers in the factories processing grain in Delhi is also difficult to evaluate. It is estimated that there are about 500 grain factories which employ an average of 10 to 20 people, meaning that their sum total would consist of some 5 to 10,000 workers.

There are, without doubt, many other people whose activities could be included in this list, but even if one considers only the few categories mentioned here, the people directly associated with this market could number anything between thirty and forty thousand. However, more interesting than their exact number is the distribution of caste, class, gender, religious and regional identities amongst them. It is noticeable, for example, that nearly all traders in the grain market are Hindu, belong to merchant castes and trace their origins to Haryana or the Punjab (more than 90 per cent of them, according to those questioned). One does not find such homogeneity among other groups. For example only 65 per cent of *dalals* and only 40 per cent of accountants are thought to belong to the merchant castes. The distribution of Brahmins in different roles in the market follows the opposite trajectory. Whilst amongst the traders there are almost no Brahmins, amongst *dalals* we find roughly 20 per cent and amongst accountants 30 per cent Brahmins.

Caste, regional origin and economic power are all significant factors of identity in the market place but their particular relevance varies in different professions. For example, although the traders share a similar background in terms of region and caste, it is their access to capital that gives them their distinctiveness in the market. Among coolies it is regional origin rather than caste identity that is emphasized. In each case what really matters are the networks that one's identity enables one to tap into both in terms of business and social relations. However one cannot fail to notice the almost total absence of Muslims in the market with the exception of a few Muslim coolies mainly from Rajasthan.

The Trade

Most of the grain which passes through Delhi is neither produced nor processed nor consumed in Delhi itself. The grain market of Delhi constitutes one of many elements in the global network which feeds the grain market of north India. Before the grain reaches the market in Delhi, most of it has already gone through the hands of local and regional traders. Moreover, in the case of rice, it will also have passed through the hands of factory owners for processing. Similarly, when it leaves Delhi, it will generally be resold to other regional traders who will go on to sell it to shopkeepers before it finally reaches the consumer.

Delhi's importance as one of the largest grain markets of Asia cannot however be understood purely in terms of economic logic. A variety of factors, political and historical as well as fiscal and cultural, come into play. Delhi's relative proximity to the most fertile tracts of the Indo-Gangetic plain and the importance of a trading community which has kept multiple links with these regions play an important role; as does the centrality of Delhi in the railway network of India and the existence of an important consumer market which guarantees the existence of a minimal demand for agricultural products. However, the importance of Delhi as the epicentre of grain transaction also rests on more fragile foundations: according to market people, one of the main reasons why most of the grain passes through the capital and is not sent directly from the producer to the consumer area is fiscal. Similarly, the importance of Delhi as the main place for the export of rice is primarily due to reasons which are more political and institutional than strictly economic. Technically, it is due to the fact that Delhi has obtained the legal and fiscal status of a 'dry port',[8] but it is no doubt also influenced by the fact that Delhi, as the capital, is also the place where political decisions are taken and policies made.

Not only are the reasons for the centrality of Delhi in the network of grain markets in north India many, but the general organization of the grain trade itself is also rather intricate. Basically, the market for grains and pulses in north India is divided into two. This is because the Indian government enforces an agricultural policy whereby a large proportion of each year's production of grain is sold to the state at prices fixed by the administration. Government institutions also have the responsibility for storing and distributing this part of the produce; or eventually selling it on the free market in order to regulate the price of agricultural goods. Such a policy is increasingly being contested nowadays, partly because of the general trend toward liberalization and partly due to accusations of inefficiency and embezzlement against the government. Nevertheless, one should not forget that it was the direct involvement of the Indian state in the grain market that helped India attain its nutritional autonomy from the 1960s; and also that in spite of its relative inefficiency, the procurement system plays a role in fighting speculation, price variations and hoarding practices in the grain market.[9] Finally, there is no guarantee that the full liberalization of the grain market would, in any sense, be more profitable for the ordinary people of India. But whatever the case may be, it is the remaining part of each year's production which is traded on a free-market basis in Naya Bazaar and in the other grain markets of north India.

The importance of this free-market should not, however, be underestimated, not only because it is one of the market places where representatives of the state intervene, often massively, in their attempt to stabilize the price and the supply of food grain in India, but also because the physical trade and turnover of a market like Naya Bazaar is far greater than what official records and statistics imply.[10] This is particularly the case because Naya Bazaar remains one of the most important markets for agricultural products which has succeeded in avoiding becoming officially a 'regulated' market.[11] The market people of Delhi are among the very few trading communities to have managed successfully to retain the entire and exclusive control of a market of such importance. This is also what makes it such an interesting place for studying the role of intermediaries.

THE INVENTION OF THE MARKET SCENE

The Making of Marketable Goods

One of the most common activities that can be seen in Naya Bazaar is the making up of grain samples. This is done by using an instrument known as a *parkhi*, which looks somewhat like a dagger with a small gutter down the centre. The instrument is inserted into the side of a bag of grain in such a way that when it is withdrawn it brings with it a few grains for inspection. According to the number of bags which have to be checked, the trader or his assistant will systematically take tiny samples of grains from each bag or from an arbitrary selection of them. Nowadays, the samples are generally kept in small plastic bags with just a few indications written on them regarding the provenance and the quantity of the grain. But in Naya Bazaar it is still possible to see intermediaries using the old technique of transporting samples in carefully knotted folds of cloth.

It might appear to some that the technique of creating samples constitutes only a small ethnographic detail which does not have much to do either with the general organization of the market or with the principles of market economy. But as I have briefly hinted before, this is not the case: in more than one sense this very simple technique of sampling could be said to define the specific space of the market more than anything else.

There are various points at stake here. The first obvious point is that grain is both voluminous and heavy in proportion to its cost and it is therefore difficult to survey precisely what each bag contains. Traders and intermediaries have to deal everyday with transactions which represent hundreds of tons of goods. This is obviously difficult to do. There are basically two ways of transmitting information: either 'analogically' by transmitting some of the physical qualities of the data through a channel of communication; or 'digitally' by coding all the relevant information. The choice of method employed in trading is no different. The use of samples can be considered as an 'analogical' technique while the use of a 'gradation' system in order to communicate the quality of the grain can be identified a 'digital' one.

In India there have been numerous attempts to introduce a system of gradation which could conveniently be used by all market people to assess more simply and more quickly the quality of grain all over the country.[12] Such a system of grading has effectively been put into use in the case of certain agricultural products but it has not been generalized until now in the case of Naya Bazaar. Market people are on the whole opposed to the idea. According to them there are just too many types of grain of too many different qualities for such a system to be functional; it would either be too imprecise or too complicated. Only the biggest traders and exporters seem to be in favour of such a system. But they are also keen that the grain production of the entire country be radically homogenized because of the specific requirement of their politic of commercialization.

The quick succession of small gestures which allow traders and commercial intermediaries to assess the quality of a grain sample have a quasi-ritual quality and it is obvious to any observer that it is at such moments that market people employ all their commercial acumen. It is on the basis of this that they will make their own estimation of the price they are ready to pay for the grain. They will also have to judge the quality of grain and calculate what the potential demand for it might be, according to its price and the evolution of the market.

Another noticeable point in the way market people use such samples is their apparent absence of doubt about whether the grain they eventually receive will correspond to the sample. One might think this irrelevant because traders generally pay for the totality of the grain they buy only after they have had the chance to check its quantity and quality. But it must also be recognized that at the time that they check it, any calling into question of the deal would certainly be contested and would become a matter of irritation and loss of time if not a direct loss of money for all the operators involved. Neither should one conclude that the possibility that a load of grain does not correspond to what is expected is so uncommon in this trade. Two examples serve to illustrate the point.

The first concerns the difficulties encountered by Indian exporters on the international market after the exceptional year of 1995-6. It so happened that in this year India was practically the only big rice-growing country to have had a good level of production while the production among nearly all the other main rice suppliers of the world was low. As a result India had the opportunity to export more than it had ever done before on the international market.[13] And because huge quantities had been kept in reserve in state granaries, which proved unnecessary because of the abundance of the crop, the government institutions in charge of these reserves were allowed to sell huge quantities of rice to exporters at the market price. At the time no one bothered much about the quality of the rice. This was the rice which was usually sold in government shops to people who are not in a position to protest.[14] But foreign importers were inevitably more fastidious. As a consequence, well-established exporters complained the following year that speculators had, within a single year, succeeded in lowering India's reputation on the international rice market.[15]

The second example takes us to the other end of the economic and geographic spectrum. Just adjacent to one side of Naya Bazaar is an unauthorized market, populated almost exclusively by immigrant Biharis. Here grain is sold to Delhites of modest income at heavily discounted prices. These shops are filled with grain, which has been sold by the traders of Naya Bazaar at a cheap rate, usually because, for some reason, it did not fit their expectations when they checked its quality. One of the petty traders of this market explained the principle of a trick which consisted of asking accomplices to add discreetly a little dirt to one or two bags of rice of good quality so that when a trader in Naya Bazaar takes his sample he is likely to reject the bags and to end up selling them very cheaply to marginal traders.

Such examples are obviously extreme; taken too far they would imply a radical contrast between how traders behave when they deal with insiders or with outsiders: while according to one example they do not hesitate to discount a bag of best quality rice if it contains a little dirt, according to the other example, they are apparently less scrupulous in dealing with public organizations or with the foreign market. Such an interpretation would surely be exaggerated. Nevertheless, knowing the difficulties linked with the assessment of the quality of the merchandise in this trade, one should not underestimate the achievement of a market organization which allows a few thousand people to make transactions which may amount to thousands of bags of 100 kg everyday, on the basis of a few handfuls of grain circulating from hand to hand. This is possible precisely because market transactions combine two sorts of interpersonal relationship. On the one hand, buyers and sellers remain largely anonymous to each other ; on the other hand, at every stage of the market process, transactions are made exclusively by persons who know each other personally. These two relationships no longer seem contradictory once we begin to recognize the role of the intermediary in the functioning of the market. It is because all transactions are mediated by them that buyers and sellers don't have to know each other; but it is also because of their presence and of their intimate knowledge of all market actors that all transactions are done between persons who know each other.

The Personification of the Market Actors

Naya Bazaar is certainly one of the most crowded areas of Delhi. But unlike many other parts of the old city this crowding is not due to the influx of clients and passers-by. As a matter of fact, one could spend days observing the activity of the market and the unfolding of transactions, without ever meeting any of the people who have either supplied or bought the grain sold in the market. If by any chance one of them happens to come to the market it is usually not to negotiate or conclude a deal but rather to socialize with traders, to check the pulse of market activity, to resolve a problem or to settle a dispute. Basically, the only people there who are not based in Delhi are commercial intermediaries who have come on behalf of factory owners or regional traders in order to sell some grain to the Delhi traders. As a consequence, one of the main characteristics of this market is the way in which it functions almost exclusively on the basis of transactions between the market people of Naya Bazaar themselves. One proof is the fact that if one were coming to the market in order to buy or to sell anything without being represented or, at least, very strongly introduced and recommended by some insider, not only would that person risk being neglected but he would also find that the only possible transaction open to him would be the direct exchange of cash against merchandise. In other words, he would not be allowed to benefit from the full potentialities of the market.

The attraction of Delhi as one of the most important market places for the grain trade is, as already pointed out, due to a variety of factors. Among them one reason which seems to have played a particularly important role is the major way in which the traders of Delhi have always assumed not only the role of trader but also that of an *adati* (commission agent). Basically, the traders of Naya Bazaar have been able to attract a large supply of grain (especially after the harvest when the prices are low) by offering to pay their clients in advance approximately 70 or 80 per cent of the sum they will get later on when their grain will be sold in the market place. Once this is done, they will give the grain seller the remaining part of the price, and only then claim their own commission.

What is remarkable about such a procedure is that large reserves of grain immediately disposable for sale are continuously stocked in the capital. And because Delhi traders generally offer credit to the buyers of the grain, Naya Bazaar benefits from the reputation of being the place where, at any given point of time, supplies are abundant and transactions swift and not too hampered by heavy administrative control. On the one hand, suppliers have some sort of guarantee that they can get almost immediately a large percentage of the price they want for their grain, without having to face the alternative of waiting for a customer or to sell their grain too cheaply; on the other hand, buyers will also be reasonably sure that at any given time they will be able to find the quantity and the quality of grain they need.

As already noted, one of the basic assumptions of the economic literature about markets is that the confrontation between buyers and sellers is the focal point in any market transaction. It is of course recognized that such a confrontation is often mediated by all sorts of intermediaries. But the latter are generally perceived to be standing in for the real partners of the exchange. If they involve themselves in a deal, they are quickly suspected of distorting the functioning of the market process. But in the case of a market like Naya Bazaar, it is practically the opposite which is true. Not only do the buyers and sellers seldom meet each other; but the distinction between a trader who buys a load of grain in order to sell it later to one of his customers and the one who does it from the beginning on behalf of one of his customers is almost imperceptible. More fundamentally, the practice of traders who are being paid only on a commission basis but who nevertheless advance most of the price of the grain to the seller before the transaction takes place, blurs practically any distinction between the main partners of a transaction (the 'real' buyers and the 'real' sellers) and the intermediaries. It does not make sense to consider a trader who has paid in advance 80 per cent of a load of grain which is stocked in a godown belonging to him and who has the charge of selling it on behalf of his client as a simple intermediary. Similarly, if he buys some grain with his own money for a client who has given precise indications of the quality and quantity of grain he wants, and if he takes only a fixed commission on the price, will he be considered as a trader or as a commission agent? Such distinctions seem somewhat immaterial at the time of the transaction.

Let us now summarize: In the streets of Naya Bazaar, not only are huge loads of grain replaced by tiny samples of grain but, as we have just seen, the people who sell the grain to Delhi and those who buy it from Delhi are 'replaced' by the market people who more or less assume their roles during the transaction. But this is not all. There is yet another aspect to the 'immateriality' of the functioning of this market that I wish to stress. One normally will not see, either at Naya Bazaar or elsewhere in Delhi, traders negotiating directly the exact terms of a transaction. If necessary, there is the possibility of contacting each other by telephone, fax or letter. But until now these remain only auxiliary channels of communication. Normally all transactions which take place between market actors are mediated by specialized intermediaries who interpose themselves not only on behalf of outsiders who cannot be present in Delhi but also on behalf of insiders within the market itself. Almost all transactions take place through intermediaries.[16] As one trader explained to me: even if he had to negotiate a deal with his immediate neighbours, he would always prefer to do it through an intermediary.

The Making of Transactions

Every morning, dozens of intermediaries will visit each trader in Naya Bazaar to enquire if they have some load of grain to be sold. After assessing the quality of the samples, they will enter into discussion with the traders to sort out what can be reasonably expected from a given load of grain. Having made their first round of the traders, they will have a certain amount of grain samples and will renew contact with certain traders, either by telephoning them or by meeting them directly. This time their aim will be not only to assess the offer of the day but also to find in the market a demand which corresponds to it. Though one should not take such estimations too seriously, I have tried to calculate the number of personal interactions which take place between traders and intermediaries in the market every working day: according to this estimate, there should be no less than 30,000 of them (and probably much more). Once market intermediaries have found a potential demand for an offer of grain on the market, they will be used as go-betweens throughout the duration of the transaction, which will normally last anything from one to three days. It is generally only after the conditions of a deal have been agreed to that the partners of the transaction will enter into a brief contact, usually by telephone, in order to confirm their agreement. But if they trust the intermediaries and know with whom they are dealing, they often will not bother making even this brief contact.

Moreover, the intermediaries function more than simply as go-betweens. Even if they are not financially or legally responsible, their reputations are at stake when they organize or supervise a deal. When they buy grain, traders consider it equally the responsibility of the intermediaries in whom they put their trust to make sure that the quality of the grain effectively corresponds to what they have been shown in the sample. And when they go on to sell it, they expect a certain guarantee that the buyers will effectively repay their credit.

Finally, in a market like Naya Bazaar, the conditions of a transaction obviously have to be agreed to by all the partners involved. Generally, there is no written contract to confirm the terms of agreement. Thus, one of the most important functions of market intermediaries is to stand as witnesses to any agreements that are made under their supervision.

THE LOGIC OF THE MARKET

What makes the importance of a market place like Naya Bazaar, and what distinguishes it fundamentally from a simple collection of individual firms, is the fact that most transactions involve at least four main protagonists: besides the ones who supply the grain to Delhi and those who buy it from Delhi, there are generally two local traders who play an intermediary role in the transaction (acting either as traders *stricto sensu* or as commission agents). Moreover, as I have already pointed out, *dalals* are also used as intermediaries to establish and maintain the contact between each of these 'main actors'.

The fact that there are two traders rather than one involved directly in most market transactions may seem yet again an insignificant detail. However, it is precisely this fact which changes the nature of the majority of transactions in the market: as long as a trader sells only what he has already bought or buys only what he will be able to sell to his own clients, the extent of his operations will necessarily be limited; but if traders do not hesitate—as appears to be the case—to sell to their own customers whatever grain is available on the market, and if they do not hesitate either to buy grain in order to sell it themselves or on behalf of their clients to other market people, then each of them is able to give their clients access to all the demands and/or supplies available in the market. Or, rather they are able to do it insofar as they are able to diffuse market information and to facilitate transactions which may involve and mobilize quickly a vast number of local traders.

What characterizes such a market, then, is the fact that it blurs the distinction which is usually made between bazaars and markets, and more generally between 'real' markets and supposedly less 'rational' institutions. Basically, in this system people only effectuate transactions with those they know. Yet, at the same time, they get access through these intermediaries to all the other resources available in the market place.

The Inevitability of Intermediaries

Intermediaries are generally ill considered in any sort of deal. It is not surprising to find that the connotations associated with the term *dalal* in India are none too flattering. The mediation of a *dalal* in any transaction rapidly evokes the image of a world of opacity, of dubious patronage and shady negotiations, if not more radically, of illegality, blackmail, and corruption. Many people in the Indian capital feel that the role of *dalals* in most domains of the social and economic life of Delhi should be deplored or perceived as some sort of social pathology. Nonetheless it is worth noting that two different criticisms are often blended in such condemnation in spite of being based on very different sets of implicit assumptions: On the one hand, the intervention of *dalals* in diverse social transactions is commonly considered a blatant symptom of the extent to which commercialization and financial greed have pervaded the social life of the whole city. In this sense they are perceived as the very personification of the logic of the market. But on the other hand, they are often also perceived to represent the proof that a particular society or a specific economic sector has not yet attained the status of a mature market. Viewed in this perspective market intermediaries are criticized for introducing a strong element of opacity into economic transactions.

What I have attempted to show in this essay is that the distinction between a market like Naya Bazaar and a simple collection of individual traders lies mainly in the existence of intermediaries who mediate between the partners of commercial transactions. It would be erroneous to assume that with the generalization of market culture, intermediaries such as those found in Naya Bazaar will disappear. In fact, the idea that markets could exist without intermediaries is really little more than an intellectual illusion or ideological mystification. The condemnation of *dalals* is little more than the condemnation of market institution itself. But of course, intermediaries can always change their tune. Perhaps the *dalals* of the future will all have degrees in marketing and advertising.

NOTES

The research for this project on the grain market of Delhi is part of a collaborative project between the French Institute of Research for Development (IRD,Paris), the Centre de Sciences Humaines (CSH, New Delhi) and the Centre for the Study of Developing Societies (CSDS, New Delhi). It has benefited from the financial support of IRD and the CNRS (action concertée en sciences sociales IRD-CNRS). I want to thank particularly the people of

Khari Baoli who have been kind enough to take interest in my research and answer patiently my questions. And I would like to thank also Rajender Singh Negi whose personal assistance has been invaluable for the ethnographic study of this market in 1997.

1. See Véronique Dupont's essay in this volume.
2. Cf. in particular, F. Braudel, *Civilisation matérielle, Economie et Capitalisme, XV-XVIIIème siecle, T. 2. Les jeux de l'échange,* Paris: Armand Collin, 1979.
3. M. Granovetter, 'Economic Action and Social Structure: The Problem of Embeddedness', in M. Granovetter and R. Swedberg (eds.), *The Sociology of Economic Life,* Boulder: Westview Press, 1992.
4. For example, cf. C.J. Fuller, 'Misconceiving the Grain Heap: a Critique of the Concept of the Indian Jajmani System', in Parry and Bloch, *Money and the Morality of Exchange,* Cambridge: Cambridge University Press, 1989 and S. Subrahmanyam 'Institutions, Agency and Economic Change in South Asia: a Survey and Some Suggestions', in B. Stein and S. Subrahmanyam, *Institutions and Economic Change in South Asia,* Delhi: OUP, 1996.
5. C. Geertz, 'The Bazaar Economy: Information and Search in Peasant Marketing', in M. Granovetter and R. Swedberg (eds.), *The Sociology of Economic Life,* Boulder: Westview Press, 1992.
6. Ibid., p. 230 (the three quotations).
7. These figures have been obtained by using a combination of quantitative and qualitative measures with the help of traders and diverse professionals associated with the market.
8. The expression 'dry port' basically means that all customs operations and formalities concerning the exportation and importation of goods can be done within Delhi itself as if it were a border. The goods, therefore, remain in sealed containers on the Indian territory before eventually being shipped abroad.
9. In contrast with the very small body of literature dedicated to the empirical functioning of wholesale markets like the one which is studied here (for an exception see the works of Barbara Harriss-White (in particular: B. Harriss-White, *A Political Economy of Agricultural Markets in South India,* Delhi: Sage, 1996), there is an abundance on the appraisal of the procurement policy by the Indian State. Cf. S.S. Acharya and N.L. Agarwal, *Agricultural Marketing in India,* Delhi: OUP, 1987, pp. 216-302.
10. 'In 1994-1995, as much as 60 per cent of the food subsidy in 1994-1995 went to finance the buffer stock, sales on the open market, or export (World Bank 1996)'. P. Balakrishnan and B. Ramaswami, *Economic and Political Weekly,* 25-31 January 1997, p. 165.
11. For an excellent study of the impact of regulation on agricultural markets in India, cf. B. Harriss-White 'Order, Order . . . Agro-commercial Micro-Structures and the State: The Experience of Regulation' in B. Stein and S. Subrahmanyam, op. cit., 1996.
12. Ibid., pp. 81-93.
13. In 1995-6, India, which only began to export rice in the late seventies, emerged as the second largest world exporter with about 5 millions of tons.
14. Cf. P. Balakrishnan and B. Ramaswami, 'Quality of Public Distribution System. Why it matters', *Economic and Political Weekly,* 25-31 January 1997, p. 162.
15. One could even find a mild echo of this polemic in the very offical magazine of the All India Rice Exports Association: 'Today, though we have managed to make our presence felt in the graph of global rice trade, yet till now we are not able to create a goodwill which USA or Thailand enjoys. However, few Indian rice shipments made last year by opportunist exporters and importers did invite some criticism on the quality front', *Rice India,* January 1997, p. 21.
16. 'I never go to meet my parties. I've "seen" Sethji also only on phone. It is for the first time that I am seeing him face to face. It's the mutual trust that makes all the difference in this trade. And I too have come here for the reasons of restoring that trust.' Excerpt of an interview during an arbitration meeting at the Delhi Grain Merchant Association, 14 April 1997.

PART III

MONUMENTS OF POWER

8

The Contemporary Architecture of Delhi: The Role of the State as Middleman

A.G. KRISHNA MENON

Delhi 'looks' different. A visitor to Delhi is struck by the nature of its physical development, which sets it apart from other urban centres in the country. In fact it is so different that it would be incorrect to generalize about other Indian cities from the Delhi experience. 'Delhi is not India, and India not Delhi' is a cautionary maxim for any would-be theorist. Yet, architectural critics have generalized indiscriminately and have been unable to distinguish the characteristics that set Delhi apart from the rest of the country. Instead of studying the diverse range of regional architectures, they have pursued pan-Indian themes and constructions of 'Indian identity' in their efforts to explain the architecture of the country as a whole and, in turn, that of Delhi. This is largely because of their Orientalist predisposition in thinking architecture[1] and also because the architecture of Delhi does, perhaps, share some characteristics with the architecture of other parts of the country.

After all, Delhi shares the same construction industry characterized by its primitive technology and archaic management practices. It also shares the same architectural culture and often the same architects who are products of a common system of education.[2] Even the attitude of the patrons is surprisingly common in the manner they deal with architects and architecture all over this diverse country, whether they be elite patrons, bureaucrats, executives in industrial and commercial organizations or the public-at-large in whose name much is built: the history of modernization in the country has to a great extent marginalized the role of the architect in the development of the built environment and contributed to unflattering perceptions of their work as professionals. These perceptions are also the outcome of the sociology of the profession as it has developed from its colonial roots.[3] People commonly believe that the services of the architect are easily substituted by the skill and knowledge of a common mason, or by a civil engineer if the safety of the structure is under consideration, or by any indigent architect available and willing to work at ridiculously low fees. Architects and architecture in Delhi share all these 'problems' with the rest of the country.

But what sets Delhi apart is the strong interventionist role of the state in the development of the profession and the physical constituents of the city. The state has been a strong presence all over the country because until recently, the government was attempting to impose a Soviet-inspired command economy to bring about development. But the influence of state control has been particularly strong in Delhi, because of its special administrative status as the capital of the country.

Until recently, Delhi was administred directly by the central government. It now enjoys political autonomy but this is still contingent on close co-ordination with the central government on all policy matters. Therefore, it is hardly surprising to find that in the past the architecture of Delhi has been decisively mediated by the agency of the state in a manner and to a scale not witnessed in other Indian cities or states. The state as middleman has brokered a disproportionately large share of the country's scarce resources for the development of Delhi, and the results of this bounty are manifestly evident: to the poor from distant crisis-prone areas in terms of job opportunities and bounty and to the better off in terms of better services, amenities and facilities. The metaphor that Delhi's roads are paved with gold rings true to many and has attracted migrants of all classes from every part of the country making it one of the fastest growing metropolises in the country.[4] But how has this munificence influenced the act of form-making and place-making in Delhi?

THE EXHIBITION PROJECT

To find out, the TVB School of Habitat Studies, New Delhi (TVB/SHS) undertook a research project during the academic year 1997-8 as an extra-curricular programme involving a large number of students and faculty. The mass of data collected and the debates they provoked are still being analysed, and will, no doubt, provide grist for much theorizing long after the project is completed. But an empirical understanding of Delhi's architecture is already emerging and taking shape in the form of a critical exhibition of contemporary architecture in Delhi. This essay is essentally a personal reflection but is derived and based on that collective exercise.

The research project was predicated on two premises: first, that Indian academics' involvement in 'thinking' architecture had been insufficient for arriving at appropriate theories; and second, the little theorizing that had been attempted was invariably cast in an Orientalist mould which homogenized a diverse range of regional architectures and architectures-in-the-making, under the overall rubric of 'Indianness'. From a methodological perspective, it was also decided that the project should focus on a part of the whole, surveying about 200 buildings built in Delhi since 1947, in an attempt to gain empirical understanding of the circumstances which governed their production, and to identify patterns and processes which would help to illuminate the specificity of the architecture of Delhi.

The understanding that is emerging from this study contests the impression one gets from the literature available on the architectures of India which implies that a single meta-narrative has dominated the architectural production of buildings of significance in the country: that is the search for 'Indianness'.[5] But one knows by common sense and also simply by looking around that this must never have been the case: deeper reflection on this point would inevitably reveal the multiplicity of narratives of architectural development during the past fifty years, each as varied as the diverse regions of the country. One would realize that the many regional architectures have been contested and redefined by different communities to create what is today a truly eclectic variety of architecture in the country; yet, the focus of architectural writing has persistently been on imagined pan-Indian themes. The cultural process of contestation and reflexive redefinition is clearly evident in the rich variety of literature found in the country[6] and in the diversity of fine arts;[7] but no one has seriously attempted to examine the existence of such variety in the field of architecture. As in the case of literature and the arts, such an attempt requires a critical shift of focus in architectural theorizing away from pan-Indian themes to more regional, context-specific ones. The need to shift the focus from the whole to the part is already acknowledged in other parts of the world where the purposeful study of regional architecture is accepted as an useful academic objective. Writing about the American scene, Rafael Maneo states,

> Today's American scene seems to reflect the decentralized, or many-centered, structure of this country more than ever. It would be impossible to speak of 'style' or 'manner' without associating these with a specific geographical location or with a very precise socio-economic group. . . . I firmly believe that if we want to understand the message that is emerging from today's American architecture, we first need to provide a free view of the panorama.[8]

The TVB/SHS project recognized the necessity of providing just such 'a free view of the panorama' in Indian architectural studies before trying to 'understand the message' that is emerging from the architecture of India as a whole.

There were several conceptual issues that dogged the project. Does Delhi constitute a 'region'? And if so, what are its boundaries? We decided to focus within the political boundaries of Delhi, though we were aware of architectural developments taking place in the hinterland. We felt that future studies could try to define the boundaries of the 'influence zone' of Delhi. We also hope that other regions of the country would be studied by other schools and scholars, and that through this process several regional narratives of architectural development might be brought forth to provide a 'free view of the panorama'. It is only after such a process that attempts might be made to develop meta-narratives to describe the synoptic 'essence' or the 'deep structure' of the contemporary architecture of India.

The period 1947-97, which delimited this study, was in many ways arbitrary, but we retained it with the view that future studies might extend the temporal boundaries. It must be admitted however, that the Golden Jubilee of India's Independence provided a convenient marker and a provocative catalyst for the project. What have we achieved in the first fifty years of our Independence? This question takes on added significance in the context of the impending millennium milestone: what are the prospects for the next fifty years?

Having established the objectives of the study, the problem of methodology remained. What criterion should be used to select buildings for the survey and what classification system should be used to present them? To begin with, only 'known' buildings were selected covering all functional types (offices, hotels, institutional buildings, commercial complexes, residences, etc.) in each of the five decadal periods being studied. This information constituted the data bank. The data bank was of course open to several interpretations. In this essay I shall focus on only one of the interpretations which can be construed from mapping the architecture of Delhi: the decisive role of the state in mediating its development.

This interpretation also offers a different insight into the development of the profession. For example, it is possible to argue that contrary to the cherished perceptions amongst architects regarding their intellectual autonomy, what emerges from the study is that such perceptions are largely unfounded, and that the development of the profession has been the outcome of the demands made on it by the state. There were no Howard Roarks[9] battling the 'system' in the history of contemporary architecture in Delhi/India—architects were the complicit agents of a powerful state.

As in Washington DC, Canberra and Islamabad, the presence of the government in Delhi is unavoidable. These are all capital cities: *prima inter urbis* and, therefore, enjoy special status not accorded to other cities in the country. In the case of Delhi, this status confined the economic role of the city to its function as an administrative centre during the decades following Independence. The economy itself was strongly state directed and investments oriented towards decentralizing development away from metropolitan centres as a broad objective. That this policy did not succeed is another story but—in the case of Delhi—the reason for its failure is precisely because of the presence and power of the bureaucracy in a strongly state-controlled economy. The bottleneck in the decision-making process inevitably subverted the overt intent to decentralize development and willy-nilly attracted commercial and industrial activity because businesses sought to benefit from proximity to the corridors of power. Thus, in spite of a strong state policy objective to decentralize development, the opposite resulted, and Delhi grew to become a diverse mega-city like any other metropolitan centre in the country, acquiring in the process the very qualities of predator-like primacy that the initial policy-makers had wished to avoid.[10] This essay argues that the agency of state policy was also significant to the development of a distinct architectural culture in the city as well.

THE 'AURA' OF DELHI

With hindsight, it might be argued that the distinctive architectural culture which developed in Delhi was historically inevitable. Without going into the history of the seven, eight, or nine Delhis—whichever way one wants to read this complex history—it can be argued that what all these past Delhis shared in common was the 'aura' of being a capital city and for centuries this characteristic persisted. School textbooks have taught generations of students that those who ruled Delhi ruled India. Each succeeding dynasty contributed to this aura through public works. Consequently, Delhi is today littered with the architectural evidence of their efforts. A recent survey conducted by INTACH recorded over 1200 extant buildings considered worth conserving for their intrinsic heritage value.[11] The modern phase in the development of Delhi's aura began in 1912 with the building of the Imperial capital of the British Indian Empire at Delhi. Edwin Lutyens' design for the new capital was deeply inflected with intimations of its imperial glory (Plate 8.1). Lutyens' baroque city plan and the setting of the capital complex on Raisina Hill invested the project with qualities of landscaped order and monumentality which were to become established as the hallmarks of the urban environment of Delhi in subsequent years; and this is largely why Delhi 'looks' different. After Independence, continuing the pursuit of these urban and architectural intentions became an article of faith with the planners of Delhi. Thus the Preamble to the Master Plan for Delhi, Perspective 2001, states:

> Delhi, the focus of the socio-economic and political life of India, a symbol of ancient values and present aspirations, the Capital of the largest democracy, is assuming increasing eminence among the great cities of the world. The city of Delhi has a distinct personality. Imbibed in it, is the history of centuries, in its parts it has the grand vistas of New Delhi and the throbbing lanes of Shahjahanabad. It is a gem with many facets.[12]

The iconic power of Lutyens' Delhi (still referred to in municipal terminology as Delhi Imperial Zone or the DIZ area) can be judged by the fact that it is the only urban ensemble in the city that is effectively protected against development—not Shahjahanabad (in fact, until recently it was classified as a notified slum) or any or the earlier Delhis (though some are declared protected).[13] This can perhaps be explained by the fact that Lutyens' Delhi is where the political and bureaucratic elite live and work and that they have a vested interest in protecting their privileged lifestyles (Plate 8.2). The aura of Delhi's urban aesthetics is also expressed in other ways, such as in the attempt to keep the city 'green', and in the conceiving of large city-building projects that are seldom attempted in other cities. Building on a grand scale is typical of Delhi's architecture, and this predilection is linked to perceptions of Delhi's aura.

But, curiously, the ancient monuments of Delhi themselves have not had a significant impact on the local architectural imagination. Architects in Delhi tend to refer to Jaisalmer and Fatehpur Sikri[14] more often than they do to the local monuments of the Khiljis, the Tughlaks, the Lodis or Mughals, all of whom contributed to the aura of Delhi before the British Empire. In fact, the architecture of British Imperial India appears to be more influential in the production of contemporary architecture in Delhi than the architecture of any of the preceding centuries,[15] although this fact is seldom acknowledged by those who write on contemporary architecture. The overwhelming reality is that contemporary architecture in Delhi suffers from amnesia. 'Tradition' in this context often does not seem to go further back than Delhi's most recent colonial history.

THE SEARCH FOR 'INDIANNESS'

However, at the time of Independence, there was an overt effort to erase the memory of the recent past and to forge a new 'Indian' architecture by looking either further into the past or into the future. The influence of the state in determining the characteristics of the new architecture was more direct and more evident at that time. Most of the buildings were being built by government architects for government use. To the government of a newly independent nation establishing an 'Indian identity' became an important political and aesthetic agenda, and architects working for the government were naturally expected to infuse their works with indigenous character. Two styles of architecture emerged in response to this imperative.

The two buildings that typify these styles are the Ashok Hotel (1956) and the Headquarters of the Council of Scientific and Industrial Research (CSIR) (1959). The Ashok Hotel (Plate 8.3) represents the revivalist position, where architects sought motifs from the past to embellish buildings which were built with contemporary materials and addressed contemporary requirements. The architect of the CSIR building, on the other hand, followed the tenets of the international style, and attempted to create an indigenous version of 'Indian modernism'.

The development of both styles grew out of state direction. The revivalist ideology had broad appeal amongst the intelligentsia and was supported by engineers, senior bureaucrats and politicians who, by virtue of their hierarchic superiority in decision-making could ensure that buildings reflected their tastes.[16] Thus, even if government architects had other ideas, they could do very little because they were then, as indeed they still are, low-level functionaries, expected to go along with their superiors' views. Naturally, architectural malapropism resulted, and this is how one would describe the numerous Krishi Bhawans and Vigyan Bhawans built by government architects at that time.

Responding to the call of the international style, under the circumstances, required enlightened patrons willing to give modernism a try. A.P. Kanvinde, who was a government architect when he designed CSIR, credits its head, Dr Shanti Swaroop Bhatnagar, for reposing faith in his 'new' architectural ideas.[17] Even here, we are faced to acknowledge the evidence of architects acceding to their hierarchic superior's views. Jawaharlal Nehru, for example, rejected Habib Rehman's first proposal for Rabindra Bhawan

(1961), saying that it did not have the spirit of Tagore, though he was pleased with the final result.[18] Like Nehru, there were other ministers, bureaucrats and other hierarchically senior decision-makers who had no compunctions about imposing their tastes on hapless architects. Even today senior bureaucrats continue to 'instruct' architects because, in their view, aesthetic matters are as much their prerogative as management issues. Perhaps this imposition reflects the Indian view that 'wisdom' in all matters is acquired through age (or superior managerial position).

It is not possible to view these architectural styles as 'theories'; they were not. In fact, they were only reflections of the prevalent social reality. This social reality was dominated by a rationalist and interventionist approach to social and economic development under state control and this ideology got transferred to the production of architecture. The country had to be modernized quickly to 'catch up' with the West. As the modernization ideology spread, the desire to modernize in almost every aspect of state action beyond the purely economic, came to be regarded as a policy goal in itself. Developments in architecture of the period must be seen in this light (Plate 8.4). Architects naturally wished to modernize the country through the medium of architecture and aligned themselves with the dominant views of state policy. Thus, the state was very much the middleman in the production of architecture during this period, determining whether architects promote continuity with the past or emulate the West.

In the meantime many architects went abroad (or were sent abroad on government scholarships) for training, learnt Western ways and returned to preach and practice their newly acquired faith. They had seen the future and were converted. On their return, they proselytized as only the newly converted could. Their precise affiliations to modernism differed, according to where they had acquired it: Harvard, MIT, or Liverpool or some other Western university where a particular brand of modernism was taught. They learnt the solution before they returned to understand the problem. They obviously made a 'difference' when they returned to practice at home, but their works were not the kind of reflexive architectural developments one would have expected from members of a confident profession after the attainment of Independence. If one compares this to developments in Russia after the October 1917 Revolution, for example,[19] one understands the dimensions of failure that characterized such architecture. Indian architects did not revolt against the colonial order. Having always collaborated with the colonial architectural project, they had no reason to critically examine its legacy on achieving freedom. Talk of revivalism under the circumstances was merely self-flagellation, and the pursuit of modernism another politically correct style-of-the-moment acquired by individual architects. Gunnar Myrdal, analysing the planning policies of this period attributed its ineffectiveness to the 'soft state'.[20] The failure of architects to achieve their desired transformative goals might equally be attributed to the fact that architecture as it developed in India after Independence, turned out to be a 'soft profession'.

UTILITARIANISM

There are two other aspects of state policy as it emerged during the early years after Independence that had a bearing on subsequent development in architecture. One was the manner in which the role of politicians and bureaucrats got consolidated in the execution of projects (here I am not referring to their pervasive influence in matters of stylistic taste) and the other was the catalytic role of state-imposed austerity in triggering off the development of the self-indulgent and flamboyant architectural styles in Delhi as a reaction.

During the 1950s and 1960s, the government undertook massive development projects in the city through the Rehabilitation Ministry and the Improvement Trust. Their works had to be undertaken on a war-footing and required dynamic leadership. Ministers like Mehr Chand Khanna were key figures during this phase of the city's development, and his style of working became a model for later authoritarian builder-administrators like the New Delhi Municipal Committee (NDMC) Commissioner, Chhabra, and the Delhi Development Authority's (DDA) Vice Chairman, Jagmohan.[21] The development of Delhi well into the 1980s was characterized by the 'contributions' made by such authoritarian administrators. Their proclivity for building-by-fiat emerges as a characteristic of Delhi's architectural culture.

Khanna established many residential colonies like Lajpat Nagar and Rajinder Nagar to house refugees. He relied on enthusiastic young government architects who, basically, learnt through doing. In those days, there was no Master Plan or precedent to follow and one can easily see how through such on-the-spot decision-making, two important characteristics of Delhi's architecture became institutionalized: one, the power of the politician and/or bureaucrat to mediate building activity, and the other, the complicity of the architect in this process. This has had long-term effects on the profession because it undermined the architect's worth and ethical responsibilities. The initial constraint of emergency 'triage', as it were, became axiomatic: only immediate action rather than systematic planning was held to be effective. Consequently, designs necessarily had to be simple for quick implementation in the field, rather than the outcome of a more complex process of contemplation and reflexive thinking. A pernicious idea became established: architecture as expediency, characterized by the attitude '*sab chalta hai*' ('anything is acceptable'). Secrecy was the best antidote to public criticism or resistance. Much of the government-produced architecture and urban planning of the 1950s and 1960s can be rationalized on the basis of this pernicious mindset which unfortunately has become ingrained in architectural consciousness. As far as the quality of government architecture is concerned, matters have hardly improved. Today the government is less noticeable simply because it is no more such a dominant player in the city.

The second aspect of state policy, the constraints of economic austerity, was concomitant with state planning strategy. The Soviet-inspired command economy in force did not allow for extravagances in the construction of buildings and the need to cut costs became an important, if not the exclusive, objective in the design of buildings. The linking of austerity with poor design specifications appears to have affected the architectural imagination as well (Plates 8.5 and 8.6). Its impact on residential architecture of the period was particularly severe. Housing of this period was characterized by the flat roofs, external surfaces finished in plain plaster with cement or lime wash, with functional sunshades providing the only relief to an otherwise bland facade. Anything else would have been 'politically incorrect'. The buildings in the government housing colonies like Bapa Nagar and Kaka Nagar are examples of this style (Plate 8.7). Formulaic utilitarian modernism evolved out of this practice and architecture reflected the same ideology that defended the virtues of the ubiquitous Ambassador car in the face of global technological development and change. Exceptions, such as they exist, were reactions to this regimen of austerity, and the results were invariably outlandish. In hindsight, one wonders why these constraints were not made the basis for developing more compelling architecture. And the greater tragedy is that today, in the face of the stylistic amorality spawned by post-modernism, architects look back on the products of architectural utilitarianism with nostalgia and invest those unimaginative products with an importance they do not merit.

The elite—who were only a small class in a government-dominated economy—reacted against this regimen of austerity, and their ideals were realized by the Austrian *émigré*, K.M. Heinz. Heinz's production of *ersatz palazzos* and Spanish villas with icing-like decorations, pompous ducal crests, baroque mouldings, curlicued metal railings, improbable corinthian capitals and other incongruous European architectural elements obviously satisfied his elite clientele who craved for things foreign in these inward looking, austere times. Other architects followed his example (Plates 8.8 and 8.9). Thus, the ascetic ideals of Nehruvian socialism may have inadvertently and unexpectedly reinforced the allure of foreignness in architectural design, as embodied in Heinz's buildings, and were a prelude to the flamboyant architecture of the middle classes, which grew to blossom in the wake of economic liberalization in the 1980s and 1990s. Buildings in newer middle-class colonies like Shivalik Enclave (south of Panchsheel Park) and along Vikas Marg in East Delhi are, for example, products of the same reactionary impulses that generated the architecture of Heinz (Plate 8.15). The exuberant, if not comic results of this peculiar form of architectural expression have been vividly captured in the writings of Gautam Bhatia, as 'Punjabi Baroque', 'Marwari Mannerism', 'Early Halwai', 'Bania Gothic' and so forth.[22]

CATALYTIC POLICIES OF THE STATE

From the 1980s onwards, two other trends in housing have become evident. Again, both can be attributed to policies of the state. One can be generically defined as 'developer housing', replacing old stock in established residential colonies, and the other, the explosion of group housing projects on the periphery of the city. The monopolistic control of land by the DDA resulted in a dramatic rise in land values, and it became attractive to replace existing individual bungalows with apartment blocks, pushing to the limits (and usually, in connivance with municipal authorities, well beyond the limits) permissible building regulations. Citizens reacted to these blatant violations of building norms through Public Interest Litigations, establishing precedence for future consumer action in matters relating to deterioration in the quality of life. Here too the instrumentality of the state is evident in the form of judicial activism in architectural matters: yet again, it was not the profession that initiated reform. As a consequence, the character and quality of life in these residential neighbourhoods are changing. Besides, the incessant building and rebuilding in some residential colonies are turning them into permanent building sites. Most of the new 'developer housing', ironically enough, uses the 'colonial style' in their elevations.

The second trend, the development of group housing projects, is dramatically changing the skyline along the periphery of the city (Plate 8.10). Again, this is a direct consequence of the DDA's development strategy. Contrary to the natural market-directed tendency for the development of high-rise buildings in the centre of the city tapering to lower levels on the periphery, Delhi is currently acquiring the reverse profile of residential building heights, taking on the form of a doughnut with bungalows and very low densities at the centre, high-rise and high densities on the periphery with low-rise and medium densities in-between. This is the result of the implementation of a strong Master Plan.

The dramatic growth of the city following the partition of the country necessitated undertaking *ad hoc* developments which created obvious infrastructural and health problems. The necessity of formulating a Master Plan to guide the further growth of Delhi became evident and was undertaken by a team of foreign experts recruited by the Ford Foundation. The plan came into force in 1962. Their proposal for a poly-nodal structure with segregated land uses was an imported town-planning concept which had nothing in common with indigenous patterns of urban development. It was as alien as Lutyens' baroque city plan.[23] Consequently, its implementation over time has been characterized by non-conforming developments, which are later 'regularized'—to use planner's parlance—through the democratic political process. This is the source of the planner's bitter lament about 'political interference' but, in reality, the need to 'regularize' development is indicative of problems relating to the ideology of planners, not the political process. The inability of planners to comprehend and address the problems of Indian urbanism is, in fact, more tragic than the issue of political interference which is only to be expected in a healthy democracy. The problem with the planner's ideology does, however, go deeper than their predilection for imported strategies and has to do with their social ideals. Faced with a choice between a 'stable' West and a transforming East, the town-planner opts for the Western brand of equilibrium and certainty. As Edmond Leach has pointed out in a different context:

> [They] tended to borrow their primary concepts from Durkheim rather than from either Pareto or Max Weber. Consequently, they are greatly prejudiced in favour of societies which show symptoms of 'functional integration', 'social solidarity', 'cultural uniformity', 'structural equilibrium'. Such societies, which might well be regarded as moribund by historians or political scientists, are commonly looked upon by social anthropologists as healthy and ideally fortunate. Societies which display symptoms of faction and internal conflict leading to rapid change are on the other hand suspected of 'anomie' and 'pathological decay'.[24]

This accounts for the attitude of the Indian town-planner as well and the tragedy of modern Indian urban planning. If Delhi 'looks' different on this account, then it must be seen as the profession's failure to come to terms with the imperatives of Indian urbanism, and not its 'success'. Yet the appearance of 'success' has inspired other cities of the country to emulate the example of Delhi, thus spreading its influence far and wide.

The Delhi Master Plan legitimized the acquisition of almost all urbanizable land within the boundaries of the city. Land consolidation was, therefore, never a problem in Delhi and permitted the construction of a number of large-scale projects: District Centres (Nehru Place, Bhikaji Cama Place (Plate 8.11), Rajendra Place, Janakpuri District Centre, and when they are all completed there will be about 27 of them in Delhi); large public housing projects (Vasant Kunj, Kalkaji, Saket); sub-cities (Dwarka and Rohini both planned for housing over one million people); large campuses for educational institutions [the Indian Institute of Technology (Plate 8.13), Jawaharlal Nehru University, the South Campus of the University of Delhi], and a good distribution infrastructural facilities and amenities including neighbourhood parks, playgrounds, regional parks and 'urban forests'. Projects of such magnitude could rarely be matched or even conceived in other cities and the fact that they are commonplace in Delhi—so common that Delhi is considered 'different'—was entirely on account of the agency of the state and the imagination of the imported experts recruited by the Ford Foundation to formulate the first Master Plan for Delhi. Many of these large projects took the form of single commissions to architects—both government and private—who were able to explore architectural themes on a monumental scale in consonance with the aura of Delhi.

It is important to note that many of these huge commissions were awarded by the DDA and other government agencies to private practitioners (Plate 8.14). In no uncertain terms, this enlightened policy has vastly contributed to the development of the architectural profession in Delhi. In addition to the award of projects related to the Master Plan, two *ad hoc* mega events—the 'Asia 72 exhibition' (Plate 8.12) and the '1982 Asian Games'—have also stocked the city with memorable architectural objects by private architects. The profession responded to these massive building opportunities by producing a truly eclectic variety of architecture. While some succumbed to the lure of current fashionable clichés, others produced works of enduring quality, which can be profitably examined along with the monuments of the past. In architectural terms, it is, of course, difficult to pinpoint or attribute specific characteristics of the architecture of Delhi to the fallout from these events or to the agency of the state, but in general, it can be stated that they engendered a feeling of optimistic self-confidence in the local architectural community and this, in turn, is reflected in their works. Observing the execution of these projects, other architects realized that the extraordinary, when integrated into a design plan, could indeed be accomplished. The negative attitude fostered in the 1950s and 1960s, exemplified by the practice of utilitarian modernism, began to recede, particularly under the liminal conditions surrounding the execution of the time bound projects for the mega-events. Under these conditions there were few limits to architectural intent and architects began to display greater confidence in developing innovative architectural themes. It would be interesting to see whether or not a similar development in architectural consciousness took place in other cities as well, and if so, whether it was infused with the same sense of purpose which binds the architecture of Delhi in the form of a recognizable 'style'—the 'Delhi style'. Again, it must be reiterated that it would be difficult to correlate specific elements of this 'style' to the agency of the state in any clear-cut way; but the point I am making is that this 'style' is identifiable and is, in a general sense, infused with the aura cultivated and enabled by the state.

For some of the major projects, the government conducted competitions to select the architect—again an enlightened practice—which also contributed to the development of architectural culture in the city. There have been several such competitions held in Delhi since the 1960s: the NDMC City Centre, Bhikaji Cama District Centre, Jawaharlal Nehru University Campus, Indira Gandhi National Open University, the National Gallery of Modern Art, Dilshad Garden and Kalkaji Lower Income Group Housing schemes, the Indira Gandhi Indoor Stadium and the Indira Gandhi National Centre for the Arts. Although it was the winner who generally got the spoils in terms of important commissions, these competitions benefited more generally the architects who participated or whose sketches were merely viewed in the post-competition exhibition of entries. These exhibitions, to some extent, mitigated the absence of dialogue in journals and books and contributed to the cross-fertilization of architectural ideas and the development of a particular architectural culture in Delhi.

The government has also actively promoted the construction of low-cost housing. The DDA is justly proud of its massive social housing programme for the poor and low-income segments of the population. The Housing and Urban Development Corporation (HUDCO) has focused on the development of alternative construction technologies and low-cost building materials in the projects they finance and has been able to lever a great deal of change. Though their work is spread all over the country, these initiatives have had a significant impact on the development of architecture in Delhi. A curious fact that emerges from studying the production of housing in Delhi is that architects have demonstrated an impoverished mind when dealing with rich clients—mindless 'post-modern' indulgences being an example—but a richness of spirit while dealing with poor clients—as evidenced by the low-rise, high density housing for the poor. It seems that the constraints of poverty are beginning to catalyse the production of a more compelling architecture in a manner which did not take place in the 1950s, 1960s and even 1970s.

Another factor in the development of the architecture of Delhi which ought to be mentioned is the role of the Delhi Urban Arts Commission (DUAC).[25] Set up in 1973 by an Act of Parliament, the DUAC is generally considered little more than a 'nuisance value'. Nevertheless, it has gradually contributed to the establishment of minimum standards, which were otherwise overlooked when civic authorities approved projects based solely on their adherence to building bye-laws. Despite its indifferent record, the fact remains that the DUAC is an independent body established by the government to oversee the quality of architecture in Delhi, and it is sometimes able to make a positive contribution to major projects. Perhaps the architecture of Delhi has been spared the excesses perpetrated by developers' lobbies in other cities because of this.

'THINKING THE PRESENT'

In this essay I have focused on the role of the state in brokering the development of an architectural culture in Delhi. I have attempted to explain why Delhi 'looks' different. Of course, in historic terms, any attempt to view events by taking only the last fifty years is myopically doomed and perhaps vitiates the possibility of achieving a significant or enduring perspective on the course of events. Nevertheless, 'thinking the present' remains an intriguing possibility both academically and for reflexive practice.[26] There are many lessons to be learnt from such an attempt. An important one pertains to understanding the role and significance of the state as middleman in the development of the architecture of Delhi. What is revealed is the tragic absence of reflexive thinking in the practice of architecture. The developments of the last fifty years have by and large remained firmly aligned and contingent on the agency of the state. Unless this is targeted as a critical agenda for architectural reform, the post-Independence ideals and objectives of producing transformative architecture will not be realized, and the architecture of the next fifty years will remain grounded in the orientalist trap which in Edward Said's words is our 'uniquely punishing destiny'.[27]

NOTES

The photographs in this essay have been taken by the author.

1. A.G.K. Menon, The 'Contemporary Architecture of Delhi: A Critical History', Proceedings of the Conference, *Discontinuous Threads: Memory, Freedom and Architecture in Contemporary India*, Mohile Parikh Centre for the Visual Arts/ Architectural Forum, National Centre for the Performing Arts, Mumbai, 10-12 December 1997.

2. A.G.K. Menon, 'Architectural Education in India in the Time of Globalisation', Proceedings of the Conference *FORUM II: Architectural Education for the 3rd Millennium*, Gazimaguza, North Cyprus, Turkey, 22-4 April 1998.
3. A.G.K. Menon and M.N. Ashish Ganju, 'The Problem', *Seminar*, New Delhi, August 1974, pp. 10-13.
4. See Philippe Cadène, 'Delhi's Place in India's Urban Structure', and Véronique Dupont, 'Spatial and Demographic Growth of Delhi and the Main Migration Flows', in this volume.
5. A.G.K. Menon, *The Contemporary Architecture of Delhi: A Critical History*, op. cit.
6. See, for example, Tejaswini Niranjana, P. Sudhir and Vevek Dhareshwar (eds.), *Interrogating Modernity, Culture, and Colonialism in India*, Calcutta: Seagul Books, 1993.
7. See, for example, Gulammohammed Sheikh (ed.), *Contemporary Art in Baroda*, New Delhi: Tulika, 1997.
8. Ralph Maneo, Introduction, in *Thinking the Present, Recent American Architecture*, K. Michael Hays and Carol Burns (eds.), New York: Princeton Architectural Press, 1990, pp. 4-5.
9. Howard Roark was the fiercely independent-minded architect—hero in Ayn Rands' cult novel, *The Fountainhead*. Generations of students of architecture have fed on this lore and vicariously constructed their future careers in a similar mould. What is starkly evident in the Indian scene is the poignant contrast between fact and fiction.
10. A.G.K. Menon, 'Imagining the Indian City', Proceedings of the Conference, *Theatres of Decolonisation*, Chandigarh, 6-10 January 1995, and *Economic and Political Weekly*, Mumbai, vol. XXXII, no. 46, 15 November 1997, pp. 2932-6.
11. Source: Indian National Trust for Art and Cultural Heritage, New Delhi.
12. Master Plan for Delhi, Perspective 2001, Delhi Development Authority, Vikas Sadan, New Delhi, August 1990, p. 1.
13. For conservation policies in Delhi, see Narayani Gupta in this volume.
14. Raj Rewal, 'The Use of Tradition in Architecture and Urban Form', in Farooq Ameen (ed.), *Contemporary Architecture and City Form, The South Asian Paradigm*, Mumbai: Marg Publications, 1997, pp. 52-63.
15. G.H.R. Tillotson, *The Traditions of Indian Architecture, Continuity, Controversy and Change since 1850*, New Delhi: OUP, 1989.
16. Jon Lang, Madhavi Desai and Micki Desai, *Architecture and Independence, The Search for Identity—India 1880 to 1980*, New Delhi: OUP, 1997.
17. In personal discussions with Author.
18. Patwant Singh, 'Rabindra Bhawan', reprinted in *Architecture + Design*, vol. XIII, no. 2, March-April 1996, p. 32.
19. Kenneth Powell, 'Modernism Divided', in Catherine Cooke and Justine Ageros (eds.), *The Avant-Garde Russian Architecture of the Twenties*, London: Academy Editions, 1991.
20. Gunnar Myrdal, *Asian Drama, An Inquiry into the Poverty of Nations*, New York: Pantheon, 1968, pp. 895-900.
21. See Emma Tarlo and Narayani Gupta, this volume.
22. Gautam Bhatia, *Punjabi Baroque and Other Memories of Architecture*, New Delhi: Penguin, 1995.
23. A.G.K. Menon, *Imagining the Indian City*, op. cit.
24. E.R. Leach, 'Political Systems of Highland Burma', in M.N. Srinivas, *Social Change in Modern India*. New Delhi: Orient Longman, 1972, p. 160.
25. See Narayani Gupta, this volume.
26. Michael Hays and Carol Burns, *Thinking the Present, Recent American Architecture*, op. cit.
27. Edward Said, *Orientalism*, New York: Vintage Books, 1979. See particularly the Introduction.

Plate 8.1 The aura of Delhi: the Capital Complex.

Plate 8.2 The aura of Delhi: the wide tree-lined avenues in Lutyens' bungalow zone.

Plate 8.3 The Revivalists: Ashoka Hotel. (Architect: B.E. Doctor)

Plate 8.4 The Modernists: the WHO building. (Architect: Habib Rehman)

Plate 8.5 Utilitarian modernism: the School of Planning and Architecture. (Architect: T.J. Manickam)

Plate 8.6 Utilitarian modernism: the AGCR building. (Architects: The CPWD)

Plate 8.7 Government housing in the 1950s: Bapa Nagar.

Plate 8.8 The reaction to utilitarian modernism: an upper-class house in Panchsheel Park.

Plate 8.9 The reaction to utilitarian modernism: an upper-class house in Defence Colony.

Plate 8.10 The self-finance housing scheme at Saket. (Architect: Kuldip Singh)

Plate 8.11 The mega projects emerging out of the implementation of the Master Plan of Delhi—1962: the Bhikaji Cama Place District Centre. (Architect: Raj Rewal)

Plate 8.12 The mega projects of the 1970s: Exhibition pavilions for the Trade Fair Authority of India provided the opportunity for experimentation. The entrance to the Hall of Nations. (Architect: Raj Rewal)

Plate 8.13 Major institutional complexes: the Indian Institute of Technology, Delhi. (Architect: J.K. Choudhary)

Plate 8.14 The mega projects of the 1980s: the SCOPE Complex. (Architect: Raj Rewal)

Plate 8.15 The post liberalization architecture of the 1990s. Plotted row-housing in Shivalik Enclave.

9

Concern, Indifference, Controversy: Reflections on Fifty Years of 'Conservation' in Delhi

NARAYANI GUPTA

Conservation of the built heritage has been an official concern in India since the creation of the Archaeological Department in 1861, and a popular concern since the 1970s. Delhi is unique in being at once a national capital and the city with the fastest growing demographic rate over the past half century, while at the same time, including in its area over 150 'monuments' 'protected' by the Archaeological Survey of India.

The present map of Delhi is one of interlocking landscapes from different points of time. Delhi, with a continuous history from the twelfth century, is used to being a capital (and therefore a refuge) and to being praised as beautiful (and therefore both coveted and invaded). Having lived in Delhi almost continuously during the past fifty years, I have seen how not only the landscape, but also the perceptions of the citizens, officials, architects and 'environmentalists' have changed. Over these last fifty years, the prices of land in different parts of Delhi have increased in quantum terms. Those who want to ensure that 'protected monuments' should not only be kept in good condition but should also have room to breathe, and that many other buildings and areas should be classified as 'heritage' and protected against demolition or modification, are in a minority. This essay will explore how in the past fifty years, the rulers of Delhi have cherished, desecrated or ignored the three main components of the city's past—pre-Mughal Delhi, Shahjahanabad and British Delhi. But first a brief overview.

THE NINTH DELHI

In 1947, just before Independence, Delhi had interlocking landscapes, but these were different from the present configuration. Elements of pre-Mughal Delhi are chiefly concentrated in the South, and at that time they were like islands in a sea of fields, hills and *jhils* (shallow tanks). Mughal Delhi by contrast was clearly recognizable by its road-and-lane network and its dense habitation. British New Delhi, on the other hand, was a quiet enclave, sparsely populated—very beautiful in winter—with formal gardens, a high water-table, and very little traffic on its wide roads. The large cantonment area to the south-west was autonomous and had little interaction with the rest of the city.

The echoing empty monuments (Plate 9.1), the stretches of rocky uncultivable land, the open areas west of the Ridge and east of the Yamuna, the houses in Mehrauli and in Shahjahanabad which had been hastily vacated by Muslim families who migrated to Pakistan at the time of partition, were an open invitation to the hundreds of thousands who continuously arrived in Delhi through the sad and frightening months of 1947 and 1948. These 'refugees' did not see themselves as refugees, but as individuals who had opted to become citizens of a new India, who had made the choice under desperate conditions at the price of being uprooted from their homes in what had become Pakistan. Their numbers and sheer visibility led to their being given whatever shelter could be mustered, and being permitted to occupy the homes of 'evacuees'. Delhi was retained as the capital. This meant that the number of government offices increased, and these had a multiplying effect, encouraging a further in-migration of people promised or hoping to get jobs. Government departments, research institutes and universities, it was assumed, would provide 'housing' and this put a lot of pressure on land.[1] A third stream of migrants was the rural poor, who hoped to find or create work for themselves in the expanding city, and were prepared to take the risk of 'squatting' on public land and building their own cheap shanty towns.

This three-fold 'colonization' of Delhi was checked by the shock of a major cholera epidemic in 1955. To prevent things getting out of hand, a supreme land controller was created for Delhi in 1957 in the form of the Delhi Development Authority (DDA). For the next thirty years Delhi's map was drawn by the DDA, which had to contend with older land-controllers, one of which was the Archaeological Survey of India (ASI). More powerful than the ASI as land-controllers were the New Delhi Municipal Committee which administered Lutyens' New Delhi, the Cantonment Board, the Municipal Corporation of Delhi and the villages near the urban areas, which numbered over a hundred and were mostly located south of New Delhi. This rural area was what the DDA planned to 'urbanize' and divided into 'zones'—residential, commercial, and institutional. A clever move led to a large swathe of farmland in South Delhi (where many monuments were located) being transferred from villages to private agencies as freehold. This land was enclaved in the vast area designated by the DDA for disposal in the form of instalments on long leases. The *abadi* (inhabited) areas of the villages themselves were not to be touched and these became defined as 'urban villages'. Many of them had monuments in their midst. The villagers rejoiced at the windfall of 'compensation money' from the DDA. Unused to such wealth, their instinct was to spend rather than invest it, and once it was gone, they had to turn to other means of livelihood—salaried jobs, setting up shops, selling skilled services, or taking in tenants. Lacking playgrounds and basic civic amenities in their villages, many chose to use the premises of the monuments, which were perfunctorily policed. Their attitude to the old buildings themselves was characterized mainly by indifference. As they watched new neighbouring housing estates spring up, usually with their backs to existing villages, the villagers saw the new as desirable and the crumbling ruins of their monuments as not worthy of care, much less pride. As for the inhabitants of the new 'colonies', they were quite oblivious of the geography of the adjacent villages, and not interested in the monuments (Plate 9.2).

This poverty of interest is partly cultural, partly generational. In 1943, Percival Spear had published his *Delhi—Its History and Its Monuments*[2] which was used in schools where, until 1958, students had to answer a compulsory question on Delhi's monuments. This meant that students born in the 1930s and 1940s had at least some acquaintance with the town's historic architecture. But things were different from the 1950s. The newcomers' lack of familiarity with Delhi's landmarks, the irrelevance of historic architecture to people building their lives afresh; the habit of associating monuments with rather shabby villages, the inhabitants of which had a different lifestyle from that of the urban dwellers—all these meant an alienation from the monuments. This could have been remedied if students of history and architecture could have been encouraged to take an interest in them but, unfortunately, 'art and architecture' was taught very perfunctorily even at university level, where the nationalist movement and economic history were considered the new frontiers. Professor Mujeeb[3] is remembered affectionately for his readiness to accompany students of the college and the school on field trips, and his generosity in sharing his enthusiasm and knowledge about Delhi's architectural past.

All the standard histories of Indian architecture, such as Fergusson's *History of India and Eastern Architecture*, Percy Brown's *Indian Architecture* and the *Cambridge History of India*,[4] have copious descriptions of Delhi's medieval buildings but 'architectural history' as an area of research did not have any takers in India. By contrast, scholars from other countries showed an interest in it. The most comprehensive work on the Sultanate architecture of Delhi (1192-1526) was that of Professors Yamamoto and Matsuo Ara, written in the 1960s and 1970s.[5] Anthony Welch of Canada, Ebba Koch of Austria, Catherine Asher of the USA and Attilio Petruccioli of Italy were other well known modern scholars who worked, *inter alia*, on Delhi. The School of Planning and Architecture, set up in 1955, did have a sketchy course on the history of architecture, but this was weighted heavily in favour of European architecture. Figures like le Corbusier and Frank Lloyd Wright were held up as idols for the new generation of aspiring Indian architects, and styles of medieval or 'colonial' architecture were considered of little interest. One of the earliest directors of the School of Architecture, Jhabwala, eventually compiled his charcoal drawings of Delhi monuments into a book,[6] but by and large students of architecture did not develop any enduring sense of affinity with the distant past. The same is true with the recent past. In the 1950s and 1960s, when the extensions and infill to Lutyens' city were being built, his own architecture, admired in his lifetime, was seen as an embarrassing piece of imperialist baggage. It certainly was not seen as 'heritage'.

Jawaharlal Nehru's influence on independent India's architecture was considerable. His widely-read *Discovery of India* (published in 1946) endorsed the received idea of 'Indian architecture' being either 'Hindu' or 'Muslim'; British/European colonial architecture was not worthy of attention. It is therefore hardly surprising that the Act of Parliament in 1958 which confirmed the powers and functions of the ASI also did not consider such buildings worthy of 'protection'.[7] It was ten years later that Sten Nilsson published his pioneering work, *European Architecture in India*,[8] which took the story up to 1850.

After the Second World War the European countries whose irreparable losses in terms of architectural properties led them to adopt policies of conservation and restoration, also found the simple unfussy lines of modernist architecture convenient for their gigantic rebuilding and housing projects. India, propelled by Nehru and its first generation of USA-trained Indian architects, took a flying leap into modernist styles.[9] Gordon Cullen was invited to Delhi to make proposals for 'modern' buildings to mask or modify the scale and style of Lutyens' work.[10] This was reminiscent of how less than forty years earlier Lutyens had tried to integrate Delhi's medieval architectural masterpieces into his baroque city.[11] As for Shahjahanabad, the Red Fort and the Jama Masjid, they were conventionally considered worth visiting, but the narrow *gulis* (lanes) and palpable congestion were plainly considered an embarrassment to Nehru. He endorsed the label of 'notified slum' that the DDA's Master Plan[12] used for Shahjahanabad. The grey area between the Mughal and British capital, where Gandhiji had proposed the establishment of a village of *khadi* (handloom) weavers,[13] and where Gordon Cullen had visualized multi-storeyed shops and plazas, was transformed, with Nehru's approval, into a narrow elongated site for public meetings, set against a new 'wall' of three-storeyed 'commercial blocks' facing New Delhi and screening Shahjahanabad. The mental as well as physical distance between the 'imperial city' and the indigenous 'slum' increased, and Dilliwallas did not see either as 'heritage'.

'CONSERVATION' OR 'DEVELOPMENT'?

We said at the outset that conservation of the built heritage became a popular concern in the 1980s. To understand how this concern developed, we have to move back to the 1970s and examine changing perceptions of the three categories of architecture mentioned—pre-Mughal buildings, the town of Shahjahanabad, and Lutyens' New Delhi. One important factor in changing attitudes was that those who had seen the completion of the building of New Delhi and those others who had borne the brunt of Partition had, by the 1970s, reached middle age. The desperation and uncertainties of the 1940s were over, and Delhi had a new and recognizable form—composed of a prosperous West Delhi built by the newcomers after 1947, a spacious South Delhi with large official houses and private homes, the pleasant Civil Lines and the Delhi University complex to the north, an increasingly commercial Shahjahanabad and of course Lutyens' New Delhi occupying the centre.

More and more people from other parts of India were opting to live permanently in Delhi. This would eventually lead in the 1980s to the expansion of 'cooperative housing' further north and east of the Yamuna, and the spillover into Haryana, from the 1980s. But in the 1970s people did not know this. It seemed, as in the USA in 1892, that the 'frontier' had 'ended' and that Delhi had taken on a stable form. When frontiers end, conservation begins. Again, the US parallel is instructive. Judging by newspaper articles from the 1970s there was a new interest in Delhi's architectural history, and in interpreting heritage. There was also a counter-current of opinion encouraged by those who felt that the medieval ruins were occupying too much valuable real estate, that the housing stock of Shahjahanabad should be destroyed and replaced by multi-storeyed flats and that Lutyens' wasteful 'garden city' should be redesigned to increase its density. Conflicting opinions resulted in a feud—largely verbal—between 'conservationists' and 'developers'. Divisions and subdivisions within these broad categories were complex: architects were not all on one side and citizens were divided through their support of different combinations. Should the aim be to conserve 'protected' buildings, but let Shahjahanabad be modernized or retain the 'period' ambience of Shahjahanabad, and let the imperial British capital be modernized? Ideally, one would like to be able to present a Conservation Master Plan for the whole city. But such a map has never been prepared. Therefore, at the risk of oversimplification, the following analysis has been divided into three topographical sections.

THE MAGNIFICENT RUINS

As early as the sixteenth century, Delhi, particularly south Delhi, was perceived as a landscape of mausolea, masjid, secular buildings and forts.[14] Interspersed with these were shrines—in particular those of Bakhtiyar Kaki (thirteenth century), Hazrat Nizamuddin and Roshan Chiragh-e Dehli (both fourteenth century) which have continuously drawn crowds of pilgrims. All three were architecturally interesting, but they were more significant as magnetic poles which attracted people and prompted them to build tombs and mausolea near them. The ASI, fortified by powers given in the 1904 Act, and encouraged by the added incentive of Delhi being selected as the capital of British India in 1912, was, in the first thirty years of the 1900s, extremely active in 'listing' ancient buildings,[15] clearing them of illegal occupants, and landscaping the surrounding areas. Some 160 structures (including over a dozen small ones located on the northern Ridge associated with the 1857 uprising) were labelled 'Grade A' and 'protected' by the central ASI. By the 1960s, all the old guidebooks to Delhi were out of print. An ASI official, Y.D. Sharma, was asked to write a new one for the Orientalists' Conference in 1964. Definitive though it is, it is a great pity that it has only been marketed through the very few outlets of the ASI.[16]

The ASI was achieving great things in Afghanistan and Cambodia, while its own backyard in Delhi was sinking under the weight of indifference and encroachments as well as the excessive burden on the central offices of the ASI which lacked the support of a state department. Such a department was set up in the 1970s, but instead of 'acquiring' 'Grade B' monuments, its role as custodian was limited to the 1857 sites, which the ASI offloaded on to it. The ASI was not very active in signposting 'protected' monuments so most of them became anonymous. As for the 'Grade B' structures, which elsewhere in India have been taken over for 'protection' by the state departments of archaeology, in Delhi these remain vulnerable, even today, because—for political reasons—Delhi still does not have a state department with the power to 'acquire' them. 'The casualty list of the well-known monuments is long', stated an article in *Design* in April 1973. 'The extensive airforce installations now abiding within yards of the ruins of Tughlakabad; the India International Centre and the Ford Foundation buildings within the precincts [*sic*] of the Lodi Tombs; a permanent fair site next to the Purana Qila; the Abdun Nabi Mosque on Bahadur Shah Zafar Marg now squashed between a pedestrian overbridge and the . . . Delhi Administration's skyscraper. . . .' The Nehru Planetarium, designed by M.M. Rana, deserves attention for its design, which is sympathetic to the adjoining Tughlaq shikar-kiosk. Till the 1950s most monuments were picturesque picnic-spots, set in open fields. As the DDA auctioned off more and more farmland for the development of new neighbourhoods, the village *abadis* and the monuments they contained became hemmed in; monuments scattered in the surrounding fields were also enclaved. The ASI realized too late that it had not fenced off areas to give breathing room. In the absence of this, it did not have a viable case for demanding that such land be left free from 'development'. Where monuments were enclosed by walls—Safdarjang's and Humayun's mausolea, for example—they sought to keep 10 yd. around them free of construction. But even this was difficult to ensure. Masjid Moth, an exquisite Lodi mosque is an example of a monument which has suffered from the absence of boundaries. Ignorance, indifference, obfuscation and collusion, all helped those whose greed for land in Delhi has been satisfied at the expense of Delhi's priceless heritage.

In the 1980s, the two opposing forces—the pressure on land, and the moves to defend monuments—suddenly gathered strength. In 1974 the unchecked building of multi-storey tower blocks in New Delhi had prompted the Prime Minister, Indira Gandhi, to establish, by an Act of Parliament, the Delhi Urban Art Commission (DUAC) which would monitor proposed additions to the city's landscape, built or natural. In 1982, the DUAC commissioned the School of Planning and Architecture to make a study of some 'protected' monuments and of the Ridge and the Yamuna. Later that year, an Environment Group was set up by Ms Kamaladevi Chattopadhyaya at the India International Centre. It had an active 'Monuments Sub-Group' which, in 1985, became the Conservation Society of Delhi (CSD). The CSD set itself the agenda of acting as the unofficial guardian of Delhi's historic architecture and as a pressure-group. Its erratic newsletter was called *Prahari* (watchman). Newspapers were quick to comment on or to report comments on 'neglected monuments', which became a frequently used term. A further refinement, aired at seminars, was the criticism of the unimaginative way in which the ASI had designed the open areas around monuments. The British formula of lawns and palm fringed avenues, which did not conform to the original Mughal gardens, had been supplemented by a standard formula of bougainvillaea and casuarinas, both colonial imports and considered equally 'un-authentic'. The DDA and the Municipal Corporation were also criticized for laying out parks near the monuments but excluding the actual monument grounds (as at Vijay Mandal and Jamali Kamali) creating the curious effect of carefully-manicured parks adjacent to areas of unkempt wilderness, the former being indicative of the resources of the DDA and the latter of the poverty of the ASI. The CSD made specific suggestions about numerous monuments and prepared slide-shows which were screened at educational institutions and for citizens' groups. The enthusiasm of the Conservation Society was considerable, given the small number of active members. Looking back, one can see the decade from 1982 as perhaps the most significant for raising the level of public awareness and a sense of local pride, and for making the ASI realize that it was not so much a proprietor of extensive properties as a custodian of heritage, and therefore accountable to the people.

It has to be admitted, however, that the CSD's suggestions were carried out only to a very limited degree. One reason was the obverse side of the new awareness. Monuments now began to be exploited as useful adjuncts to the marketing of specific products. Another was the exploitation of the 'urban villages' which were exempt from the building bye-laws controlling the rest of the city. There was a great increase in the number of people living in these villages, without a corresponding expansion of infrastructure. For the desperately needed open spaces, villagers turned to the monuments. The resultant degradation of the surroundings and sometimes also the interiors discouraged people from visiting many of them or walking through them, as they do in Lodi Garden. A snobbish upper middle-class Delhi started distancing itself from its past and from 'rural' pockets within the city. At the same time, the very shabbiness, the disconcerting coexistence of world-class architecture and rubbish dumps came to acquire a new attraction. This has been reinforced by the publication of evocative photographs and illustrated books.[17] Words like 'ethnic' became popular, as did perceptions of 'villagers' as 'simple' and 'unspoiled'. The monuments began to be used as backdrops for commercial propaganda; the villages as milieus for 'happenings', for 'boutiques' and restaurants serving 'ethnic' food. 'Site chosen by Alauddin Khilji/ Restaurant established by X' proclaims a poster near Hauz Khas Village, which has come to serve as a cautionary tale of villagers and boutique-owners both trying to take advantage of each other while the nearby monuments get increasingly marginalized[18] (Plate 9.3). The web of issues involved is often highly complex with politicians taking their cut and official agencies making partisan interventions. It is not difficult to distinguish 'real' champions of heritage from 'fake' ones, disinterested agitators from predators, but the latter are usually more powerful. They can be checked only with media support or by legal injunction, which calls for alertness, good timing and the sacrifice of time. One instance when the CSD did succeed was when it stopped the owner of a sixteenth century tomb demolishing it in order to build a block of flats. This was achieved by a prompt legal injunction with the cooperation of the ASI. But in another instance—the demolition of the Tehsil of Bahadur Shah 'Zafar' at Mehrauli—the CSD did not learn about it early enough to stall it.

In a city getting steadily more congested and polluted, the monuments of a distant past could offer the promise of green areas and tranquillity. If the endless discussions (many of which go over well-trodden ground) about methods of conservation and the restoration of gardens, water-bodies and waterways could be translated into time-bound projects, we would win the gratitude of generations to come. At the same time, we need to ensure a quality of permanence, adopting the philosophy of the Mughal rulers who planted shade-giving trees in spite of the fact that they were slow-growing, rather than the policy of contemporary agencies who in recent years have planted useless eucalyptus trees and the not always appropriate casuarina, simply because they are fast-growing. There is room for cautious optimism: students of architecture have become more sensitive to historic architecture in the past fifteen years; the DDA has, for the first time in its revised Master Plan (Delhi 2001) made token references to 'Conservation Areas' (in 1995); two monuments in Delhi—the Qutb Minar and the mausoleum of Humayun—have been designated as World Heritage sites. While it is sadly true that one-third of the early medieval (twelfth to sixteenth century) buildings photographed by Professor Ara in the late 1960s have 'disappeared', those that remain are the more substantial ones and are unlikely to be demolished. The chief 'danger' is of a different order—vandalism in the name of gentrification, ruins being smartened up in a superficial manner. For some years in the 1970s a person of vision, Kamaladevi Chattopadhyaya, encouraged the use of the Mughal palace, Zafar Mahal in Mehrauli, as a workshop for craft persons. In an excess of zeal, the ASI asked them to vacate the building. Today, the Mahal is bare and desolate, often locked. Admittedly, a thin line separates 'use' from 'misuse'. But it may be better to ensure careful and appropriate use rather than simply leaving buildings empty. The laughter of children diving into Ugrasen's *baoli* (stepwell) or the quiet voices of participants at a calligraphy workshop in Khirki Masjid are infinitely preferable to echoing silences.

SHAHJAHANABAD: HERITAGE CITY OR SLUM?

Shahjahanabad has been designated a 'Conservation Area' by the DDA in its report: *Delhi 2001*.[19] This belated gesture has come after forty years (1945-85) of 'damage' of various kinds. The most serious of these was its being labelled a 'slum' in 1962, and being dumped under the same administrative department as shanty towns and 'unauthorized colonies'. Since the 1930s there have been proposals to 'decongest' the crowded south-western sections of the city. In the 1950s, this became difficult because of the construction of Asaf Ali Road, which was built in alignment with the former city wall. In 1975, Jagmohan, Vice-Chairman of the DDA, published his book, *Rebuilding Shahjahanabad*,[20] which repeated the suggestions of the 1930s, adding a gloss of nostalgia and suggesting it was possible to recover the ambience of the Mughal city. This idea had been evoked in 1973 by Maheshwar Dayal, who belonged to an old Delhi family. He had written a series of newspaper articles, which were later published as a book, *Rediscovering Delhi*, also in 1975.[21] But in the previous two decades much of this ambience had already been destroyed as the old *havelis* (mansions) were partitioned between large numbers of families, *gulis* (lanes) choked with modern vehicles and the avenue of Chandni Chowk narrowed by shop verandas and disfigured by hoardings and streamers (Plate 9.4).

A year after Jagmohan's book was published, he had the opportunity to begin trying to put the plan into action. With the callousness that many officials found so easy to assume during the Emergency, many houses near Turkman Gate, in south-western Shahjahanabad, were bulldozed in spite of the horrified resistance of their owners.[22] This was part of a larger campaign to make Delhi free of 'slums', the inhabitants of which were sent to distant 'resettlement colonies'.[23] The area around the Jama Masjid was cleared of shops and redesigned as parks and walkways at various times. In 1980, Max Mueller Bhawan worked with the School of Planning and Architecture to conduct a seminar on urban renewal in Shahjahanabad.[24] The fundamental issue concerning this Mughal city was whether conservation was for or against the local people.

Another political factor in this locality is the involvement of the Imam of the Jama Masjid who sees the area around the mosque as being under his authority. One recent occasion when this caused controversy was in 1994-5 when he ordered the construction of a structure for ablution purposes (a *wuzu-khana)* near the southern entrance, pleading that the tank in the courtyard was inadequate on days when the congregation was very large. The CSD and the DUAC (which at that time had two CSD members on its board) were successful in persuading the courts that this new structure should be demolished. The hesitant attitude of the ASI (in view of the fact that the masjid's maintenance is their responsibility, though its custodians are the Waqf Board) and the DDA (since Shahjahanabad falls under the purview of their 'Slum Board') suggested that in any prolonged conflict of interests, the Imam would be unlikely to lose and might actually gain. For officials to take a firm stand, they would need to show commitment, which would mean not being diverted by the numerous other (more important) claims on their time. This example served to highlight the significant role that could be played by an alert 'conservation' lobby. It also showed that the local inhabitants' bark was far more impressive than their bite; while they endorsed the cause of beautiful architecture with enthusiasm, they were not willing to fight for it. What is disturbing is that the Jama Masjid, one of the finest examples of Mughal architecture in India, is getting increasingly hemmed in by shops and barriers. The gardens and walkways laid out on the east side are not connected to the mosque, and some are even kept locked on the grounds that they would be vandalized if left open.

The inhabitants of Greater Delhi who were preoccupied with their 'plots' and flats, with setbacks and service-lanes, hedges and flower beds, with a yearning for the perfect 'government quarters', had little interest in the compact homes of Shahjahanabad. But the glamorization, particularly in cinema, of the Mughal/Mughlai cuisine, costume, music (*ghazal*) and etiquette, has now extended to habitat. A new interest in *gulis* was followed by an interest in *havelis*.[25] Popular books[26] made an important contribution to this trend—as they did with 'urban villages'. Scholarly interest having been, at best, sporadic, has now become almost constant as students of architecture are encouraged to study the layout of *gulis* and *kuchas* (cul-de-sacs), and houses (Plate 9.5). During the forty years following Independence most of the *havelis* had been destroyed by being partitioned, their courtyards roofed and extra floors built. Those that survived in recognizable form did so usually because their owners preferred to be poor and proud. The Indian National Trust for Artistic and Cultural Heritage (INTACH), formed in 1984, launched a programme to list 'heritage buildings'. The Delhi list (begun in 1985, and completed, after a stop-go history, in 1997) includes many *havelis* but also suggests that area conservation is as important as that of individual buildings (Plate 9.6). Parallel to this has been the rapid conversion of old buildings for commercial use. If the second generation of Greater Delhi residents became sentimental about *gulis* and *havelis*, their contemporaries in Shahjahanabad, are by contrast disenchanted with their crowded city and, given the opportunity, a majority of them would choose to migrate to the more 'open' neighbourhoods beyond. Any effective conservation plan will, therefore, need intelligent and sensitive coordination between the needs of local inhabitants, the opportunities for tourism and the demands of commerce. Facades, street furniture and traffic lanes, need to be blended into a pleasing yet workable whole.

Sometimes one has the impression that Shahjahanabad is becoming increasingly schizophrenic, with its attraction to tourists on the one hand and to the promoters of commerce on the other. In an unplanned but intuitively balanced fashion, it seems to save itself from ruination. Its vitality makes nonsense of the planners' talk of 'revitalizing' it, and those who frequent it could be surprised to learn that another old city, Venice, begs its visitors to view it in silence!

The Mughal citadel (the Red Fort) has, in the 1990s, become a subject of study for students and senior architects seeking to understand what it was like before much of it was wantonly destroyed after 1857,[27] and try to identify parts of it which might be 'restored'. The conservation versus restoration arguments can be seen at their best here. One example is the barracks built by the British army after 1857. In the 1980s it was unanimously agreed that these barracks which pierce the skyline incongruously should be demolished as soon as possible (in 1981, Parliament ordered the army to vacate the fort). However in the 1990s tables turned as some architects argued for retaining the barracks as classic examples of British military architecture!

Another feature unique to the Red Fort is that it has become imbued with a host of patriotic symbols. These are celebrated daily in the *Son-et-Lumière* programme, annually when the Prime Minister unfurls the national flag from its ramparts on Independence Day, and are conveyed implicitly through the museum's celebration of the nationalist movement and in the museumification of the barracks in Salimgarh where the Indian National Army prisoners were incarcerated in 1945. The fort is increasingly becoming a shell to house symbols of the nationalist movement. The impact on the 10,000 people who visit it daily can well be imagined. In contrast to the detailed interpretation offered by the museums of the 'Freedom Movement', there is almost no explanation of the gardens, chambers and museum of the Mughals which are only minimally signposted and not explained, thus giving free rein to the imagination of the so-called 'guides'. The fort could potentially be a great source of income, which could then be spent on making it spectacularly beautiful. But this will not happen as long as the tourism agencies are content with the money they earn from the *Son-et-Lumière* show, the ASI continues to make a virtue of not being 'money-minded', the army refuses to vacate the fort (though it did give part of Salimgarh to the ASI in 1995) and INTACH thinks its job is done once it has produced its elegant reports. Even while these reports were being written, the Municipal Corporation of Delhi was going ahead with its plans to widen the road east of the fort, which serves as a major national highway, oblivious to the long-term damage which trucks cause as they thunder past the fort walls at a distance of a few yards, simultaneously polluting Shahjahan's marble pavilion with diesel fumes. As far as the people of Delhi are concerned, they remain satisfied with things as they are. Unless made aware of what could be done to present the fort as architectural heritage, they will not be able to demand anything different.

The integration of the Red Fort, Jama Masjid, *gulis* and *havelis* into the organic city it once was remains a distant dream, but research and discussions that have been going on over the past fifteen years have at least brought it within the realm of the desirable. Even this had been impossible before the 1980s.

LUTYENS GETS HIS DUE

Lutyens' capital would have been subject to the same pressures of real estate as the two areas discussed earlier, were it not for the restraints exercised by the New Delhi Municipal Committee, a nominated body controlled by the central government. It is an area overlaid with nationalist political connotations. Reactions to this defiantly baroque city have been mixed from the time of its inception. After 1947, despite Gandhiji's suggestion that the Viceroy's Palace be transformed into a hospital and the President live in a bungalow, Nehru successfully argued for the necessity of grandeur which he thought appropriate to a great, albeit young, country. According to this logic, it made good sense to recycle the British buildings, and to use Kingsway/ Rajpath for processions. In the 1950s, Gordon Cullen was invited to make suggestions for further architectural development in Delhi. His book, *The Ninth Delhi,* daringly proposed high-rise buildings at the base of Raisina Hill, near Parliament House, and in the area between Lutyens' New Delhi and Shahjahanabad. Another area which many architects and planners wished to 'redevelop' was the 'bungalow zone'. But the low-rise houses which made Delhi one of the greenest cities in the world, were coveted by senior officials and ministers. Ironically, it was this that helped retain the verdant quality of the 996 acres of Lutyens' New Delhi. In 1973, the Design Group had accurately projected a population of ten million for Delhi by the end of the century which, they felt, justified a fourfold densification of the 'bungalow area'. There was strong protest from Patwant Singh who, through his journal *Design* (1957-87) consistently pleaded for a regard to aesthetics as well as 'development' and who had, as early as 1971, suggested a City Commission on Art similar to those in historic towns in Europe. 'We are under no illusions about the resistance which would be put up against this idea by those civic and other bodies who would see in it a possible threat to their own sovereignty. Yet, in reality it would be threatening nobody's sovereignty, but would be safeguarding the interests of the city which, ideally speaking, every citizen should have at heart.'[28] It was his insistence, and in particular his objection to the skyscrapers near Connaught Place, that led Indira Gandhi to persuade Parliament to institute the Delhi Urban Art Commission in 1974. Though sections of Lutyens' city have been disfigured by plotwise 'development' (read 'high-rise buildings'), large areas still retain their original quality. The roundabouts, which had at one point of time been suggested as suitable for commercial development ('Another Connaught Place at Windsor Place!') have become emerald islands, which in winter bloom riotously with flowers in a friendly spirit of competition. The danger of 'development' seems to have been staved off, with young architects ready to admire Lutyens' skill as a town-designer who worked on a human scale.

Around 1980 the architecture of Lutyens, like that of earlier 'Indo-Saracenists,' came to be regarded as 'good', and no longer as kitsch. That year, an exhibition on New Delhi by the School of Planning was very well received,[29] as was Robert Irving's book on the building of New Delhi, published one year later.[30] When the Penguin Guide to Indian Monuments, Volume Two (*Islamic, Rajput and European*) was published, it had a generous section on Lutyens.[31]

Controversy has periodically bubbled over the question of which symbols should be highlighted on the Central Vista. Iconoclasm in free India has targeted not buildings but statues of the 'men who ruled'. As the busts and figures of preceding sovereigns and viceroys were removed, there was a clamour for replacing them with statues of Indian leaders. One instance where this caused remarkable controversy was after the removal, in 1968, of the statue of George V from the cupola on Rajpath where it had stood for thirty years. The empty cupola seemed to demand an occupant, and the obvious person to be commemorated was Mahatma Gandhi (Plate 9.7). However, he himself had always been resolutely opposed to the practice of naming roads and installing statues to immortalize leaders. Furthermore, there were already several Gandhi statues in Delhi, the best one being the bas-relief sculpture, situated at the top of Sardar Patel Marg, depicting Gandhi and his followers on the Salt March. But the Central Vista was seen as a far more prestigious location. In 1989, a seated Gandhiji was cast in bronze but turned out to be too big to fit the cupola; it was then decided that the cupola itself should go. A protest from the CSD triggered off a surprising number of articles, letters to editors and cartoons. Young students of architecture were in agreement with older people in wanting to retain the cupola—the former on the ground that it was good architecture, integral to Lutyens' overall design, the latter out of sentiment. Sensing the general feeling, the cabinet abandoned the plan to remove the cupola, and the Gandhi statue was installed in the precincts of Parliament House.[32] A few years later, the question came up again, with the All-India Freedom Fighters' Association anxious to transform India Gate's gardens into a park to commemorate the heroes of the 1942 Quit India Movement. This time the CSD, along with INTACH, got a court injunction to prevent any modification of the area, and in particular to suggest that Gandhiji's statue (a standing one this time) could be installed anywhere but not along the main Vista.[33] There was a *déjà vu* feeling about the whole episode, and the DUAC, when asked for comments, simply quoted what had been said by its members back in 1975. What remains disquieting is that, despite so many 'final' decisions, successive governments see nothing wrong in reopening the issue, and that the calculations are purely political—to hijack Gandhiji—rather than aesthetic. It is clear that the Central Vista is seen as the axis of national political power, and that Gandhi's Samadhi at Rajghat will never have the same significance.[34] It is also clear that architects now accept Lutyens' buildings as well as his city-plan as canonical. Neo-colonial architecture has become fashionable, as have 'colonial' furniture, prints and even cuisine.

One of the regrets of Lutyens' admirers is that the official obsession with national security prevents them having access to all but three rooms of Rashtrapati Bhawan or to Hyderabad House. The third stately home, Baroda House, has been carved up into cubicles by the Railway Ministry. Baker's Secretariat buildings also suffer from a combination of overuse and lack of concern for their exquisite tiled floors, niches and inscriptions. Like 'colonial' buildings in other towns, they have become degraded through their continuous use as offices.

GETTING DOWN TO BUSINESS

'Conservation' needs vision, policy and agency. Delhi's various pasts have been objects of visitors' attention for centuries. Tourists have become numerically significant in the last fifty years. The threats to historic buildings—pollution, encroachments, misuse, neglect, lack of repair—have been noticed and commented on, with the assumption that the official custodians/occupants would respond. This has not happened to any significant degree. Therefore, while vision shines through in speeches and articles, clear-cut policy has not been spelt out. Amenity groups like the CSD are regarded as having nuisance value. INTACH, with its high-profile image, is at best treated with occasional deference but the custodians can play Delhi's favourite game—'passing the buck'.

At the popular level is the fundamental dilemma faced in so many spheres in India—is the modern not more desirable than the old? The members of a family on a recent visit to Delhi were strolling on the spacious platform of Humayun's mausoleum, camera at the ready, when one of them spotted a newly built place of worship at some distance, its new marble surface glowing in the sun. 'Take a photograph of that', he urged. 'It is so new and beautiful, not old like this building' (Plate 9.8). Conservation advocacy can be awakened by nostalgia and sustained by the prospect of economic gain. However, nostalgia often becomes compartmentalized and easily acquires communitarian overtones; and more immediate economic gain seems to lie in demolishing and replacing old buildings rather than conserving them. Against the indifference of the majority is the concern of the few. The faith of the few has been known to move, if not mountains, at least endangered heritage buildings. In Delhi, attitudinal change has begun, and the third generation of independent Indians will achieve and gain more from it. The gain will not be something quantifiable. To be aware of the history of the place where one lives helps one situate oneself in that history and overcome rootlessness, the commonest disease of city-dwellers. It also brings that sense of joy that only good, well-maintained architecture can give.

NOTES

1. V.K.R.V. Rao and P.B. Desai, *Greater Delhi: A Study in Urbanization*, Delhi: Asia, 1965.
2. Percival Spear, *Delhi: Its Monuments and History* (updated and annotated by Narayani Gupta and Laura Sykes), Delhi: OUP, 1997.
3. M. Mujeeb was the author of the well-known book *Indian Muslims*, Delhi: Munshiram Manoharlal, 1985.
4. J. Fergusson, *History of India and Eastern Architecture*, 2 vols., London: John Murray, 1876, reprinted Delhi: Munshiram Manoharlal, 1967; Percy Brown, *Indian Architecture (The Islamic Period)*, Bombay: DBT, 1990; John Marshall, 'The Monuments of Muslim India', in *Cambridge History of India*, vol. 3, CUP; Delhi: S. Chand & Co., 1970.
5. T. Yamanoto, M. Ara and T. Tsukinowa, *Delhi: Architectural Remains of the Delhi Sultanate Period* (in Japanese), 3 vols., Tokyo: University of Tokyo Press, 1967-70.
6. C.S.H. Jhabwala, *Delhi: Stones and Streets*, Delhi: Ravi Dayal, 1990.
7. S. Bhattacharya, 'The Management of the Past', *Biblio*, Delhi: July-August 1997, pp. 31-2.
8. Sten Nilsson, *European Architecture in India 1750-1850*, London: Faber and Faber, 1968.
9. Jon Lang, Madhavi Desai and Miki Desai, *Architecture and Independence: The Search for Identity—India 1880 to 1980*, Delhi: OUP, 1997. See also A.G. Krishna Menon, this volume.
10. Gordon Cullen, *The Ninth Delhi*, Delhi: Town and Country Planning Organization, 1960.
11. R.G. Irving, *Indian Summer—Lutyens, Baker and the Making of Imperial Delhi*, Delhi: OUP, 1982.
12. Delhi Development Authority, *Draft Master Plan for Delhi*, 2 vols., Delhi: Government of India, 1960.

13. I am grateful to Professor K.T. Ravindran for this information.
14. *The Baburnama,* Memoirs of Babur, Prince and Emperor, trans., ed. and annotated by Wheeler M. Thackson, New York: OUP, 1996, p. 327.
15. J.A. Page, *List of Mohammedan and Hindu Monuments, Delhi Province,* 4 vols., Calcutta: Government of India Press, 1916-22, popularly called the 'Zafar Hasan Volumes' after the ASI official who did the survey. These have been reprinted with a wrong title—*Monuments of Delhi: Lasting Splendour of the Great Mughals and Others,* Delhi: Aryan Books International, 1997.
16. Y.D. Sharma, *Delhi and its Neighbourhood,* Delhi: Director General of Archaeology in India, 1964, Archeological Survey of India, 1990.
17. For example, Karoki Lewis, and Charles Lewis, *Delhi's Historic Villages,* Delhi: Ravi Dayal, 1997; and M.M. Kaye (ed.), *The Golden Calm,* Exeter, Devon: Webb and Bower Publishers Ltd., 1980.
18. For a discussion of this, see Emma Tarlo, *Clothing Matters,* London: Hurst and Co., 1996, Chapter 9.
19. Delhi Development Authority, *Delhi 2001,* Delhi: DDA, 1985.
20. Jagmohan, *Rebuilding Shahjahanabad,* Delhi: Vikas Publishing House, 1975.
21. M. Dayal, *Rediscovering Delhi,* Delhi: S. Chand & Co., 1975.
22. J. Dayal and A. Bose, *Delhi under the Emergency,* Delhi: Ess Ess Publishers, 1997.
23. For information on resettlement policy during the Emergency, see Emma Tarlo, this volume.
24. *Shahjahanabad: Improvement of Living Conditions inTraditional Housing Areas,* Delhi: School of Planning and Architecture and Max Mueller Bhavan, 1980.
25. P.K. Varma, and S. Shankar, *Mansions at Dusk: The Havelis of Old Delhi,* Delhi: Spantech, 1992.
26. G. Barton and L. Malone, *Old Delhi: Ten Easy Walks,* Delhi: Rupa, 1988.
27. Narayani Gupta, *Delhi Between Two Empires 1803-1931,* Delhi: OUP, 1981, 1998.
28. Patwant Singh and Ram Dhamija, *Delhi: The Deepening Crisis,* Delhi: Sterling, 1989.
29. E.F.N. Ribeiro and A.K. Jain (eds.), *The Future of New Delhi,* Delhi: DDA, 1984.
30. For R.G. Irving, cf. note 11.
31. P. Davies, *Monuments of India,* vol. 2, London: Penguin, 1989.
32. Narayani Gupta, 'From Kingsway to Rajpath—the Democratization of Lutyens' New Delhi', in C. Asher and T.R. Metcalf (eds.), *Perceptions of South Asia's Visual Past,* Delhi: Oxford and IBH, 1994.
33. K.D. Alley, 'Gandhiji on the Central Vista: A Post Colonial Refiguring', *Modern Asian Studies,* 31, 4, Cambridge: 1997, pp. 967-97.
34. For a sense of the political connotations of the Central Vista, see Satish Sharma's photographic essay in this volume.

Plate 9.1 'Echoing empty monuments.' Entrance to Najaf Khan's Tomb (*c.* 1782), opposite Safdarjang Airport. (Photograph: Rohit Krishan Gulati, February 1999.)

Plate 9.2 'Oblivious to the geography of adjacent villages.' Humayunpur, a village engulfed by Safdarjang Enclave. (Photograph: Rohit Krishan Gulati, February 1999.)

Plate 9.3 'Villagers and boutique owners trying to take advantage of each other.' Hauz Khas Village. (Photograph: Rohit Krishan Gulati, February 1999.)

Plate 9.4 'The avenue of Chandni Chowk narrowed with veranda-shops.'
(Photograph: Rohit Krishan Gulati, February 1999.)

Plate 9.5 'Students of architecture were encouraged to study the layout of *gulis*.' Naugharana, Shahjahanabad. (Photograph: Rohit Krishan Gulati, February 1999.)

Plate 9.6 'The Delhi list includes many *havelis.*' *Haveli* in Guli Khazanchi. (Photograph: Rohit Krishan Gulati, February 1999.)

Plate 9.7 'The empty cupola seemed to demand an occupant.' Canopy at Rajpath. (Photograph: Rohit Krishan Gulati, February 1999.)

Plate 9.8 'It is so new and beautiful.' Gurdwara adjoining Humayun's Tomb. (Photograph: Rohit Krishan Gulati, February 1999.)

10

Delhi through the Eyes and Lenses of a Photographer

SATISH SHARMA

'Delhi through the eyes and lenses of a photographer.' That is what I intend to portray, present my own subjective view of the capital, show how my image of the street Delhi differs from the idealized image of Delhi—the capital city of India. I hope to define those differences in the various ways the city has been imagined and imaged. At the same time, I want to contemplate the issue of power: the political games and actor's strategies that featured in the seminar, Delhi Games, and recur in this book.

This theme fascinates me because I have recently started seeing photography as a physical site—a geographical space that is the site of power games and politics. The photograph has, for me, become the site of a battle of sights and spectacles. It is a stage on which actors act out roles just for cameras—cameras which then extend the reach of their theatricals in ways which are unbelievable even in a world which seems to be becoming increasingly constructed and controlled by the camera. There are, somebody once said, more photographs in the world today than there are bricks. The camera was invented at a time when industrialization and colonization were fostering the rapid growth of metropolitan cities and giving them a power that the camera was used to describe and, in fact, inscribe. One can hardly separate the camera from the whole phenomenon of modernity.

In Delhi, the capital of the world's largest democracy—a nation, with a multitude of languages and a huge number of illiterate people—the power of photography cannot be underestimated. It is perceived as a 'universal language', that needs no translation, that cuts through regional and language barriers and has an ever expanding and insidious reach. The camera's images—whether as television bytes, still photographs or film footage, are perceived as documents of reality and often accepted as being more real than the reality they construct. Photographs have a veracity that gives them a power, which then has to be used and, more importantly, controlled. And control and use is what photography in Delhi is all about.

Walk the streets around the Central Vista and try to shoot pictures of the DIZ area ('Delhi Imperial Zone'—fifty years after independence it still retains its name) and you will find the police and security agencies on your back in no time—especially if you seem to be shooting the exteriors of 'Government buildings'. Private security guards, chowkidars and even doormen will be equally vocal and physical in performing their 'duty' of protecting the city, even if they are just manning the doorway of a commercial showroom you are trying to photograph in the capital's commercial centre—Connaught Place. It seems that everyone is scared of the photographic image they don't control.

Photographic access even to tourist sites, which do not fall under Defence of India Rules, is controlled by the powers that be. If you want to photograph them a little more seriously than a tourist you have to get the ASI's (Archaeological Survey of India's) permission. And even with official permission your access is still limited. The 'out of bounds' areas remain out of bounds. The special permission to shoot the interior of the Taj Mahal, for example, cannot be signed even by the Director General of the ASI. That is something only the Union Minister can sign.

What has the ASI got to hide? Nothing hopefully though public monuments in India are often contested sites. Maybe it's just a matter of having power and loving to exercise it. Or maybe its a colonial hangover coupled with lessons independent India learnt from her Big Brother—the former Soviet Union.

I want to go back to my early days as a budding photojournalist, in 1975—the days of the Emergency. *India Today* was then a new-born newsmagazine for which I freelanced—shooting images of politicians who dressed up in Gandhi caps and Nehru jackets just for the photographs. When a minister sent for a cap and insisted that I take just a head shot that would not show the casual polo-neck sweater he was wearing below, I decided that I would no longer be a party to controlled photo ops—shooting pretty pictures of politicians and participating in the image creating exercise that mainstream news photographers were, and still are, a part of. Properly accredited by the Press Information Bureau, they alone have any real access to the top rungs of the political ladder. Accredited photographers are the pampered pets of the powers that be. Besides exclusive access to the top rungs of power, they are given subsidized housing in the best parts of Delhi's Babu domains and are the only professional photographers who have been allowed duty free import of photographic equipment from abroad. And if they don't have the money to buy the equipment they can easily get low interest loans. Rajiv Gandhi made sure of that when he rose to power on the strength of his 'Mr. Clean' image created by the advertising agency hired to sell him.

As an amateur photographer himself, Rajiv Gandhi was quite camera savvy and well versed in the American style of selling good looking Presidents. The camera and television have, since the days of John Fitzgerald Kennedy, given good looking and photogenic candidates a definite edge. Sonia Gandhi now seems the ideal candidate for success. The interest in photographs of the 1998 Indian Lok Sabha elections seemed almost nil in the largely visual foreign press until Sonia appeared on the scene. Suddenly the elections came alive for the media. They were now visually viable—complete with a good looking and saleable face.

The saleability of an image definitely has a lot to do with the making of personas. Icons are increasingly created by the market. The tourist market for colourful coffee table books of the 'places and faces' kind has definitely defined the way destinations like Delhi are photographed. Publishers only print books they know they can sell to foreign tourists who seem interested mainly in reinforcing preconceptions of the places they plan to visit. This has meant the use of colour even by photographers whose self-confessed forte was and is black and white photography. But the black and white reality of tourist destinations has no ready market. Colour is what is demanded from 'the Orient' and that is what profit-oriented publishers want from photographers. And is mostly what they get.

Consider two of the most well-known books on Delhi. Both are by the same photographer—Raghu Rai.[1] Both contain a mixture of colour and black and white photographs. The first was published by Delhi Tourism but is not entirely touristy—half the images are black and white. They are from Raghu Rai's *Statesman* days. A lot of them were shot as 'human interest' pictures that newspapers love. The second book was supposed to be much more 'personal' and is more about photography as a formalist frame—again apparently non-touristy. But here again there is a continued, almost conscious stress on a Delhi defined by its monuments, a city celebrated by its material constructions, a cliché that photography has created over the 150 years of its existence. Delhi's 'monumental' visual history apparently forecloses any attempt to see and show it as anything else. My recent, personal attempt to see and show a slightly different Delhi when commissioned as photographer for the *Eicher City Guide*[2] was met with an abrupt 'I am the editor' response. An editorial diktat that ensured yet another stereotypical view of the city. There seems no escaping the monumentality of Delhi's picture perfect past. Is it, I wonder, that this is the only image of Delhi that sells, or is this simply a mindset and a market demand that Delhi photographers have yet to break?

The mindsetting begins early in every young photographer's career. They learn primarily from a guru-like older generation of photographers who have yet to break the influence of colonial photography's desire for a 'picturesque' Orient. The gurus train their chelas (followers) by sending them out to shoot pictures of romantic and picturesque monuments or, at best, if the gurus are photojournalists, to photograph the people around the Jama Masjid—people who are seen and shown as exotic 'others' by citizens of the same city. 'Others' are always more interesting and easier to shoot—especially if they are lesser others—people who are not supposed to control their own images. Control over images of the self is a privilege of the privileged few who can control their imaging by denying access to all but the controlled image-maker—someone they pay, someone who works to satisfy them.

I have recently moved away from a 'social documentary' photography of just the underbelly of Indian society to what I call the mink coat of the same society. Every third world has its first world and every first world its third world, someone said. To photograph the first world of our third world demanded a changed strategy. I started with assignments for an interiors magazine. That got me access to otherwise private, rather exclusive and definitely excluding spaces. A Delhi that is as out of bounds to serious documentary photography as Delhi's politicians. This is the Delhi of Playboy bars, the Delhi which has chandeliers in its bathrooms.

From being a literal outsider walking the public streets I decided I needed a different insight—that of an 'insider' photographing the homes of the upper crust and shooting my own middle class society. In the homes of the ultra rich I was still an outsider with limited access, but in the art world of Delhi I am comparatively speaking, an insider. An insider with better access, better understanding and, I hope, incisive insight.

I have begun to understand the power and politics of photography and I am fascinated by the way photography has been used to construct power. My photography has consequently become to a large extent an oppositional practice that quietly challenges and hopes to counterpoint mainstream media imagery with my own rather personal and subjective vision and images.

I began to look at the imaging of politicians more than a decade ago—from the post-independence valorizing of them in books published by the Government's own Publications Division through to books like Raghu Rai's *A Life in the Day of Indira Gandhi* published by *The Statesman*. Photographs construct a heroism that is never really challenged, not even after Mrs. Gandhi declares the Emergency. Her greatness is redoubled when she is assassinated and a second, equally eulogising, book is produced. And at Mrs Gandhi's funeral it is the orchestrated scenarios around Teen Murti which received visual prominence in print. The inhuman massacres in Trilokpuri that followed were hardly shot or have been safely edited out of Delhi's visual history. But then there is a difference between the *murtis* (figures) that photography is used to make and the *lok* (people) that it generally looks down on.

Post-independence photography has been used to produce a visual history biased towards the construction of a nationalist image of the nation—from the point of view of the state and its leaders. Looking at the archives and permanent collections of institutions like the Nehru Memorial Library gave me quite a shock last year as I was compiling the visuals for India Today's Independence special. The bias of government collections towards the Congress Party and the 'first family' is loud and clear—hardly surprising but certainly shocking. There are many images by Homai Vyarawalla in the archives, but the more unflattering ones of Nehru that she shot are just not there. They are incredible images but visual worth has never been the deciding factor in state archives. What is shocking, though, is the fact that even the archives of supposedly independent and autonomous art institutions are carefully censored. A fantastic, though rather unflattering image of Nehru with the Mountbattens was not shown at Cartier-Bresson's Exhibition of Indian Photographs at the National Gallery of Modern Art in 1992. Bresson has presented a set of his Indian photographs to the biggest and best funded art institution of the country—the Indira Gandhi National Centre for Art. The IGNCA seems to believe that control and censorship are central to the construction of a photographic archive. But one can not blame just the state institutions for constructing and compiling a safe nationalist archive. Photographers themselves are doing their own bit.

Most pictures of demonstrations and riots are invariably shot from the point of view of the state and its police—simply because photographers place themselves safely behind the police cordon thus 'choosing' an angle that is the viewpoint of the police. Facing the police in a riot situation is not easy, as I know to my cost. I paid for a photograph a split second later, when the lathi (policeman's stick) landed on me. Photographers generally want a different kind of payment—the Padma Shri kind, probably. And that comes with constructing icons and not deconstructing them. What I find interesting is that all the Padma Shri awardees in photography have done their share of service to the state or the politicians in power.

I have watched how photography has been used to construct and sell an iconic image of the politician. When I first saw the arrival of Rajiv Gandhi on the streets I decided to watch the construction of his image through his posters on Delhi's walls. What I saw over a period of a decade was literally the deconstruction of his image. These were some of the images in my exhibition, *Deconstructing the Politician* (Eicher Gallery, New Delhi, 1997).

The politician is carefully constructed and projected at state expense. The guns that surround the leaders and create sacred spaces around them to define their importance are just the obvious creators and symbols of power. The Press Information Bureau daily distributes countless photographs of official 'functions' free of charge to the print media. Combine these with the images of controlled photo ops that the agencies and print media produce and you have an image-building exercise that, through sheer repetition, creates not images of the events that occurred but of the importance of the politician who seems to be central to almost every event. You can organize a conference on post-colonialism but the image that goes out to the press and the public is of the political stars who graced the occasion and gave it its importance. Conference organizers know that all too well. They invite the politicians to enhance the importance of their conferences and to get a place in the media the next day. They play the game as well as the photographers who shoot images that they know the news editors will use. And news editors know only too well where the interests of the press and its owners lie.

My interest in photography as a medium has meant that I have begun to look at the different photographies that a society produces. About ten years ago I started to collect photographs from local studios and from family albums. The idea was to see what happened to photography at a subaltern level—in a non-western society. I wanted to understand photography's social and political spaces—see, for example, what happened when it came into a society that did not really subscribe to the whole discourse of realism that came with western photography; look at the little *leelas* (religious theatrical performances) that are enacted in little studios for little postcard-sized prints. And the image of Delhi in these personal projections in studios and in private family albums is as interesting and important a document of Delhi as the one produced by the media. Interestingly enough the media images definitely influence the former. Many of the ideas of what a visual Delhi means are drawn from the images the media projects—in the news and in coffee table books. Birla Mandir is part of the postcard-city constructed by the tourist industry. But in the world of one Birla Mandir photographer, the temple is the backdrop to a different kind of theatrical performance. The photograph here becomes a projection of an imagined self and a wish fulfilment for the photographer's subject—his client. What is presented here is another photography. Another space that photography occupies in a subaltern India.

NOTES

1. Raghu Rai, *Delhi: A Portrait,* Delhi: Oxford University Press & Delhi Tourism Corporation, 1983; *Raghu Rai's Delhi,* Delhi: Indus, an imprint of Harper Collins, India, 1994.
2. *Eicher City Guide. Delhi,* New Delhi: Eicher Goodearth, 1998.

Plate 10.1 Beating the Retreat: dress rehearsal on Vijay Chowk.

Plate 10.2 Bofor's gun on Raj Path.

Plate 10.3 Rajiv Gandhi poster, Safdarjang Airport.

Plate 10.4 Rajiv Gandhi's cut-out, New Delhi.

Plate 10.5 Rajiv Gandhi: popular constructed photograph.

Plate 10.6 Political cut-out of a leader, India Gate.

Plate 10.7 Rafi Marg, New Delhi.

Plate 10.8 Parliament House.

Plate 10.9 Political cut-out of a leader, Connaught Place.

Plate 10.10 Indira Gandhi as Durga: post 1984 elections, New Delhi.

Plate 10.11 1984 riots, Trilokpuri.

Plate 10.12 Riot control, Raj Path.

Plate 10.13 Netaji Subhas Chandra Bose, Jama Masjid, Old Delhi.

Plate 10.14 Tilak Marg, New Delhi.

Plate 10.15 Election graffiti, Old Delhi.

Plate 10.16 Election graffiti, New Delhi.

Plate 10.17 Commercial hoarding, New Delhi.

Plate 10.18 Street children, Jama Masjid, Old Delhi.

Plate 10.19 Chandelier in a bathroom, Old Delhi.

Plate 10.20 Vision of Delhi in popular photography: Birla Mandir.

Plate 10.21 Vision of Delhi in popular photography: Qutb Minar.

Plate 10.22 Vision of Delhi in popular photography: Bahai Temple.

PART IV
IDENTITIES AND POLITICS

11

The Hindu Nationalist Movement in Delhi: From 'Locals' to Refugees—and towards Peripheral Groups?

CHRISTOPHE JAFFRELOT

The Bharatiya Janata Party (BJP) suffered a major setback during the 1998 assembly elections in Delhi when it won only 15 seats to Congress' 51. However, this defeat can be attributed largely to the then growing unpopularity of Vajpayee's government at the centre. Not long before, during the last two general elections, held in 1991 and 1996, the BJP had recorded its highest ever scores in Delhi (49.6 per cent and 53 per cent respectively) and its popularity was not a new phenomenon. In fact, in contrast to the adjoining states, Delhi is perhaps the oldest electoral stronghold of the Hindu nationalist movement. As early as the autumn of 1951, the Bharatiya Jana Sangh emerged as the main rival to the Congress during the Delhi municipal elections with 25 per cent of the valid votes as against Congress' 33 per cent.[1] And during the 1952 assembly elections, it still performed reasonably well taking 22 per cent of the valid votes.[2] Since then, the Jana Sangh and later the BJP have continued to be the main challenger to the Congress or even the ruling party in Delhi (see Tables 11.1 and 11.2).

The exceptional strength of the Hindu nationalist parties in Delhi has often been attributed to the circumstances and implications of Partition: communal feelings were exacerbated in a city which had been badly affected by Hindu-Muslim riots and which harboured so many refugees from Pakistan.

TABLE 11.1. PARTY-WISE COMPOSITION OF DELHI MUNICIPAL CORPORATION

Party	*1958*	*1962*	*1967*	*1971*
Congress	42	73	42	44
Jana Sangh	25	9	52	53
Communists	7	2	2	1
Others	1	–	2	1
Independents	9	3	3	3
TOTAL	84	87	101	102

Source: Delhi Gazetteer, New Delhi, Delhi Administration, 1976.

TABLE 11.2. PERCENTAGE OF VOTES POLLED IN STATE ELECTIONS AND DELHI METROPOLITAN COUNCIL ELECTIONS

Year of election	*Congress*	*BJS/BJP*	*Swatantra/Janata Party*
1952	52.1	21.9	–
1972	48.5	38.5	0.1
1977	36.1	–	52.6
1983	47.5	37.0	3.7

Source: D. Gupta, *The Context of Ethnicity*, Delhi: OUP, 1996, p. 37.

This approach can be substantiated by facts but it needs to be supplemented and refined. First, the Hindu nationalist movement had already some support before 1947 in Delhi, as suggested by the pre-independence development of the Rashtriya Swayamsevak Sangh (RSS), which relied on the collaboration between local notables (who were often big merchants) and activists from the intelligentsia (who, originally, were Maharashtrian Brahmins). Second, the influx of so many Punjabis who resented the Congress' so called 'appeasement' policy towards Muslims did help the Jana Sangh, but this was partly because many of the refugees had already imbibed Hindu nationalism in the Punjab. Furthermore, while the Jana Sangh depended on the refugees (for its organization as well as at the time of elections), it did not become *the* party *of* the refugees. In fact, refugees voted in large numbers for the Congress while it was the local business community who provided strong support for the Jana Sangh, and the BJP. In a way, these parties were primarily representative of the 'middle world'. The BJP has retained this social profile today even though it tries to reach the rural periphery of Delhi.

THE RSS ORGANIZATION—BUILDING PATTERN IN DELHI

The RSS was not the first Hindu nationalist organization in Delhi. Kenneth Jones considers that Delhi 'became the centre of a new type of Hinduism—organized, structured Hinduism'[3] as early as the late nineteenth century, especially after Dayananda founded a branch of the Arya Samaj there in 1878 and after Din Dayal Sharma established the headquarters of the Bharat Dharm Mahamandal, a Sanatanist (orthodox) association in 1890, followed by the founding of the Hindu College in 1899. In 1909 the Arya Samaj also transferred its main office to Delhi with the creation of the Sarvadeshik Arya Pratinidhi. The Delhi Provincial Hindu Sabha was later founded by Arya Samajists and Sanatanists in 1918 and the headquarters of the Hindu Mahasabha was transferred from Varanasi to Delhi in 1925, after Lajpat Rai became its president. The Hindu Sabha movement was never a mass movement in Delhi—it polled only 179 votes, as against Congress' 6,261 during the 1945 Legislative Assembly elections when the winning candidate and his runner-up were both Muslims.[4] But its modest resources helped the RSS take root in Delhi in the 1930s.

In its formative phase, the RSS developed its network by sending *pracharaks* (full-time propagandists) from Nagpur to most cities, in particular to those with substantial student populations since the educated youth was its priority target (and the *pracharaks* could approach students after registering themselves as students). As K.R. Malkani explains, 'In town after town the Sangha *pracharak* would arrive with a few letters of introduction to the local leaders, whether belonging to Congress, Hindu Mahasabha, Arya Samaj or whatever. He would put up in the local Bhavan of any of these organisations or in a temple or with any well-wisher.'[5] This modus operandi is well illustrated by an example from Delhi in the 1930s.

The *pracharak* who was sent to Delhi was Vasant Rao Oke. A Chitpavan Brahmin from Nagpur, he had joined the RSS in 1927 and had served as secretary to Hedgewar for sometime. He had completed his Instructors' Training Camp (ITC) in 1929-30 and his Officers' Training Camp (OTC) in 1931 and organized the first OTC outside of Nagpur in Poona in 1934.[6] After this he was sent to Delhi where he received the support of Padam Raj Jain, a notable from the Hindu Mahasabha. This Marwari from Calcutta had been impressed by the Nagpur *shakha* (RSS branch) which he had visited after the session of the Hindu Mahasabha in Poona in 1935. He told Hedgewar how much he appreciated his 'silent but highly important work'[7] and suggested that the RSS start a branch in Delhi. Vasant Rao Oke was sent there in November 1936 and as general secretary of the Hindu Mahasabha, P.R. Jain helped him establish the Delhi *shakha* by authorizing him to set up his general headquarters—and the first *shakha*—in the central office of the Mahasabha.[8]

This office was close to Birla Mandir and Jugal Kishore Birla who patronized the temple extended his help to Oke.[9] The latter found his first recruits in the premises of the temple. One of them recalls:

> We used to go to Birla Mandir to play and once Vasant Rao Oke was on the road. He was on the lookout for young people to start the *shakha*. He saw us play. He called us and asked why we were playing there and would we want to learn how to wield a *lathi* [stick], to wield a sword. We said, 'Yes'. We went to the *shakha* and got enrolled there, in 'Hindu matri bhavan'. It was the first branch in Delhi. It was opened in 1936.[10]

In 1937, there were six *shakhas* in Delhi but ten years later, at the time of Partition, there were as many as one hundred, according to Oke who had become *prant* (provincial) *pracharak* (in charge of the Delhi province) in 1938 and kept this position for ten years. It was a big unit, compared to others in Uttar Pradesh and elsewhere. Oke was especially successful at attracting government servants, students from the three main colleges (Hindu College, St Stephen's and Ramjas) and Banias, as the social profile of his patrons testifies.

Each branch of the RSS used to benefit from the support of local patrons who were soon referred to as *sanghchalaks* (literally, directors). They functioned mostly as counsellors or even guides and conferred a certain respectability to the movement by sponsoring the *pracharaks'* activities. In Delhi, Padam Raj Jain could not play this part for long because of the deteriorating relations between the RSS and the Hindu Mahasabha, especially after Madhav Sadashiv Golwalkar took over as *sarsanghchalak* of the RSS in 1940. This role was played in 1937-40 by Prakash Dutt Bhargava, an advocate who had met Golwalkar at the Banares Hindu University (BHU) when he was a student but who was originally from Ajmer and was not very influential—not even a notable in the true sense of the word.[11] For these reasons he could not fulfil the conditions for being a good *sanghchalak* and ended up contacting Lala Harichandra Gupta, who was to become the first Delhi *sanghchalak* in 1940. As a zamindar (landlord) who owned orchards in Uttar Pradesh, and a rich businessman with a factory in Delhi, he had 'a social public life'[12] and had been elected to the Municipal Council. An RSS old timer described him as a *rais*, a wealthy notable. When he came to Delhi, Golwalkar would stay in Lala Harichandra Gupta's house situated in Sitaram Bazaar.[13]

A bigger *rais*, Lala Hans Raj Gupta, became *prant sanghchalak* in the late 1940s. Though he had an MA (Master of Arts) and an LLB (Bachelor of Laws) degree, Hans Raj Gupta never practised law because he had joined his father-in-law's business in the mid-1920s and had soon after inherited important firms from both him and his own father. He had settled in Delhi in the 1930s when his father had already built a bungalow at 20 Barakhamba Road. The family made a fortune from the steel industry and by renting sugar cane crushers to the peasants of western Uttar Pradesh. In 1937, the responsibility of the iron syndicate fell on him and he started an iron forgery, a distillery in Meerut as well as factories making cycles and fans in the 1940s.[14] He looked after the Delhi-based business of M. Vishveshwarya, a civil engineer from Mysore who had built a big dam there and was the founder president of the All India Manufacturers Association of Delhi, an institution of which Hans Raj Gupta was made the chairman in 1945.[15]

In addition to his business, Hans Raj Gupta had inherited ideological inclinations from his father. The latter had been a staunch Arya Samajist who had sent his son to Arya Samaj prayer meetings every Sunday as well as Arya Samajist schools. One of his teachers, Mohan Singh Mehta, had initiated him into the scout movement and Hans Raj Gupta remained supportive of the Hindustan Scouts Association all his life. In 1935 he joined the Congress but he soon considered that its so-called 'appeasement policy' towards Muslims was responsible for Jinnah's militancy and he shifted to the RSS in 1944-5. Oke contacted him first:

> I met Hans Raj Gupta because in every area we used to arrange meetings with good people [*sic*]. In Barakhamba Road there were several good people: some businessmen, some contractors. From every house we used to call on one man every month at one place where I would go to address them about the Sangh's ideas. They were invited to visit at least one *shakha* to see our work.[16]

Hans Raj Gupta was thus requested to visit a *shakha* and then to preside over the RSS function of Raksha Bhandan in 1945. These details are revealing of the way the RSS penetrated the establishment of Delhi. In 1946, H.R. Gupta attended an ITC in Vrindavan, where he met Golwalkar. He became the *prant sanghchalak* in 1947, and in 1948 chairman of Bharat Prakashan, the publisher of the RSS mouthpieces, *The Organiser* and *The Motherland* (in the 1970s).

As a true notable, Hans Raj Gupta succeeded in occupying posts of responsibility without contesting elections. He became the mayor of Delhi in 1967 after being selected as one of the six eldermen by the hundred elected members of the Municipal Corporation. He was re-elected up to 1973 and his son, Rajendra Gupta, reached the same position in 1977-9. By then, Hans Raj Gupta had given up party politics in order to devote more time to what he called 'social work'. In fact, he patronized caste associations (he supported the Aggarwal Sabha's efforts to organize this merchant caste and reform its social habits) and educational institutions [he was chairman of the DAV (Dayananda Anglo-Vedic) Higher Secondary School of Yusuf Sarai and gave financial assistance to Indraprastha College, the Hindu College, Bal Bharati Public School, etc.]. He also contributed to the scout movement (in the 1970s he was still director of the Delhi branch of the Bharat Scout and Guides). Rather than social, these activities were more akin to philanthropy than social work. They were in fact well in tune with the traditional function of the *rais*.[17]

In his work on Allahabad, C.A. Bayly suggests that the Indian National Congress was first established at the local level thanks to the collaboration of *rais* and publicists—educated Brahmins (or Kayasthas) fluent in English and able to present the claims of the *rais* to the British.[18] The *rais* would support the publicists in their efforts to defend Hindu society and culture (especially festivals such as the Magh Mela of Allahabad) from British interference. Bayly points out that the publicists gradually emancipated themselves from the *rais* after the reforms of 1909 and 1919 and became full-fledged politicians.[19] However, such a schema still seems relevant to the study of the RSS even after 1947. In this case, the publicists were primarily *pracharaks* whose main purpose was to propagate the ideology of the movement. Most were educated Brahmins who seemed more prepared than 'modern' Congressmen to seek the guidance of conservative notables whose patronage they needed.

In Delhi, the *rais*-publicist combination was successively embodied first by the pair formed by Lala Harichandra Gupta and Vasant Rao Oke; then by Hans Raj Gupta and Oke, and from the mid-1950s onwards, by Hans Raj Gupta and Madhav Rao Muley. The latter, again a Chitpavan Brahmin, had been sent from Nagpur to Lahore in 1940 to occupy the newly created post of *prant pracharak* for the Punjab province which included Delhi according to the RSS map of India.[20] In this capacity, Muley tended to eclipse Oke, especially after the latter developed a keen interest in the creation of the Jana Sangh despite Golwalkar's initial reservations about the implication of *pracharaks* entering party politics.

Thus, one of the main assets of the RSS in Delhi was the support which it gathered from *rais* of the business community. Besides the elite of this milieu, many other Delhi Banias took an interest in the movement. Kanwar

Lal Gupta was one of them. This rich merchant, educated at Delhi University in the 1940s, joined the RSS, and later became the first general secretary of the Delhi Pradesh Jana Sangh in 1951. He was elected to the Delhi Vidhan Sabha in 1953, to the Municipal Corporation in 1958 and to the Lok Sabha from Sadar constituency—its base—in 1967.[21] Another Bania, Shyam Charan Gupta, an Arya Samajist who joined the RSS in 1940, was also president of the Delhi branch of the Boy Scouts Association and of the Delhi Provincial Aggarwal Sabha. He was elected MLA (Member of the Legislative Assembly) on a Jana Sangh ticket in 1952 and was then made Municipal Councillor in 1967 and 1972.[22] In fact, the merchant castes were well represented among the RSS and Jana Sangh leadership both before and after Partition, something which can be explained in various ways.

First, the Arya Samaj—whose organization had always been strong among the merchant castes of the Punjab—had prepared the ground for Hindu nationalism. In 1931, out of about 4,00,000 Hindus there were more than 50,000 Arya Samajists in Delhi.[23] Most of them probably belonged to the merchant communities; in the Punjab the merchant castes (Khatris, Aroras, Agarwals) and Brahmins together represented about half of the 1,00,846 Arya Samaj members in 1911.[24] The merchant castes appreciated the Aryas' notion of 'self-help' which suited their sense of enterprise and perhaps even stemmed from it. Arya Samajists were the first to set up indigenous undertakings such as the Punjab National Bank and the Bharat Insurance Company in the 1890s.[25]

The Arya Samaj's success story in the Punjab had a lot to do with the specific social structure of the province. The Kshatriyas who had seen their power being taken away by Sikhs and Brahmins and felt deprived of patrons, had to take recourse to the support of the merchant castes.[26] The Banias came to occupy the forefront of Hindu society more and more exclusively as the British allowed them to extend their economic dominance and to translate it into socio-economic terms through education.[27] Barrier argues that the Arya Samaj's attraction to the Banias stemmed from the fact that in spite of all these changes the Banias remained the last of the 'twice born': 'Dayananda's claim that caste should be determined primarily by merit not birth, opened new paths of social mobility to educated Vaishyas who were trying to achieve social status commensurate with their improving economic status.'[28] Dipankar Gupta has suggested more convincingly that the Arya Samaj gained much support in the Punjab, especially from Banias, because the local society was free from brahminical control and orthodoxy.[29]

While the Arya Samaj had prepared the ground for Banias joining the RSS in Delhi as it had in the Punjab, there were some Delhi Banias who joined the RSS without having any Arya Samaj background. One RSS veteran, who admits the over representation of Banias in the RSS, considers that it provided a good opportunity for Banias to practise sports in the light of the fact that they spent most of their time sitting down in their shops: 'Businessmen would join the RSS,' he argued, 'because it would give them something in terms of exercise.'[30] The need for physical strength was even more acutely felt in the 1940s when Muslim organizations demanding the creation of Pakistan, began to acquire a similar para-military dimension.

Thus Delhi's magnates such as Hans Raj Gupta and, more generally, a number of local Banias, contributed to the growth of the Hindu nationalist movement in the city, even before independence. However, the main factor influencing the rise of the RSS and later the Jana Sangh after independence was the influx of refugees from the Punjab.

AMBIVALENCE OF REFUGEES' SUPPORT

Partition and the influx of thousands of refugees into Delhi in 1947 enabled the Hindu nationalist movement to organize mass mobilizations in the city for the first time. In 1947 about 4,50,000 people from west Punjab settled in Delhi. They composed almost one-third of the urban population.[31] Many of them had lost everything and some had been victims of communal violence. The Hindu Mahasabha and the RSS presented themselves as organizations catering to their needs and exploited their resentment.

On 7 December 1947, about 50,000 people attended a meeting held by the two organizations. The main speakers were the Maharaja of Alwar, Gokul Chand Narang and Jugal Kishore Birla, both close to the Hindu Mahasabha and Golwalkar who eulogized the role of his movement in protecting Hindus in Punjab. He also criticized the 'satanic' attitude of Nehru's government for its 'appeasement' policy *vis-à-vis* Pakistan.[32] Refugees had already openly expressed their resentment of Gandhi on several occasions,[33] especially when he announced what was to be his last fast in January 1948. Immediately, refugees demonstrated in front of Birla House, shouting slogans such as 'Blood for blood!' and 'Let Gandhi die!'[34] In addition to the Rs. 550 million for Pakistan, Gandhi wanted local representatives of the different communities to sign a 'peace-pledge' before he suspended his fast. Interestingly, Hans Raj Gupta did so on behalf of the Hindus. However, on 25 January, the Hindu Mahasabha and the Delhi branch of the Arya Samaj organized a procession against Gandhi's fast and two days later the Hindu Mahasabha held a meeting, allegedly attended by 50,000 people, in which Gandhi and the Congress were aggressively accused of being responsible for Partition.[35] A few days later, on 30 January 1948, Mahatma Gandhi was assassinated in Birla House by Nathuram Godse.

Besides orchestrating the refugees' protest and exploiting their resentment, the Hindu Mahasabha and RSS tried to project themselves as their benefactors. The Hindu Mahasabha Bhawan was opened to refugees and food as well as clothes were distributed while the Hindu Mahasabha established a refugee camp near the railway station.[36] However, it was short of funds and after some time the Mahasabha contented itself with having lists of job seekers circulated among local businessmen.

The *sangh parivar* or the *sangh* family—an expression designating the RSS and its offshoots—played a more important part after the ban imposed on the RSS because of its links with Gandhi's assassin was lifted in 1949. In fact, it could by this stage appear more convincingly as the protector of the refugees because most of its leaders, especially in the newly created Jana Sangh, came from Punjab. While Oke, Muley and 'locals' such as Hans Raj Gupta remained at the helm of the RSS, an increasing number of Punjabis were taken on as their lieutenants and the Delhi unit of the Jana Sangh recruited most of its cadres from this milieu. Men such as Balraj Madhok, Bhai Mahavir, Vijay Kumar Malhotra, Kedar Nath Sahni and Har Dayal Devgun were among the most prominent figures and they shared a similar background.

Madhok came from a Jammu-based Khatri family with Arya Samajist leanings.[37] He joined the RSS in 1938 while he was studying in DAV College in Lahore. According to him, 'the Arya Samajists were closest to Dr Hedgewar's way of thinking'.[38] He became a *pracharak* in 1942 and was sent to Kashmir in this capacity. Bhai Mahavir, the son of Bhai Parmanand, a staunch Arya Samajist who had been President of the Hindu Mahasabha in 1933, was one of his fellow-students in DAV College in Lahore and he joined the RSS at the same time.[39] He too was a Khatri. He had spent a couple of years, from 1942 to 1944, as a *pracharak* in Jalandhar before working as office secretary of the RSS in Lahore from 1944 to 1947. After 1947 he settled down in Jalandhar and then in Karnal where he worked as a lecturer. He came to Delhi in 1956 when he was offered a job in Punjab University College, an institution specially created for Punjabi refugees, where Madhok was already teaching. Madhok had come to Delhi soon after Partition. He had taken part in the foundation of the Praja Parishad[40] in Jammu in November 1947 and had been expelled from Jammu and Kashmir soon after because of his political activities. In 1948 he settled in Delhi.

The moving spirit behind the creation of the Jana Sangh was Syama Prasad Mookerjee but his colleagues in this enterprise were either Delhi-based Hindu nationalists or refugees from Punjab. After he resigned from Nehru's government because of the Liaqat-Nehru Pact in April 1950, he was given a welcome ceremony by a group of prominent Delhi citizens, including Hans Raj Gupta, Vasant Rao Oke, Mauli Chandra Sharma (the son of Din Dayal Sharma, a co-founder of the Hindu Mahasabha, who had worked in the administration of several Princely States before settling in Delhi)[41] and Lala Yodhraj Bhalla, the son of Hans Raj, one of the founders of DAV College in Lahore and the president of the Punjab National Bank. Mookerjee immediately launched a campaign for the defence of refugees which culminated in July with an All India Refugee Conference which attracted 15,000 participants in Delhi.[42] Several months later, in January 1951, Mookerjee discussed the possibility of founding a new party with the same group: Madhok, Bhai Mahavir, Dharmavir (Bhai Parmanand's son-in-law, a former lecturer in English in Lahore and the Punjab *prant pracharak*), Balraj Bhalla (Yodhraj's brother) and Mahasha Krishnan (an Arya Samajist who edited *Pratap* in Lahore before Partition and who continued to do so in Delhi after 1947).[43] On 27 May 1951, one month after the creation of the West Bengal branch of the Jana Sangh by Mookerjee, a meeting was held in

Jalandhar at the instigation of Madhok, to launch the Jana Sangh which would represent Punjab and Delhi.[44] Balraj Bhalla was elected its first president, M.C. Sharma its vice-president and Balraj Madhok its secretary.[45]

Madhok and Bhai Mahavir were appointed to important posts in the All India Jana Sangh which was founded in Delhi on 21 October 1951, with Bhai Mahavir becoming general secretary and Madhok a member of the working committee (and in 1958 national secretary in charge of north India), but they continued to play a part in the party-building process in Delhi too—with Madhok presiding over the local branch of the Jana Sangh in 1959 and winning the Lok Sabha seat for New Delhi in a bye-election in 1961. Other refugees were also very active in the local party apparatus.

Refugees with an RSS background gradually took over the party apparatus in the 1950s and displaced leaders who either had no RSS background—like the Hindu Sabhaites—or were not from west Punjab. The turning point occurred in 1954 when Vaid Guru Dutt, the president of the Delhi Jana Sangh, expressed his resentment of RSS interference in party affairs. An Arya Samajist and teacher of History in the Government College, Lahore, before he migrated to Delhi where he became a writer and practised Ayurvedic medicine, Guru Dutt had no links with the RSS. Ironically enough, K.L. Gupta, vice-president of the Delhi Jana Sangh, and V.R. Oke, its Organizing Secretary, supported him, even though they were from RSS cadres. This local conflict crystallized at the same time that similar developments were occurring in the party central headquarters where M. Sharma, who had succeeded Mookerjee as party president in 1953, also objected to RSS interference, but in vain. Eventually, like Dutt, Gupta and Oke, he resigned. The Delhi Jana Sangh was dissolved[46] and then re-constituted with former RSS *pracharaks* from Punjab at the helm. While Madhok was president, he had so many responsibilities at the national level that the day to day affairs fell to K.N. Sahni's share.

Sahni had just settled in Delhi in 1954. He came from Jalandhar where he had worked as *pracharak*. A native of Punjab, he was born in Rawalpindi and studied in Multan Arya Samaj School. Like Madhok, he considers that in Punjab, the 'Arya Samaj prepared the ground for the RSS to work'. He had been sent to Kashmir as a *pracharak* in 1946 and later to east Punjab after having been expelled from Jammu and Kashmir in 1948.[47] In 1954 he was appointed to the key post of organization secretary of the Delhi Jana Sangh. He became general secretary four years later when Lal Krishna Advani took over from him. Advani was not from Punjab, but was a refugee from Sindh, like another RSS figure in Delhi, Kewalram Ratanmal Malkani.[48] Advani had joined the RSS in Hyderabad (Sindh) in 1942, had been sent to Karachi as a *pracharak* in 1947 and had migrated to Rajasthan, where he worked as *pracharak* after Partition.[49] He came to Delhi in 1957 and became secretary and later vice-president of the Delhi Jana Sangh. Thus, the key posts of the party unit were gradually occupied by refugees with an RSS background. In addition to this sociological change, the *sangh parivar* worked for the cause of refugees—or pretended to do so.

Hans Raj Gupta initiated a Hindu Sahayata Samiti which worked almost as a front for the RSS. Though it was especially active in Delhi, it also had some existence elsewhere in India—in Gwalior for instance. Its main work consisted of distributing clothes and blankets in refugee camps and enrolling children in the new Hindu Sahayata Samiti schools.[50] However, the refugees gradually became less concerned with emergency measures and more interested in issues such as the cost of rent and the rate of loans. In the *sangh parivar,* Vimal Kumar Malhotra devoted comparatively more time to these issues in the framework of a 'welfarist tactic' well in tune with the RSS tradition of selective relief-work: its activists' network has always enabled the *sangh parivar* to do a kind of social work which, in fact, was intended to help the movement to build pockets of influence among poor, displaced persons and the like.

Malhotra had a profile similar to Madhok and Mahavir: a Khatri by caste, he had joined the RSS in Lahore while in the 7th class at DAV College and had been sent to Jammu as a *pracharak* in 1947. Not long after, he had come to Delhi to study at Punjab University College—the college specially created for Punjabi refugees. He later taught there—like Madhok and Mahavir he was a teacher by training—till the college closed down in 1958.[51] Malhotra then joined DAV College. As a student leader he became secretary of Delhi University Student Union (DUSU) in 1951[52] and later all India organizing secretary of the RSS backed student union, the Akhil Bharatiya Vidyarthi Parishad (ABVP) till 1952 when he shifted to the 'refugees front'. He was then the founder-president of the Kendriya Chamarti Sabha (Central Refugees Association) and one of the three convenors of the United Refugees Front, the two others being Balraj Khanna (then a member of the Hindu Mahasabha) and Bishamdar Kapur (close to an ex-Hindu Sabhaite from the Congress, Mehr Chand Khanna—see below). This organization, which had been set up 'under the initiative of Delhi Pradesh Jana Sangh'[53] lobbied in favour of the refugees. It fought against the elevation of rents in government-built residential quarters and shops in refugee colonies like Lajpat Nagar, Kingsway Camp, Malaviya Nagar, Moti Nagar, Ramesh Nagar and so forth. The Delhi Jana Sangh supported the agitation of the United Refugees Front against the government decision to recover full payments on refugees' properties within three years—K.N. Sahni asked for thirty years.

Being a party with refugees at its helm and defending the cause of refugees from Punjab, the Jana Sangh was well placed for getting the refugees' votes. A study of refugees from the Dehra Dun district shows that about 40 per cent of them remained very hostile to Muslims and considered that the Congress had done no good for the country. In a place like Rishikesh, this attitude combined with support for the RSS and Jana Sangh.[54] Gita Puri came to a similar conclusion in her study of the Jana Sangh in Delhi. Among the four Jana Sangh MLAs elected in Delhi in 1952 were G.D. Salwan, the president of the Refugees Relief Committee in Jhandewalan (where the RSS headquarters was situated and where so many refugees had settled), Shyam Charan Gupta in Daryaganj (again a constituency with many refugees) and

Rana Jang Bahadur Singh (in Kingsway Camp—a former refugee camp). During the 1954 elections to the Municipal Corporation, the Jana Sangh won 10 of its 15 seats in refugee-dominated constituencies,[55] and during the 1958 elections to the Municipal Corporation, the Jana Sangh won 16 (out of 25) seats in refugee-dominated constituencies.[56] In the 1962 municipal elections, when the party suffered a severe setback, it won 6 of its 9 seats in constituencies with a substantial percentage of refugees. In 1967, 23 of its 52 seats and in 1971, 23 of its 53 seats were won in Punjabi-dominated constituencies.

However, to consider the Jana Sangh of Delhi as 'the party of refugee people'[57] is incorrect. First, Punjabis probably voted for the Jana Sangh not only because of the hardships they suffered as refugees but also because of their backgrounds: many of them were already supporters of the RSS before 1947. Indeed, the movement saw a dramatic increase in the 1930s and 1940s in eastern and western Punjab as well as in Delhi. In fact, of all the Indian provinces, Punjab was the one state where the RSS developed most quickly. While the first *shakhas* had started there in 1935 with the help of Arya Samajists turned Hindu Sabhaites (like Bhai Parmanand), the movement swelled in greater Punjab (Delhi and Himachal Pradesh included, but west Punjab excluded) to reach 14,000 members by 1940[58] and 1,25,000 members by 1951.[59] The fortunes of the RSS in Punjab were undoubtedly linked to the rise of separatism among local Muslims. At that time, the organization tended to function as a militia for both offensive and defensive purposes.[60]

More important, the Jana Sangh cannot be considered the party of the refugees, not only because its strength in the city-capital was not purely based on refugee support, but also because there were refugees who did not vote for this party. A large number of refugees did in fact remain close to the Congress, not least because they already saw it as a Hindu party even before Partition. Almost since its inception in the late nineteenth century, there had been a strong Hindu traditionalist current in the Punjab Congress. Lala Lajpat Rai epitomized this school of thought till his death in 1928, as did several other extremists from the Arya Samaj. One of his lieutenants, Gopichand Bhargava, took over from Rai in the 1930s, and after Partition, Gopichand's brother, Thakurdas Bhargava, became one of the main advocates of Hindu traditionalism in the Constituent Assembly. He objected to the recognition of religious minorities as 'communities'[61] and to the granting of rights of citizenship to non-Hindu immigrants from Pakistan. He was also one of the staunchest advocates of cow protection and the promotion of Hindi as a national language.[62]

Many Delhi-based Punjabi Congressmen had similar Hindu leanings. Jagat Narain, who had been a student of Bhai Parmanand and remained a staunch Arya Samajist, was a Congressman. He was the editor of *Milap*, an Arya Samaj paper with a strong inclination towards the Congress.[63]

In addition to this tradition, Mehr Chand Khanna, the key figure of Hindu politics in the North-West Frontier Province before 1947, was co-opted into the central government soon after Partition. Khanna—Rai Bahadur since 1927—was a *rais* of Peshawar who had been elected to the Municipal Council as early as 1922 and who was appointed by the British to the NWFP (North-West Frontier Province) Franchise Committee in 1932. He had been elected to the Legislative Council in 1933 on a Hindu Mahasabha ticket.[64] He shifted to the Congress after Partition and worked first as an advisor for the Ministry of Rehabilitation and later as its minister. At the same time, he was at the helm of a powerful refugees' lobby, the Delhi Refugees Federation. In 1962, Khanna was the Congress candidate for the prestigious Lok Sabha seat of New Delhi against Madhok (who had wrested it from the Congress in 1961) and he won with 57 per cent of the valid votes, as against Madhok's 38 per cent. He had been nominated owing to the support of other refugee representatives within the Congress, notably Jag Pravesh Chandra.[65]

Generally speaking, the refugees from the North-West Frontier Province tended to maintain their allegiance to the Congress party. They had been close to the party before Partition, not least because Muslim politics in this area had been dominated by Abdul Ghaffar Khan, the so called 'Frontier Gandhi', rather than the Muslim League.

Interestingly, the percentage of members of the Metropolitan Council of Delhi (MCD) who came from west Punjab did not fluctuate in accordance with Jana Sangh election results: in 1967 when the party won a majority, 34 per cent of its members were from Pakistan; in 1972 when it lost heavily, refugees still represented 33 per cent of the metropolitan councillors; in 1977 when the Janata Party (of which the former Jana Sangh was a major component) swept the polls, the proportion of refugees in the MCD dropped to 26 per cent and in 1983 when the Congress party won the elections the proportion of refugees stabilized at 25 per cent.[66]

The Congress retained strong support among Punjabi refugees partly because it was perceived as a Hindu party, but also because Nehru's government helped them a lot. The Ministry of Rehabilitation, established on 6 September 1947, set up three refugee camps: Kingsway, Tibia College (in Karol Bagh) and one in Shahdara. The number of inmates started to decline by mid-1948, which meant that the refugees were finding new jobs and places to live,[67] largely due to the government's policy. While 1,90,000 refugees were accommodated in houses which had been left by Muslims, 1.2 million were given new houses. Parallel to these special measures, 4752 shops and stalls were built by the government and local bodies.[68] In 1948, a loan of Rs. 42,62,075 was sanctioned for refugees and by March 1952, 1800 of the displaced secured jobs through the employment exchange set up by the government.[69] The refugees who benefited from this rehabilitation scheme were naturally grateful to the Congress government. Malkani himself admits that Nehru's government was very helpful to refugees:

> The government has done relatively well. I would not attack the government on this. There was only one problem: the government was not firm enough with Pakistan. They should have asked for more compensation because the property the Hindus

left there were about ten times the property left by the Muslims. But apart from that, the government did well. I had no particular grievance.[70]

Some refugees therefore voted for the Congress because they were not unhappy with the government's policy, but also because they depended on Congressmen for getting things done. Since many of them were traders, they had to ask the government for licences, electricity connections and so on. In Delhi as elsewhere, the Congress could rely on its bargaining power and operated within a framework of clientelism.

The Jana Sangh was thus not 'the party of the refugees' because refugees did not vote only for this party and because the party did not recruit its support only from refugees. This point was made as early as 1951 during the first local elections to the Delhi Municipal Corporation: although the refugees were just settled and could not take part in great numbers in the poll, the Jana Sangh won one-quarter of the valid votes. This figure reflected the influence the *sangh parivar* had gained among 'locals' after 25 years of groundwork in Delhi. Not surprisingly, its following was especially strong among traders. In the Chandni Chowk unit of the party, where, in the 1970s, three-quarters of the office bearers were 'locals', 55 per cent of them were Banias and 29 per cent Kshatriyas—probably Khatris working as businessmen.[71] The Jana Sangh had indeed a strong following among 'locals' and if it won a majority of its seats to the Municipal Corporation in refugee-dominated constituencies, a substantial number of them were obtained in 'local' Hindu dominated constituencies: 3 out of 9 in 1962, 18 out of 52 in 1967—the first elections after K.L. Gupta (still very influential in Delhi Sadar), rejoined the Jana Sangh in 1964—and 15 out of 53 in 1974.[72] In the 1967 municipal elections in the Sadar district the Jana Sangh won more votes than the Congress (43 per cent as against 41 per cent) in the Hindu 'local'-dominated wards, partly because it was able to nominate 'local' candidates.[73]

In fact, the Jana Sangh was weak only in the rural and the reserved constituencies where the Congress, in contrast, was very strong. One of its main leaders, Brahm Prakash Choudhury, a Yadav, who had been chief minister of Delhi in 1952, was elected to the Outer Delhi seat of the Lok Sabha four times successively from 1962 onwards. The Jana Sangh, by contrast, did not win any rural seat to the Municipal Corporation in 1958 (for the good reason that it had not even fielded a candidate), and won only one in 1962 in Alipur where, interestingly, more than half of its office-bearers were Punjabi refugees with an urban background. In 1967 it won 4 seats and in 1971, 2 seats.[74] The urban bias of the party was still evident in the 1983 elections.

So far as reserved seats were concerned, the Jana Sangh could not win any seats in Karol Bagh in the 1958 municipal elections largely because it could not attract Scheduled Caste voters in this Dalit-dominated constituency. This weakness affected its prospects for a long time since it could win only 4 reserved seats in the elections to the Delhi Municipal Corporation in 1971. Even in the reserved constituencies where it won, the Jana Sangh owed its success mainly to non-Scheduled Caste voters as Saini and Andersen have shown in their detailed study of the voting pattern for the Scheduled Caste seat of Sadar Bazaar.[75] The only Jana Sangh representative elected in a reserved and rural constituency in the 1971 municipal elections, S.P. Sumnaskar, defected to the Congress party in 1975 because 'high caste members dominated the Jana Sangh and displayed superiority complex and wanted to keep Scheduled Castes members at a distance'. He considered that there was 'no opportunity for those who [were] outside this Punjabi-Banya alliance'.[76] The only Scheduled Caste leaders who remained in the Jana Sangh had an RSS background and had inherited an impulse to 'Sanskritize' from their training. Its successful candidate in Karol Bagh in 1967 (and its unsuccessful candidate in 1971) was an advocate advisor to the All India Scheduled Castes Uplift Union, but with an RSS background and the second Jana Sanghi who, after Sumnaskar succeeded in winning a reserved and rural seat, Kalka Dass, had a similar profile. He had joined the RSS in 1946 in Mehrauli, his birth place, while his father—the headman of several villages—was close to Ambedkar (he called himself a Jatav). For Kalka Dass, who won the Mehrauli Municipal Council seat in 1977 and 1983 and the Karol Bagh parliamentary seat in 1989 and 1991 on a BJP ticket, the *sangh parivar* was the only movement fighting against the caste system on behalf of nationalistic—and therefore supposedly egalitarian—values.[77] The Jana Sangh failed to attract Scheduled Caste leaders who had not been trained in the RSS mould and who were truly representative of their group.

One may conclude from the aforesaid argument that the Jana Sangh was not so much 'the party of the refugees' as the party of the urban Hindu middle classes. Punjabi refugees did not vote exclusively for the Jana Sangh and when they did, it was not only because they were refugees but also because of the political culture they had acquired before 1947 and their ethos and interests as businessmen. Meanwhile many 'locals' voted for the Jana Sangh because of an ideological background they had acquired before Partition, and because of their professional activities as merchant castes. Instead of looking at the Jana Sangh as 'the party of the refugees' it may then be more relevant to study it as the party of businessmen, provided one includes within this category anybody independently involved in trade, industry (including cottage-industries) and other manufacturing.

FROM THE 'MIDDLE WORLD' TO THE 'OUTER WORLD'?

The distinction between 'locals' and refugees is probably less important than the one between businessmen and others. In his study of the 1972 elections to the Delhi Metropolitan Council, Raj Chandidas emphasizes that 'the Jana Sangh draws heavily for its support on petty traders and small businessmen'.[78] This description was also true of the Jana Sangh candidates to the Delhi Municipal Corporation and the Delhi Metropolitan Council among whom Banias and Khatris, both merchant castes, represented 42.5 to 44.5 per cent of the total. While 20 per cent of the members of the council were businessmen (as against 22 per cent in 1967[79]), 47 per cent of the Jana Sangh candidates had this background.

Many Jana Sangh candidates in 1971 and 1972 were probably Punjabi refugees since most of them were businessmen. The 1971 Census indicates that 31 per cent of these refugees were involved in 'trade and commerce', 16 per cent in 'manufacturing, processing, servicing and repairs (other than household industry)', and 11 per cent in 'transport, storage and communication'.[80] In 1971, almost 60 per cent of the Punjabi refugees (and even more if one takes into account the 2 per cent involved in 'construction') belonged to what Bruce Graham has called 'the middle world'—the middle classes, threatened from above by the state's intervention and from below by an increasing awareness of the backward classes.[81] Therefore, the Jana Sangh's relative success in Delhi may have less to do with the large refugee population than with its social profile. The 'middle world'—whether among 'locals' or refugees—voted for the party because it defended their interests. Indeed, Deendayal Upadhyaya, the general secretary of the Jana Sangh from 1952 till his death in 1968, never ceased to criticize the Nehruvian view of a state-owned economy and the Congress' priority towards industrialization. In 1958 he wrote that 'By taking up programmes of heavy industries the [Planning] Commission intended to bring about a structural change in our society. . . . But we cannot build a pyramid from the top downwards.'[82] He

TABLE 11.3. CASTE AND COMMUNITY OF THE JANA SANGH CANDIDATES TO THE DELHI MUNICIPAL CORPORATION IN 1971 AND TO THE DELHI METROPOLITAN COUNCIL IN 1972

Castes and communities	*1971*	*%*	*1972*	*%*
UPPER CASTES	*54*	*62*	*32*	*59.3*
Brahmin	11	12.6	7	13.0
Bania	18	20.7	11	20.4
Khatri	19	21.8	13	24.1
Arora	5	5.7	–	–
Other	1	1.1	1	1.8
INTERMEDIATE CASTES	*2*	*2.3*	*2*	*3.7*
Jat	2	2.3	2	3.7
OTHER BACKWARD CLASSES	*11*	*12.6*	*5*	*9.3*
Gujjar	5	5.7	2	3.7
Yadav	4	4.6	2	3.7
Saini/Mali	1	1.1	–	–
Julaha	1	1.1	1	1.8
Other	–	–	–	–
SCHEDULED CASTES	*6*	*6.9*	*2*	*3.7*
SIKH		–	*1*	*1.9*
MUSLIM	*1*	*1.2*	*1*	*1.9*
EUROPEANS/ANGLO-INDIANS	–	–	–	–
NON-IDENTIFIED/OTHER	*13*	*15*	*11*	*20.4*
TOTAL	*87*	*100*	*54*	*100*

Source: Interviews with BJP and Jana Sangh old timers.

TABLE 11.4. OCCUPATIONAL BACKGROUND OF THE JANA SANGH CANDIDATES TO THE DELHI MUNICIPAL CORPORATION IN 1971

Occupation	*Absolute numbers*	%
Agriculturist	6	6.9
Lawyer	4	4.6
Medical profession	4	4.6
Business	41	47.2
Executive/employee	4	4.6
Teacher/Principal	6	6.9
Journalist	3	3.5
Trade unionist/Social worker	2	2.3
Politician/Pracharak	2	2.3
Landlord	1	1.2
Unknown	13	14.9
TOTAL	87	100

Source: Interviews with BJP and Jana Sangh old timers.

criticized the lack of investment in 'decentralised small scale industry' which, in his view should have been the main route to economic development.[83] From 1951, the Jana Sangh advocated a division of tasks between the state (which would run heavy industry) and the private sector: the production of consumer goods, for instance, would be reserved for the latter, and the state would be required to prevent economic conglomeration so that family enterprises might flourish.[84]

The Jana Sangh tried to defend the 1,00,000 small-scale enterprises of India in a very concrete way. It objected to the imposition of sales taxes which hampered the functioning of these enterprises. In 1958, merchants were forced to accept the establishment of state control over the grain trade, a measure intended to reduce inflationary shortages by promoting a centralized regional distribution of the produce. The Jana Sangh condemned this decision, arguing that it would lead to the nationalization of small businesses[85] and the disappearance of 30,000 wholesalers and 3 millions retailers.[86] Thus, those who belonged to the 'middle world' could be attracted to the Jana Sangh simply because of its right-wing agenda.

The over-representation of the 'middle world' in the ranks of the Hindu nationalist party remained true in 1983 within the Delhi Municipal Corporation: while this institution had 20 per cent of businessmen, the BJP group had 60 per cent.

Ten years later, the over-representation of the upper castes in the BJP was still very much in evidence, as testified by the large number of upper-caste candidates, especially Banias and Khatris, fielded by the party during the 1993 state assembly elections. While the Congress nominated almost as many upper-caste candidates (though more Brahmins than Banias) as the BJP, it also nominated a larger number of Jat candidates, a sign of the rural reach of the Congress in Outer Delhi.

The larger number of Jat candidates in the Congress is of course

TABLE 11.5. OCCUPATIONAL BACKGROUND OF THE BJP MEMBERS OF THE DELHI MUNICIPAL CORPORATION ELECTED IN 1983

Occupation	*BJP*	%
Agriculturist	3	8.6
Lawyer	2	5.7
Business	21	60.0
Ex-civil servant	1	2.9
Teacher	4	11.4
Trade unionist/Social worker	2	5.7
Unknown/Other	2	5.7
TOTAL	35	100

Source: Interviews with local cadres and office bearers in the office of the Delhi Pradesh BJP.

congruent with the larger proportion of agriculturists among its assembly candidates. However, the share of businessmen—by far the largest—is slightly more important within the Congress, whereas in the BJP, the teachers are second to the businessmen with more than 11 per cent (see Table 11.7).

The social composition of the BJP Delhi State Executive suggests that the party is slowly promoting Jats in its apparatus since the Jat share of seats grew slightly between 1993 and 1995 at the expense of the upper castes. The erosion of high-caste seats is especially marked among the Brahmins. However, the proportion of Other Backward Classes and Scheduled Castes in the party structure remains nominal.

The social profile of the office-bearers of the district and local units of the BJP and the Congress show a similar picture. All in all, the BJP remained slightly more Punjabi, more urban and more elitist (from the caste point of view at least) than the Congress, and by and large as business-oriented as the latter but then the differences between both parties are often not significant.

After winning the 1993 assembly elections, the BJP appointed Madan Lal Khurana as chief minister, who was clearly representative of this milieu. Khurana joined the RSS in 1943, in Lyallpur in west Punjab, even before he was a teenager. His family, Khatri by caste, migrated to Jammu after Partition and then settled in Delhi. M.L. Khurana, who used to live in Paharganj, started his career as a teacher with a modest income of Rs. 400 per month till 1967, the year when he was first elected member of the Metropolitan Council. He then set up a goods truck transport and bus company.[87] Khurana is, therefore, typical of the post-Partition *sangh parivar* leadership, made up of upper-caste teachers and/or businessmen from Punjab. He became general secretary of the Delhi Jana Sangh in 1965 and kept this charge till 1975. In 1977 he was elected executive councillor of Delhi and in 1980, general secretary of the Delhi branch of the BJP of which he became the president in 1985. He was succeeded by Om Prakash Kohli, another Khatri teacher from Punjab, but in 1993 was elected chief minister when the BJP won the elections.

Khurana had to resign in February 1996 owing to his alleged involvement

TABLE 11.6. CASTE AND COMMUNITY BACKGROUND OF THE BJP AND CONGRESS CANDIDATES TO THE ASSEMBLY ELECTIONS IN 1993

Castes and communities	*BJP*	%	*Congress*	%
UPPER CASTES	*33*	*47.1*	*26*	*35.7*
Brahmin	8	11.4	11	15.1
Rajput	3	4.3	–	–
Bania	11	15.7	4	5.5
Khatri	9	12.9	9	12.3
Arora	–	–	1	1.4
Other	2	2.9	1	1.4
INTERMEDIATE CASTES	*9*	*12.9*	*15*	*20.5*
Jat	9	12.9	15	20.5
OTHER BACKWARD CLASSES	*7*	*8.6*	*5*	*6.8*
Gujjar	–	–	2	2.7
Yadav	1	1.4	3	4.1
Jhangi	4	5.7	–	–
Soni	1	1.4	–	–
Other	1	1.4		
SCHEDULED CASTES	*13*	*18.6*	*13*	*17.8*
SIKH	*1*	*1.4*	*1*	*1.4*
MUSLIM	*3*	*4.3*	*1*	*1.4*
EUROPEANS/ANGLO-INDIANS	–	–	–	–
NON-IDENTIFIED/OTHER	*5*	*7.1*	*12*	*16.4*
TOTAL	*70*	*100*	*73*	*100*

Source: Interviews in the party offices.

in the 'hawala affair'. His successor, Sahib Singh Verma, was from a different background. An RSS activist since childhood, he had worked as a college librarian till 1993. Verma, a Jat from the periphery of Delhi and unlike most Jats not a farmer, was put in charge of rural development and education in Khurana's cabinet. While Verma was probably appointed for a variety of other reasons such as power equations within the party, the Delhi BJP certainly chose him partly in order to expand its social base in Outer Delhi where it used to be very weak. In August 1997, Verma commissioned a survey to identify more OBCs in Delhi. Press reports suggested that it was aimed at trying to include new castes, such as the Jats and the Jaiswals in this category.[88] Indeed the BJP may well be tempted to play 'the OBC card', from which it might be able to derive electoral dividends in the post-Mandal context.

CONCLUSION

While the coming to Delhi of hundreds of thousands of refugees after Partition helps to explain the Jana Sangh's electoral fortunes in the capital as early as 1951, it is not in itself a sufficient explanation. Many of the Punjabis who settled in Delhi may well have voted for the Jana Sangh because they had lost everything after Partition, a catastrophe they attributed to the Congress. But others, especially those from the NWFP, still preferred the ruling Congress party because they perceived it as a Hindu party anyway and

TABLE 11.7. OCCUPATIONAL BACKGROUND OF THE BJP AND CONGRESS CANDIDATES TO THE ASSEMBLY ELECTIONS IN 1993

Occupation	*BJP*	*%*	*Congress*	*%*
Agriculturist	8	11.4	10	14.3
Lawyer	–	–	3	4.3
Medical professions	4	5.7	2	2.9
Business	28	40.0	29	41.4
Ex-civil servant/Service/Engineer	3	4.3	4	5.7
Teacher/Principal	8	11.4	3	4.3
Journalist/Writer	1	1.4	3	4.3
Trade unionist/Social worker	5	7.2	13	18.6
Politician	6	8.6	–	–
Landlord	1	1.4	–	–
Unknown/Other	6	8.6	3	4.3
TOTAL	70	100	70	100

Source: Interviews in the party offices.

TABLE 11.8. CASTE BACKGROUND OF THE BJP DELHI STATE EXECUTIVE AND OF THE DELHI CONGRESS PRADESH COMMITTEE

Castes and communities	*BJP 1993*	*%*	*BJP 1995*	*%*	*Cong 1992*	*Cong 1994*
UPPER CASTES	*99*	*70.8*	*63*	*69.2*	*11*	*6*
Brahmin	33	23.6	12	13.2	3	2
Rajput	2	1.4	3	3.3	1	–
Bania	28	20.0	21	23.1	4	1
Khatri	32	22.9	21	23.1	3	3
Kayastha	3	2.1	–	–	–	–
Other	1	0.7	6	6.6	–	–
INTERMEDIATE CASTES	*5*	*3.6*	*8*	*8.8*	2	2
Jat	5	3.6	8	8.8	2	2
OTHER BACKWARD CLASSES	*12*	*8.6*	*3*	*3.3*	–	–
Gujjar	6	4.3	–	–	–	–
Saini			1	1.1	–	–
Julaha	–	0.7	–	–	–	–
Other	–	–	1	1.1	-	-
SCHEDULED CASTES	*12*	*8.6*	*6*	*6.6*	*5*	*1*
SIKH	*3*	*2.1*	*1*	*1.1*	*1*	–
MUSLIM	*4*	*2.9*	*7*	*7.7*	*3*	*1*
NON-IDENTIFIED/OTHER	*5*	*3.6*	*3*	*3.3*	–	–
TOTAL	*140*	*100*	*91*	*100*	*26*	*10*

Source: Interviews in the party offices.

depended on it for rehabilitation. The Punjabi refugees who opted for the Jana Sangh often did so because they had already been won over by the RSS in Punjab where the movement had grown rapidly in the 1940s. In other words, the trauma of Partition acted not to convert them to right-wing Hindu politics but to reconfirm their existing inclination.

More important, the base of the Jana Sangh was never confined to Punjabi refugees. The party also recruited strong support from 'local' businessmen, partly because of the early groundwork of the RSS and, before that, the Arya Samaj. In fact, the Jana Sangh and the BJP were probably less parties of refugees than parties of traders—Banias and Khatris (a caste whose members are often engaged in commercial activities). This interpretation is all the more convincing as about one-third of the refugees started businesses in Delhi. However, the social profile of the BJP cadres and MLAs is not significantly different from that of the Congress equivalents, even though the Jana Sangh and the BJP have perhaps been more consistently and constantly elitist.

Today, the BJP seems eager to expand its base in the rural periphery of the Delhi state where the Hindu nationalist movement has always been weak. The selection of a Jat, Sahib Singh Verma as chief minister in 1996, may be analysed in this perspective and the inclusion of his arch rival, M.L. Khurana, in Vajpayee's government might have been an attempt to remove him from the local scene. However, Verma's own dismissal shortly before the 1998 state assembly elections and his replacement by Sushma Swaraj (a Brahmin) have antagonized the rural voters of the Delhi state. The resignation of Khurana from Vajpayee's government in early 1999 has also heralded his return to local Delhi politics. In October-November 1999, he contested an MP seat. Interestingly, Sahib Singh Verma was also nominated by the BJP to contest in Outer Delhi, a Jat-dominated constituency where the party had only fielded upper-caste candidates till then. Both of them won their seat. In fact all the BJP candidates won the seven seats of Delhi for the first time, a reconfirmation of the party's traditional influence in this old stronghold of Hindu nationalism.

NOTES

This research would not have been possible without financial support from the ORSTOM-CNRS programme and the constant help of Mrs Bhalla from the Centre of Human Sciences (New Delhi) who collected some of the data presented in the last part of this essay. I am also most grateful to Dipankar Gupta for his comments as discussant of my paper. Certain nuances and insights can be attributed to him. I would also like to thank Dirubhai Seth for his constructive remarks following the oral presentation of this paper.

1. *The Statesman* (Delhi), 29 September 1954, p. 1.
2. *Delhi Gazetteer*, New Delhi: Delhi Administration, 1976, p. 972.
3. K. Jones, 'Organized Hinduism in Delhi and New Delhi', in R.E. Frykenberg (ed.), *Delhi Through the Ages*, Delhi: OUP, 1986, rpt. 1993, p. 203.
4. D. Gupta, *The Context of Ethnicity*, Delhi: OUP, 1997, p. 21.
5. K.R. Malkani, *The RSS Story*, New Delhi: Biblia Impex, 1980, p. 43.

6. Interview with Vasant Rao Oke, 12 August 1992, New Delhi.
7. Savarkar Papers, Reel no. 3, File no. 1, Letter of 27 July 1936, NMML (Nehru Museum & Memorial Library).
8. Ibid., Reel no. 4, File no. 1, Letter of Padam Raj Jain to Savarkar, 29 November 1936, and interview with V.R. Oke.
9. In fact the building of this office was, like the temple, financed by Jugal Kishore Birla who acted as a traditional patron in both cases.
10. Interview with Ratan Bhattacharya, 6 November 1997, Agra.
11. Max Mueller convincingly defines notables as persons '(1) whose economic position permits them to hold continuous policy-making and administrative positions in an organization without (more than nominal) remuneration; (2) who enjoy social prestige of whatever derivation in such a manner that they are likely to hold office in virtue of the members' confidence, which at first is given and then traditionally accorded' (*Economy and Society*, New York: Bedminster Press, 1988, p. 290).
12. Interview with V.R. Oke.
13. Interview with Ratan Bhattacharya. He was elected in the Lal Darwaza-Suiwalan ward on a Jana Sangh ticket in the 1958 Delhi municipal elections.
14. Ramashankar Mishra, 'Jivan vritt', in *Vinay Aur Vivek*, Delhi: Sri Hansraj Gupta Abhinandan-Prant Samaroh Samiti Prakashan, 1972, pp. 1-11.
15. Hans Raj Gupta's reminiscences in ibid., p. 26 and interview with his son, Rajendra Gupta, 25 February 1995, New Delhi.
16. Interview with V.R. Oke.
17. See, for instance, D.E. Haynes, 'From Tribute to Philanthropy: the Politics of Gift Giving in a Western Indian City', *The Journal of Asian Studies*, 46 (2), May 1987.
18. C.A. Bayly, 'Patrons and Clients in Northern India', *Modern Asian Studies*, 7(3), 1973, pp. 349-88.
19. C.A. Bayly, *Local Roots of Indian Politics*, Oxford: Clarendon Press, 1975.
20. *Organiser*, Varshapratipada Special, 1979, p. 13.
21. B.R. Gupta, *The Aggarwals*, New Delhi: S. Chand, 1975, p. 85.
22. Ibid., p. 130.
23. *Census of India, Delhi*, vol. 16, Lahore: Civil and Military Gazette Press, 1933, p. 120.
24. *Census of India, Punjab Census Report*, 1891, p. 172 and 1911, p. 138.
25. See P. Tandon, *Banking Century. A Short History of Banking in India and the Pioneer: Punjab National Bank*, New Delhi: Penguin Books, 1989, pp. 152-4.
26. P.H.M. Van Den Dungen, 'Changes in Status and Occupation in 19th Century Punjab', in D.A. Low (ed.), *Soundings in Modern South Asian History*, Berkeley: University of California Press, 1968, p. 75.
27. Ibid., p. 81.
28. N.G. Barrier, 'The Arya Samaj and Congress Politics in the Punjab—1894-1904', *The Journal of Asian Studies*, 26(3), May 1967, p. 364.
29. I am grateful to Dipankar Gupta for this comment.
30. Interview with Rajendra Gupta.
31. V.N. Datta, 'Panjabi Refugees and the Urban Development of Greater Delhi', in R.E. Frykenberg (ed.), *Delhi Through the Ages*, Delhi: OUP, 1993, p. 288.
32. *Report of the Commission of Inquiry into Conspiracy to Murder Mahatma Gandhi*, Part 2, New Delhi: Government of India, 1970, p. 66.
33. In Kingsway Camp, for instance, he had been criticized for reading excerpts of the Koran to refugees. Pyarelal, *Mahatma Gandhi—The last phase*, vol. 2, Ahmedabad: Navajivan Publishing House, 1957, p. 441.
34. *Report of the Commission of Inquiry into Conspiracy to Murder Mahatma Gandhi*, Part 1, New Delhi: Government of India, 1970, p. 141.
35. Ibid., Part 2, p. 57 and Hindu Mahasabha Papers (NMML—Manuscript section) C-160 Press Statement, dated 18 January 1948.
36. Interview with Hardayal Devgun, 17 October 1995, New Delhi.
37. Interview with B. Madhok, 10 November 1990, New Delhi.

38. B. Madhok, *RSS and Politics*, New Delhi: Hindu World Publications, 1985, p. 23.
39. Interview with Bhai Mahavir, 4 September 1992, New Delhi.
40. An organization supported by the RSS and close to the Dogras (Hindu landlords), the Praja Parishad was the first incarnation of the Jana Sangh in Jammu and Kashmir.
41. Oral History Transcript, interview with M.C. Sharma (Hindi), NMML, pp. 154, 162 and 175.
42. *Sunday News of India*, 30 July 1950, pp. 1 and 3.
43. B. Madhok, *RSS and Politics*, op. cit., p. 50.
44. *Organiser*, 10 September 1951, p. 14.
45. G. Puri, *Bharatiya Jana Sangh—Organisation and Ideology: Delhi, A Case Study*, New Delhi: Sterling, 1980, p. 27.
46. *The Times of India*, 5 January 1955, p. 3.
47. Interview with K.N. Sahni, 20 November 1990, New Delhi.
48. Malkani, a *swayamasevak* since 1942, had settled in Delhi in January 1948, arriving from Hyderabad (Sindh). He joined the *Organiser* in October 1948. Interviews with K.R. Malkani, 16 November 1989 and 11 August 1992, New Delhi.
49. Interview with L.K. Advani, 11 February 1994, New Delhi.
50. *Organiser*, 1 January 1948, p. 7 and 8 January 1948, p. 9 and *Hitavada*, 9 January 1948.
51. Interview with V.K. Malhotra, New Delhi, 24 November 1990.
52. The *sangh parivar* was especially active and reasonably successful among students of Delhi University after Partition. In July 1948, Madhok founded the Akhil Bharatiya Vidyarthi Parishad in Delhi, which became the first affiliate of the RSS.
53. G. Puri, *The Bharatiya Jana Sangh*, op. cit., p. 63.
54. R.N. Saksena, *Refugees—A Study in Changing Attitudes*, Bombay: Asia Publishing House, p. 21.
55. Yogesh Puri, *Party Politics in the Nehru Era—A Study of Congress in Delhi*, New Delhi: National Books Organisation, 1993, p. 186.
56. G. Puri, *The Bharatiya Jana Sangh*, op. cit., p. 154.
57. V.L. Pandit, *Elites and Urban Politics—A Case Study of Delhi*, New Delhi: Inter-India Publications, 1984, p. 58.
58. 'Notes on the Volunteer Movement in India', prepared by the Intelligence Bureau, 27 January 1940 and 23 August 1940, in L/P&J/Coll. 17—C 81 IOLR.
59. J.A. Curran, *Militant Hinduism in Indian Politics—A Study of the RSS*, Institute of Pacific Relations, 1951 (duplicated), pp. 14 and 43.
60. Hardayal Devgun, who was to be elected MP in east Delhi in 1967 on a Jana Sangh ticket and who had joined the RSS in Lahore to become a *pracharak* in 1940, said that 'he organized the Hindus against Muslim rioters' but underlines that his 'people attacked Muslim shops and so on' when they heard a false rumour suggesting that *I had been killed* (Interview with H.D. Devgun).
61. *Constituent Assembly Debates*, New Delhi: Lok Sabha Secretariat, 1989, vol. VII, p. 899.
62. S.P. Sen (ed.), *Dictionary of National Biography*, Calcutta: Institute of Historical Studies, 1973, vol. 1, p. 175.
63. The Arya Samaj people at large distanced themselves from the Jana Sangh in the 1950s. Immediately after Partition, the RSS and the Arya Samaj had advocated the formation of a Greater Punjab, amalgamating PEPSU (Patiala and East Punjab States Union), Himachal Pradesh and east Punjab, with Hindi as its official language—something the Sikhs could not accept. The Delhi-Punjab unit of the Jana Sangh adopted a much more moderate position by conceding that Punjabi and Hindi should be recognized as the languages for education and administration. Furthermore, in support of the notion of a Greater Punjab, the party alleged that Punjabi, which the Akali Dal considered peculiar to the west of the province—a region they wanted to separate off for themselves—was in fact spoken throughout. This cause and its supporting arguments were highly unpopular with the Arya Samajists who regarded Hindi as the sole language of the eastern part of the province where they were in a majority and who at times aspired to hive off this region from the western half of Punjab and have Delhi as its capital. The Delhi Jana Sangh could attract strong public support from the Arya Samaj only in 1967 when its president, Hardayal

Devgun, persuaded R.S. Shawlwale, a prominent local Arya Samajist to contest in Chandni Chowk as a Jana Sangh candidate.

64. Moonje Papers NMML (Microfilm Section), Reel no. 9, Letter from Moonje to the Secretary of the Joint Select Parliamentary Committee (dated 10 July 1933).
65. Jag Parvesh Chandra, who arrived in Delhi on 17 August 1947 from Lahore where he had worked as a journalist since 1938, was inducted into the ruling party by Rajendra Prasad. He was elected to the Legislative Assembly in 1952 and ended up as Chief Executive Councillor from 1983-90.
66. K.N. Seth and G.C. Malhotra, *Delhi Metropolitan Council—A study (1966-1989)*, Delhi: Metropolitan Council, 1989, p. 127.
67. V.N. Datta, 'Panjabi Refugees', op. cit., p. 290.
68. Ibid., p. 292.
69. Ibid., p. 294.
70. Interview with K.R. Malkani.
71. G. Puri, *The Bharatiya Jana Sangh*, op. cit., pp. 80-1.
72. Ibid., pp. 158-75.
73. M.K. Saini and W. Andersen, 'The Congress Split in Delhi', *Asian Survey*, 11(11), November 1971, pp. 1084-1100.
74. Ibid., pp. 84, 92 and 158-75.
75. N.K. Saini and W. Andersen, 'The Basti Julahan bye-election', *The Indian Journal of Political Science*, July-September 1969, pp. 266-76.
76. Cited in G. Puri, *The Bharatiya Jana Sangh*, op. cit., p. 57.
77. Interview with Kalka Dass, 23 November 1990, New Delhi.
78. R. Chandidas, 'Elections to Delhi Metropolitan Council—An Analysis of Electoral and Ecological Variables', *Economic and Political Weekly*, p. 970.
79. K.N. Seth and G.C. Malhotra (eds), *Delhi Metropolitan Council*, op. cit. Kilawat gives somewhat different figures: 33 per cent of businessmen and 15 per cent teachers in the 1972 Delhi Metropolitan Council. S.C. Kilawat, *The Government of the Federal Capital of India (Delhi)*, Jaipur: Publication Scheme, n.d., p. 268.
80. *Census 1971—Delhi*, General Report, p. 96.
81. B. Graham, *Hindu Nationalism and Indian Politics*, Cambridge: CUP, 1990, p. 165.
82. D. Upadhyaya, *The Two Plans—Promises, Performances, Prospects*, Lucknow: Rashtradharma Prakashan, 1958, p. 258.
83. Ibid., p. 268.
84. 'Manifesto—1951', in Bharatiya Jana Sangh, *Party Documents*, vol. 1, New Delhi, 1973, p. 52.
85. *Hindustan Times*, 8 March 1959, pp. 1-2.
86. Resolution passed at the party's annual session, 28 December 1958 (*Party Documents*, vol. 2, op. cit., p. 163).
87. Hardayal Devgun, *Corruption and Bharatiya Janata Party*, New Delhi: Democratic Vigilance Committee, n.d., p. 6 and interview with M.L. Khurana, 8 December 1990.
88. *The Times of India*, 25 July 1997.

12

Political Profile of Delhi and Support Bases of Parties: An Analysis

V.B. SINGH

Invaders have come and gone and yet Delhi continues to attract people. This is not to comment on history nor meant to add a further footnote to the biography of Delhi, but rather to refer to the problem of the unabated influx of people rolling into Delhi. Registering a very rapid growth, Delhi's population has gone up by more than six times, from a mere 17,44,072 in 1951 to 94,20,644 in 1991 and must by now have reached 12 million. A spiralling increase in the population residing in slums and ghettos; mounting pressure on already overcrowded residential areas; congested streets and choked markets; and a host of problems resulting from all of these have made Dilliwallas (the residents of Delhi) a miserable lot. Lack of imaginative planning and an indifferent administration have aggravated the problem further. In brief, Delhi is fast becoming a chaotic place to live, and yet this does not deter new migrants from coming in. Unlike earlier invaders, today's newcomers have come not for loot nor with the lust to rule but only to earn their livelihood, in the hope of improving their chances in life by coming to the capital.

The purpose of this essay is not to discuss civic amenities. Neither is it intended to find faults with the planning and administrative wings of the Delhi government. I have referred to these only to show how vulnerable the city of Delhi has become due to its ability to attract people from all parts of the country. The nature and composition of its population is changing very fast. About 1,00,000 people come to reside in Delhi every year. While promises of opportunities pull people to Delhi, the living conditions, marred by the acute shortage of civic amenities for most in-migrants, remain far from satisfactory. The 'dream land' of Delhi has become a nightmare. Earning a livelihood is perhaps easier here than finding a decent shelter. Despite all this, people still keep streaming into Delhi, struggling to survive and trying to improve their chances in life.[1] Though they have the pride of residing in the capital, very few of them actually become Dilliwallas—people who live and feel as if they really belong to Delhi.

Even though most people come to Delhi through existing primordial ties and linkages, the moment they settle in they begin a fresh search for identity. Their perception of the outside world changes. Like water seeking its own level, individuals become members of one group or the other. Reference points also begin to change. Irrespective of people's native backgrounds their views and attitudes are, by and large, affected by the surroundings they live in. Delhi, with nearly half of its population consisting of in-migrants, constantly faces this problem. Though the formation of new groups or divisions into older ones inevitably occurs in all societies, in Delhi these changes take place at an alarming rate. Groups are formed or broken on the strangest of grounds. Think of any issue and one can find groups formed around it. These informal groups which are hardly visible in the normal course get activated during elections. From a state of anonymity the members of such groups are suddenly transformed to realize their citizenship by leaders who would hardly take notice of them as citizens when approached for the redressal of problems at any other time. While a large part of Delhi's population suffers from disabilities to the extent it is forced to live under subhuman conditions,[2] there are other people whose interests are always pampered. In brief, the composition of Delhi's population is very diverse; disparity in every sphere of life is very wide and the system's response, be it government, political parties or local representatives, is partisan and selective. Despite all of these factors there exists a feeling of oneness to the extent that all are residents of Delhi and relationships with the outside world and the system have to be mediated through this fact.

In view of these factors I decided to use the occasion of the 1996 Lok Sabha elections (elections to the House of People, i.e. Parliamentary elections) to capture some of these peculiarities of the National Capital Territory and to see the extent to which voters' views and attitudes are affected by them. Do people living in different localities of Delhi behave differently or is it their native origin that makes the difference? Which of these two contextual situations (present locality or native origin) is more important in determining a person's behaviour particularly during the elections? Before seeking answers to these and some other system-related questions, I shall begin by presenting a brief description of Delhi's population followed by details of all the Lok Sabha and Vidhan Sabha (state legislature, i.e. assembly) constituencies of Delhi. Here, I shall attempt to characterize constituencies in terms of their electoral size, the composition of localities, literacy, workforce, etc., and to see if any voting patterns are discernible from them. Aggregate descriptions of constituencies and trends emerging from them will also be compared with the data collected through the 1996 survey of Lok Sabha elections. While the survey findings help explain the preferences of Delhi voters, they will also be used to examine some long-term questions concerning the system. That is, given the material conditions of Delhi voters, how do they evaluate the functioning of governments at different levels? What views do they hold about different institutions and the actors associated with them? What hopes and fears do they have for themselves and their children? And, finally, how do all of these relate to the issues of governance and the sustenance of democracy?

COMPOSITION OF DELHI'S POPULATION

Registering nearly a 2 per cent (1.98 per cent) decadal growth in its population, the National Capital Territory of Delhi at the beginning of the twentieth century was a quiet place. Between 1901 and 1911 it registered a slow increase in population, from 4,05,819 to 4,13,851. However, with the transfer of the capital from Calcutta to Delhi in 1911, the city's population began to increase at a much faster rate, witnessing decadal growth rates of 18.0 per cent, 30.3 per cent and 44.3 per cent during the periods 1911-21, 1921-31 and 1931-41 respectively. From 1941 to 1951 Delhi almost doubled its population, increasing from 9,17,939 persons in 1941 to 17,44,072 in 1951—a growth rate of over 90 per cent. Such a steep rise during the 1941-51 decade can of course be attributed in part to the mass influx of refugees following Partition. However, a steady growth rate of 52.4 per cent during 1951-61; of 52.9 per cent during 1961-71; of 53.0 per cent during 1971-81 and of 51.5 per cent during 1981-91 can only be explained in terms of the gravitating influence that radiates from the National Capital Region of Delhi.

The proportion of in-migrant population was, not surprisingly, the highest in 1951. According to the 1951 Census only 41 per cent of its total population were 'born in Delhi' with the remaining 59 per cent registered as 'migrants'. Roughly half of the total migrants (i.e. 47 per cent) came to Delhi as refugees from Pakistan following Partition. Thereafter the share of the native population (those born in Delhi) shows an increase in every successive census year. That is, persons born in Delhi increased to 44 per cent, 52 per cent, 55 per cent and 61 per cent during the periods 1951-61, 1961-71, 1971-81 and 1981-91 respectively. Consequently, the migrants' share in Delhi's population has declined. But although this represents a downward trend in percentage terms, a look at the same figures in absolute terms shows an increase of about 1,00,000 in-migrants to Delhi every year. For example, between 1981 and 1991 Delhi added 8,90,172 more migrants to its total population.

As far as the proportion of migrants from different regions/states is concerned, the northern region accounts for most of the migrants to Delhi. As much as four-fifths of them come from this region alone, of which 57 per cent are from Uttar Pradesh. In order of significance, the states of Haryana, Bihar, Rajasthan and Punjab account for the remaining migrants from the northern region. Migrants from the western, southern and eastern and north-eastern regions do not constitute a large proportion but nevertheless there are 1,31,636, 1,25,719, and 1,06,491 migrants from these regions respectively (see figures for 1991 Census in Table 12.1). Moreover their share in Delhi's in-migrant population has been increasing in every subsequent census year.

The in-migrant population reported in Table 12.1 includes only those not born in Delhi. This figure does not include the offspring of migrants who, though born in Delhi, are often socialized in families and neighbourhoods which retain socio-political values similar to those held in their parents' places of origin. Hence, when broad categories of identification like Bihari, UPwalla (persons from Uttar Pradesh), Rajasthani, Punjabi and

TABLE 12.1. IN-MIGRANT POPULATION OF THE NATIONAL CAPITAL TERRITORY OF DELHI, 1951-91

	1951	*1961*	*1971*	*1981*	*1991*
Total population	17,44,072	26,58,612	40,65,698	62,20,406	94,20,644
Born in Delhi	717,310	11,59,958	21,04,876	33,99,684	57,09,750
	(41.1)	(43.6)	(51.8)	(54.6)	(60.6)
Total in-migrant	1,026,762	1,498,654	1,960,822	28,20,722	37,10,894
	(58.9)	(56.4)	(48.2)	(45.4)	(39.4)
Distribution of in-migrants from different regions and states[1]					
North	5,08,522	8,84,664	13,06,078	20,93,230	29,69,315
	(49.5)	(59.0)	(66.6)	(74.2)	(80.0)
Bihar	1,303	9,723	23,012	96,902	2,67,567
	(0.1)	(0.7)	(1.2)	(3.4)	(7.2)
Uttar Pradesh	2,62,098	4,21,220	6,73,241	11,71, 404	17,04,197
	(25.5)	(28.1)	(34.3)	(41.5)	(45.9)
Punjab[2]	1,89,417	3,40,604	1,86,904	2,18,729	2,35,142
	(18.5)	(22.7)	(9.5)	(7.8)	(6.3)
Haryana[3]	–	–	2,33,831	3,43,657	4,40,275
			(11.9)	(12.2)	(11.9)
Rajasthan	48,592	94,902	1,36,413	1,90,415	2,31,856
	(4.7)	(6.3)	(7.0)	(6.8)	(6.3)
West	20,007	30,111	51,677	1,00,309	1,31,636
	(1.9)	(2.0)	(2.6)	(3.6)	(3.5)
East & North East	6,466	18,144	31,211	61,657	10,6491
	(0.6)	(1.2)	(1.6)	(2.2)	(2.9)
South	7,977	38,806	64,032	96,426	12,5719
	(0.8)	(2.6)	(3.3)	(3.4)	(3.4)
Pakistan	4,79,744	5,08,490	4,87,289	4,26,948	3,20,210
	(46.7)	(33.9)	(24.9)	(15.1)	(8.6)
Other countries	4,046 (0.4)	18,439 (1.2)	20,535 (1.0)	42,152 (1.5)	57,523 (1.6)

Notes: 1. States included in different regions are: North: Bihar, Haryana, Himachal Pradesh, Jammu & Kashmir, Rajasthan, Uttar Pradesh, Chandigarh; West: Gujarat, Goa, Madhya Pradesh, Maharashtra and Daman & Diu; East & North East: Assam, West Bengal, Orissa, Tripura, Nagaland, Meghalaya, Manipur, Mizoram, Sikkim and Arunachal Pradesh; South: Andhra Pradesh, Karnataka, Kerala, Tamil Nadu, Pondicherry, A & N. Island, Dadra & Nagar Haveli and Lakshdweep.

2. Including Pepsu (Patiala and East Punjab States Union) in 1951.

3. Till 1961 the state of Haryana was part of Punjab.

Percentages are indicated in brackets.

Source: Census of India, Migration Tables (Table D-1) of 1961, 1971, 1981 and 1991, Series I, India.

Madrasi are used, they include not only the people originating from these geographical areas but also their offsprings who were often born in Delhi. In this sense, non-Dilliwallas form a much larger social group than the census figures imply. Later in my analyses I shall try to identify the elements of this social group and to examine the political preferences of people from different regions.

PROFILE OF DELHI LOK SABHA CONSTITUENCIES

Delhi has had seven Lok Sabha constituencies since 1967. Earlier, in the 1957 and 1962 elections, there were five constituencies and in the first Lok Sabha election held in 1952 they were only four. Tables 12.2 and 12.3 present the social and political profiles of these constituencies respectively.

The rapid growth in population and the unplanned expansion of residential areas wherever possible, have made Delhi Lok Sabha constituencies very uneven in size. While constituencies like Chandni Chowk, New Delhi, Sadar and Karol Bagh (reserved for Scheduled Castes), with very little scope of geographical expansion, have remained more or less static in size, the rest have become very large. A comparison between Chandni Chowk (5,33,844 persons) and Outer Delhi (28,78,023 persons) reveals a gap of 23,44,179 persons according to the 1991 Census.

Apart from numerical size, these constituencies vary in terms of socio-economic composition as well. For example, with 72 per cent literates, the constituency of East Delhi is placed on the lowest educational rung as against the highest of 82 per cent in South Delhi. Interestingly, South Delhi also has the lowest proportion of Scheduled Castes. On the other hand, East Delhi, which has maximum number of illiterates, also has the largest share of non-working population, thereby indicating a greater degree of unemployment and dependency ratio which characterizes the constituency as poorer than others.

TABLE 12.2. SOCIAL PROFILE OF LOK SABHA CONSTITUENCIES IN DELHI

Name of Constituency	*Population*	*% of Literates (6 yrs +)*	*% of Scheduled Caste*	*% of workers*		
				Total	*Male*	*Female*
1. New Delhi	6,70,475	79.1	17.3	35.2	29.8	5.4
2. South Delhi	13,48,698	81.6	12.9	34.5	29.4	5.1
3. Outer Delhi	28,78,023	72.6	22.2	30.4	27.4	3.0
4. East Delhi	26,48,659	71.8	19.8	29.3	27.1	2.3
5. Chandni Chowk	5,33,844	73.5	13.9	32.0	29.6	2.4
6. Delhi Sadar	6,69,945	79.2	15.2	32.7	29.7	3.0
7. Karol Bagh	6,71,002	76.6	28.7	33.1	29.6	3.5
TOTAL	94,20,646	75.0	19.3	31.5	28.2	3.3

Source: Census of India, 1991.

As compared to voters located in far-flung areas of the countryside, Delhi's voters until recently showed a greater degree of participation in elections ever since universal adult franchise was first introduced in India. In the very first general election of 1952, Delhi registered a 58 per cent voter turnout as against the national average of a mere 46 per cent. With the subsequent increase in the national average, the level of participation in Delhi has also increased. Turnout figures in Delhi remained higher than the national average in all elections held until 1984. In 1989, when the franchise was expanded by lowering the qualifying age from 21 to 18 years, Delhi for the first time registered a lower turnout (54 per cent) than the national average (62 per cent). Thereafter, it has not touched the national average. In both the 1996 and 1998 Lok Sabha elections, Delhi fell behind the national average by about 7 per cent and 12 per cent respectively. The inclusion of younger voters in the list, the majority of whom are students, may be one likely factor influencing the lower turnout in Delhi but one has to look for other factors too.

A second observation that can be made from Table 12.3 concerns the uneven growth in the electoral sizes of different constituencies. In 1967, Chandni Chowk with an electorate of less than 2,00,000, was the smallest constituency whilst South Delhi, with an electorate of about 3,00,000, was the biggest. This difference has since widened. As of 1998, Chandni Chowk still remained the smallest constituency (3,68,226 electors). However, two constituencies—Outer Delhi and East Delhi with 29,26,563 and 22,64,600 electorates respectively—have grown to sizes which are unmanageable both for representatives and for the electorate. This illustrates the short-sightedness of the Parliament's decision in 1976 to postpone the next delimitation of constituencies until after the year 2001.

Third, the data presented in Table 12.3 clearly shows the emergence of a two-party system in Delhi. The Bharatiya Jan Sangh (BJS), the earlier incarnation of the present Bharatiya Janata Party (BJP), polled 26 per cent of votes in the very first election of 1952 as against 49 per cent votes polled by the Congress party. Barring two elections (1957 and 1984), in all subsequent elections the BJS/BJP or the Bharatiya Lok Dal/Janata Party secured more than one-quarter of the total votes polled in Delhi. As far as the number of seats is concerned, the BJS won six of the seven seats in Delhi in the 1967 elections. In 1977 the Congress drew a blank and all seven seats were cornered by the Janata Party of which the BJS was almost the sole constituent. As part of the Janata Party, it polled 38 per cent of votes and won only one seat in 1980. After 1971, 1984 turned out to be the worst election for the BJP. Having suffered a humiliating defeat in 1984 the BJP gained supremacy over the Congress in all subsequent elections. In alliance with the Janata Dal it won five seats (4 BJP + 1 JD) in 1989 and in both the 1991 and 1996 Lok Sabha elections it won five seats. In the 1998 elections, while both the major parties improved their share in votes, only the BJP benefited in terms of seats, winning six out of seven. Since 1989 the voters in Delhi seem to have polarized into two camps, namely the Congress and the

TABLE 12.3. POLITICAL PROFILE OF LOK SABHA CONSTITUENCIES (1952-96)

Year of election	*New Delhi*	*South Delhi*	*Outer Delhi*	*East Delhi*	*Chandni Chowk*	*Delhi Sadar*	*Karol Bagh*	*Total*
1952: Electors	1,82,293	-	7,75,706	-	1,74,522	-	-	11,32,521
% Turnout	56.1		58.3		58.2			57.9
% INC vote	39.2		26.2+23.2		59.6			49.4
% BJS vote	-		16.4+13.0		36.6			25.9
1957: Electors	1,92,753	-	8,79,582	-	1,71,563	1,72,245	-	14,16,143
% Turnout	53.9		53.7		68.8	67.9		57.8
% INC vote	73.7		26.7+26.1		43.0	54.6		54.3
% BJS vote	21.9		5.9+5.2		30.8	41.2		19.7
1962: Electors	2,68,661	-	3,31,600	-	2,01,891	2,34,520	3,08,688	13,45,360
% Turnout	64.4		66.7		71.4	71.3	71.1	68.8
% INC vote	56.7		44.3		50.0	48.4	54.4	50.7
% BJS vote	38.1		34.1		29.2	33.8	28.3	32.7
1967: Electors	2,08,755	2,98,699	2,58,107	2,65,230	1,94,661	2,25,517	2,33,745	16,84,714
% Turnout	73.3	67.1	68.5	67.3	72.7	71.1	68.6	69.5
% INC vote	38.6	35.8	40.8	45.5	31.2	41.3	37.3	38.8
% BJS vote	55.4	54.5	35.2	48.8	44.1	47.5	40.2	46.7
1971: Electors	2,17,319	4,08,392	3,48,585	3,58,046	1,94,732	2,34,764	2,54,558	20,16,396
% Turnout	59.2	66.7	62.9	64.8	72.0	67.5	64.1	65.2
% INC vote	64.4	62.4	66.1	64.1	64.2	62.5	67.9	64.4
% BJS vote	29.4	35.9	13.9	31.7	31.5	35.3	30.0	29.6
1977: Electors	2,70,702	3,82,219	4,43,858	5,11,716	3,13,714	3,09,550	3,15,305	25,47,064
% Turnout	65.8	69.5	71.3	70.1	83.0	71.0	68.9	71.3
% INC vote	27.6	29.0	32.6	30.4	27.0	29.6	34.2	30.2
% JNP vote	71.3	69.8	66.1	67.9	71.9	66.2	64.3	68.2
1980: Electors	3,01,071	5,04,959	6,07,825	6,77,955	2,99,479	3,33,500	3,44,847	3,06,936
% Turnout	65.1	63.2	62.8	62.4	71.7	69.2	65.7	64.9
% INC vote	45.9	47.8	50.4	55.0	47.3	47.4	55.3	50.4
% JP vote	48.5	46.5	24.1	33.9	39.2	43.9	39.7	37.9
1984: Electors	3,04,123	5,22,980	8,54,302	8,32,324	2,83,849	3,67,575	3,31,628	34,96,781
% Turnout	64.7	68.3	59.8	61.4	71.8	68.8	67.1	64.5
% INC vote	67.9	61.1	72.8	76.9	60.5	62.1	68.8	68.7
% BJP vote	30.4	37.0	23.1*	14.7	37.2	35.8	29.5	18.8
1989: Electors	4,29,535	8,51,780	15,74,973	14,78,000	3,81,491	5,06,017	4,81,032	57,02,828
% Turnout	55.0	56.7	50.2	49.7	66.5	61.1	60.1	54.3
% INC vote	41.9	37.4	42.7	49.8	36.0	43.2	47.3	43.4
% BJP vote	53.5	59.4	49.5*	5.3*	32.1	53.8	49.7	47.2
1991: Electors	4,56,073	9,04,489	18,66,074	15,82,516	3,99,737	5,34,335	5,09,932	60,73,156
% Turnout	47.9	46.6	41.4	48.2	57.2	53.6	50.3	48.5
% INC vote	42.7	37.8	45.4	32.1	34.5	48.6	39.2	39.6
% BJP vote	43.4	50.0	34.0	40.3	35.7	43.6	40.2	40.2
1996: Electors	5,05,445	1,10,39,548	28,21,566	22,21,193	3,62,555	5,00,633	5,43,590	80,58,941
% Turnout	51.7	5.0	48.1	50.5	57.5	60.2	53.7	50.6
% INC vote	31.7	34.1	35.1	34.9	44.9	46.6	52.5	37.3
% BJP vote	54.3	55.6	52.5	48.7	34.1	47.2	38.0	49.6
1998: Electors	5,17,319	1,15,607	29,26,563	22,64,600	3,68,226	5,11,403	5,53,436	82,97,622
% Turnout	50.2	49.3	49.0	51.4	61.8	58.5	54.5	51.3
% INC vote	41.7	38.1	43.4	44.9	33.9	40.6	48.8	42.6
% BJP vote	54.4	58.8	50.3	48.8	35.3	56.9	47.2	50.7

Note: In 1984 and 1989 the BJP contested the election in alliance with the Lok Dal and Janata Dal respectively. Figures marked with an asterisk under the constituency column denote their respective shares while the rest are clubbed with the BJP vote in the state total.

Abbreviations: INC: Indian National Congress; BJS: Bharatiya Jana Sangh; JNP: Janata National Party; JP: Janata Party; BJP: Bharatiya Janata Party.

Source: V.B. Singh and Shanar Bose, *Elections in India: Data Handbook on Lok Sabha Elections, 1952-85*, New Delhi: Sage Publications, 1987; V. Singh, *Election in India: Data Handbook on Lok Sabha Elections, 1986-91*, New Delhi: Sage Publications, 1994; and Election Commission of India *Statistical Report on General Election, 1996 and 1998*.

Bharatiya Janata Party, both polling about 40 per cent votes each. That is to say that between the two of them, these two parties share 80 per cent of the total votes in Delhi.

Finally, a closer scrutiny of election results at the constituency level suggests that the BJP, which appears to have consolidated its position at the state level is still weak in some constituencies. For example, Chandni Chowk and Outer Delhi are two constituencies where the BJP has lost most of the elections. In these constituencies only in 3 of the 11 elections held so far, have the results gone in its favour, whereas in other constituencies the BJP has either fared better than the Congress or represented the constituency on more or less an equal number of occasions. The weaker performance of the BJP in Chandni Chowk and Outer Delhi may be attributed to the nature of the social composition of these constituencies. While the former has a large concentration of Muslims, the latter includes a substantial rural population within it, the majority of whom belong to lower socio-economic groups. Interestingly, these are the social groups generally considered to be hostile to the BJP. As elsewhere in the country, while Muslims have strong reservations about the pro-Hindu stance of the BJP, so too do some sections of the majority community. Depending on local conditions the same social group may support the party in one area but oppose it vehemently in others. As far as Delhi is concerned, both parties—the Congress and the BJP—have, over the years, stabilized their support bases in different sections of society. This is evident at least from the aggregate data presented in Table 12.3. However, there have been noticeable shifts in voters' loyalties as well. Had this not been the case, voters' verdicts in different elections would have remained stable through time. With these peculiarities, the case of Delhi provides an excellent opportunity for examining stability and change in the support bases of parties. The pages that follow explore this crucial aspect of voting behaviour by analysing the post-poll survey data from Delhi.

1996 ELECTION SURVEY IN NEW DELHI

Delhi formed a part of the national sample of the all-India study of the 1996 Lok Sabha elections. However, its representation with 212 cases selected from 2 Vidhan Sabha constituencies was too small to enable analysis at the state level. Coverage in the state was therefore increased and 12 more Vidhan Sabha constituencies were selected to form a larger sample size for the state (see note on sampling, Appendix I). In all, 932 cases were selected from 14 segments (see Map 12.1) and interviews with 563 respondents were completed. Considering urban mobility the completion rate of 60 per cent for a survey like this was quite respectable.

The representation of male electorates in Delhi is higher than the national average. Accordingly, there are more male respondents in the sample. Out of 563 cases for which data were collected, 55 per cent were males. It may be noted that the proportion of males in the Delhi population is also 55 per cent (see Table 12.4). Delhi's electorate is also better educated

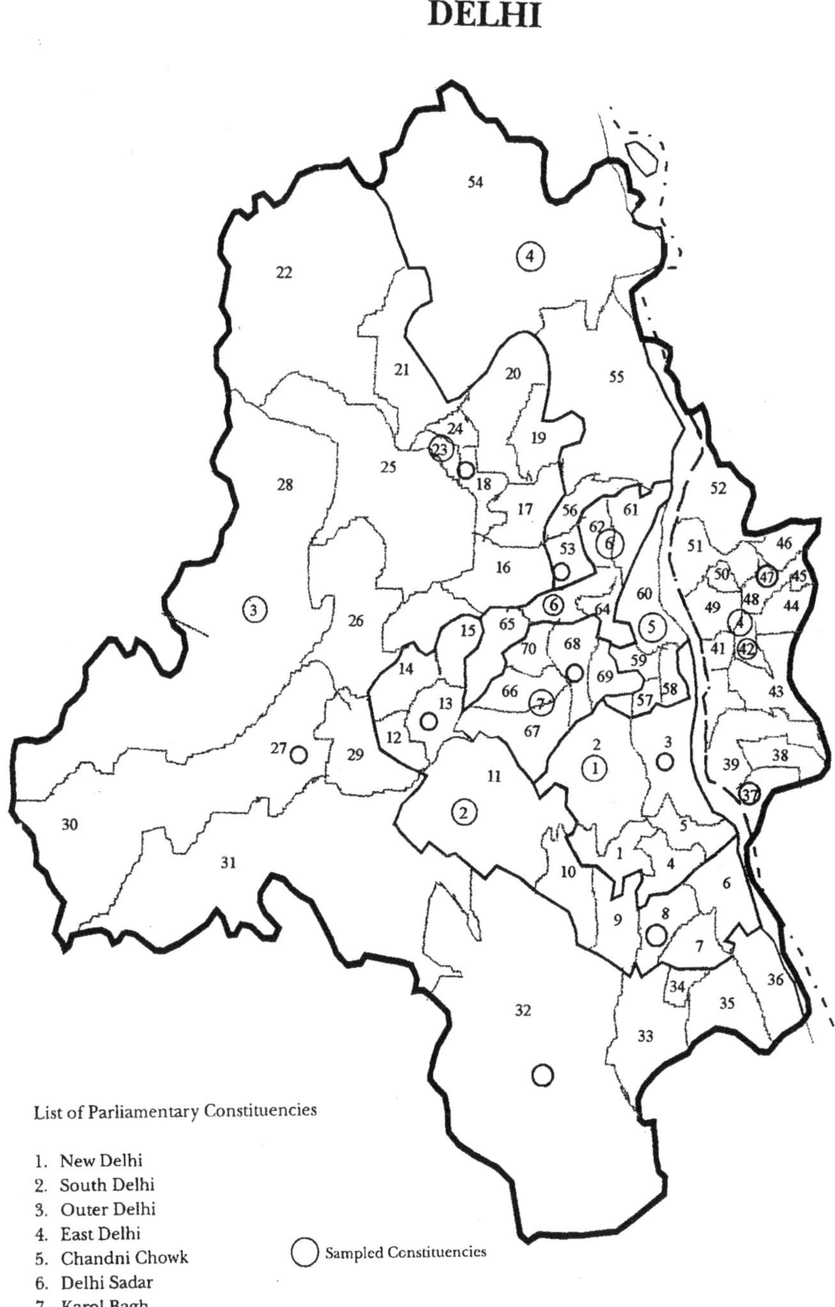

Source : CSDS Data Unit.

MAP 12.1. PARLIAMENTARY CONSTITUENCIES OF DELHI.

than electorates elsewhere. As against 42 per cent illiterates in the national sample, Delhi has only 22 per cent which is about 3 per cent less than the census figure of 1991. But the fact that the literacy level has increased during the last six years means the proportion of illiterates in our sample comes much closer to the reality. Among the literate, 48 per cent have done nine or more years of schooling, and of these about 20 per cent are graduates or post-graduates. Similarly, the proportion of people pursuing business, white collar or professional jobs is also quite high. Corresponding roughly to the state average, Hindus represent 87 per cent of the sample, Muslims 8 per cent and Sikhs 4 per cent. Roughly half of the Delhi electorate, according to the survey, belong to upper castes while only 12 per cent of Delhi's total sample belong to Other Backward Classes (OBC) castes. There is, however, an over-representation of Scheduled Castes in our sample. They represent 27 per cent in the sample, but only 19 per cent in the total population of Delhi. Apart from this, the close resemblance between the sample and the total population of Delhi as reflected in Table 12.4 makes the sample quite representative and enhances confidence in the survey findings.

In spite of the large proportion of Scheduled Castes (27 per cent), the Delhi sample consists of people belonging mainly to the upper economic strata. Roughly one-sixth of those questioned own a car or jeep and a little less than half own a scooter or motor cycle. As many as 90 per cent of them own televisions; 78 per cent have radios or transistors and 77 per cent live in pukka (brick or cement) houses. The proportion of those living in huts or kutcha (mud) houses is very small (9 per cent). Newspaper readership is also quite high (53 per cent). This is second only to Goa (58 per cent) and higher than Kerala (52 per cent). On other indicators like 'listening to the Radio' and 'TV viewing', Delhi also ranks at the top of the scale. Considering this background, the interest level of Delhi voters was found to be quite low. Only 43 per cent took an interest in the 1996 election campaign as against much higher proportions in Pondicherry (81 per cent), Kerala (73 per cent) and Tamil Nadu (60 per cent). This low level of interest in elections in Delhi, especially among people who are well educated and better exposed to the information system than in many other parts of the country, does not augur

TABLE 12.4. BACKGROUND CHARACTERISTICS OF RESPONDENTS AND THE TOTAL POPULATION OF DELHI (*in per cent*)

Background Characteristics	*Distribution in Sample Characteristics*	*Distribution in Population*
Male	54.5	54.7
Rural	9.1	10.1
Illiterate	21.3	24.7
Scheduled Caste	27.4	19.3
Muslim	7.9	9.4
Sikh	3.6	4.8

Source: Post-Poll Survey, 1996; and 1991 Census Reports.

well for the health of democracy in the long run. The short-term fallout in the form of lower voter turnouts in recent Delhi elections has already been seen.

THE SOCIAL BASES OF THE TWO MAIN PARTIES

Except in 1984, when the Congress swept the poll, riding the sympathy wave following the assassination of Indira Gandhi, popular support for the BJP has not dropped below 38 per cent in any election held from 1971 to 1998. Similarly, the Congress party's share of votes has always remained above 30 per cent. However, 1977 was the only election when it could not win any seat and when its share of votes came down to the lowest of 30 per cent. Losses and gains in seats notwithstanding, both parties have done quite well in sustaining popular support above 30 per cent. While a casual look at Table 12.3 clearly shows the crystallization of the support bases of both parties, a comparison of trends in the share of votes held by the Congress (decreasing) and the BJP (increasing) during the last four elections of 1989, 1991, 1996, and 1998, suggests a shift in voters' loyalties. Who votes for whom and what distinguishes the supporters of one party from those of the other are questions I would like to answer from the data collected in the post-poll survey of 1996.

Data presented in Table 12.5 conform to the general trend. While Muslims, Scheduled Castes and people belonging to lower socio-economic groups tend to support the Congress party, the opposite is true in the case of the BJP. In fact the lower the status in terms of caste, the further the distance from the BJP. In the 1996 Lok Sabha elections in Delhi 74 per cent of upper castes voted for the BJP as against only 42 per cent of Scheduled Castes. The BJP could not get any votes from Muslims and the majority of OBC voters favoured non-BJP candidates. If these were to be added together with other groups who oppose the BJP like Scheduled Castes and Christians, then this would constitute a serious threat to the BJP. But since Delhi's population contains such a high percentage of upper castes (over 50 per cent), votes in the capital are heavily biased in favour of the BJP.

Caste hierarchies are not merely levels of social ranking. They have an economic aspect too. People belonging to higher castes are on the whole endowed with better economic standing by way of inheritance, better education, and better occupations. As a result, the relationship between caste hierarchy and vote preferences is more or less reflected in economic variables as well. That is, support for the Congress comes largely from illiterates and lower levels of literate, manual workers and those involved in other low-level occupations while support for the BJP comes from people placed higher in terms of education and occupation. For example, 56 per cent of illiterates vote for the Congress while 70 per cent of those having college and university education vote for the BJP. Similarly, more than two-thirds of professionals and business people vote for the BJP while the majority of the Class IV workers and manual labourers lend their support to the Congress (see Table 12.5).

TABLE 12.5. VOTE PREFERENCES BY RESPONDENTS' BACKGROUNDS

Background characteristics	*INC*	*BJP*	*Others*	*Total*
A. *Caste & Religion*				
Upper Castes	25.1	71.9	3.0	231
Other Backward Classes	39.0	52.5	8.5	59
Scheduled Castes/Tribes	52.0	39.3	8.7	150
Muslims (all categories)	706	–	29.4	34
Others	38.5	53.8	7.7	13
Chi-Square: 93.58; Df.: - 8; Probability: <.01				
B. *Education*				
Illiterate	55.7	34.0	10.4	21.9
Primary School & below	51.6	41.9	6.5	12.8
Middle School	37.5	52.3	10.2	18.1
High school	33.0	63.3	3.7	22.5
College-undergraduate	20.0	70.0	10.0	6.2
Graduate & above	24.4	70.0	5.6	18.6
Chi-Square: 41.00; Df.: 8; Probability: <.01				
C. *Occupation*				
Professional	27.7	66.2	6.2	13.6
Trader/Shopkeeper	2.8	68.2	3.0	27.6
White-collar skilled worker	32.1	56.0	11.9	22.8
Class IV employee & semi-skilled worker	50.0	39.8	10.2	18.4
Unskilled worker	57.7	36.6	5.6	14.8
Others	50.0	35.7	14.3	2.9
Chi-Square: 40.21; Df.: 10; Probability: <.01				
D. *Ownership of House or Flat*				
Yes	33.9	60.7	5.4	75.8
No	53.4	33.1	13.6	24.2
Chi-Square: 29.49; Df.: 2; Probability: <.01				
E. *Economics Class**				
Very Poor	57.1	32.1	10.7	6.0
Poor	52.0	38.8	9.2	21.0
Middle	41.6	50.4	8.0	29.4
Rich	25.6	69.0	5.4	43.6
Chi-Square: 33.65; Df.: 6; Probability : <.01				
TOTAL: N	188	263	36	487
per cent	38.6	54.0	7.4	100.0

Note: Vote shares are calculated row-wise, i.e. for each social or economic group separately while the figures reported in the total column denote shares of specific groups in the total sample of Delhi who marked their vote preferences.

* For details on the construction of class variables, see Appendix II.

Source: Post-Poll Survey, 1996.

The relationship between voters' preferences and their social status as reflected by the four variables of caste, education, occupation and ownership of a house or flat is amplified when we examine the question of 'economic class'. Since all of these attributes have economic connotations, I decided to construct an index of 'economic class' using composite information concerning a person's income, assets, occupational status and type of residential accommodation. I then used the index to see how different classes of people in Delhi voted in the 1998 elections.

As expected, the BJP got its main support from the upper economic classes while the Congress got the majority of its support from the poorer sections of society (see E, Table 12.5). The secret of the BJP's success in Delhi lies in the nature of the distribution of Delhi's population in different socio-economic categories. That is, Delhi has a fairly large share of people belonging to the upper economic class, many of whom are from high castes, well-educated backgrounds and work in high-ranking occupations. If one excludes the 44 per cent of people belonging to this (rich) class, then one can see that the Congress polls more votes than the BJP from amongst the other three classes including the 'middle' class. Of the 263 voters belonging to either the very poor, poor or middle class categories, the Congress gets 124 votes (47 per cent) as against the BJP's 116 (44 per cent). But the fact that the BJP gets 69 per cent of its support from the rich (who constitute 44 per cent of the total voters) turns the tide in its favour.

The BJP's capacity to attract voters from the upper classes is clearly demonstrated by the data presented in Table 12.5. The higher the status of the people, the greater their propensity to vote for the BJP whereas the opposite dynamic is true for the Congress. Exactly the same relationship is found at an all India level as well. Figures 12.1 and 12.2 present the comparative data. While the basic trend remains the same, degrees of support from various segments of society have changed. The BJP which managed to get about one-third of its support from the lowest class in Delhi, failed miserably in attracting voters in the same proportion from this class of people in other parts of the country. As a result, it received only 15 per cent of votes at all India level from the 'very poor' class. Even from the 'poor' it got only 22 per cent. Since these two classes (very poor and poor) between them account for 62 per cent of the total voters of the country, the BJP's share of votes at an all India level came down to 24 per cent despite its success in mobilizing the support of 42 per cent of the 'rich'.

The idea of an upper-class support base for the BJP may satisfy its supporters, particularly those who come from this section but its opponents can rest assured that in a game of numbers it can never take the party to majority status. The hype of 'majoritarianism' propagated through the BJP's *Hindutva* plank is baseless unless it manages to expand its appeal and acceptance among the lower segments of society, both economic and social. A look at the all-India graph (Figure 12.1) presenting the class-based support of the three major political groupings (Congress, BJP and Others) reveals that the other parties, major constituents of which are the regional parties

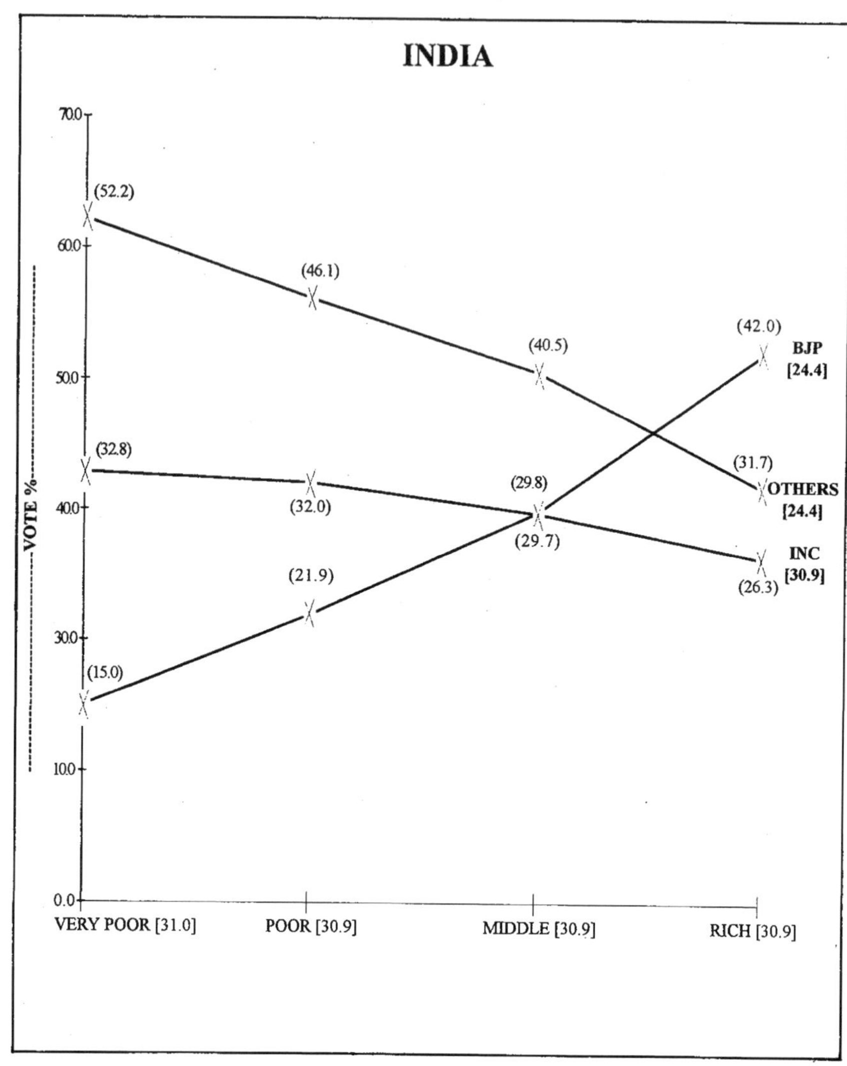

Note: All figures in percentages. Figures presented in round brackets () denote the percentage of vote preferences within each class while those in square brackets [] present the shares of voters in the total sample.

* For details on the construction of class variables, see Appendix II.

Source: Post-Poll Survey, 1996.

FIGURE 12.1 VOTE PREFERENCES BY ECONOMIC CLASS (ALL INDIA), 1996

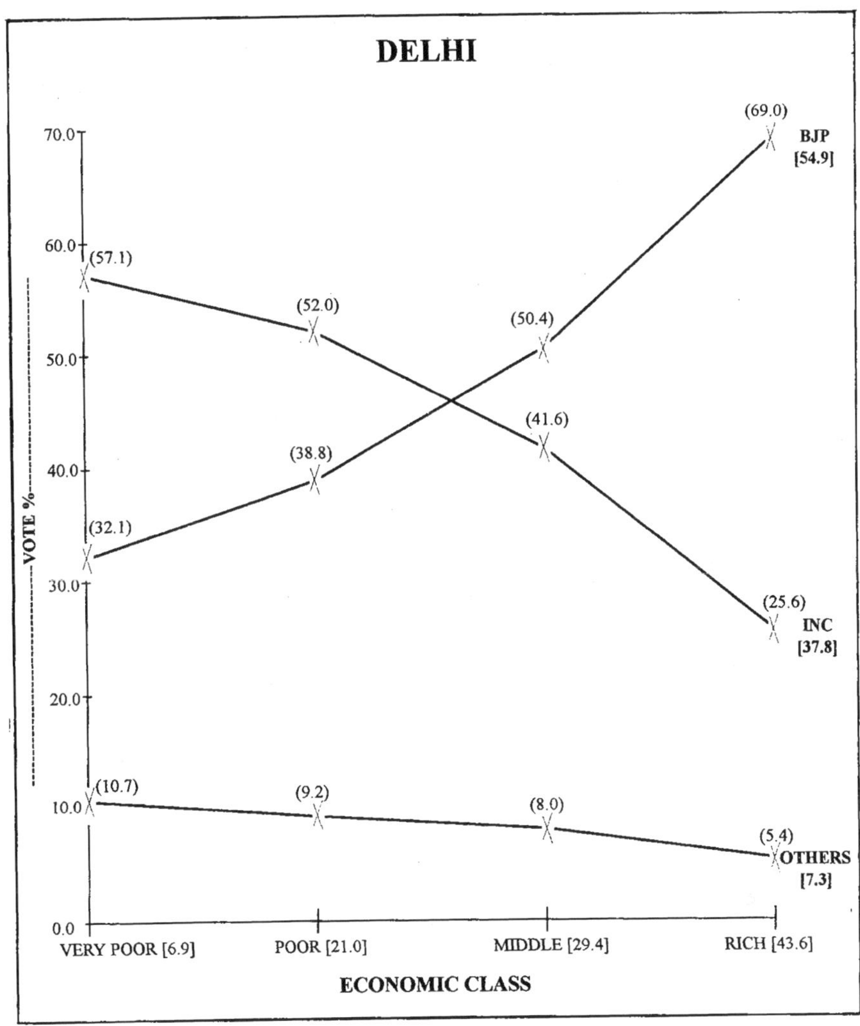

Note: All figures in percentages. Figures presented in round brackets () denote the percentage of vote preferences within each class while those in square brackets [] present the shares of voters in the total sample.
* For details on the construction of class variables, see Appendix II.

Source: Post-Poll Survey, 1996.

FIGURE 12.2. VOTE PREFERENCES BY ECONOMIC CLASS (DELHI), 1996.

and of course the Left Front and National Front, enjoy a definite edge over both the national parties (the Congress and the BJP) when it comes to attracting 'very poor' and 'poor' voters. Between the Congress and the BJP the former is still much better placed than the latter in this respect. The miserable performance of the BJP in attracting voters from the lowest economic class, the majority of whom come from Scheduled Castes and Tribes and lower OBCs, constitutes the main weakness of the party. Considering present political developments and patterns of support, as reflected in the survey data, the void created by the decline of Congress is likely to be filled mostly by non-BJP parties at least among the lower classes of people. Meanwhile, the BJP is likely to garner support largely from amongst the upper segments of society, the composition of which varies from region to region.

Considering the overarching influence of caste in Indian politics, especially during elections, I decided to analyse voting preferences by caste group within each of the four classes separately in Table 12.6 (at the all-India level).

Although caste plays an important role in influencing people's voting preferences, class appears to be an equally important factor. For example, if we take Scheduled Castes, a group usually hostile to the BJP, we find that the higher they move up the class ladder, the more likely they are to vote for the BJP. While the party's support is only 11 per cent from the 'very poor', it increases to 19 per cent among the 'poor', 25 per cent among the 'middle' rank and 41 per cent among the 'rich'. This pattern is also discernible with other castes and with tribes. The class factor is equally important for the Left Front which gets as high as 13 per cent of upper-caste votes from among the 'very poor' and only 4 per cent from among the 'rich'. More or less the same trend is found in the case of the National Front. From this it may be concluded that it is the economic status rather than the caste position as such (though the two are often closely related) which plays the greatest role in influencing a person's voting preference.

Turning back to Delhi I have also tried to examine the voting preferences of in-migrants who constitute a large chunk of Delhi's population. Out of the total number of voters in Delhi, 67 per cent are Delhi-born, 19 per cent indicate that they have come either from Uttar Pradesh or Bihar and the remaining 14 per cent from other states (see Table 12.7). Interestingly, the BJP receives its maximum support from amongst the people coming from other states. In-migrants from Uttar Pradesh and Bihar are found to vote for the Congress and the BJP in equal proportions.

The myth that voters from Bihar and Uttar Pradesh form a special group and tend to vote for a particular party or candidate *en masse* is unfounded as they are equally divided in their voting preferences. They may come from the same place, live together in slums, resettlement colonies or other types of residential areas and share many things in common, but their voting decision is largely guided by their socio-economic status and the political background they have come from. Since caste is the most important factor

TABLE 12.6. VOTE PREFERENCES BY CASTE AND CLASS (*in per cent*) (ALL INDIA)

Class / *Party*	*Upper Caste*	*Other Backward Classes*	*Scheduled Caste*	*Scheduled Tribe*	*Muslim (all categories)*	*Total*
Very Poor						
INC+	31.5	28.0	34.4	43.8	42.0	33.5
BJP+	29.2	23.7	10.7	19.0	2.0	18.2
NF	8.8	16.9	7.8	8.1	18.0	12.1
LF	13.4	8.9	15.9	12.4	23.3	12.9
BSP	0.9	2.9	11.4	1.7	–	5.0
Other	16.2	19.5	19.9	15.0	14.7	18.4
TOTAL	216	931	730	347	150	2,374
	(9.1)	(39.2)	(30.7)	(14.6)	(6.3)	(100)
Chi-Square: 261.43; Df.: 20; Probability: <.01						
Poor						
INC+	33.4	24.0	35.9	47.6	47.4	32.4
BJP+	45.0	26.5	19.0	25.2	2.9	26.7
NF	4.2	19.4	4.1	8.0	18.3	12.2
LF	8.2	5.6	11.5	3.6	15.4	7.8
BSP	0.7	3.1	19.2	1.2	1.1	5.5
Other	8.5	21.4	10.3	14.4	14.9	15.5
TOTAL	449	1,018	468	250	175	2,360
	(19.0)	(43.1)	(19.8)	(10.6)	(7.4)	(100)
Chi-Square: 533.17; Df.: 20; Probability: <.01						
Middle						
INC+	30.7	20.7	39.3	52.7	41.0	29.6
BJP+	49.6	30.6	25.3	24.7	3.8	35.9
NF	4.3	21.9	5.2	6.5	32.4	12.7
LF	6.8	5.8	7.0	1.1	12.4	6.5
BSP	0.4	1.9	13.1	–	2.9	2.6
Other	8.2	19.1	10.0	15.1	7.6	12.8
TOTAL	776	729	229	93	105	1,932
	(40.2)	(37.7)	(11.9)	(4.8)	(5.4)	(100)
Chi-Square: 429.76; Df.: 20; Probability: <.01						
Rich						
INC+	26.3	19.6	26.5	47.8	54.2	26.6
BJP+	57.2	34.9	40.8	43.5	2.1	47.9
NF	4.7	17.9	6.1	–	39.6	9.6
LF	3.8	5.1	8.2	–	2.1	4.1
BSP	0.2	–	8.2	–	–	0.5
Other	7.8	22.6	10.2	8.7	2.1	11.3
TOTAL	612	235	49	23	48	967
	(63.3)	(24.3)	(5.1)	(2.4)	(5.0)	(100)
Chi-Square: 235.17; Df.: 20; Probability: <.01						
GRAND TOTAL	26.9	38.2	19.3	9.3	6.3	100
	(2,053)	(2,913)	(1,476)	(713)	(478)	(7,633)

Note: Figures in parentheses denote row percentages.

Abbreviations: INC+: Indian National Congress and its allies, namely All India Anna Dravida Munnetra Kazhagam in Tamil Nadu and partners of United Democratic Front in Kerala; BJP+: Bharatiya Janata Party and its allies, namely Shiv Sena in Maharashtra, Samata Party in Bihar and Haryana Vikas Party in Haryana; NF: National Front consisting of Janata Dal, Samajwadi Party; LF: Left Front consisting of Communist Party of India (Marxist), Communist Party of India, Revolutionary Socialist Party and Forward Bloc; BSP: Bahujan Samaj Party.

Source: Post-Poll Survey, 1996.

in Uttar Pradesh and Bihar I decided to examine their voting preferences by caste and found that 67 per cent of upper castes from Uttar Pradesh and Bihar voted for the BJP while the majority (57 per cent) from other castes and communities voted for the Congress (see Table 12.7). On the other hand, in-migrants from other states have shown greater and wider support for the BJP, not just among the upper castes but among other groups as well. Therefore, one may safely conclude that the voting choices of in-migrants are largely influenced by their economic status and caste affiliation and not by their place of origin. Since in-migrants from Uttar Pradesh and Bihar are constituted largely by non-upper castes (51 per cent), their support for the Congress equals that for the BJP.

As far as the attitudes and opinions of Delhi voters are concerned, they are found to be more critical of their representatives, political parties and the electoral system than people in the country as a whole. Among the Delhi voters 78 per cent feel that elected representatives do not care about the people they represent as against 63 per cent in the nationwide sample. Similarly, 35 per cent of Delhi voters (as opposed to 27 per cent in the national sample) feel that political parties are not very helpful in making the government pay attention to the people. A similar attitude is found when it comes to elections. All of these factors contribute to the comparatively low turnout in Delhi elections. The majority of Delhi voters (55 per cent as against only 21 per cent in the national sample) reject the idea of loyalty to one's region above loyalty to India, thereby showing a metropolitan frame of mind.

TABLE 12.7. VOTE PREFERENCES BY PLACE OF BIRTH

Place of Birth	*INC*	*BJP*	*Others*	*Total*
Uttar Pradesh or Bihar	45.7	45.7	8.7	92
Upper Castes	33.3	66.7	–	45
Others	57.4	25.5	17.0	47
Chi-Square: 19.11; Df.: 2; Probability: <.01				
Other States	33.8	58.8	7.4	68
Upper Castes	18.5	74.1	7.4	27
Others	43.9	48.8	7.3	41
Chi-Square: 4.87; Df.: 2; Probability: <.09				
Born in Delhi	37.6	55.4	7.0	327
Upper Castes	23.9	73.0	3.1	159
Others	50.6	38.7	10.7	168
Chi-Square: 39.46; Df.: 2; Probability: <.01				
TOTAL	38.6	54.0	7.4	487

Source: Post-Poll Survey, 1996.

Interestingly, about 60 per cent of Delhi voters claim to have found the demolition of the Babri Masjid in Ayodhya unjustified and 46 per cent of them voted for the BJP. From among those who considered the demolition justified the BJP got 77 per cent of votes as against the Congress' 20 per cent. Finally, those Delhi voters who are economically better off reveal a higher level of optimism about the future. They anticipate good economic prospects and foresee better opportunities for their children. As expected, the BJP gets a larger share of votes from these people which reconfirms the upper-class bias in favour of the party.

In the final analysis, it can be concluded that Delhi presents a picture of the development of a two-party system in which the Congress and the BJP compete for supremacy. Between the two, the Congress' support appears to be dwindling. Having polled 69 per cent of votes and won all seven seats in 1984, its share of both votes and seats has registered a gradual decline in subsequent elections. Meanwhile, the BJP share has increased accordingly. Analysis of their support bases, however, suggests that the Congress, despite a gradual loss in popularity, still enjoys a broader base than the BJP. Apart from the upper strata, the Congress has attracted more than average support from all other social groups; by contrast, the BJP has no support whatsoever among Muslims and less than its state average support among OBCs, Scheduled Castes and other religious groups like Christians. Similarly, the BJP has received much less votes from illiterates, Class IV employees and manual workers, thereby indicating the upper caste and class bias of its supporters. This narrower support base of the BJP is further substantiated by the fact that it has received less support in the rural areas of Delhi (as compared to rural areas nationally) and its fate in the Outer Delhi constituency continues to fluctuate.

With this inability to attract voters from lower social groups, the BJP still faces uncertainty in sustaining its newly acquired superiority over the Congress in Delhi politics. Similar trends are also discernible from the all-India data. This brings into question the future prospect of the BJP at the all-India level. Yet, in Delhi, since its record for attracting voters from the upper segments of society is fairly high, the BJP does not have to worry much about its prospects as large proportions of the population are classified as 'well educated', 'upper caste' or 'upper class'. Since these groups appear to be expanding in Delhi, it is likely that the BJP will be able to retain its support base here in the near future. This may be the reason why, unlike in Maharashtra and Rajasthan, the incumbency factor did not adversely affect the BJP's performance in Delhi in the 1998 Lok Sabha elections. Finally, those Delhi voters who are well educated, better informed and capable of taking a critical stand on issues, can also be characterized as being volatile in their behaviour. The low turnout among the upper segments of society is a mild way of expressing resentment. However, if resentment increases, the same voters could potentially turn to vote in large numbers against their usual party or candidate. This makes the BJP more vulnerable than it appears.

APPENDIX I. NOTE ON SAMPLING

In order to draw a representative sample of the Delhi electorate a multi-stage stratified random sampling procedure has been used wherein it was decided to select 20 per cent of the total assembly constituencies of Delhi, that is, out of 70 assembly constituencies a total of 14 were selected. The selection of different sample units was made in different stages:

Stage One: Selection of Assembly Constituencies

1. All assembly constituencies with their electorates were serialized according to the Election Commission's Delimitation order;
2. The cumulative total of the electorate was assigned against each constituency in ascending order;
3. In order to avoid selection of contiguous constituencies, the total electorate in the state was divided by the number of constituencies to be selected, i.e. 14. It helped to create as many geographical zones as the number of sampled constituencies. Figures thus obtained represent the total electors of one zone and are hereafter called a 'constant';
4. Finally, to select individual assembly constituencies, a random number (using Random Number table) was chosen from within the constant and compared with the cumulative total of electorate listed against each constituency. In whichever cumulative total it fell, the constituency listed against that was chosen as the first sample and subsequent assembly constituencies were selected by adding the constant to the random number. That is, one addition of constant would give a second constituency, two additions would give a third one and so on.

This procedure, while providing adequate coverage (geographical) of the state, also ensures a proportional chance to every constituency with a larger electorate to enjoy a greater chance of selection in the sample.

Stage Two: Selection of Polling Booths

Two polling booths from each of the 14 assembly constituencies were selected by simple random procedure, that is the PPS (probability proportionate to size) method was not followed in the selection of polling booths. However, care was taken to avoid selection of contiguous units. To do so:

1. The total number of booths in an assembly constituency was divided by two to make two geographical groups and to obtain a number (constant) that would determine the distance between the two sample booths;
2. The first polling booth was selected by picking a random number from the first half;
3. The second polling booth was selected by adding the constant to the serial number of the first sample booth.

Stage Three: Selection of Respondents

To select individual respondents from the sampled booths, the following steps were followed:

1. The most recent electoral roll of the sample booth was obtained from the election office;
2. If required, the electoral roll was serialized for any deletions and additions in the roll;
3. The total number of electors in the sample booth was divided by 53 for the four booths which formed part of the national sample and by 30 for the remaining booths to obtain a constant to divide the electors in as many sub-units;
4. A random number was chosen from within the constant to select the first respondent from that booth. The constant was added to the random number to select the next respondent and this exercise was repeated till the last respondent from that booth was selected.

This procedure was repeated for all the 28 polling booths and a list of 932 respondents was prepared to form a representative sample for the National Capital Region of Delhi.

APPENDIX II. NOTE ON CONSTRUCTION OF SCALE ON 'ECONOMIC CLASS'

Economic Class is computed by summating the score assigned to each respondent on four indicators, namely, monthly household income, occupational status, asset holding status and type of residential accommodation. First, a value of 1, 2, 3, 4 or 5 (low to high) was assigned against each indicator for each respondent. A sum total of these values ranging between a lowest of 4 and highest of 20 was obtained in the second step. And, finally, considering the frequency distribution, mean score and standard deviation for the total, four class intervals were created to make four classes labelled as 1: very poor; 2: poor; 3: middle; and 4: rich.

NOTES

1. This paper was written in March-April 1998 and it ends with the analysis of the results of the 1998 Lok Sabha elections and not beyond.
2. See Véronique Dupont's essay in this volume for the example of houseless migrant workers.
3. For details of the living conditions in squatter settlements, see Saraswati Haider's essay in this volume.

PART V

MAPPINGS

13

Spatial and Demographic Growth of Delhi since 1947 and the Main Migration Flows

VÉRONIQUE DUPONT

SPATIAL AND DEMOGRAPHIC GROWTH OF DELHI

The development of Delhi and its metropolitan area reflects a major trend in India's urbanization process which is the growing concentration of the urban population in metropolises of a million or several million inhabitants. Yet the domination of the Indian urban scene by these 'megalopolises' takes place within the context of a country which is predominantly rural and is likely to remain so in the medium term (in 1991 only 26 per cent of the population lived in urban areas).

The demographic evolution of the city of Delhi during the twentieth century is closely linked to the history of the country. Following the promotion of Delhi as the capital of the British Indian Empire in 1911, the population grew from 2,38,000 in 1911 to 6,96,000 in 1947. On the other hand, the spatial expansion of the city according to a widely spread pattern of urbanization led to a dramatic decrease of residential densities from 55 inhabitants per hectare in 1911 to 18 in 1921, followed by a gradual increase up to 40 in 1941 (see Table 13.1).

After Independence in 1947 Delhi became the capital of the newly formed Indian Union and had to face a massive transfer of population following the partition of India. Thus, just after 1947 Delhi, whose population was about 9,00,000 at the time, received 4,70,000 refugees from western Punjab and Sindh, while 3,20,000 Muslims left the capital and migrated to Pakistan. Not surprisingly, 1941-51 is the period of the highest demographic growth in the history of the capital which expanded from almost 7,00,000 inhabitants in 1941 to 1.4 million in 1951, corresponding to an annual growth rate of 7.5 per cent which has not been equalled since.

Such a demographic growth occurred together with the spatial expansion of the urban zone in all directions, including to the east of the Yamuna river. The 'official' urban area almost doubled between 1941 and 1961 (see Table 13.1). The geographical location of Delhi in the Gangetic plain, and, moreover, the absence of any significant physical barrier to the progress of urbanization (the Aravalli hills—the Delhi Ridge—in the west and the south do not constitute an effective obstacle) favoured multi-directional urban

TABLE 13.1. POPULATION, AREA AND DENSITY OF DELHI URBAN AGGLOMERATION FROM 1911 TO 1991

Year	Population			Area		Density
	Number	Decennial growth rate %	Annual growth rate %	sq. km	Decennial growth rate %	Pop/ha
1911	2,37,944	–	–	43.25	–	55
1921	3,04,420	27.94	2.49	168.09	288.64	18
1931	4,47,442	46.98	3.93	169.44	0.80	26
1941	6,95,686	55.48	4.51	174.31	2.87	40
1951	14,37,134	106.58	7.52	201.36	15.52	71
1961	23,59,408	64.17	5.08	326.55	62.07	72
1971	36,47,023	54.57	4.45	446.26	36.76	82
1981	57,29,283	57.09	4.62	540.78	21.17	106
1991	84,19,084	46.94	3.92	624.28	15.44	135

Source: Census of India, Delhi, 1951, 1961, 1971, 1981 and 1991.

expansion, and this trend continued in the decades that followed (see Map 13.1).

Delhi is the third largest Indian metropolis, overshadowed only by Mumbai and Calcutta. Furthermore, of the 12 Indian metropolises with a population of over one million in 1981, Delhi has experienced the highest rate of demographic growth despite this having slowed down in recent decades: 5.1 per cent per year from 1951 to 1961, 4.5 per cent to 4.6 per cent per year from 1961 to 1981, and 3.9 per cent per year from 1981 to 1991. The population of Delhi urban agglomeration had reached 8.4 million at the time of the 1991 Census, and by 2000 it has certainly crossed the 10 million figure.

This overall growth of the urban agglomeration conceals acute differences at a more desegregated level (see Maps 13.2 and 13.3). In particular, the peripheral zones exhibit faster rates of growth whereas a process of deconcentration is occurring in the historical city core known as Old Delhi—a densely populated area which contained as many as 740 inhabitants per hectare within the Walled City in 1961, and 616 in 1991 (as compared to 135 in the entire urban agglomeration for the same year).

In order to understand better the spatial dynamics of urban growth, it is interesting to contrast the centrifugal pattern of population growth with the spatial pattern of residential densities (see Map 13.4).[1] The latter conforms largely to a classical model of population density gradients characterized by high densities in the urban core and a sharp decline towards the periphery, the original causes of which were summed up in three words by J. Brush: 'protection, prestige, and proximity'.[2] Thus, the superposition of the two maps—population growth and densities—for the 1981-91 period suggests a negative correlation between these two variables. This is confirmed by statistical tests although the extent of association is moderate (correlation coefficient = -0.292). Nevertheless, this suggests that high population densities tend to deter new dwellers from settling and even to induce exits towards less crowded areas.

The centrifugal pattern of urban growth in Delhi was first highlighted by J. Brush for the decade 1961-71.[3] This spatial pattern of population dynamics has not only persisted, but extended beyond the limits of the urban agglomeration. Thus, the rate of population growth between 1981 and 1991 was faster in the rural hinterland of the National Capital Territory than in Delhi's urban agglomeration: 9.6 per cent per year as against 3.8 per cent respectively (in the urban/rural limits as defined in the 1991 Census). These figures can be compared to the rate of natural growth during the same period, that is 2.5 per year on an average in rural areas and 2.1 per cent in urban areas, which underscores the contribution of net in-migration. Admittedly, population densities remain considerably lower in rural areas than in the urban agglomeration (12 inhabitants per hectare as against 135 in 1991); moreover, although the rural zones cover 54 per cent of the total area of 1483 sq. km which constitutes Delhi's National Capital Territory, they harbour only 10 per cent of the total population of the territory. The number of new settlers in the rural parts of Delhi's territory remains small as compared to those choosing to settle in urban areas. Nonetheless, these population moves are revealing of the effective appeal of the capital's rural hinterland to migrants coming from other states, and to those city dwellers who choose to leave the Delhi urban agglomeration in search of less congested and/or cheaper places to live.

The process of metropolization and rurbanization around the capital is also reflected in economic terms. Hence, the sectorial employment structure of the working population residing in the so-called 'rural Delhi' resembles that of Indian urban areas more than rural ones: for example, only 19 per cent of workers in rural Delhi work in the primary sector as compared to 83 per cent of the rural population and 15 per cent of the urban population at the national level according to the 1991 Census. Although the administrative limits of the Delhi urban agglomeration have been extended several times, with an almost twofold increase in the urban area between 1961 and 1991 (see Table 13.1), the rapid growth of the rural population in the National Capital Territory as well as its economic characteristics underline the gap between the administrative delimitation of the urban agglomeration and the actual modalities of the urbanization process.

FACTORS CONTRIBUTING TO URBAN DECONCENTRATION

Beyond the negative relationship between population growth and residential densities, the pattern of population distribution and growth is related to a number of factors: patterns of land-use, the availability and price of land or residential property, and the accessibility of employment opportunities and urban services. If, as mentioned earlier, this last factor helps explain the centripetal force of the past, the actual centrifugal tendency is certainly associated with the scarcity of land for new residential constructions and its consequent appreciating value in central areas. The less congested peripheral zones provide more affordable housing possibilities, as well as more accessible sites for squatting. Finally, the expansion of the urban periphery is the outcome of the relationship between planning attempts made by the Delhi Development Authority (the central administration in charge of the implementation of the Master Plan and of land development) and private initiatives and responses.

The Delhi Development Authority has played a direct role in the urban spread of the capital through its large-scale acquisition of agricultural land geared towards the implementation of various housing programmes: the construction of flats for sale to private households of different income groups; the development of land and the allotment of plots on a 99-year leasehold basis to private households and cooperative group housing societies; the servicing and allotment of land for the resettlement of slum dwellers and squatters evicted from central areas of the city. This last policy which resorts to coercive measures including the demolition of slum and squatter settlements was pursued most actively during the 'Emergency' (1975-7) during which time about 7,00,000 persons were forcibly evicted and sent to resettlement colonies, all located—at that time—on the urban outskirts (see Map 13.5).

In some cases, these various schemes of flat and plot allotments are part of 'mega-projects' aimed at developing new peripheral zones and leading to the creation of satellite townships. For example, the Rohini project (in the north-western suburb) launched in 1982 was planned to accommodate 8,50,000 inhabitants whilst the Dwarka-Papankala project (in the south-western suburb), launched in 1988 and still under development, is planned to receive ultimately one million inhabitants.

However, these public housing policies have failed to respond to the demands of large sections of the urban population, in particular the lower-middle classes and the poor who have had to resort to the informal housing sector. Hence, the proliferation of unauthorized colonies in the urban-rural fringe on agricultural land not meant for urbanization according to the stipulations of the Delhi Master Plan. In 1983, 736 such colonies were enumerated, housing an estimated 1.2 million people, that is almost 20 per cent of the population of the capital;[4] in 1995, their official number had reached 1300.[5] A policy which aimed at regularizing 567 unauthorized colonies up until 1990 is again on the agenda of the town planners, but it has not succeeded in preventing the unabated proliferation of such irregular settlements. Furthermore, it seems that this regularization policy had the opposite effect of indirectly encouraging the development of new unauthorized colonies, since prospective buyers hoped their settlement would obtain regular status in the future, thereby guaranteeing the long-term economic profitability of their investments.

As for the poorer sections of the urban population, they are relegated to squatter settlements and precarious forms of habitat (locally known as *jhuggi-jhonpri*), which have also continued to proliferate despite the 'slum clearance' and resettlement programmes.[6] In 1994, according to official estimates, about 4,81,000 families lived in 1080 so-called '*jhuggi-jhonpri* clusters' which varied in size from a dozen dwelling units to 12,000.[7] This figure corresponds to about 2.4 million persons—that is 20 to 25 per cent of the total population of Delhi. The population density in the big clusters can be very high owing to the cramming together of families in one-room huts and very narrow lanes. Although some of the largest clusters are located in the urban periphery, squatter settlements are found all over the capital, occupying not only vacant land in the urban fringes (at the time of their emergence), but also all the interstices of the urban fabric wherever there is vacant land and where surveillance by the legal authorities is limited (see Map 13.6).

Nevertheless, the uncontrolled urbanization of the outskirts of Delhi is the effect of the residential strategies implemented not only by low-income groups, but also to some extent by high-income ones. For example, the construction in the southern urban-rural fringe of very luxurious and spacious 'farmhouses', built on agricultural land often without respecting the land-use pattern and floor-area ratio stipulated for such zones, has resulted in the emergence of rich unauthorized colonies.[8]

PROCESS OF METROPOLIZATION: THE DEVELOPMENT OF SATELLITE TOWNS

The slowdown of the population growth rate within Delhi's urban agglomeration (without any decline in the rate of natural increase)[9] coincides with a redistribution of the population in favour of fast growing peripheral towns. This centrifugal population dynamic stretches out beyond the administrative limits of the National Capital Territory, thereby extending the trend of population deconcentration already observed in the urban agglomeration and its rural hinterland. Thus, the ring towns in the Delhi metropolitan area have increased at a much faster rate than the Delhi urban agglomeration. The difference was already noticeable during the 1961-71 period; it reached a peak during the 1971-81 period (8.6 per cent per year as against 4.6 per cent) and still was remarkable during the 1981-91 period (6.5 per cent as against 3.9 per cent) (see Map 13.7 and Table 13.2).

The development of ring towns was encouraged by the regional policy of town and country planning initiated in the 1960s in order to control the growth of the capital and to curb in-migration flows by reorienting them towards other towns in the region.[10] However, the initial stress put on the development of this first ring of towns around Delhi had the effect of strengthening the attraction of the capital and encouraging intensified commuting within the metropolitan area. Due to their proximity to the capital, these ring towns did not emerge as autonomous, alternative growth centres, and most of them can be considered satellite towns.

The fact that the Delhi administration is in direct control of land suitable

TABLE 13.2. POPULATION GROWTH OF CITIES, TOWNS AND RURAL AREAS IN DELHI METROPOLITAN AREA FROM 1951 TO 1991

Towns/zones	*Population*					*Annual growth rate (%)*			
	1951	1961	1971	1981	1991	1951-61	1961-71	1971-81	1981-91
Delhi NCT	17,44,072	26,58,612	40,65,698	62,20,406	94,20,644	4.31	4.34	4.34	4.24
(i) Delhi UA	14,37,134	23,59,408	36,47,023	57,29,283	84,19,084	5.08	4.45	4.62	3.92
(ii) other census towns	–	–	–	38,917	52,541	–	–	–	3.05
(iii) rural Delhi	3,06,938	2,99,204	4,18,675	4,52,206	9,49,019	–0.25	3.42	0.77	7.69
Ghaziabad UA	43,745	70,438	1,37,033	2,87,170	5,11,759	4.88	6.88	7.68	5.95
Loni	3,622	5,564	8,427	10,259	36,561	4.39	4.24	1.99	13.55
Noida	–	–	–	35,541	1,46,514	–	–	–	13.31
Faridabad CA	37,393	59,039	1,22,817	3,30,864	6,17,717	4.67	7.60	10.42	6.44
(i) Faridabad	31,466	50,709	1,05,406	–	–	4.89	7.59	–	–
(ii) Ballabgarh	5,927	8,330	17,411	–	–	3.46	7.65	–	–
Gurgaon UA	18,613	3,868	57,151	1,00,877	1,35,884	7.36	4.20	5.85	3.02
Bahadurgarh UA	11,170	14,982	25,812	37,488	57,235	2.98	5.59	3.80	4.32
Kundli	1,073	1,681	2,669	3,354	5,350	4.59	4.73	2.31	4.78
Total ring towns	1,15,616	1,89,572	3,53,909	8,05,553	15,11,020	5.07	6.44	(a) 8.57 (b) 8.08	6.49

Abbreviations : NCT: National Capital Territory; UA: Urban Agglomeration; CA: Complex Administration.
(a): including population of Noida; (b): excluding population of Noida.

Source : Census of India, 1951, 1961, 1971, 1981 and 1991.

for urbanization within the National Capital Territory has encouraged some large-scale private property developers to implement residential housing schemes outside the administrative limits of the territory of Delhi, in the neighbouring states of Haryana and Uttar Pradesh. Given the lack of a mass transport system in Delhi and the surrounding region, it is the tremendous increase in private means of transportation that has allowed the emergence of such distant townships suitable for those who can afford the price of commuting daily by car, or who compensate for the increased transport cost by the cheaper housing costs.

SIGNIFICANCE OF MIGRATION TO THE POPULATION GROWTH OF DELHI

The dramatic influx of refugees in Delhi following the partition of the country has already been underlined. In the post-Independence era, internal migration played a major role in the demographic expansion of the capital, although the relative contribution of migration has tended to decrease over the last decades. Thus, the share of net migration to the total population growth of Delhi National Capital Territory (urban and rural areas included) was 62 per cent for the 1961-71 period, 60 per cent for 1971-81 period, and declined to 50 per cent for the 1981-91 period. Migrants born outside the Capital Territory constituted 50 per cent of the population of Delhi urban agglomeration in 1971, 47 per cent in 1981 and 40 per cent in 1991. In the five years preceding the 1991 Census, about 8,83,500 in-migrants settled in the Territory of Delhi, almost 90 per cent of whom settled in the Delhi urban agglomeration.

Catchment Area of Migrants in Delhi

The trauma of partition and the massive flow of refugees is directly reflected in the composition of migrants found living in Delhi in 1951, 47 per cent of whom were born in Pakistan. With the direct demographic impact of this specific migration flow fading out over time, the contribution of migrants from foreign countries has declined. At the 1991 Census, 9 per cent of the total migrants in Delhi were recorded as having come from abroad, and only 3 per cent of those who had arrived in the last 5 years.

For a better appraisal of the composition of internal migratory flows, certain salient characteristics of the Indian urban system need to be recalled. The network of Indian cities is quite elaborate without primacy of a single metropolis at the national level. In 1991, 23 Indian cities had more than one million inhabitants. Of these, 5 had a population of over 5 million with Delhi ranking third in size. It is this 'competition' with other big metropolises at the national level that explains why the catchment area of Delhi is mainly regional. More than two-thirds of the migrants (whatever their duration of residence) living in Delhi in 1991 come from the neighbouring states of north India: Haryana, Punjab, Rajasthan and Uttar Pradesh. This last giant state (the most populous in India) accounts for as much as 46 per cent of Delhi's migrants. This can be explained largely by its size. In 1991 Uttar Pradesh had a population of 139 million, that is 1.7 times more than the population of the other three states put together. Only 20 per cent of Delhi migrants came from the remaining parts of India (beyond the Delhi National Capital Territory and its four neighbouring states) despite the fact that this vast area contains three-quarters of the total population of the country. With the exception of Bihar, the other Indian states have contributed only marginally to the migrant population in Delhi (see Figure 13.1).

While the contribution of the neighbouring states of Delhi was already predominant in previous decades, the emergence of Bihar in the catchment area of Delhi migrants is more recent. This phenomena is best highlighted by examining the evolution of the distribution of recent migrants (with less than 5 years of residence)[11] according to their place of origin[12] (see Maps 13.8, 13.9, 13.10 and 13.11). Among the recent migrants residing in Delhi in 1991, 11 per cent had come from Bihar, as against only 1 per cent in 1961.

Rural/Urban Origin of Migrants

Although majority of the migrants in Delhi come from rural areas, it is worth noting that as many as 44 per cent of the total migrants residing in the territory of Delhi in 1991 were from urban areas. This is all the more remarkable given that India is a predominantly rural country (in 1991, 74 per cent of the population of India were living in rural areas). The relative proportion of migrants coming from rural and urban areas varies according to both the state of origin and distance from the capital. With the exception of Punjab,[13] migrants coming from Delhi's neighbouring states and from Bihar are mostly from rural areas: for example, 71 per cent of migrants from Bihar, 61 to 63 per cent of those from Haryana, Rajasthan and Uttar Pradesh. On the other hand, the majority of migrants (67 per cent) from the rest of India come to Delhi from urban places. A similar pattern of rural/urban differentiation according to state of origin was also found in previous decades.

Demographic and Socio-Economic Characteristics of the Migrant Population in Delhi

As in other big Indian metropolises, majority of the migrants in Delhi are male, due to the large numbers of men who come to the capital in search of work, leaving their families behind in their native places. For example, 54 per cent of the total migrants residing in the territory of Delhi in 1991 were male, and this proportion has remained almost unchanged since 1961 (56 per cent).

The age structure of the migrant population in Delhi reveals an over-representation of the age group 15-29 years among both males and females: hence in 1991, 51 per cent of migrants residing in Delhi for less than 5 years belonged to this age group, as against only 30 per cent of the total population of the territory of Delhi. This is also a common characteristic of migration flow towards other Indian cities.

In terms of educational level, the comparison between migrants living in Delhi for less than 5 years and the total population of the National Capital Territory reveals two interesting features. In the population aged 15 and above, the percentage of illiterates among migrants is higher than among the total population, although the gap is not very wide (25 per cent as against 20 for males, and 41 per cent as against 38 for females in 1991). At the top of the educational scale, the proportion of migrants educated up to graduate level or above is almost similar to that observed in the total population (16 per cent as opposed to 17 per cent). These characteristics underline the diversity of the migrant population in terms of educational capital, and reveal that Delhi attracts not only large number of illiterate migrants but also highly qualified sections of the population.

The socio-economic diversity of the migrant population in Delhi is confirmed by the occupational structure of migrants, as analysed on the basis of the 1981 Census data on migrants who have come to Delhi for employment reasons[14] (a group which represents 51 per cent of male migrants, but only 5 per cent of female migrants). A comparison between the occupational structure of the total working population of urban Delhi and that of migrants who had been in the capital for less than 5 years in 1981 revealed no salient distortions between the two distributions, although migrant workers were proportionally over-represented in production, transportation and construction work (54 per cent as against 41 per cent) and in service work at the expense of clerical and sales work. As one would expect of a multi-functional diverse capital of the size of Delhi, the urban labour market attracts very diverse categories of workers, from unskilled casual labourers and construction workers to highly qualified civil servants and professionals.

Reasons for Migration: The Specific Pull of the Labour Market

Employment constitutes the most significant factor of migration for men: 68 per cent of migrants of rural origin residing in the territory of Delhi in 1991 and 59 per cent of those of urban origin had come to Delhi for employment reasons. Yet, among female migrants only 4 per cent had migrated for this reason, without any particular variation between those of rural and urban origin. The main reasons for female migration were families moving house and marriage which altogether accounted respectively for 48 per cent and 40 per cent of the female migrants living in the territory of Delhi in 1991.

The migration survey conducted by the National Sample Survey

Organization in 1987-8 (forty-third round) revealed clearly the specific pull of the capital's labour market, by comparison to other Indian towns and cities. Whereas 66 per cent of male migrants who arrived in the last 10 years came for employment reasons, only 49 per cent of those arriving in other Indian towns and cities gave employment as their main reason for migrating; the corresponding proportions among female migrants were 10 and 5 per cent respectively.

To conclude, let us synthesize the main characteristics of the process of metropolization at work in and around Delhi. The population growth of the capital in the post-Independence period has been remarkably rapid for an urban agglomeration of this size, notwithstanding its slowdown over the last decades. This took place along with a trend of population deconcentration, including depopulation of the old city core, combined with a process of suburbanization which is reflected in the fast growth of peripheral zones. This centrifugal pattern of population dynamics has spread beyond the administrative boundaries of the National Capital Territory with the rapid development of satellite towns. Migration has played a major role in the demographic evolution of Delhi. As expected of a large multi-functional metropolis providing ample employment opportunities, the capital city has attracted a great diversity of migrants, both in terms of their socio-economic backgrounds and their rural/urban origin. Yet, the catchment area of the capital remains dominated by the neighbouring states.

SOURCE OF POPULATION STATISTICS

Census of India 1951, 1961, 1971, 1981 and 1991.

Census of India 1951, Punjab Population Sub-zone, General Population, Age and Social Tables.

Census of India 1961, vol. XIX, Delhi, Migration Tables.

Census of India 1971, Series 27, Delhi, Migration Tables.

Census of India 1971, Series 27, Delhi, *District Census Handbook*, Delhi: Directorate of Census Operations, 1972.

Census of India 1981, Series 28, Delhi, *District Census Handbook*, Delhi: Directorate of Census Operations, 1983.

Census of India 1981, Series 28, Delhi, Migration Tables, Socio-cultural Tables.

Census of India 1991, Series 31, Delhi, *District Census Handbook*, Village and Townwise Primary Census Abstract, Delhi: Directorate of Census Operations, 1992.

Census of India 1991, Series 31, Delhi, Migration Tables, Social and Cultural Tables, Delhi: Directorate of Census Operations (*on floppies*).

National Sample Survey Organization, 'Internal migration (All India): NSS 43rd round (1987-88)', *Sarvekshana*, 51st Issue, vol. XV, no. 4, April-June 1992.

NOTES

1. A detailed analysis of the spatial differentials of population growth and densities at the charge (census division) level according to 1981 and 1991 Census data can be found in V. Dupont and A. Mitra, 'Population Distribution, Growth and Socio-economic Spatial

Patterns in Delhi. Findings from the 1991 Census Data', *Demography India*, vol. 24, 1995, nos. 1 and 2, pp. 101-32.

2. J. Brush, 'Growth and Spatial Structure of Indian Cities', in A.G. Nobel and A.K. Dutt (eds.), *Indian Urbanization and Planning, Vehicles of Modernization*, New Delhi: Tata McGraw Hill, 1977, pp. 64-93.
3. J. Brush, 'Recent Changes in Ecological Patterns of Metropolitan Bombay and Delhi', in V.K. Tewari, J.A. Weistein and V.L.S.P. Rao (eds.), *Indian Cities: Ecological Perspectives*, New Delhi: Concept, 1986, pp. 121-49.
4. Ch. J. Billand, *Delhi Case Study: Formal Serviced Land Development*, New Delhi: USAID, 1990, pp. 2-7.
5. Government of National Capital Territory of Delhi (Planning Department), 'Backgrounder', State Level Seminar on Approach to Ninth Five Year Plan (1997-2002), Delhi: Government of National Capital Territory of Delhi, December 1996, p. 11.
6. For a glimpse of everyday life in a squatter settlement, see Saraswati Haider's essay, and for insight into the development of slum clearance and resettlement programmes, see Emma Tarlo's essay, in this volume.
7. Slum & Jhuggi-Jhonpri Department, Municipal Corporation of Delhi.
8. For insight into the development of rich unauthorised colonies, see Anita Soni's essay, in this volume.
9. According to estimates from the Sample Registration System, the average natural rate of increase in the urban areas of Delhi was 2.0 per cent per year from 1971 to 1980, and 2.1 per cent from 1981 to 1990.
10. National Capital Region Planning Board, *Regional Plan 2001, National Capital Region*, Delhi: Ministry of Urban Development, Government of India, 1988, p. 9.
11. Except in the 1961 Census where it corresponds to a duration of residence in Delhi of 5 years or less.
12. 'Place of origin' refers to the place of birth in the 1961 Census and to the place of last previous residence in subsequent censuses (1971, 1981 and 1991). The Maps 13.3, 13.9, 13.10 and 13.11 pertain only to migrants whose place of origin was located in India. For an appraisal of the evolution of the share of foreign countries among the migrants' places of origin, see Figure 13.1.
13. Only 28 per cent of migrants coming from Punjab are of rural origin.
14. The corresponding table for the 1991 Census has not been released.

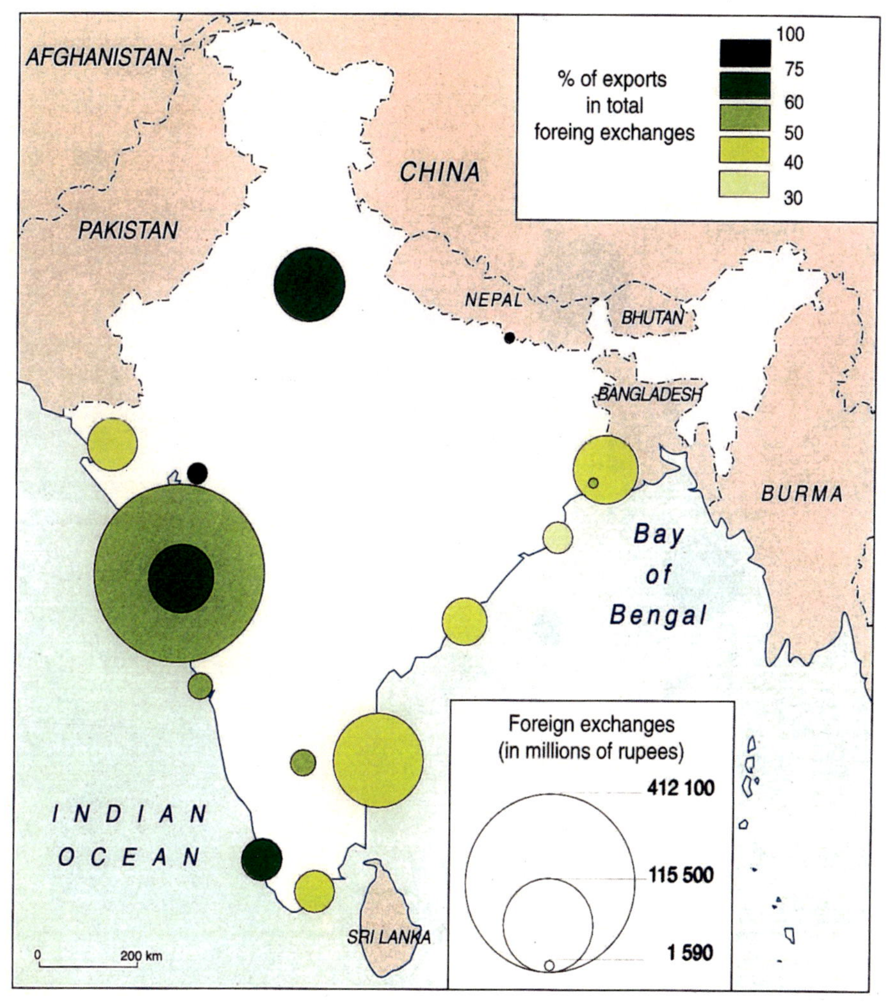

MAP 14.10 FOREIGN EXCHANGES.

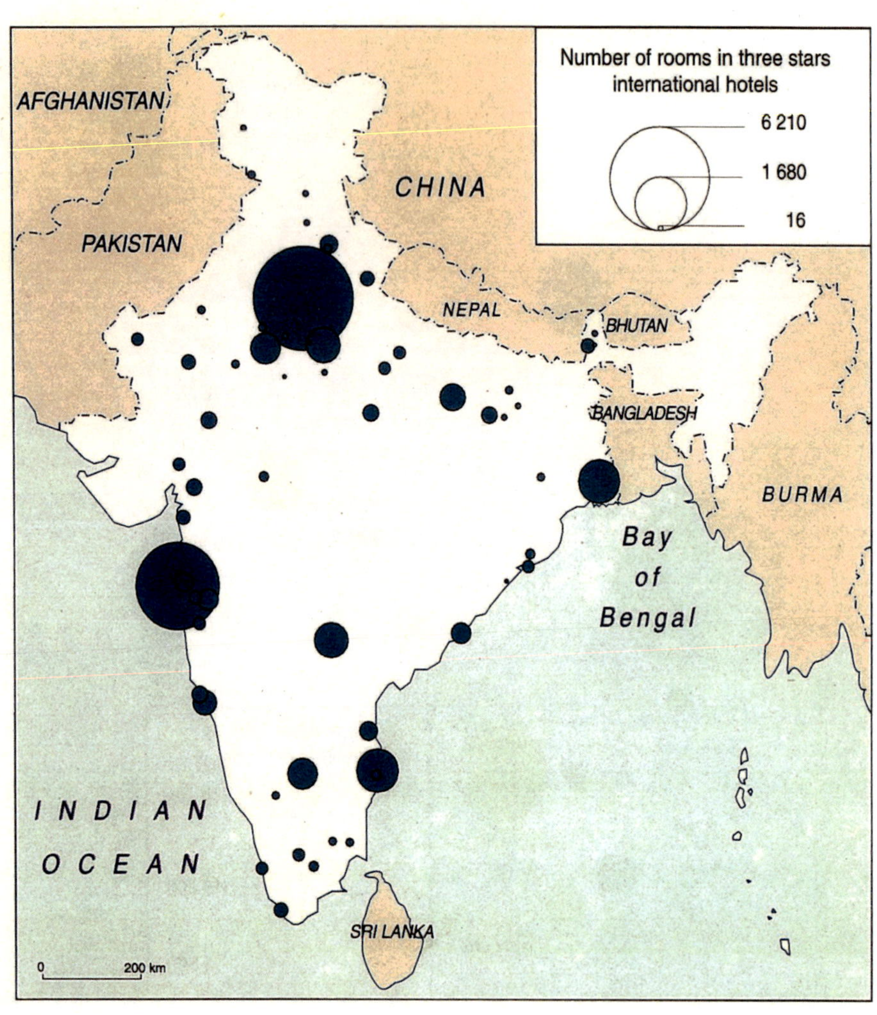

© UMR ESPACE, Ph. Cadène, 1999 *Source of data :* Federation of Hotels and Restaurants Associated of India, 1993

MAP 14.9 INTERNATIONAL HOTELS.

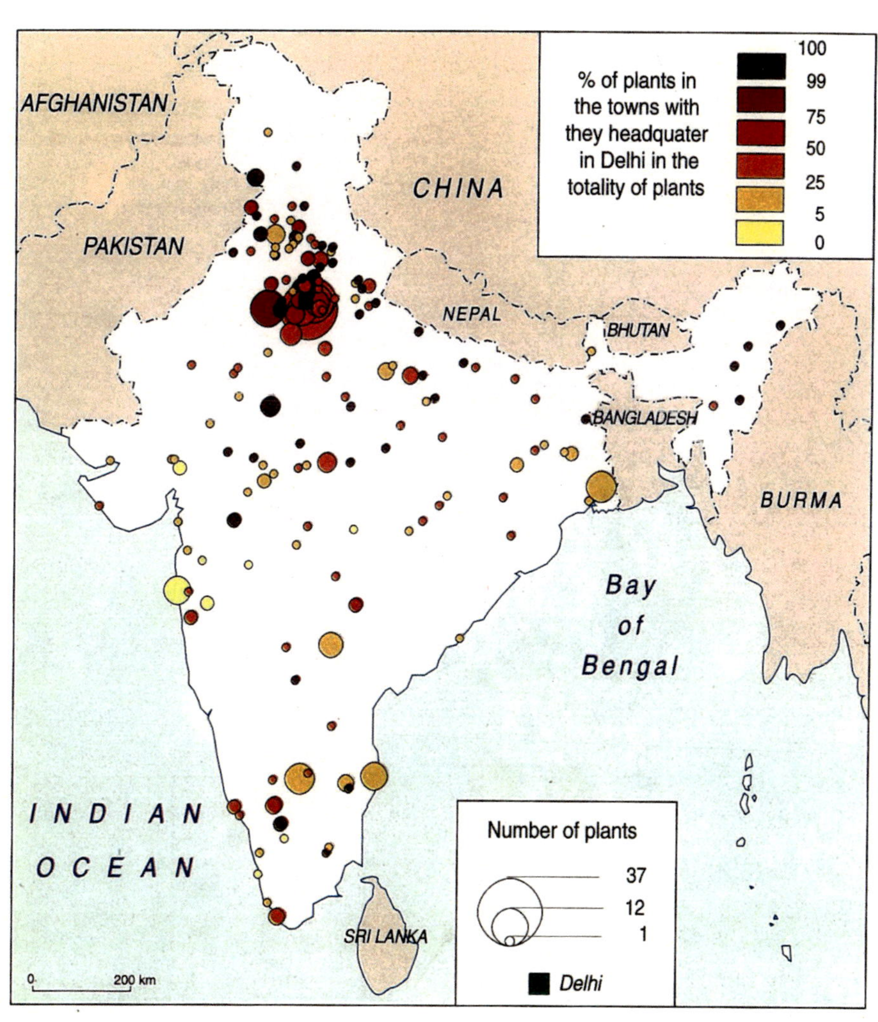

Source of data : C.M.I.E., 1992 - 1993

MAP 14.8 ECONOMIC PLACES CONTROLLED BY DELHI.

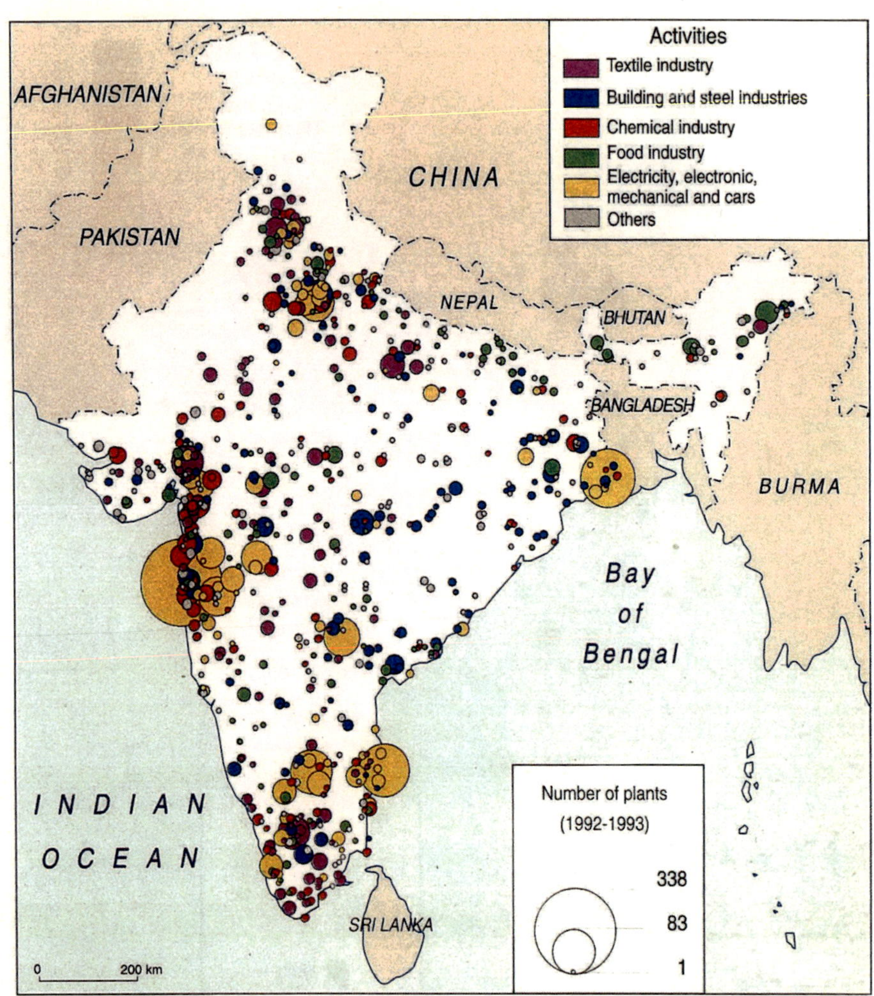

MAP 14.7 PRODUCTION UNITS BY ECONOMIC ACTIVITY.

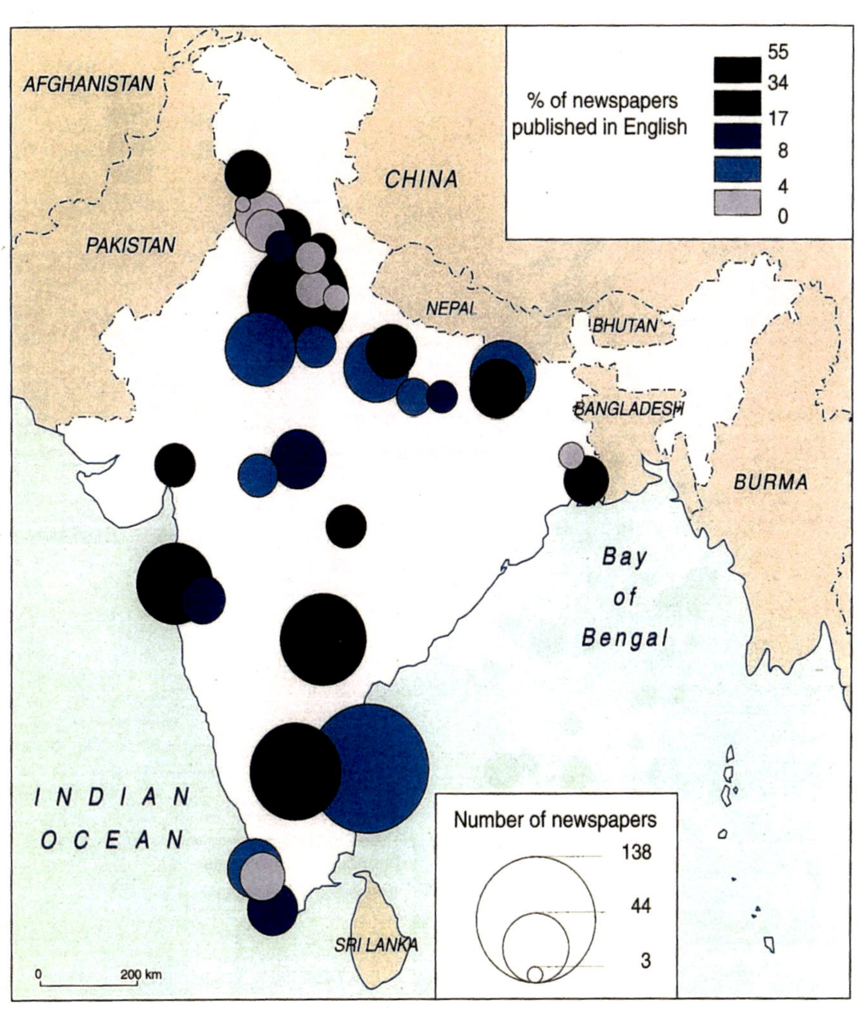

Source of data : Mass Media in India, Ministry of Information and Broadcasting Government of India, 1994

MAP 14.6 CITIES AND TOWNS WITH MORE THAN 100 NEWSPAPERS IN 1989.

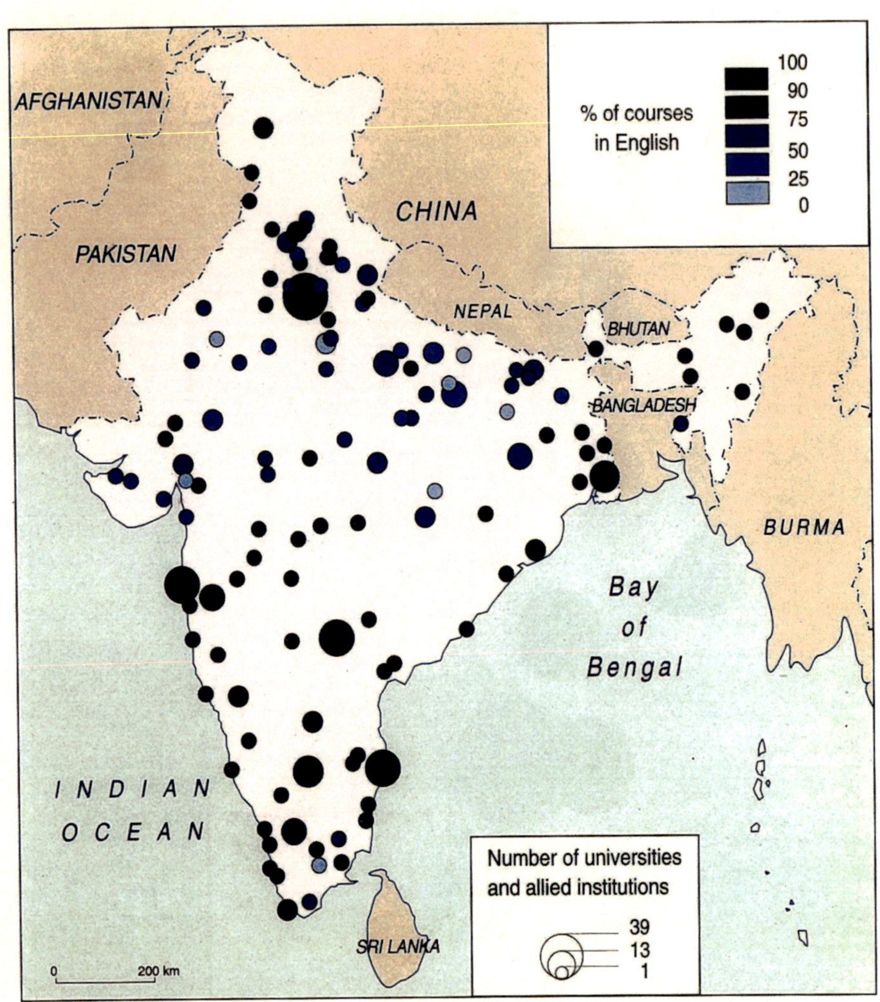

© UMR ESPACE, Ph. Cadène, 1999

Source of data : University Handbook, 1990, Association of Indian University

MAP 14.5 THE UNIVERSITIES.

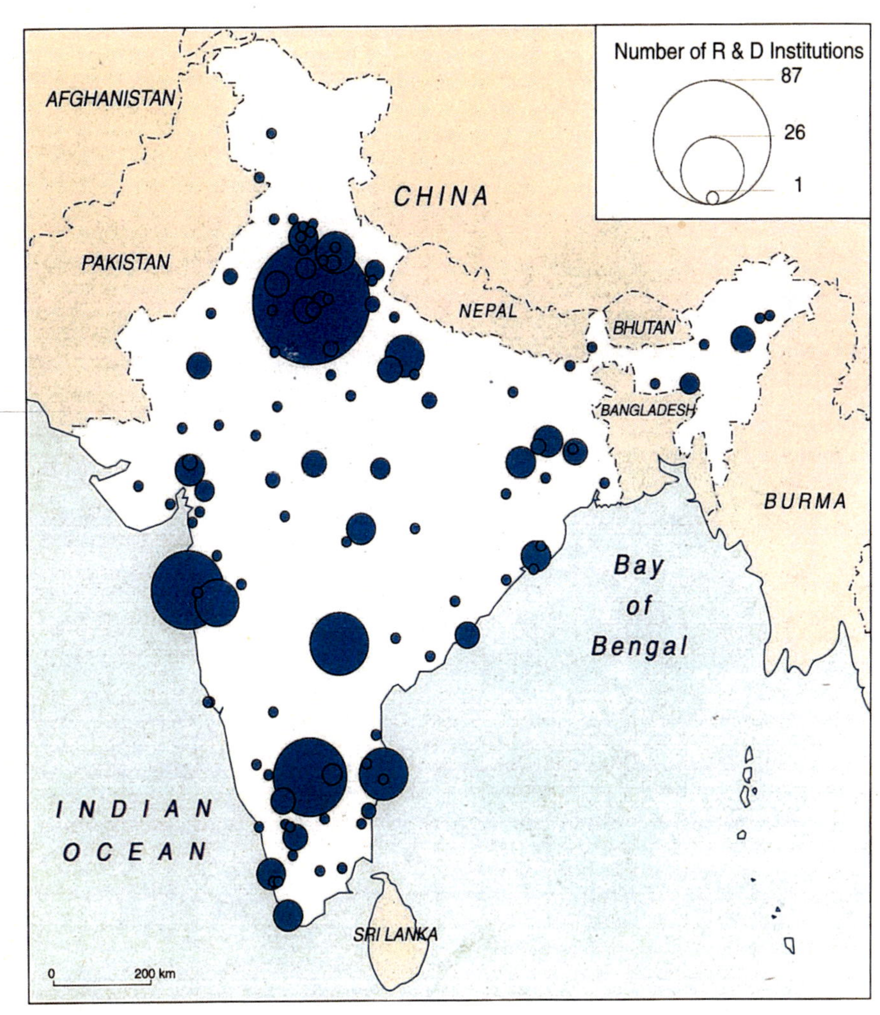

Source of data : Research and Development, 1991-92

MAP 14.4 RESEARCH AND DEVELOPMENT INSTITUTIONS CONTROLLED BY THE CENTRAL GOVERNMENT.

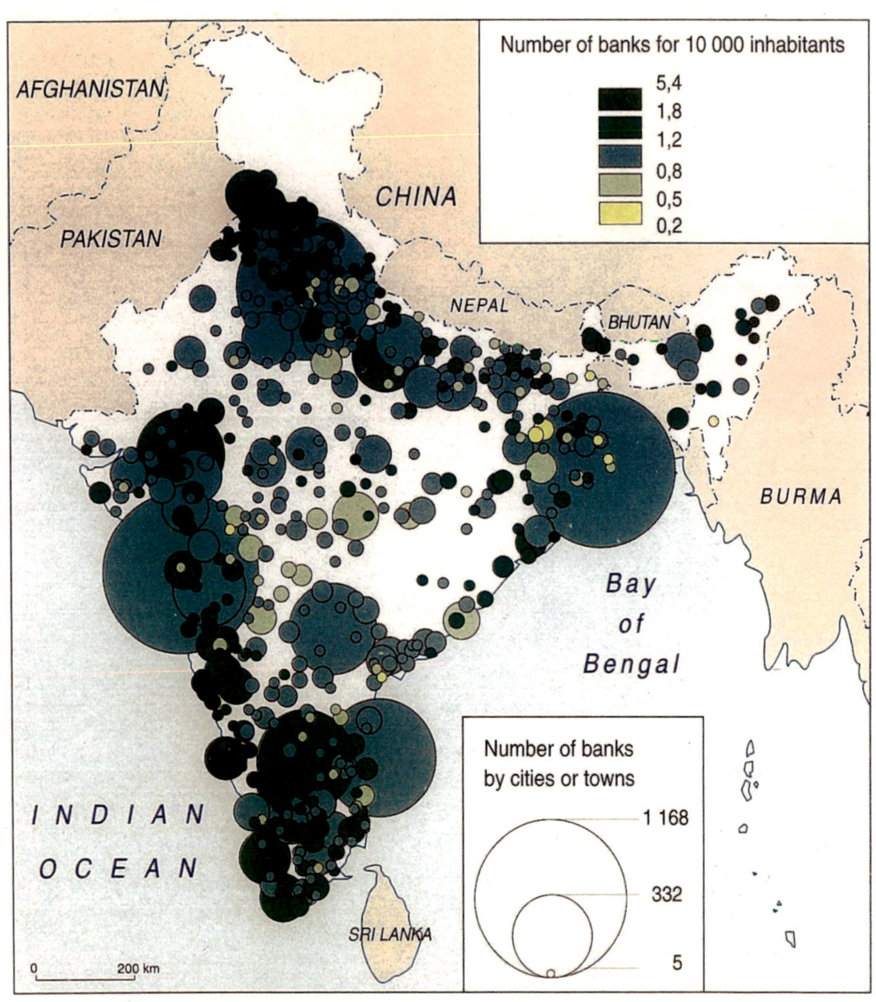

MAP 14.3 THE DENSITY OF BANKS IN CITIES AND TOWNS LARGER THAN 50,000 INHABITANTS.

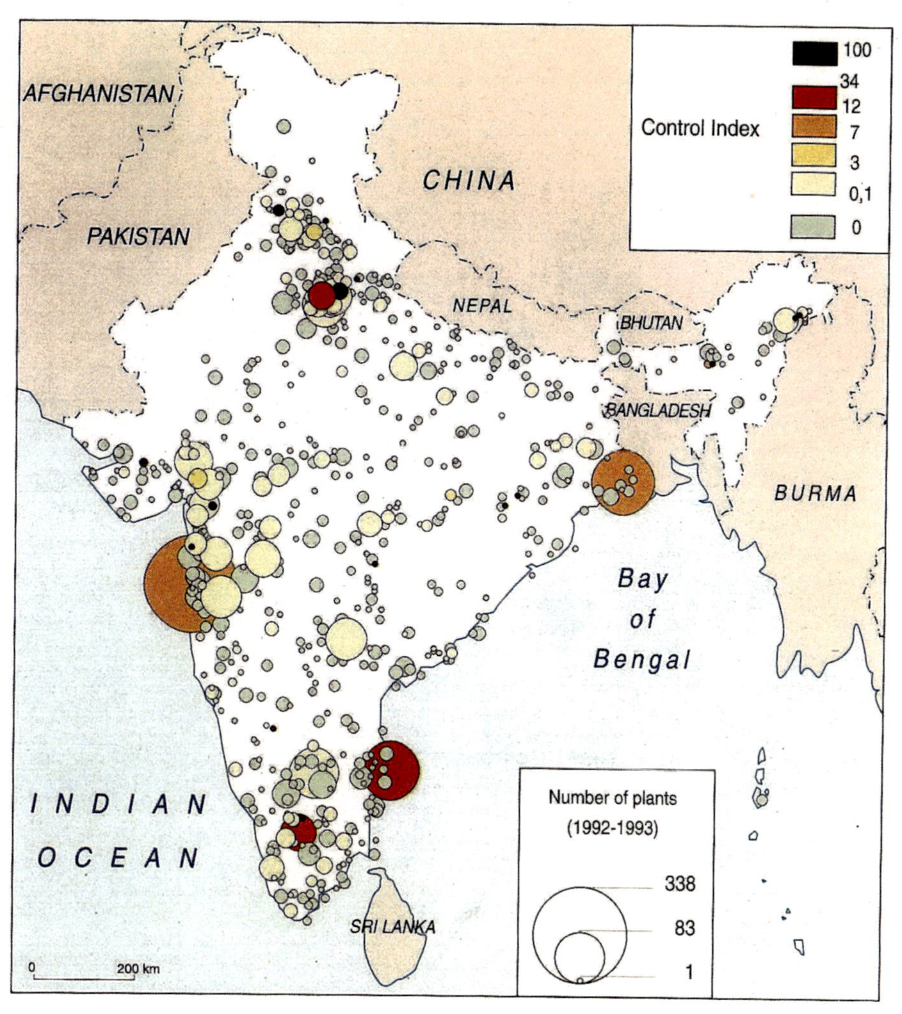

Source of data : Institut Français de Pondichéry, Centre for Monitoring of India Economy

MAP 14.2 LOCAL CONTROL OF INDUSTRIAL PRODUCTION.

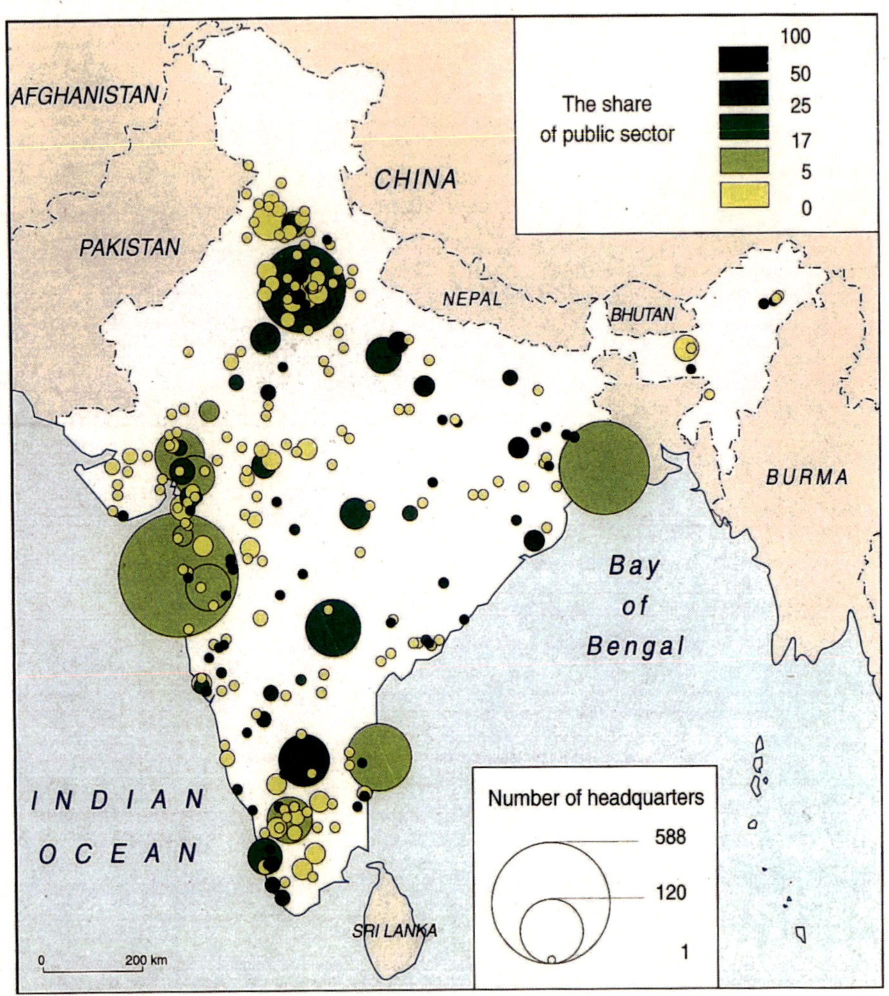

© UMR ESPACE, Ph. Cadène, 1999

Source of data : C.M.I.E., 1992

MAP 14.1 HEADQUARTERS OF LARGE-SCALE FIRMS: THE SHARE OF THE PUBLIC SECTOR.

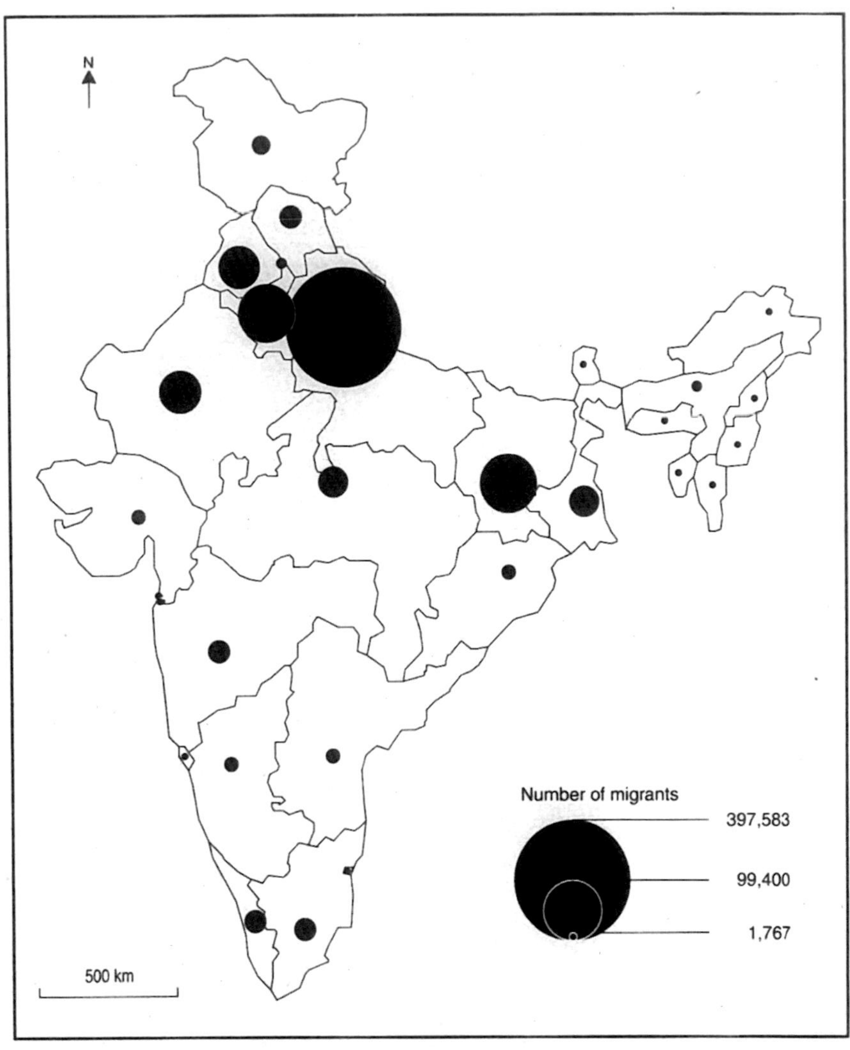

Source of data: Census of India 1991, Series 31 Delhi, Migration Tables.
Digitized map: Ph. Cadène at the French Institute of Pondicherry, Laboratoire de Cartographie IRD (Bondy), F. Dureau (UMR Regard CNRS-IRD, Bordeaux).

MAP 13.11 NUMBER OF RECENT MIGRANTS IN THE NATIONAL CAPITAL TERRITORY OF DELHI IN 1991 BY STATE OF ORIGIN (DURATION OF RESIDENCE: LESS THAN 5 YEARS).

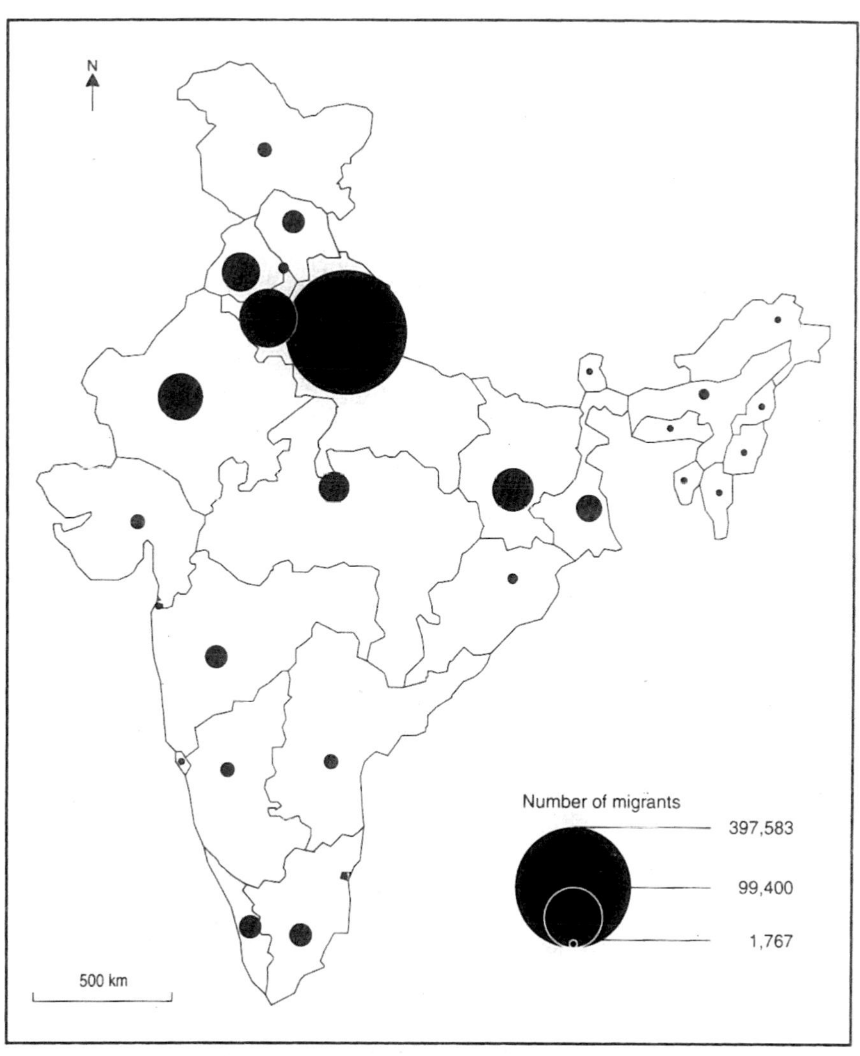

Source of data : Census of India 1981, Series 28 Delhi, Migration Tables. © V. Dupont, IRD
Digitized map : Ph. Cadène at the French Institute of Pondicherry,
Laboratoire de Cartographie IRD (Bondy),
F. Dureaù (UMR Regard CNRS-IRD, Bordeaux).

MAP 13.10 NUMBER OF RECENT MIGRANTS IN THE NATIONAL CAPITAL TERRITORY OF DELHI IN 1981 BY STATE OF ORIGIN (DURATION OF RESIDENCE: LESS THAN 5 YEARS).

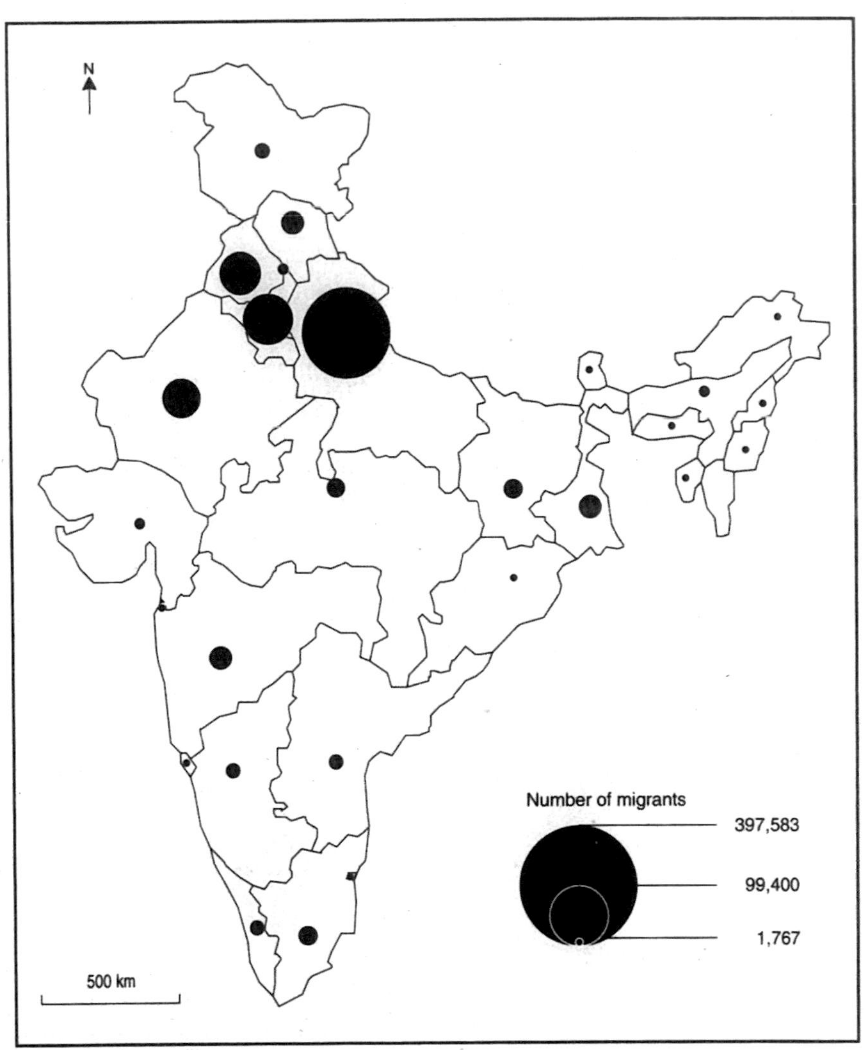

Source of data: Census of India 1971, Series 27 Delhi, Migration Tables. © V. Dupont, IRD

Digitized map: Ph. Cadène at the French Institute of Pondicherry,
Laboratoire de Cartographie IRD (Bondy),
F. Dureau (UMR Regards CNRS-IRD, Bordeaux).

MAP 13.9 NUMBER OF RECENT MIGRANTS IN THE NATIONAL CAPITAL TERRITORY OF DELHI IN 1971 BY STATE OF ORIGIN (DURATION OF RESIDENCE: LESS THAN 5 YEARS).

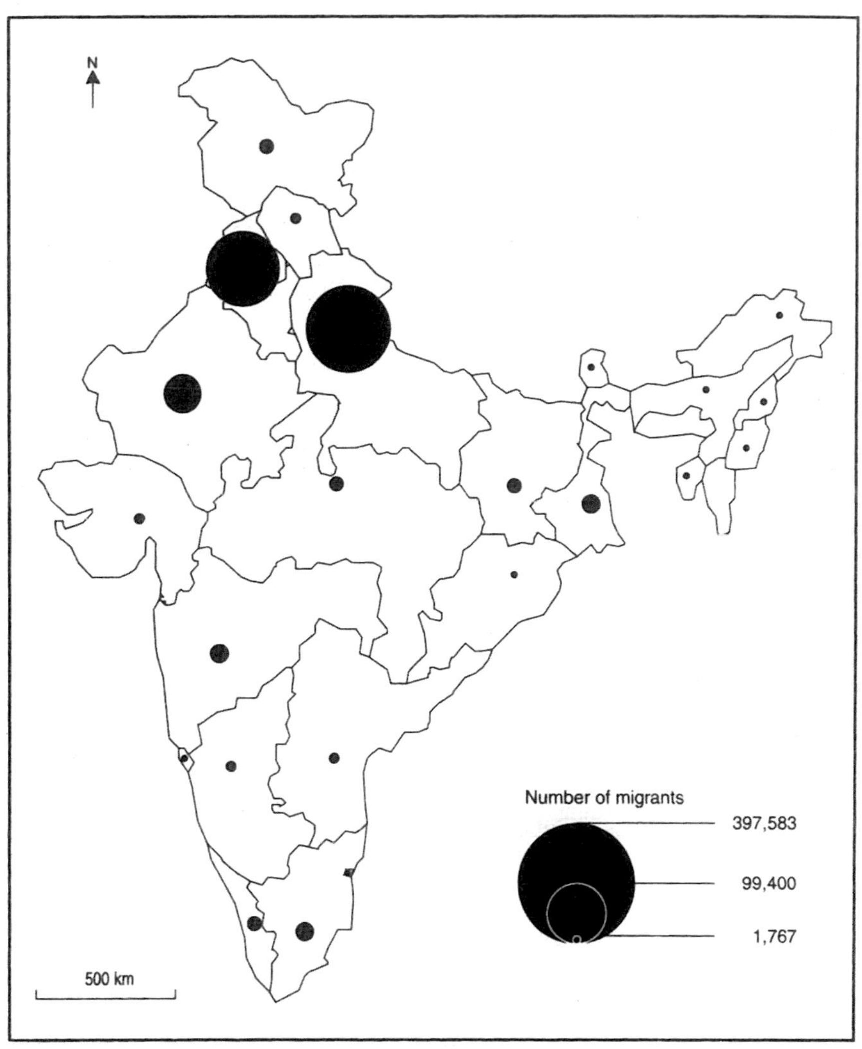

Source of data : Census of India 1961, Vol. XIX Delhi, Migration Tables. © V. Dupont, IRD
Digitized map : Ph. Cadene at the French Institute of Pondicherry, Laboratoire de Cartographie IRD (Bondy), F. Dureau (UMR Regards CNRS-IRD, Bordeaux).

MAP 13.8 NUMBER OF RECENT MIGRANTS IN THE NATIONAL CAPITAL TERRITORY OF DELHI IN 1961 BY STATE OF ORIGIN (DURATION OF RESIDENCE: 5 YEARS OR LESS).

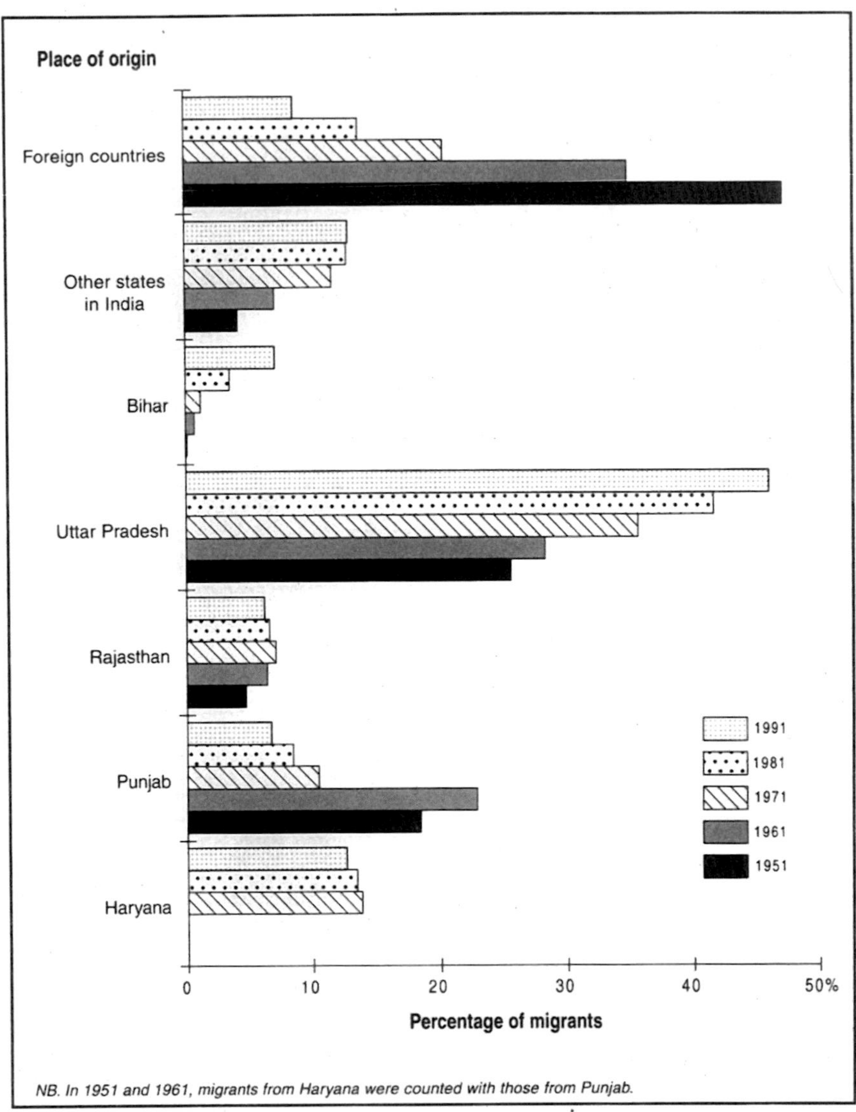

Source: Census of India, Migration Tables, 1951, 1961, 1971, 1981, 1991. © V. Dupont, IRD

FIG. 13.1 PERCENTAGE DISTRIBUTION OF MIGRANTS IN THE NATIONAL CAPITAL TERRITORY OF DELHI BY PLACE OF ORIGIN (1951-91).

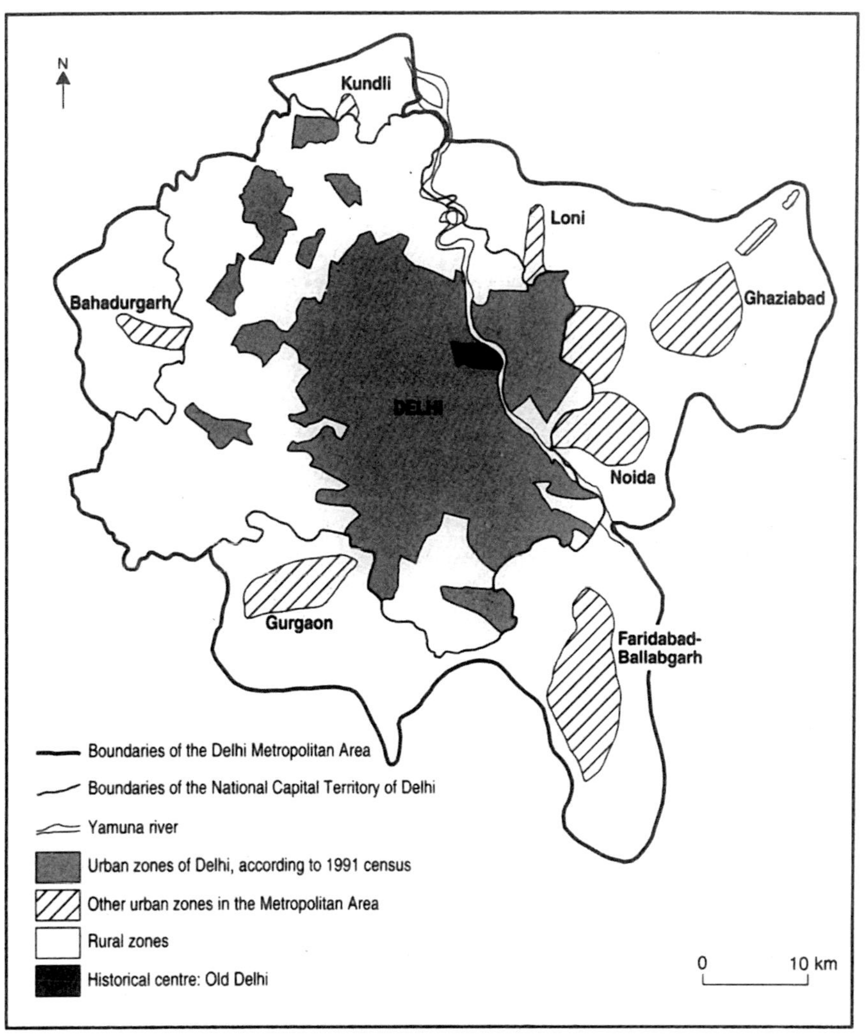

Sources : Composed on the basis of the following maps: © V. Dupont, IRD
'Map of Delhi' in *Census of India 1991, District Census Handbook*, Delhi, Directorate of Census Operation, Delhi;
'Land use 1986-87' in *Regional Plan 2001, National Capital Region*, National Capital Region Planning Board, New Delhi, Dec. 1988;
'Delhi Metropolitan Area' in *Master Plan for Delhi, Perspective 2001*, Delhi Development Authority, New Delhi, August 1990;
Eicher City Map of Delhi, Eicher Goodearth Ltd. New Delhi, 1996.

Digitized map : R.M.S.I. (New Delhi),
Laboratoire de Cartographie IRD (Bondy),
F. Dureau (UMR Regards CNRS-IRD, Bordeaux).

MAP 13.7 DELHI METROPOLITAN AREA: THE CENTRAL URBAN AGGLOMERATION AND ITS PERIPHERAL TOWNS.

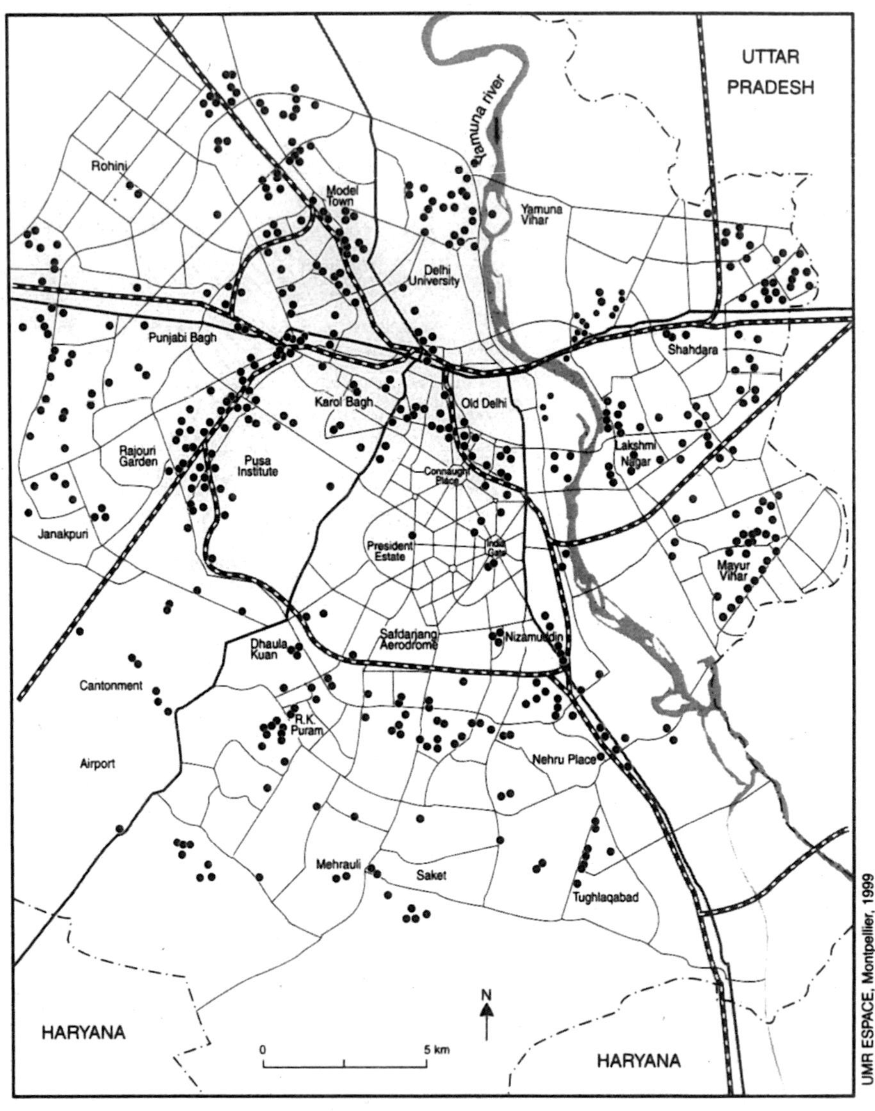

Source: Slum & Jhuggi Jhonpri Department, Municipal Corporation of Delhi. © V. Dupont, IRD

MAP 13.6. LOCATION OF SQUATTER SETTLEMENTS IN DELHI URBAN AGGLOMERATION.

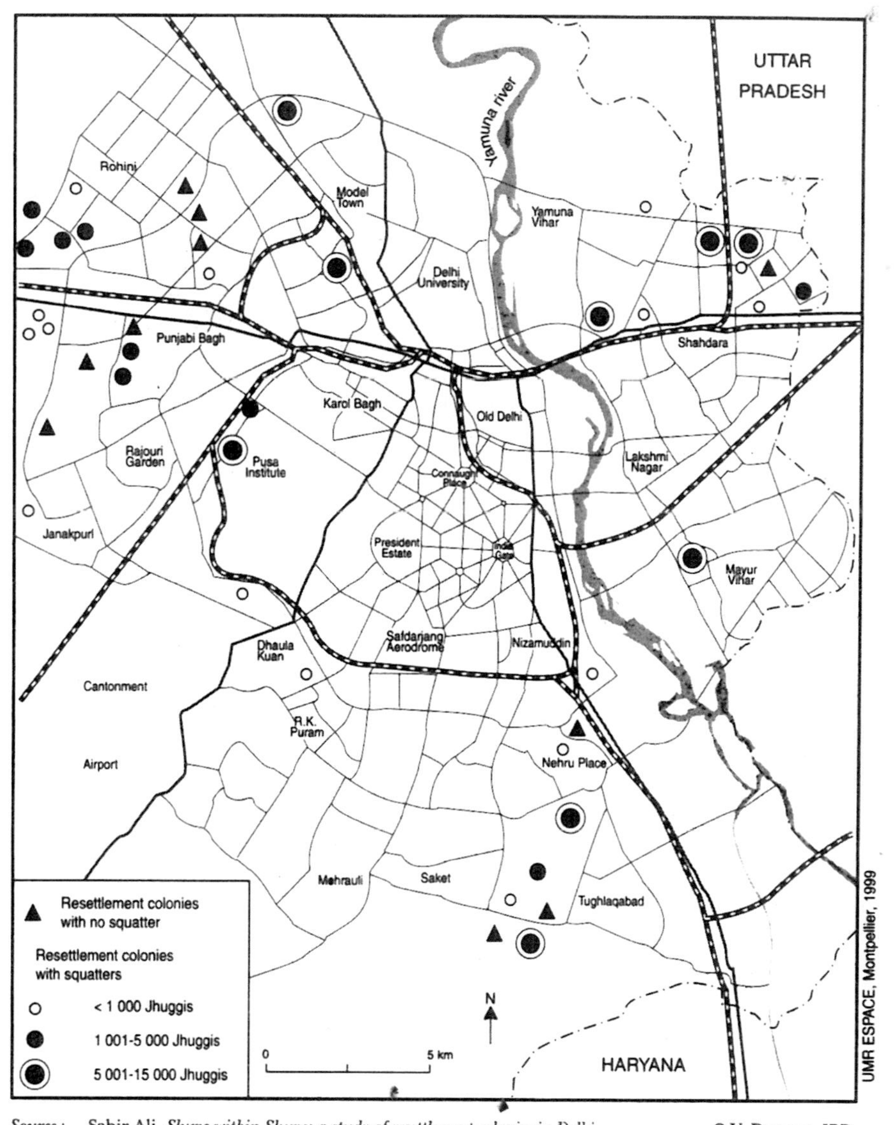

Source : Sabir Ali, *Slums within Slums: a study of resettlement colonies in Delhi*, New Delhi: Council for Social Development, 1990.

MAP 13.5 LOCATION OF RESETTLEMENT COLONIES IN DELHI URBAN AGGLOMERATION.

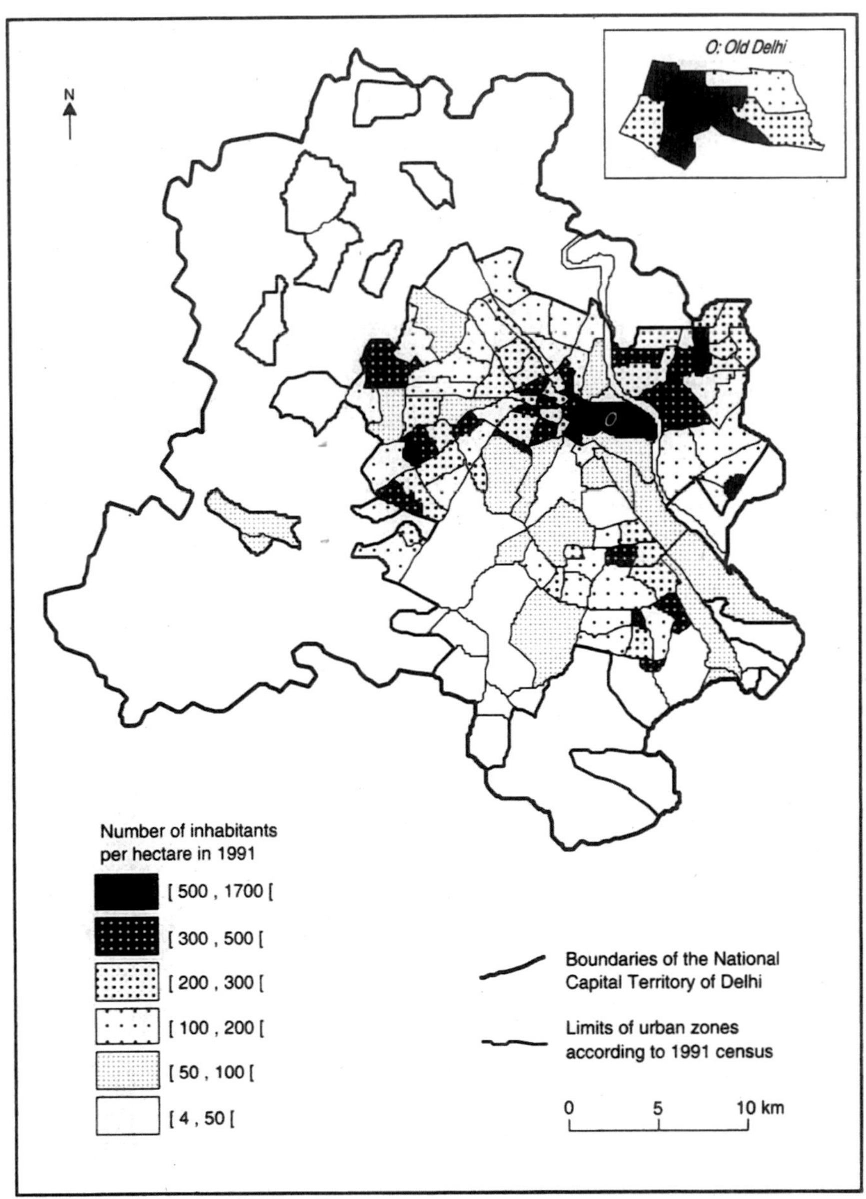

Source of data : Census of India 1991, District Census Handbook, Delhi. © V. Dupont, IRD

Digitized map : R.M.S.I. (New Delhi),
Laboratoire de Cartographie-IRD (Bondy),
F. Dureau (UMR Regards CNRS-IRD, Bordeaux).

MAP 13.4 POPULATION DENSITIES IN DIFFERENT ZONES OF THE NATIONAL CAPITAL TERRITORY OF DELHI IN 1991.

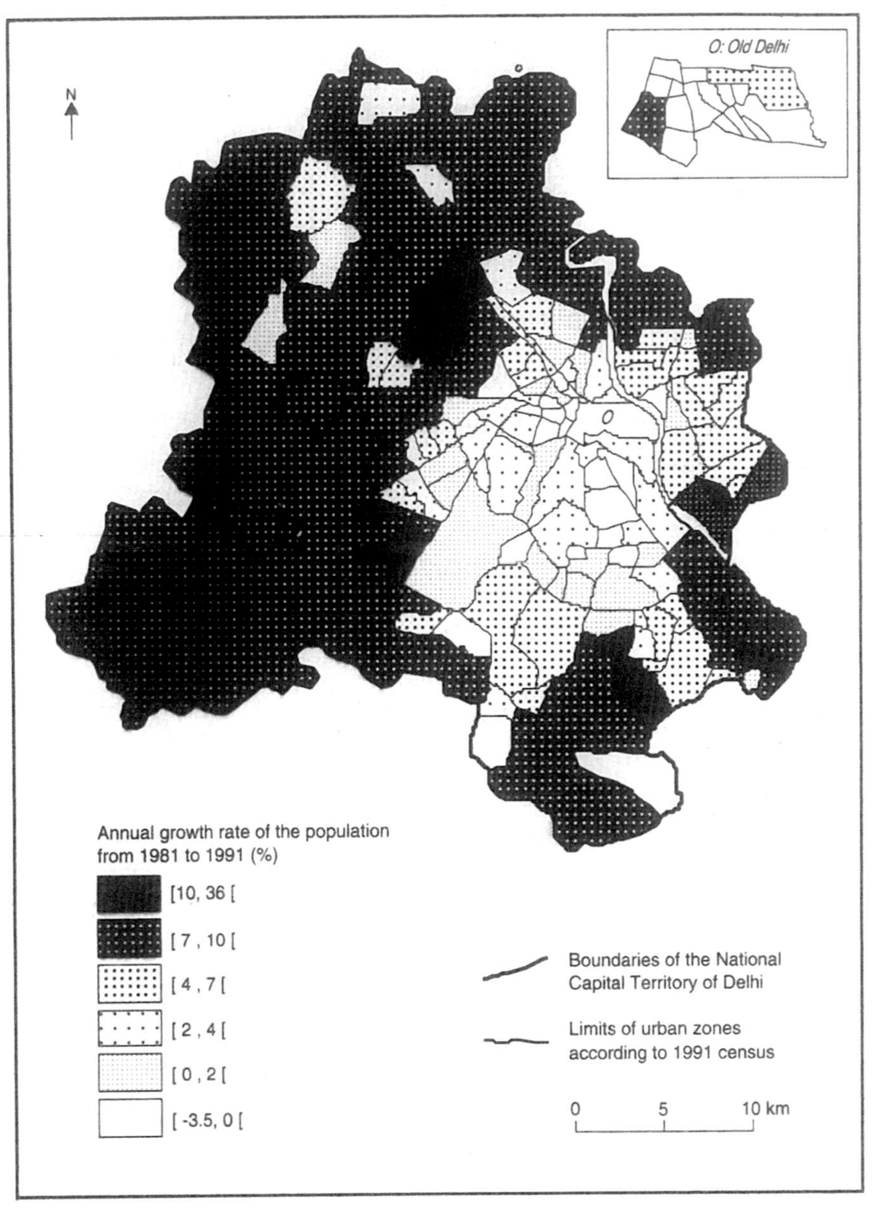

Source of data : Census of India, District Census Handbook, Delhi, 1981 & 1991. © V. Dupont, IRD

Digitized map : R.M.S.I. (New Delhi),
Laboratoire de Cartographie-IRD (Bondy),
F. Dureau (UMR Regards CNRS-IRD, Bordeaux).

MAP 13.3 ANNUAL GROWTH RATE OF THE POPULATION FROM 1981 TO 1991 IN DIFFERENT ZONES OF THE NATIONAL CAPITAL TERRITORY OF DELHI.

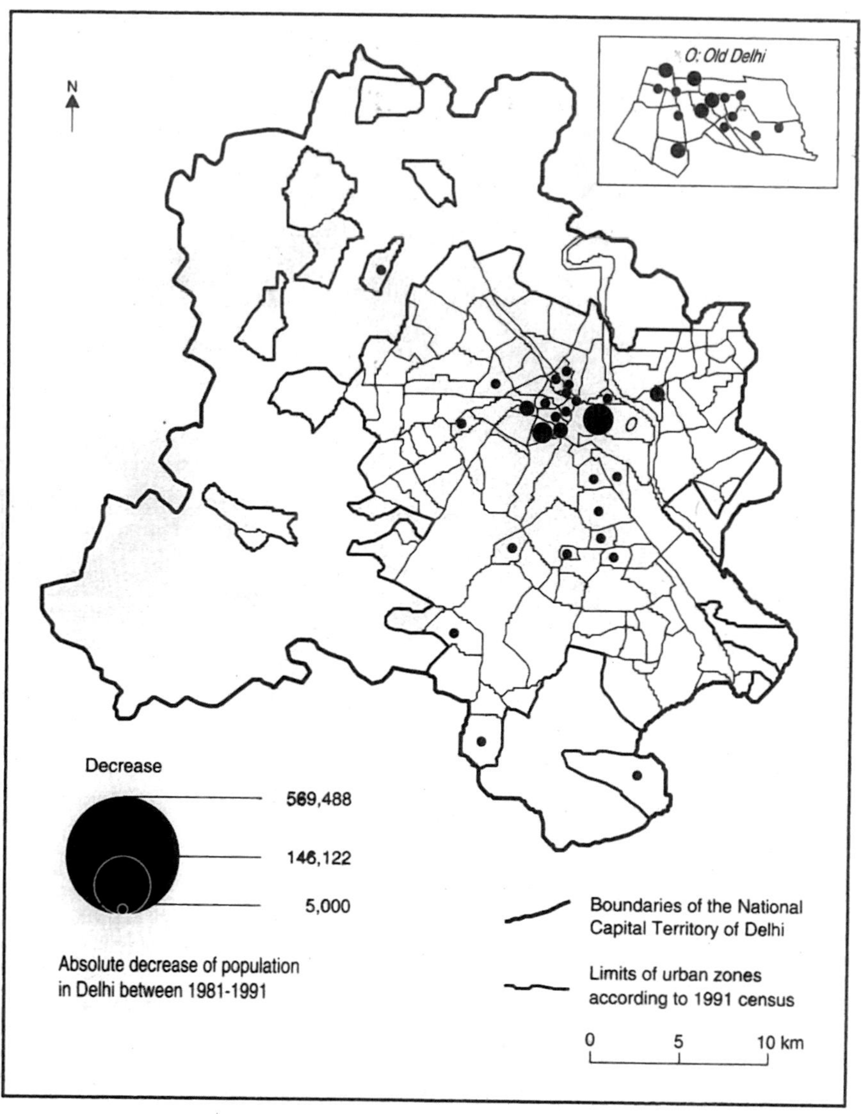

Source of data: Census of India, District Census Handbook, Delhi, 1981 & 1991. © V. Dupont, IRD
Digitized map: R.M.S.I. (New Delhi),
Laboratoire de Cartographie IRD (Bondy),
F. Dureau (UMR Regards CNRS-IRD, Bordeaux).

MAP 13.2b INCREASE AND DECREASE OF POPULATION FROM 1981 TO 1991 IN DIFFERENT ZONES OF THE NATIONAL CAPITAL TERRITORY OF DELHI.

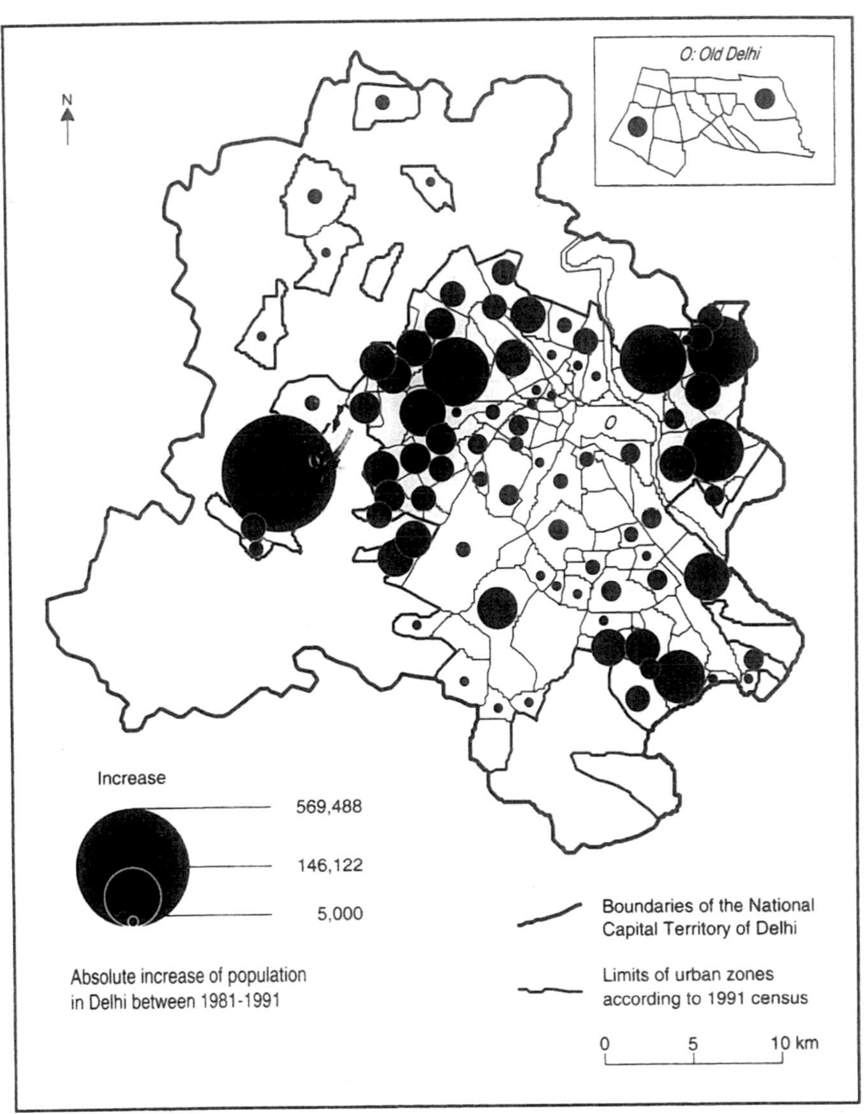

Source of data: Census of India, District Census Handbook, Delhi, 1981 & 1991. © V. Dupont, IRD
Digitized map: R.M.S.I. (New Delhi),
Laboratoire de Cartographie IRD (Bondy),
F. Dureau (UMR Regards CNRS-IRD, Bordeaux).

MAP 13.2a INCREASE AND DECREASE OF POPULATION FROM 1981 TO 1991 IN DIFFERENT ZONES OF THE NATIONAL CAPITAL TERRITORY OF DELHI.

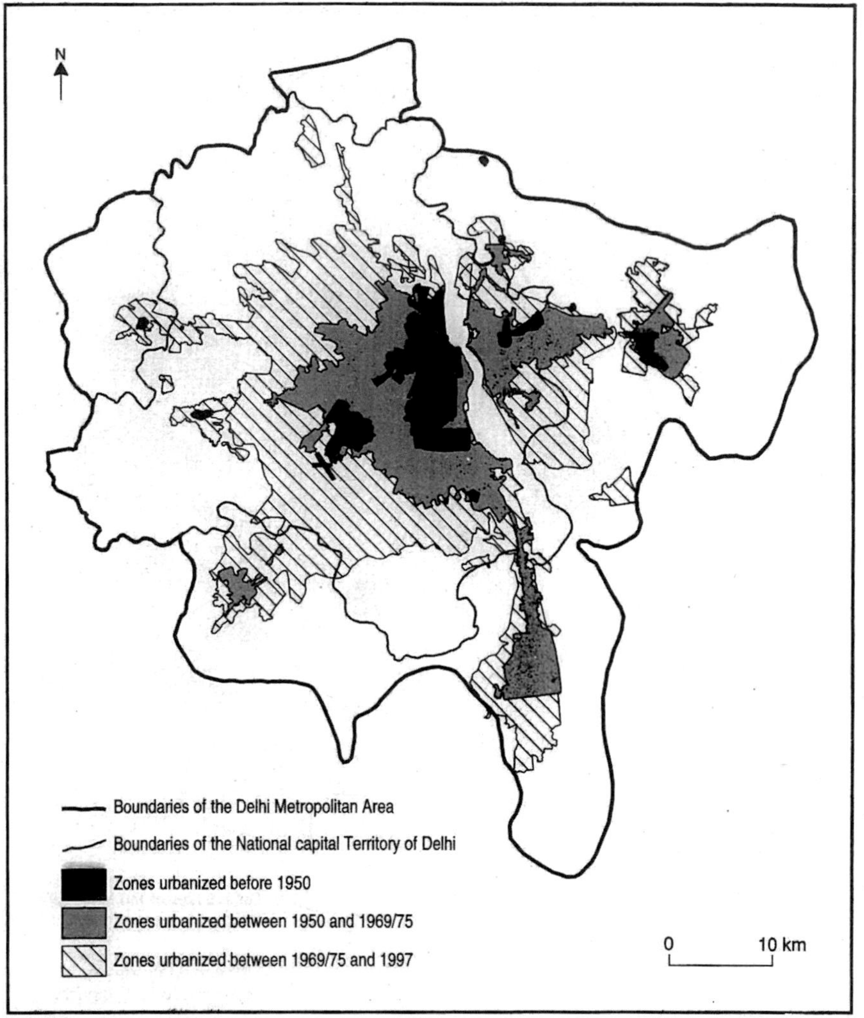

Sources : Survey of India, 1950, scale 1:63,360,
Survey of India, 1970, 1976, 1980, scale 1:50,000,
Image IRS1-C 1997.

Interpretation : Bernard Lortic

Digitized map: R.M.S.I. (New Delhi),
Laboratoire de Cartographie IRD (Bondy),
F. Dureau (UMR Regards CNRS-IRD, Bordeaux).

MAP 13.1 SPATIAL EXPANSION OF URBANIZED ZONES IN THE DELHI METROPOLITAN AREA FROM 1950 TO 1997.

14

Delhi's Place in India's Urban Structure

PHILIPPE CADÈNE

Delhi's history since Independence charts the gradual emergence, first of a national capital, and second of a great international agglomeration. It also highlights the affirmation of a new regional capital in a country, the organization of which had until then been carried out from three ports built by and for the British colonial regime: Calcutta, Mumbai and Chennai. Examined in this essay are the stages and processes leading to Delhi's new status as part of the network of towns and spatial organization of the country. The aim is also to present the economic, social, political and spatial dynamics of the capital of the Indian Union during the 1990s.

This decade has been crucial for the evolution of Delhi as it had been for the Indian society and indeed the world order. It has seen the emergence of a new system of capital accumulation which benefits major financial institutions and companies, but threatens entire sectors of activities, raising unemployment to a very high level in many areas of the world. Shaking the basis of the former divide between developed and developing countries, it creates a new world in which regions (and other countries) are ranked in a hierarchy according to their degree of integration within the global economy. The 1990s began with the fall of the Soviet Union and heralded the triumph of the liberal model. But it is also notable for the reconstruction and restoration of balances at the planetary level, the setting up of a new system of capital accumulation and the integration of societies and regions within the global dynamic.

The emergence of Delhi on the national and international scene, as also the emergence of a vast region centred around the agricultural and industrial plains of Haryana and Punjab (it was to the east of this that the ancient capital of the Mughal Empire was built) must be considered in this global context. It is a case of illustrating the place and the role of this agglomeration of nearly ten million inhabitants, first within the process of the unification of national space and second within the process of the integration of Indian urban places and regions into global networks.

This reflection is based on an analysis of a series of maps. These are presented in the illustrations' section preceding this chapter. The maps have been taken from an economic atlas of India, which is currently in press. The image which emerges of Indian territory and of the place of Delhi within the urban structure is built from an analysis of the maps taken as a whole. A map should not be considered independent from the series in which it is included just as a town should not be isolated from the others within a map. The data used presents only the main shape of the Indian territory and the main structure of the activities it describes. In each map, only the biggest companies and economic actors are represented. The numerous small-scale units and household producers, so important to Indian development, are excluded due to the non-accessibility of adequate data. But most of them, in most parts of the country, are closely located within the areas of development shown in the maps. Hence, their absence does not radically change the image of the economy presented here. Finally, the social consequences of development, whether good or bad, are not presented in the maps; this is beyond the scope of this exercise.

The sources of information are varied: national census data; data bases compiled by professional organizations from both the public and private sectors; and professional almanacs. All figures refer to the period 1991 to 1994. They are strictly economic in nature and have already been published. They provide a measure of economic development at a particular point in history, and give a picture of the distribution of economic activities at an all-India level.

EMERGENCE OF A NATIONAL CAPITAL

In the Indian political and administrative system, Delhi stands out clearly as the capital, the city in which is concentrated the totality of institutions, directly or indirectly connected to this function. Delhi is the city of ministries, of the Parliament, of the ruling bodies of all major political parties of the country, of the representative bodies of the twenty-five states that form the Indian Union. Delhi is also the city where the headquarters of public sector companies are located, such as the national airlines, the national railway board and the census board. All foreign delegations and international organizations are also located here.

With regard to economic power, calculated on the basis of the location of the headquarters of major companies, Delhi cannot compare with Mumbai. Mumbai's role in this sphere has been vital ever since the collapse of Calcutta, caused partly by the departure of British settlers who formed the backbone of entrepreneurial force in the city and partly due to the creation of East Pakistan (later Bangladesh), which separated companies responsible for the wealth of the city from the jute growing areas which provided the raw material.

Whereas Mumbai clearly dominates the urban landscape, Delhi apparently competes with Calcutta for second place in the hierarchy of Indian cities. This fact emerges from an analysis of the headquarters of the principle enterprises based in these cities. Delhi and Calcutta are practically on a par if we consider the location of the headquarters of 2,000 major companies, but Delhi has an edge when 500 of the most important companies are considered, especially those with linkages to foreign firms. Delhi owes its position in this sphere partly to its status as the capital city. The headquarters of the main public sector companies, in fact, account for half of the headquarters based in the agglomeration. This proportion is superior to that of other cities, although in absolute numbers Mumbai wins hands down and Calcutta and Delhi share second place (see Map 14.1).

If economic activities are taken into consideration, Delhi, like Calcutta, Chennai or Bangalore, is favoured by companies manufacturing capital goods, whereas Mumbai is preferred as the headquarters of chemical companies. The specific characteristics of the different sectors nevertheless show that the Delhi agglomeration, though it rarely dominates, holds a significant place in the totality of sectors, with the exception of the pharmaceutical industry where Mumbai dominates over Calcutta and Bangalore. Delhi, alongside Mumbai, occupies the top position as the headquarters of fertilizer and construction companies; it comes second after Mumbai in the field of transport equipment and electronics; second after Calcutta for mechanical consumer goods; third after Mumbai and Calcutta in the case of metallurgy, machine tools, chemicals, electrical goods, and agro-food companies; fourth alongside Calcutta in the field of textiles, but behind Mumbai, Ahmedabad and Coimbatore. True, certain branches carry greater weight than others and a sectoral analysis shows the importance that long-established economic development confers on Mumbai and Calcutta.

The capacity to control the economy—calculated as the correlation between the number of headquarters in one place and the number of manufacturing companies that it has and controls in the territory—similarly illustrates Delhi's place among the major Indian cities (see Map 14.2). If Chennai's strength is even more evident, Delhi, like Mumbai and Calcutta, nonetheless exerts its influence on the entire country. Furthermore, unlike Mumbai—which clearly dominates the scene—and to a greater extent than Calcutta, Delhi has a greater number of manufacturing companies, the headquarters of which are situated elsewhere.

This last point is confirmed by an analysis of the locational patterns of manufacturing units, which show how far removed Delhi is from Mumbai and even Calcutta and Chennai with regard to industrial employment. In this respect, Delhi is closer to two second-level agglomerations in the Indian industrial hierarchy, Bangalore and Hyderabad. Industrial economy is not, however, the only factor on which the power of a metropolis can be judged. Delhi is, in fact, strongly placed in the banking sector (see Map 14.3). It has as many banks as its two chief rivals and even outdoes Calcutta, but remains second to Mumbai with regard to the volume of transactions conducted. It concentrates visibly on monetary values, disbursing more credit and receiving fewer deposits.

In the field of education, research and communication, Delhi plays a major role largely because of its political position (see Maps 14.4, 14.5 and 14.6). If research and development in the private sector takes place mainly in Mumbai, Delhi clearly dominates in research and development initiated by the central government. Similarly, if Mumbai comes first with regard to the number of doctorates obtained in the sciences, and Delhi's universities only manage an equal position with the universities of Chennai, Bangalore, Varanasi and Kanpur, nevertheless, the universities of the Delhi region show considerable prowess. Besides, the capital can boast of many other excellent institutes of learning. While management institutes are not its strong point, it is in the forefront in the fields of humanities, communications, social and political sciences. This is explained partly by the political and administrative institutions in Delhi as well as by its role in the televisual, radiophonic, journalistic and literary spheres. Delhi occupies first place with regard to the English language dailies. It is overwhelmingly the major player in the publishing industry more generally, with more than one-third of its publications being printed in English. Delhi is also an important centre in the health sector. With institutions like the All India Institute of Medical Sciences located there, the city can offer a particular high quality of health services.

Political institutions, headquarters of major companies, universities, prestigious research institutes, national television channels, principle dailies and publishing houses, state-of-the-art hospitals—in brief, all the factors necessary to enable Delhi to become part of the national and international economic network are present. However, this situation would not have been possible if, during the period Delhi was consolidating its position in the country, this great agglomeration of the Indo-Gangetic plain had not also been establishing itself as the pivot of a powerful region undergoing development.

THE POWER-POTENTIAL OF A RAPIDLY GROWING ECONOMIC REGION

Delhi is situated in the heart of a tightly knit group of towns of various sizes, found to the west of an immense, fertile and densely populated plain which stretches from the Pakistani frontier to the Gangetic Delta. This part of the Indo-Gangetic plain is constituted mainly by the Punjab, which was divided between India and Pakistan at the time of Partition. The Indian side is itself divided into two states—Punjab and Haryana, to the south-east of which the National Capital Territory of Delhi is situated.

In the course of history, this region has received the highest investments in the field of agricultural irrigation. It was the first to try out new techniques brought in by the Green Revolution in the 1960s, and it is in this region that agricultural yields are highest, whether in rice, wheat, maize or cotton. It consumes the maximum amount of fertilizers and has the highest rate of mechanized agriculture.

Industrial development in the region is not far behind. Many enterprises have located themselves in the area, their density enabling one to talk about the existence of a vast industrial corridor of 400 km, which forms a sort of circular arc, encompassing the districts of west Punjab near the Pakistani border, north-east Rajasthan and south-east Uttar Pradesh. Less dense and less powerful than the corridor measuring 600 km which follows the coast of the Arabian Sea, north of Ahmedabad to south of Mumbai, this industrial corridor of north-west India seems to possess a greater manufacturing capacity than the third and last industrial corridor situated to the south of the Deccan, and centred around the towns of Bangalore in Karnataka, Coimbatore in Tamil Nadu and Cochin in Kerala.

The specific characteristics and inherent power of the industrial corridor of which Delhi is a part, lies in the diversity of the economic activities present there. Like the industrial corridor in which Mumbai is situated, and unlike the industrial sector of the Deccan, the north-west corridor includes areas of specialization as diverse as agro-food industries, textiles, capital goods industries, metallurgy, construction and chemicals. The differences appear along the length of a corridor which is constructed around two pivotal points: the western pivot is the city of Ludhiana, and the eastern pivot is Delhi. The articulation between the two occurs in Chandigarh which is the capital of the two neighbouring states of the Punjab, where Ludhiana is located, and Haryana to the east of which lies the territory of Delhi. The agro-food industries are equally distributed between the two. The construction industry is mostly concentrated in Delhi and its neighbourhood. The metallurgical industry is located in the east and stretches across Haryana to Rajasthan in the west, and to the south of Delhi. Machine tools are manufactured in Delhi and its periphery, but also in Ludhiana and its neighbourhood. Industries manufacturing transport equipment are distributed in various places in the corridor. Mechanical consumer goods industries are concentrated in the city of Delhi and in the small Punjabi industrial complex of SAS Nagar. Chemical industries are to be found everywhere, but the greater part of their production is concentrated in Delhi. Fertilizer manufacturing units are relatively well distributed in the corridor. However, pharmaceutical industries are generally not well represented. Electric equipment is mainly to be found in Delhi and its periphery, while the electronics industry is very much present in the two core areas (see Map 14.7).

Through the headquarters of the various companies located there, Delhi exerts strict control over this entire industrial space. Mumbai and Calcutta businessmen are present, but are not particularly powerful in this corridor. The difference between Mumbai and Calcutta resides only in the fact that whereas Mumbai has a small but definite presence in the Punjabi towns, Calcutta's influence is more or less limited to the capital. Inversely, Delhi exerts its influence on practically all the towns and, as distance from the capital increases, so too does its influence (see Map 14.8). Few industrial centres of the Indo-Gangetic plain seem capable of deciding their own economic futures. From this point of view, political power seems to contribute to the creation of an urban hierarchy. Chandigarh, because of its status as the capital of two states, or SAS Nagar, the industrial complex set up as part of the policy decisions taken with regard to national development, harbour many company headquarters, particularly in the sectors of metallurgy, machines tools, mechanical consumer goods, chemicals and pharmaceuticals. Some towns, less influenced by power, have one or sometimes two company headquarters, but only in those sectors in which the relationship with the local environment is primordial, such as agro-foods or textiles. Although headquarters confine themselves to political centres or industrial towns created out of nothing, the private character of the big companies in the Punjab is a well-established fact, and some of their dynamism rubs off on the Punjabi business community, very much in evidence in the economic life of Delhi. Ever since the influx of Punjabis to the capital as a result of the Partition of India, the flow of migrants, this time from the Indian side of the Punjab, has been continuous, creating very strong links between Delhi and the towns and villages of Punjab and Haryana.

Though situated at the extreme south-east end, Delhi, at the beginning of the twenty-first century, is the pivot of a powerful region, not only as the result of the industrial and agricultural developments but also for its varied activities in the service sector, developed within a tight network of towns of various sizes. These activities certainly coincide with economic development, but are also very significant indicators of the close linkages which exist within the region. Apart from Delhi which clearly dominates with its 84,19,084 inhabitants (1991 Census), the plains of the Punjab can boast of a very structured network of towns, controlled by a series of big agglomerations of which the most powerful are Ludhiana with 10,12,062 inhabitants (according to the 1991 Census), Amritsar, the religious centre of the Sikhs with 7,09,456 inhabitants, and Jalandhar with 5,19,530 inhabitants. In the state of Haryana, Faridabad has 6,13,828 inhabitants and lastly, Chandigarh, a capital of two states and a Union Territory, has 5,74,646 inhabitants.

These towns and many others smaller in size, offer numerous service activities which give them an important role in the economic structuration of the region. Banking institutions are specially numerous, dense, powerful, not only in the region but also in relation to the number of inhabitants. Universities and other institutions of higher education are numerous and highly active, particularly at the doctorate level, as also are the public research and development institutions. There are many dailies, and the publishing industry in general is flourishing with a major portion of literature published in the English language.

Everything contributes to making the region a highly dynamic one, benefiting from an urban network in which human resources, money, goods and information circulate and where Delhi, fully integrated in this dynamic, plays a pivotal role and provides an opening to the outside world.

DELHI: PIVOT TO THE WORLD OUTSIDE

Delhi would not have acquired legitimacy as the national capital without its integration within a region experiencing rapid growth. But it is also its capacity for exchanges and interactions at the international level that has enabled it to play a major role in the urban structure of the country. For Delhi to assume this role, the expansion of the air transport sector was necessary and this sector now dominates long-distance international passenger travel and has a considerable share in the transportation of goods. This phenomenon can be perceived through the activity of Delhi's airports. Though second to Mumbai in respect of international and domestic air traffic, no other town compares with the capital.

The intense activity at Delhi airports is due to the dynamism of the region, its status as the political capital and the importance of India in the world. Delhi offers the largest number of hotel rooms of international quality (see Map 14.9). Foreign tourists are conspicuous here, and the Indian capital is described at great length in guide books. The city has, indeed, a lot to offer thanks to its unique heritage—a result of its chartered history as the capital of two great empires, the Mughal and the British. Much remains to be done to enhance the tourist potential of this huge city constructed on the ruins of seven ancient capital cities. Whether in front of the Red Fort, near the gigantic bazaar of Old Delhi or walking in Connaught Place (city centre of Imperial Delhi), or whether relaxing in Lodi Gardens where Muslim mausoleums rub shoulders with business centres and luxurious modern houses in one of the most posh residential areas, tourists can capture something of the force that the capital of independent India represents.

Apart from tourism, Delhi also plays host to many national and international conferences. In this regard, it dominates other cities, organizing as many conferences in the field of pure sciences as in the field of economics and social sciences and religion. These conferences are, in turn, a source of business for the hotel industry. This activity is rendered possible because of the existence of numerous conference halls. Conferences are mainly organized by Indian institutions. However, in order of importance, Germany, France, Great Britain, the United States and Canada also initiate conferences in Delhi. Mumbai, which ranks second, has links only with Great Britain for organizing conferences while Bangalore which has the same ranking as Mumbai, has links with many European countries, especially France.

Leisure, tourism and conferences may be highly visible but we should not forget business travel. The latter is at the centre of the liberalization experienced by India since the early 1980s, a period in which there was a re-thinking of the old development model promoted by Nehru, based on a drastic policy of import substitutions and accompanied by the economic isolation of the country. The liberal model which advocates a multiplicity of exchanges and the promotion of exports is now favoured. It is responsible for an acceleration of growth but, at the same time, it threatens existing equilibria as well as vested interests. It also widens income discrepancies amongst the population. In India as elsewhere in the world, this economic liberalism places the big urban agglomerations at the centre of economic dynamics. The bigger cities increasingly become a place for privileged interactions and exchanges; and business travellers become important actors in the new economic system which is slowly emerging.

The volume of financial exchange with foreign countries appears to be the classic indicator of the role of various localities (see Map 14.10). According to available data, Mumbai with its two ports comes first among the Indian port-towns, outstripping Chennai and Calcutta. Despite being situated in the interior of the country, Delhi exceeds Calcutta in the value of goods exchanged and is quite close to Chennai. Bangalore, another exporting city, plays a relatively minor role. The capital, on the other hand, has a very well-developed export sector as nearly two-thirds of the total value of commercial exchange comes from exports.

Delhi seems to play a key role, along with Mumbai, with regard to the new policy which has placed exports in the forefront of economic development. The presence of major export companies in these two cities alone offers proof of the dynamism, with Mumbai outstripping Delhi. However, a product specialization study of export companies, in relation to the sites where they are located, reveals important differences. The Delhi agglomeration dominates the export of a single product (rice) whereas Delhi and Mumbai are together in the forefront of textile and marble exports. These two cities along with Goa, also control copper exports and, along with Calcutta and Cochin in Kerala, tea exports. Delhi along with Calcutta and Chennai is at the forefront of leather exports, leaving Mumbai lagging. Delhi also plays an important role in the export of carpets but several towns in Bihar control the market as this state in the Indo-Gangetic plain houses a large part of the national production. For other products, if Mumbai has a greater number of export companies, affirming its status as the economic capital of India, Delhi comes off as a serious rival. This is the case with embroidery and silk where Delhi has the same standing as Calcutta; food products in which many coastal towns of Kerala taken together play an important role; jewellery for which both Delhi and Jaipur come in second position after Mumbai. In pharmaceuticals Delhi and Mumbai share the same position though Mumbai's sphere of influence extends to many Gujarati towns who support this activity. In the manufacture of machine tools, the two regions controlled by their respective metropolises play a key role, but the Mumbai region still dominates due to the forces and antecedents of industrial development. In software production Mumbai, Delhi, Calcutta and Chennai have the same ranking. It is, however, interesting to note that Delhi does not have any major labour recruitment firms sending personnel abroad, Mumbai monopolizing all the headquarters with regard to this activity.

Taking into account all of the factors examined so far: the importance of Delhi's links with the hinterland; the potential of economic development in this portion of the Indo-Gangetic plain; the weight of the Punjabi diaspora and Delhi's important place as a production centre of the country, it seems possible to consider the Delhi agglomeration a powerful place and, above all, a transit base that the vast area in the north-west of the country can use for transactions outside India. Delhi's influence clearly outstrips its hinterland, over which it wields direct sway as seen in the maps dealing with urban structure and the distribution of activities.

DELHI, AN INTERNATIONAL CITY?

To conclude, the question that arises is what is the status of Delhi as an international city? The purpose of this notion of 'the international city', according to its use by geographers, is to categorize cities which are at the top of an urban system (generally national ones) and can serve as a relay or transit base for other towns of this system, enabling the whole to integrate within global economic networks. Such international cities, also, necessarily have many superior tertiary functions which help them reinforce economic exchanges with exchanges in the field of culture, information and the arts. Thus, we are concerned with towns capable of acting as catalysts in the dynamics taking place at the global level, leading to the development of a new economic system based on the multiplicity of exchanges with regard to men, capital and information.

The demographic weight which India represents, reinforced by a powerful diaspora, an age-old civilization and its capacity to develop the most advanced technologies, contributes to the potential emergence of 'international cities'. Actively participating at the economic level but also in education and information in the building of a national urban system, Delhi can obviously be defined as an 'international city', supported as it is by a powerful and growth-oriented hinterland and playing an important role in exports. Promoting industrial and cultural products as well as Indian values in the world, this is one of the cities which enables India to take part in the massive exchanges induced by the process of globalization. The only agglomeration which rivals and in fact appears to dominate Delhi is Mumbai. But the power that India represents makes it possible for both metropolises to play a vital international role. Delhi, however, holds the trump card which enables it to challenge the economic superiority of the Maharashtrian port, by its position as the centre of political power, and because of its domination in the fields of information and communications. Due to the recent emergence of Delhi at the regional and national levels, the capital appears capable of assuming the role of a veritable 'international city', at the head of a solid national urban system and of a powerful region.

Chronology of Significant Events in Delhi

NARAYANI GUPTA

1192	Delhi Sultanate established
1648	Shahjahanabad founded
1803	English East India Company captured Delhi
1857	The Great Revolt (India Mutiny)
1858	Mughal rule ended. Delhi made part of Punjab Province
1863	Delhi Municipality established
1911-12	Delhi made capital of British India. Delhi a separate Province
1931	New Delhi inaugurated
1936	Delhi Improvement Trust established
1943	Delhi Rent Control Act
1946-8	Migration of 'refugees' to Delhi
1947	Independence and Partition
1947-64	Jawaharlal Nehru Prime Minister
1956	Delhi Slum Clearance and Improvement Act
1957	Delhi Development Authority set up
1962	First Master Plan for Delhi
1966-84	Indira Gandhi Prime Minister
1974	Delhi Urban Art Commission set up
1975-7	The Emergency
1984	Anti-Sikh riots in Delhi
1984	Indian National Trust for Artistic and Cultural Heritage (INTACH) set up
1985	Conservation Society of Delhi registered
1985	National Capital Region Planning Board Act
1997	INTACH completes list of 'heritage' buildings in Delhi

Contributors

PHILIPPE CADÈNE is a Professor of Geography at the University Paul Valéry, Montpellier, France. He has done extensive research on Indian and French cities and towns, and contributed to several edited books in geography and sociology. He recently co-edited *Webs of Trade: Dynamics of Business Communities in Western India* (Delhi: Manohar, 1997, with Denis Vidal) and *Decentralized Production in India. Industrial Districts, Flexible Specialization and Employment* (New Delhi: Sage, 1998, with Mark Holmström).

VÉRONIQUE DUPONT is a Research Fellow in economic-demography at the French Institute of Research and Development (IRD, Paris), and a member of the French Centre for the Study of South Asia (CEIAS, Paris). She has carried out research on population mobility and the urbanization process in Gujarat and Delhi where she was affiliated with the Institute of Economic Growth and the French Centre for Human Sciences. Her recent publications include *Decentralized Industrialization and Urban Dynamics. The case of Jetpur in West India* (New Delhi: Sage, 1995).

SYLVIE FRAISSARD is an independent French photographer, whose work focuses on social topics including working conditions, migration issues and popular culture. She contributes to various magazines.

NARAYANI GUPTA is a Professor of History at Jamia Millia Islāmia, New Delhi. She has written on urban history and conservation. Her *Delhi Between Two Empires 1803-1931* was published in 1981 (paperback 1998). She was a founder-member of the Conservation Society of Delhi and a member of the Delhi Urban Art Commission.

SARASWATI HAIDER is a research scholar at the Centre for the Study of Social Systems, School of Social Sciences, Jawaharlal Nehru University. Her on-going dissertation is a sociological study of a *jhuggi-jhonpri* cluster (squatter settlement) in the metropolis of Delhi. She has published several academic articles and is also a freelance writer publishing in newspapers, journals and magazines on topics such as gender, politics, media and social problems.

CHRISTOPHE JAFFRELOT is a Research Fellow at the CNRS and Deputy Director of the Centre d'Etudes et de Recherches Internationales (CERI) in Paris. He teaches South Asian politics at the Institut d'Etudes Politiques of Paris. He is the Editor-in-Chief of *Critique Internationale.* His recent publications include *The Hindu Nationalist Movement and Indian Politics, 1925 to 1990s* (New York: Columbia University Press; London: Hurst; and New Delhi: Viking, 1996), and *La démocratie en Inde - Religion, Caste et Politique* (Paris: Fayard, 1998). He has also edited *L'Inde contemporaine - de 1950 à nos jours* (Paris: Fayard, 1996) and with T.B. Hansen, *The BJP and the Compulsions of Politics in India* (Delhi: Oxford University Press, 1998).

A.G. KRISHNA MENON is the Director of the TVB School of Habitat Studies, New Delhi. He is also a consulting architect and urban planner. His publications include *Cultural Identity and Urban Development*, and *Historic Towns and Heritage Zones.*

SATISH SHARMA is an independent photographer, photography critic and photography curator. He is interested in the sociology and politics of photography and is working on a subaltern history of Indian photography.

V.B. SINGH is a Senior Fellow and Director of the Centre for the Study of Developing Societies, Delhi. Besides having contributed numerous articles to academic journals, he has written *Profiles of Political Elites in India*; *Political Fragmentation and Electoral Processes: 1991 Election in Uttar Pradesh*; and *Elections in India: Data Handbook on Lok Sabha Elections, 1986-91*, volume 2, and has co-authored *Elections in India: Data Handbook on Vidhan Sabha Elections, 1952-85* (five volumes); *Between Two Worlds: A Study of Harijan Elites*; and *Hindu Nationalists in India: The Rise of the Bharatiya Janata Party.*

ANITA SONI is a Polish-born Indologist and Social Anthropologist (formerly associated with the Institute of Oriental Studies, University of Warsaw). Since 1978 she has been permanently based in India and works as a freelance researcher and grassroots activist among migrant labourers in the un-organized sector in semi-urban areas. She is currently collaborating with the Joint Women's Programme, an all-India social action group linking gender issues to the emancipation of dalits and minorities.

EMMA TARLO is a Lecturer in Social Anthropology at Goldsmiths College, University of London. She has carried out research in Gujarat and in Delhi where she was affiliated with the Centre for the Study of Social Systems, JNU. Her recent publications include *Clothing Matters: Dress and Identity in India* (Delhi: Viking, London: Hurst and Chicago: University of Chicago Press, 1996) and *Unsettling Memories: Narratives of the Emergency in Delhi* (forthcoming with Hurst & Co., London).

DENIS VIDAL is a Research Fellow in Social Anthropology at the French Institute of Research and Development (IRD, Paris) and an Adjunct Fellow of the CSDS. He teaches South Asian Studies at Paris University (Paris VII). He is a member of the French Centre for the Study of South Asia (CEIAS,

Paris) and adjunct fellow of the Centre for the Study of Developing Societies (Delhi). He is currently an Associate Fellow at the London School of Economics and Political Science. He has carried out research in Himachal Pradesh, Rajasthan and Delhi. His recent publications include: *Violence and Truth: a Rajasthani Kingdom Confronts Colonial Authority* (Delhi: OUP, 1997) and *Webs of Trade: Dynamics of Business Communities in Western India*, edited with Ph. Cadène (Delhi: Manohar, 1997).

Index